The College at
BROCKPORT
STATE UNIVERSITY OF NEW YORK

DRAKE MEMORIAL LIBRARY

ALUMNI

PUBLICATIONS

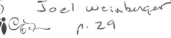

Joel Weinburger
p. 29

Bringing Psychotherapy Research to Life

Bringing Psychotherapy Research to Life

Understanding Change Through the Work of Leading Clinical Researchers

EDITED BY **Louis G. Castonguay,
J. Christopher Muran, Lynne Angus,
Jeffrey A. Hayes, Nicholas Ladany,
and Timothy Anderson**

American Psychological Association • Washington, DC

Published by
American Psychological Association
750 First Street, NE
Washington, DC 20002
www.apa.org

To order
APA Order Department
P.O. Box 92984
Washington, DC 20090-2984
Tel: (800) 374-2721; Direct: (202) 336-5510
Fax: (202) 336-5502; TDD/TTY: (202) 336-6123
Online: www.apa.org/books/
E-mail: order@apa.org

In the U.K., Europe, Africa, and the Middle East, copies may be ordered from
American Psychological Association
3 Henrietta Street
Covent Garden, London
WC2E 8LU England

Typeset in Goudy by Circle Graphics, Inc., Columbia, MD

Printer: United Book Press, Baltimore, MD
Cover Designer: Mercury Publishing Services, Rockville, MD

The opinions and statements published are the responsibility of the authors, and such opinions and statements do not necessarily represent the policies of the American Psychological Association.

Library of Congress Cataloging-in-Publication Data

Bringing psychotherapy research to life : understanding change through the work of leading clinical researchers / edited by Louis G. Castonguay . . . [et al.].
   p. cm.
 ISBN-13: 978-1-4338-0774-9
 ISBN-10: 1-4338-0774-2
 1. Psychotherapy—Research—History. I. Castonguay, Louis Georges. II. American Psychological Association.

 RC337.B73 2010
 616.89'14—dc22

                      2009046125

British Library Cataloguing-in-Publication Data

A CIP record is available from the British Library.

Printed in the United States of America
First Edition

To the Society for Psychotherapy Research,
one of many generative and nurturing sources of psychotherapy
research, without which this book would not have been possible.

CONTENTS

CONTRIBUTORS

J. Stuart Ablon, Massachusetts General Hospital and Harvard Medical School, Boston
Timothy Anderson, Ohio University, Athens
Lynne Angus, York University, Toronto, Ontario, Canada
John S. Auerbach, James H. Quillen Veterans Affairs Medical Center, Mountain Home, TN, and East Tennessee State University, Johnson City, TN
Jacques P. Barber, University of Pennsylvania, Philadelphia
Michael Barkham, University of Sheffield, Sheffield, United Kingdom
Larry E. Beutler, Palo Alto University, Palo Alto, CA
Arthur C. Bohart, Saybrook Graduate School, San Francisco, CA
Thomas D. Borkovec, Penn State University, University Park
Meredith Glick Brinegar, University of Illinois, Urbana–Champaign
Franz Caspar, Bern University, Bern, Switzerland
Louis G. Castonguay, Penn State University, University Park
John F. Clarkin, Weill Cornell Medical College, New York, NY
Michael J. Constantino, University of Massachusetts, Amherst
Kenneth L. Critchfield, University of Utah, Salt Lake City

Paul Crits-Christoph, University of Pennsylvania, Philadelphia

Louis Diguer, Laval University, Quebec City, Quebec, Canada

Robert Elliott, University of Strathclyde, Glasglow, United Kingdom

Barry A. Farber, Teachers College, Columbia University, New York, NY

Héctor Fernández-Álvarez, Fundación Aiglé, Buenos Aires, Argentina

Peter Fonagy, University College London, London, United Kingdom

Rhonda N. Goldman, Argosy University, Schaumburg, IL and the Family Institute at Northwestern University, Evanston, IL

Brin F. S. Grenyer, University of Wollongong, Wollongong, Australia

Alan S. Gurman, University of Wisconsin School of Medicine and Public Health, Madison

Gillian E. Hardy, University of Sheffield, Sheffield, United Kingdom

Jeffrey A. Hayes, Penn State University, University Park

Steven D. Hollon, Vanderbilt University, Nashville, TN

Martin Grosse Holtforth, University of Zürich, Zürich, Switzerland

Tai Katzenstein, Massachusetts General Hospital, Harvard Medical School, Boston

Sarah Knox, Marquette University, Milwaukee, WI

Merton S. Krause, Northwestern University, Evanston, IL

Nicholas Ladany, Lehigh University, Bethlehem, PA

Michael J. Lambert, Brigham Young University, Provo, UT

Kenneth N. Levy, Penn State, University Park

Robert J. Lueger, Creighton University, Omaha, NE

Wolfgang Lutz, University of Trier, Trier, Germany

Paulo P. P. Machado, University of Minho, Braga, Portugal

Karla Moras, Merion Station, PA

J. Christopher Muran, Adelphi University and Beth Israel Medical Center, New York, NY

Fredrick L. Newman, Florida International University, Miami

John C. Norcross, University of Scranton, Scranton, PA

Benjamin M. Ogles, Ohio University, Athens

John S. Ogrodniczuk, University of British Columbia, Vancouver, British Columbia, Canada

David E. Orlinsky, University of Chicago, Chicago, IL

Katerine Osatuke, Veterans Health Administration National Center for Organization Development, Cincinnati, OH

Glenys Parry, University of Sheffield, Sheffield, United Kingdom

Rhea Partyka, Cross Junction, VA

William E. Piper, University of British Columbia, Vancouver, British Columbia, Canada

Alberta E. Pos, York University, Toronto, Ontario, Canada

David L. Rennie, York University, Toronto, Ontario, Canada

P. Scott Richards, Brigham Young University, Provo, UT
Michael Helge Rønnestad, University of Oslo, Oslo, Norway
Jeremy D. Safran, New School for Social Research, New York, NY
Carrie E. Schaffer, Charlottesville, VA
M. Tracie Shea, Veterans Affairs Medical Center and Brown University, Providence, RI
Anne D. Simons, University of Oregon, Eugene
Bernhard Strauss, Institute of Psychosocial Medicine and Psychotherapy, Jena, Germany
Margarita Tarragona, Universidad Iberoamericana, Mexico City, Mexico
Christopher C. Wagner, Virginia Commonwealth University, Richmond
Bruce E. Wampold, University of Wisconsin, Madison
Jeanne C. Watson, University of Toronto, Toronto, Ontario, Canada
Joel Weinberger, Adelphi University, Garden City, NY
Ulrike Willutzki, Ruhr-Univerität Bochum, Bochum, Germany
Hadas Wiseman, University of Haifa, Haifa, Israel

PREFACE

In describing how one of their early collaborations began, David Orlinsky and Ken Howard[1] wrote that "some good things start over soup" (p. 477). In the early 1960s, the founders of the Society for Psychotherapy Research (SPR) did in fact develop the Therapy Session Report (a comprehensive measure of psychotherapy process) while meeting for light dinners at an old hotel in Chicago. The idea for the present book also emerged around dinner. It was 40 years later, the soup had been replaced by steak frites, and we suspect that much more wine was involved—we were, after all, in a French bistro! This dinner took place at the 2005 SPR meeting in Montreal, and while we joyfully exchanged funny stories and laughed a lot (wine will make you do that), there was also a wave of sadness over part of the evening (wine will also make that happen). Although the six of us fervently discussed many exciting findings of psychotherapy research, we also talked about the fact that SPR was at an important point in its history. A number of its leaders (including Howard) had recently died, and the health of many other luminaries in our

---

[1]Orlinsky, D. E., & Howard, K.I. (1986). The psychological interior of psychotherapy: Explorations with the therapy session reports. In L. S. Greenberg & W. M. Pinsof (Eds), *The psychotherapeutic process: A research handbook* (pp. 477–501). New York, NY: Guilford Press.

field was deteriorating. In addition to the impact that this had on a personal level (all of us had interacted with and/or been mentored by some of these legendary figures), we were also saddened by the strong possibility that the contributions of these and other influential researchers, whose work served as the foundation of our own, may not be known by young scholars or by psychotherapy researchers primarily active in organizations other than SPR. Particularly worrisome for the six of us was the thought that many clinicians might not be aware of clinical implications of the research that giants of our field had conducted for the last 50 years—a painful reminder of the tenuous connection between practice and science.

There is no doubt that a gap exists between what researchers write about and what practitioners do in therapy. Clinicians do not find much guidance for their practice in the empirical literature. This, however, does not mean that clinicians are not interested in research. What they are not interested in are studies (including investigations that they may have conducted themselves as part of their master's and/or dissertation theses) that fail to be clinically relevant or meaningful. Our experience in working collaboratively with clinicians, in the context of training graduate students, conducting studies in practice research networks, and practicing psychotherapy ourselves, is that clinicians are thirsty for empirical knowledge that can help them better understand the complexity of therapy and improve the impact of their own interventions. Although they may not be avid readers of original empirical papers, clinicians (both novice and experienced) are very eager to attend talks or workshops by "well-known" researchers whose significant contributions to psychotherapy research and practice have been made via peer-reviewed journals. Yet clinicians are rarely motivated to seek these findings through methodologically detailed research reports found in these scientific journals or even dry summaries of these research reports. They would rather seek out the "big picture" of findings from a full career of scientific labor. Why?

While clinicians are eager to learn what researchers have to say about psychotherapy, they tend not to be particularly enthralled with the mechanism by which most researchers choose to communicate their understanding. Although the methodological and statistical sections in journal articles are crucial for evaluating the scientific validity of the findings they report, they most often overshadow the clinical implications of these findings. From a purely clinical standpoint, the papers published in these journals frequently fail to deliver substantive and detailed practical guidelines. One would be hard-pressed to learn how to practice psychotherapy by relying primarily on such a prestigious periodical as the *Journal of Consulting and Clinical Psychology*—even though not publishing in this type of journal can be the kiss of death for the career of many professional psychologists in academia.

Yet clinicians seek out iconic psychotherapy researchers first and foremost because they are interested in research. These researchers often have a central and clear message about research—one that readily can be applied to the practice of psychotherapy. Many clinicians want to hear what researchers have found about what types of patients benefit from therapy, how relationship problems can best be handled, under which circumstances emotions can be deepened, how to foster insight, and/or how to facilitate behavioral activation—just to name a few clinically relevant issues. Therapists want to learn about the major findings of leading researchers and the lessons one can derive from years of empirical investigations—fully knowing that elsewhere they can find the methodological and statistical procedures used in the investigations. They also want to know what led these researchers to investigate particular aspects of psychotherapy, how their findings have been influenced by (and have impacted) their respective clinical practice and teaching, and how their research programs reflect some milestones of their careers. When it comes to research, many clinicians want to hear scientifically rich and clinically relevant messages that are embedded in meaningful stories.

This book brings together a large number of influential research programs that have changed the way we think about and practice psychotherapy. It presents the main findings derived by such scholarly and empirical endeavors in a way that, we hope, is conceptually meaningful and clinically relevant. These findings are also described in the context of the personal and professional journeys within which they originated; they are, in other words, historicized to some extent. We believe that such conceptualizing of scientific work can bring research to life and, in doing so, may help many clinicians to get back in touch with the excitement toward science that many of us felt as we first entered graduate school.

The marriage between research and practice has been long recognized as a troubled one. There are clinicians who reject research, and there are researchers who refuse to practice. There are, however, researchers who practice, and there are certainly practitioners who conduct research. This volume presents the contributions of those who are the embodiment of the scientist–practitioner model and depict this marriage at its best.

The volume describes findings that will resonate with many clinicians' observations and reflections. In addition, it presents empirical results that will challenge some therapists' habitual ways of thinking about clients and their work with them. We hope that, ultimately, it will provide new directions to improve practice. This attempt of ours to make empirical findings clinically relevant, and thus to reduce the gap between research and practice, is one of the two overarching goals of this book. The other goal is to pay tribute to pioneers in the field of psychotherapy research.

A number of outstanding individuals have transformed the modern field of psychotherapy, and we believe that the time is ripe for a book that would provide a brief summary of the research contributions of at least some of them. Clearly, this book could not cover all of the major contributors to psychotherapy research in the last 50 years. Specifically, it focuses on the legacies of several leading researchers who have been associated with the foundation and early growth of SPR—via their direct involvement in the society, the importance of their research program, and/or the generative value (in terms of shaping current research trends or methods) of their work. The editors recognize that, as current and past members of the executive council of the North American chapter of SPR, the selection of the researchers celebrated in this book reflects regional bias. We hope, however, that our consultation with colleagues within and outside of North America has attenuated this bias.

We are also aware that the research programs highlighted in this book are predominantly anchored in psychodynamic and humanistic traditions. While this reflects the roots of SPR, it fails to do justice to the major contributions that leaders of other orientations (especially cognitive–behavioral) have made to psychotherapy research, let alone to the influence that these researchers have had on the research of many SPR members. In an attempt to capture such contributions, as well as to pay tribute to their own theoretical allegiance, the first two editors of this book (L. G. Castonguay and J. C. Muran) are currently working on a companion book to celebrate and bring to life the research of prominent figures in the cognitive–behavioral therapy tradition. Dividing psychotherapy researchers across two books may still be viewed by some as reflecting, if not perpetuating, arbitrary barriers between theoretical allegiances. This, however, is not our intention, and we hope that the combination of the two books will, eventually, allow for broad coverage of clinical researchers who have played an important role in understanding and developing psychotherapy, irrespective of the concepts they have focused on and the research methods they have favored.

The task of selecting the researchers to be featured in this book, even when restricting ourselves to individuals who have contributed to or substantially influenced the development of SPR, was an arduous one, both intellectually and emotionally. As for any book, we were allowed a limited number of pages. Within those limits, we also wanted to devote sufficient space for each chapter to capture the major contributions of recognized scholars, the clinical implications of their empirical accomplishments, and the developmental and personal contexts within which their work has evolved. Thus, we had very difficult choices to make. We spent long conference calls brainstorming and weighing possible options. We also devoted many hours going over leading textbooks, handbooks, and published reviews of empirical literature to compile list after list of possible "candidates." We also consulted with several senior colleagues who provided us with suggestions that were very helpful in guiding our selection process. In the end, though, we had to make painful decisions about whom not to feature. Several well-known SPR contributors, including some of our own mentors, did not make the final list despite our profound respect for the quality and heuristic value of their work. We will have to live with the choices we made and hope that those not selected, at least for this first edition of the book, will understand the difficulty of our task.

We also carefully chose the authors for each of the chapters, who in return provided truly remarkable, eloquent, and inspiring tributes to the work and legacy of the researchers they were asked to write about. We primarily chose authors based on their relationships, as mentees or close colleagues, with the featured researchers (after consulting with each of them, whenever possible). We also chose authors based on their own contributions to the field. The majority of these authors are reputed psychotherapy researchers from all over the world, and many of them will, we hope, have their own work recognized in future editions of this book.

The preparation of this book has been facilitated by the help of many individuals. In particular, we want to express our gratitude to Susan Reynolds (senior acquisitions editor at APA Books), not only for her trust and support but also for her crucial help in creating the outline that guided each of the chapters in this volume. We are also thankful to many friends and colleagues who provided us with advice and suggestions regarding the general structure of the book, as well as the selection of featured researchers and selected authors. These include Jacques Barber, Larry Beutler, Franz Caspar, John Clarkin, Paul Crits-Christoph, Irene Elkin, Marvin Goldfried, Martin Grosse Holtforth, Paulo Machado, Erhard Mergenthaler, John Norcross, David Orlinsky, Glenys Parry, David Rennie, and Bernhard Strauss. We are also grateful to many of the featured researchers and chapter authors who provided us with much needed encouragement and support during the completion of our task. Such warmth has been experienced by us as a reflection of the sense of connection that is prevalent in SPR.

We hope that this book will further contribute to this spirit of affiliation and collaboration by celebrating the work and impact of some of its leaders and by encouraging the integration of research and practice. We also hope that it will foster stronger connections between different generations of researchers. One of our goals was to raise the awareness of new scholars about the sources of some of the current themes and methods of research while highlighting some future research directions they can take in advancing psychotherapy. In the current stage of our careers, we see ourselves, like so many of our peers and colleagues in SPR, as part of a cohort that should facilitate the advancement of our field by creating links between newer and older generations of psychotherapy researchers. With this role in mind, we would like to dedicate this book to our mentors, who have shown us the way, and to our students, who have not only helped us in our quests but have and will continue to contribute to the growth of SPR and psychotherapy research.

Bringing Psychotherapy Research to Life

1

A BRIEF INTRODUCTION TO PSYCHOTHERAPY RESEARCH

J. CHRISTOPHER MURAN, LOUIS G. CASTONGUAY, AND BERNHARD STRAUSS

Like many histories, the story of psychotherapy research is one repeatedly marked by creative advances, inherent tensions, and paradigm shifts. As one of the first, Freud (1916/1963) himself struggled with the question of how best to study psychotherapy: On the one hand, he promoted the case study method to demonstrate evidential support for his new psychological treatment; on the other hand, he criticized the use of statistical procedures to understand complex clinical processes and to make comparisons among them (see Strupp & Howard, 1992). Freud's struggle is one not too different from what continues today for contemporary psychotherapists and researchers. To understand this struggle, it is important to recognize that "every scientific method rests upon philosophical presuppositions" (May, 1958, p. 8) and that for the most part Western science (psychology included) has been shaped by two major traditions (Allport, 1955).

AN INTELLECTUAL–CULTURAL VIEW OF THE FIELD

American and British psychology has been dominated by the empirical or realist tradition, with its origins traced to Newton and developed in Lockean/Humean thought. It is a tradition marked by various analytic methods, including operationism and pragmatism, and most notably by logical positivism with its emphasis on confirmation based on objective data and quantitative or statistical analysis. In contrast, Continental European psychology has been more pluralistic, though largely dominated by the rationalist or idealist tradition, with its origins in Cartesian principles and developed in Leibnizian/Kantian thought. From this tradition, methods such as phenomenology, hermeneutics, and structuralism emerged that privilege the subjective and interpretive and promote exploratory and qualitative approaches to research, such as case studies.

There has been a long-standing tension between these two traditions that can be boiled down to the fundamental epistemological question *How do we know?* From the empirical perspective, our knowledge is a posteriori, dependent on sense experience. The mind is seen as tabula rasa and as essentially passive in nature. From the rationalist perspective, our knowledge can be intuited or deduced from intuitions and thus exists a priori to sense experience. In this regard, the mind is seen as having a potentially active core of its own. The empirical sees knowledge as socially derived, the rationalist as individually driven. There have been many challenges to these views in the past few decades collectively described as *postmodern*, which suggest a more complex and critical perspective, a more both/and sensibility, and a more skeptical approach to knowing (see Muran, 2001a).

Despite this tension, the empirical tradition has mostly dominated scientific method in psychotherapy research, probably because of to the extensive role that North American and British researchers have played in the field. This dominance can also be attributed to socioeconomic factors regarding evidence-based practice and cost containment in Western health care, as well as an overall cultural shift toward the values of instrumentality, efficiency, and conformity (Cushman & Gilford, 2000). There have been challenges to this dominance, however, especially in the form of attempts to blend the two perspectives (e.g., attempts to quantify subjective states and to develop both exploratory and confirmatory models, as well as challenges to their authority altogether: that is, attempts to promote methodological plurality and contextual analyses; see Muran, 2001b, 2002).

A BRIEF HISTORY OF THE FIELD

There have been a number of histories written about psychotherapy research (e.g., Lambert, Bergin, & Garfield, 2004; Orlinsky & Russell, 1994; Strupp & Howard, 1992). Most trace the origins back to the 1920s, when several psychoanalytic institutes first addressed the basic question *Does treatment work?* by logging outcomes and reporting impressive improvement rates (see Otto Fenichel's 1930 report from the Berlin Institute, Ernest Jones's 1936 report from the London Institute, and Franz Alexander's 1937 report from the Chicago Institute)—a practice that was effectively discontinued by analytic institutes following World War II. The behavioral tradition also began in the early 1920s to assess treatment response (e.g., Jones, 1924). From the very beginning, the question *How best to measure change?* was a great challenge.

The Third Force, the humanistic tradition, entered the psychotherapy research fray in the 1940s, when Carl Rogers began a research program, first at Ohio State University and then at the University of Chicago. In addition to conducting controlled outcome studies of client-centered therapy, he pioneered the use of recorded sessions, which marked the beginning of process research. He also experimented with novel measurement strategies and multivariate statistical procedures. Perhaps most significant, he mentored an impressive list of psychotherapy researchers (including Allen Bergin, Sidney Blatt, Irene Elkin, Eugene Gendlin, Donald Kiesler, Laura Rice, Reinhard Tausch, and Charles Truax) who went on to become quite innovative and influential with regard to the study of psychotherapy process. In the 1950s, Rogers and his group moved to the Department of Psychiatry at the University of Wisconsin to study the treatment of the more severely disturbed. He also published one of the first books devoted to the topic of psychotherapy research, as well as a seminal article about the role of relationship factors that has had a long-lasting impact on process-outcome research (see Chapter 2, this volume).

Subsequent to the start of Rogers's research program, two other early programs of note were established. In the context of developing his clinic, Karl Menninger attracted a number of talented investigators, including Robert Wallerstein, Otto Kernberg, Robert Holt, and Lester Luborsky, who made significant contributions to a naturalistic 30-year longitudinal study of the psychoanalytic treatment of 42 patients that began in the mid-1950s (see Wallerstein, 1986). Around the same time, Jerome Frank and colleagues (see Chapter 3, this volume) initiated a program in the Phipps Clinic at Johns Hopkins University. They designed a series of studies of 54 patients (including 20-year follow-up evaluations) aimed at understanding the common healing factors of psychotherapy, rather than focusing on the effect of a specific treatment approach.

In 1952, Hans Eysenck published a review of the psychotherapy outcome literature that would become a major impetus to the field. He reviewed 24 studies and concluded that there was no evidence demonstrating that psychotherapy works (i.e., that psychotherapy produces no more changes than what would be expected by spontaneous remission) and that psychoanalysis even was less effective than no treatment. This critique resulted in a number of rejoinders that criticized Eysenck's analysis and provided further reviews (e.g., Bergin, 1971; Lubosky, Singer, & Luborsky, 1975), which culminated in the emergence and application of meta-analytic statistical techniques that subjected reviews to more systematic quantitative analysis. The first example of this, conducted by Smith, Glass, and Miller (1980) on 475 studies, demonstrated that psychotherapy was superior to no treatment and placebo controls (these authors also concluded that different psychotherapies seemed to have equal effects across a variety of disorders, which became an important influence to the psychotherapy integration movement and the study of common factors in psychotherapy; see Chapter 11, this volume).

The late 1950s and early 1960s marked the beginning of incredible growth in the field of psychotherapy research. There was a proliferation of psychotherapy research programs: Lester Luborsky established the Penn Psychotherapy Research Project, and Hans Strupp launched his Vanderbilt Studies—both efforts to study their respective time-limited dynamic therapies; Bruce Sloane and colleagues (Sloane, Staples, Cristol, Yorkston, & Whipple, 1975) conducted the first controlled clinical trial comparing behavior therapy, dynamic psychotherapy, and a waiting-list control as part of the Temple Psychotherapy Project. Other noteworthy programs included Edward Bordin's at the University of Michigan, William Snyder's at Penn State University, David Orlinsky and Kenneth Howard's Chicago/Northwestern Project, Mardi Horowitz's Langley Porter Projects, David Malan's at Tavistock, David Barlow's Center for Stress and Anxiety Disorders (State University of New York–Albany/Boston University), Harold Sampson and Joseph Weiss's Mount Zion Psychotherapy Research Group, David Shapiro's at Sheffield University, and Arnold Winston's Beth Israel Psychotherapy Research Program.

There were also important developments with regard to the organizational structure of the field: First, there were three American Psychological Association (APA) conferences on psychotherapy research—in 1958 (Washington, DC: Rubinstein & Parloff, 1959), 1961 (Chapel Hill: Strupp & Luborsky, 1962), and 1966 (Chicago: Shlien, Hunt, Matarazzo, & Savage, 1968). Subsequent to these conferences, Kenneth Howard and David Orlinsky concluded that the field had grown to the point that there was a need for a new organization and took preliminary steps to develop it, which culminated in the first meeting of the Society for Psychotherapy Research held in Chicago in 1970. Around the same time, several behaviorists, including Joseph Cautela, Cyril Franks, Arnold Lazarus, Andrew Salter, and Joseph Wolpe, founded the Association for the Advancement of Behavior Therapy (AABT; now the Association for Behavioral and Cognitive Therapies), which held its first meeting in Washington, DC, in 1967. The establishment of AABT marked a distinct increase in interest in behavior therapy and the study of its efficacy (see DiLoreto, 1971; and Paul, 1967, as seminal studies). The only downside to the development of two separate communities with overlapping interests was the unfortunate splitting of the field that is still felt today.

Second, the field was further organized by new journal and book publications. In 1963, *Psychotherapy: Theory, Research, and Practice* was established, soon to be followed by several new journals focusing on behavior therapy—for example, the *Journal of Applied Behavioral Analysis* in 1968 and *Behavior Therapy* and the *Journal of Behavior Therapy and Experimental Psychiatry* in 1970. (Other notable journals that were established much later on and had great influence on the field include *Cognitive Therapy and Research* in 1980 and *Psychotherapy Research* in 1992.) Of course, the APA journals *Journal of Consulting Psychology* (1937, which later became the *Journal of Consulting and Clinical Psychology*) and *Journal of Counseling Psychology* (1954), the American Psychiatric Association's *American Journal of Psychiatry* (1844) and the American Medical Association's *Archives of General Psychiatry* (1919) were important outlets for psychotherapy research.

Various book projects also played an organizing role. Arguably the most important was Allen Bergin and Sol Garfield's *Handbook of Psychotherapy and Behavior Change*, which is now in its fifth edition (most recently edited by Michael Lambert; see Chapters 9, 12, and 26, this volume). Other noteworthy books that provided substantive reviews of the research literature in psychotherapy included J. Meltzoff and M. Kornreich's *Research on Psychotherapy* (1970), and Alan Gurman and Andrew Razin's *Effective Psychotherapy* (1977). Two other landmark books described instruments then available to conduct empirical investigation: Donald Kiesler's *The Process of Psychotherapy: Empirical Foundations and Systems of Analysis* (see Chapter 18), and Irene Elkin Waskow and Morris Parloff's *Psychotherapy Change Measures* (1975). These books set the foundation for further innovative instruments and psychotherapy research programs, with several of them later captured by Leslie Greenberg and William Pinsof's *The Psychotherapeutic Process: A Research Handbook* (1986) and Larry Beutler and Marjorie Crago's *Psychotherapy Research* (1991): For example, Enrico Jones's Berkeley Psychotherapy Research group, Leonard Horowitz's Stanford University Collaborative project, Clara Hill's and Bill Stiles's respective verbal response systems, William Pinsof's Family Therapist Coding System, and Adam Horvath and Leslie Greenberg's Working Alliance Inventory. The influence of these early methodological contributions can also been seen in newer empirical programs that have continued to expand our understanding of therapeutic change (see Chapter 11, this volume).

Finally, the National Institute of Mental Health (NIMH) exerted a great deal of influence on shaping the field of psychotherapy research, and the late 1960s saw significant developments at NIMH that laid the groundwork for this influence to increase. NIMH had provided funding for the mentioned APA conferences on psychotherapy research. By 1966, it established the Clinical Research Branch, within which the Psychotherapy and Behavioral Intervention section had responsibility for grants and contracts concerned with psychotherapy research. By 1980, this section was elevated to branch status as the Psychosocial Treatments Research Branch, with Morris Parloff as its first chief. Although NIMH has since gone through several reorganizations, which resulted in the integration of this branch into a new structure, its development did set the stage for the NIMH Treatment of Depression Collaborative Research Program (TDCRP)—a multisite controlled clinical trial initiated in the late 1970s by Morris Parloff and Irene Elkin. The TDCRP compared the relative efficacy of two psychotherapies (cognitive behavioral therapy and interpersonal psychotherapy) and a pharmacological intervention (imipramine) with a placebo + support condition (see Chapter 7, this volume). It was a state-of-the-art randomized clinical trial that included treatment manuals and adherence checks and that became the standard by which other outcome studies were subsequently judged and developed.

Many of the clinical trials that followed provided the bases for what came to be known as the *empirically supported treatment (EST) movement* (Chambless & Ollendick, 2001). Consistent with the epistemological assumptions underlying their approach to therapy, a large number of cognitive–behavioral-oriented researchers have contributed to the EST movement (e.g., Stewart Agras, Nathan Azrin, Aaron Beck, David Barlow, Edward Blanchard, Thomas Borkovec, Kelly Brownell, David Clark, Edward Craighead, Gerald Davison, Robert DeRubeis, Paul Emmelkamp, Christopher Fairburn, Edna Foa, Steven Hayes, Richard Heimberg, Steven Hollon, Neil Jacobson, Robin Jarret, Alan Kazdin, Terence Keane, Philip Kendall, Peter Lewinsohn, Marsha Linehan, Isaac Markus, Alan Marlatt, Daniel O'Leary, Gerald Patterson, Stanley Rachman, Paul Savolsky, Linda Sobell, Terence Wilson). Although researchers from the other orientations have conducted outcome studies providing empirical support to their approaches (e.g., see Chapter 16, this volume), to a great extent these communities, namely, the analytic and humanistic, have not fully embraced and participated in the development of EST (see Safran & Aron, 2001).

The 1970s marked a critical intellectual turn or paradigm shift in psychotherapy research as investigators moved toward more intensive analyses and methodological pluralism in their study of psychotherapy. Gordon Paul's (1967) and Donald Kiesler's (Chapter 18, this volume) respective calls for greater specificity, for multidimensional analysis of "what treatment, by whom, is most effective for this individual with that specific problem, and under which set of circumstances" (Paul, 1967, p. 111) spurred researchers to investigate, over several decades, how therapeutic interventions could be matched with clients' characteristics (see Chapters 10, 27, 28, and 29, this volume). Perhaps as a result of the postmodern milieu that was taking hold of our intellectual culture, there was an increased emphasis on intensively studying the psychotherapy process, including relationally oriented and contextually sensitive investigations. Among those analytically and humanistically oriented, this took the form of studying the patient–therapist interaction (e.g., see Chapters 4, 17, and 19, this volume). These efforts paved the way for the establishment of empirically supported therapeutic relationships (Norcross, 2002), which countered the EST movement and included the study of such variables as the working alliance (Horvath & Bedi, 2002), alliance rupture and repair (Safran & Muran, 1996), empathy (Bohart et al., 2002), positive regard (Farber & Lane, 2002), and countertransference reactions (Gelso & Hayes, 2002). Among behaviorists, the increased emphasis on intensive analyses involved the refinement and application of single-case experimental designs (e.g., Kazdin, 1978). This inspired the development of case formulation methods in all the traditions as well (e.g., Eells, 2008).

This intellectual turn also led to a number of methodological innovations that expanded the horizons of psychotherapy research. These included the quantification of subjectivity, that is, the use of subjective ratings of the patient and therapist, which was a rebellion against positivism and its emphasis on the exclusive study of overt behavior (e.g., Strupp, Horowitz, & Lambert, 1997). In addition, these innovations involved the use of complex statistical analyses to measure change, including Howard and colleagues' (see Chapter 8, this volume) dose–effect and outcome phase model, patient-focused research, and expected treatment response, as well as Lambert's (see Chapter 12) research on assessment and reduction of non-responders, therapist effect (e.g., Wampold, 2001), and interaction between technical and relational variables (Barber et al., 2006; Crits-Christoph et al., 1988). In addition, it manifested in increased interest in discovery-oriented, exploratory, qualitative, and narrative-based methods (e.g., Mowrer, 1988; Toukmanian & Rennie, 1992; see also Chapters 13, 24, and 25, this volume). Especially noteworthy examples of this were the introduction of the task analytic method to psychotherapy research by Laura Rice and Leslie Greenberg (see Chapters 15 and 16, this volume) and programmatic linguistic analyses of psychotherapy narratives that have been conducted by Wilma Bucci and Horst Kächele and the Ulm research group (including Erhard Mergenthaler). Involving a sophisticated blend of qualitative and quantitative methodologies, these programs demonstrate the feasibility and fruitfulness of integrating epistemological traditions (Castonguay, 1993) that, as we mentioned at the beginning of this chapter, are at the roots of psychotherapy research. Taken together, these methodological and statistical innovations are likely to help researchers better understand how clients, therapists, and a host of process variables are involved in patterns of interaction and interdependence that lead to or interfere with therapeutic change (Castonguay & Beutler, 2006).

OUR PURPOSE AND RATIONALE

With this chapter, we have provided a brief narrative history of psycho-therapy research, including some background on the intellectual and cultural currents of the times, as well as a summary of the major developments and con-tributions of the important figures in the field. Our objective was to set the stage for the next chapters of this book, in which psychotherapy research is brought to life through a series of biographical sketches. In other words, consistent with a postmodern sensibility (e.g., Cushman, 1995; Miller, 1991), this book aims to make psychotherapy research more accessible to clinicians and other researchers by personalizing and contextualizing the significant findings in the lives of the major figures who found them.

REFERENCES

Alexander, F. (1937). *Five year report of the Chicago Institute for Psychoanalysis, 1932–1937.*

Allport, G. W. (1955). *Becoming: Basic considerations for a psychology of personality.* New Haven, CT: Yale University Press.

Barber, J. P., Gallop, R., Crits-Christoph, P., Frank, A., Thase, M. E., Weiss, R. D., & Connolly Gibbons, M. B. (2006). The role of therapist adherence, therapist com-petence, and the alliance in predicting outcome of individual drug counseling: Results from the NIDA Collaborative Cocaine Treatment Study. *Psychotherapy Research, 16,* 229–240. doi:10.1080/10503300500288951

Bergin, A. E. (1971). The evaluation of therapeutic outcomes. In A. E. Bergin & S. L. Garfield (Eds.), *Handbook of psychotherapy and behavior change* (pp. 217–270). New York, NY: Wiley.

Beutler, L. E., & Crago, M. (Eds.). (1991). *Psychotherapy research: An international review of programmatic research.* Washington, DC: American Psychological Association. doi:10.1037/10092-000

Bohart, A. C., Elliott, R., Greenberg, L. S., & Watson, J. C. (2002). Empathy. In J. C. Norcross (Ed.), *Psychotherapy relationships that work: Therapist contributions and responsiveness to patients* (pp. 89–108). New York, NY: Oxford University Press.

Castonguay, L. G. (1993). "Common factors" and "nonspecific variables": Clarification of the two concepts and recommendations for research. *Journal of Psychotherapy Integration, 3,* 267–286.

Castonguay, L. G., & Beutler, L. E. (2006). *Principles of therapeutic change that work.* New York, NY: Oxford University Press.

Chambless, D. L., & Ollendick, T. H. (2001). Empirically supported psychological interventions: Controversies and evidence. *Annual Review of Psychology, 52,* 685–716. doi:10.1146/annurev.psych.52.1.685

Crits-Christoph, P., Cooper, A., & Luborsky, L. (1988). The accuracy of therapist's interpretations and the outcome of dynamic psychotherapy. *Journal of Consulting and Clinical Psychology, 56*, 490–495. doi:10.1037/0022-006X.56.4.490

Cushman, P. (1995). *Constructing the self, constructing America: A cultural history of psychotherapy*. Reading, MA: Addison-Wesley.

Cushman, P., & Gilford, P. (2000). Will managed care change our way of being? *American Psychologist, 55*, 985–996. doi:10.1037/0003-066X.55.9.985

DiLoreto, A. O. (1971). *Comparative psychotherapy*. New York, NY: Aldine-Atherton.

Eells, T., ed. (2008). *Handbook of Psychotherapy Case Formulation*, 2nd ed. New York, NY: Guilford Press.

Eysenck H J. (1952). The effects of psychotherapy: an evaluation. *Journal of Consulting and Clinical Psychology, 16*, 319–324.

Farber, B. A., & Lane, J. S. (2002). Positive regard. In J. C. Norcross (Ed.), *Psychotherapy relationships that work: Therapist contributions and responsiveness to patients* (pp. 175–194). New York, NY: Oxford University Press.

Fenichel. O. (1930). *Ten years of the Berlin Psychoanalytic Institute, 1920–1930*.

Freud, S. (1916/1963). Analytic therapy. In J. Strachey (Ed.), *Standard edition of the complete works of Sigmund Freud* (Vol. 16, pp. 448–463). London, England: Hogarth Press.

Gelso, C. J., & Hayes, J. A. (2002). The management of countertransference. In J. Norcross (Ed.), *Psychotherapy relationships that work: Therapist contributions and responsiveness to patients* (pp. 267–283). New York, NY: Oxford University Press.

Greenberg, L. S., & Pinsof, W. (1986). *The psychotherapeutic process: A research handbook*. New York, NY: Guilford Press.

Gurman, A. S., & Razin, A. M. (Eds.). (1977). *Effective psychotherapy: A handbook of research*. New York, NY: Pergamon.

Horvath, A. O., & Bedi, R. P. (2002). The alliance. In J. C. Norcross (Ed.), *Psychotherapy relationships that work: Therapist contributions and responsiveness to patients* (pp. 37–69). New York, NY: Oxford University Press.

Jones, E. (1936). *Report of the clinic work (London Clinic of Psychoanalysis): 1926–1936*.

Jones, M. C. (1924). A laboratory study of fear: The case of Peter. *Pedagogical Seminary, 31*, 308–316.

Kazdin, A. E. (1978). Methodological and interpretative problems of single-case experimental designs. *Journal of Consulting and Clinical Psychology, 46*, 629–642. doi:10.1037/0022-006X.46.4.629

Lambert, M. J., Bergin, A. E., & Garfield, S. L. (2004). Introduction and historical overview. In M. J. Lambert (Ed.), *Bergin and Garfield's handbook of psychotherapy and behavior change* (5th ed., pp. 3–15). New York, NY: Wiley.

Lambert, M. J. (Ed.). (2004). *Bergin and Garfield's handbook of psychotherapy and behavior change* (5th ed.). New York, NY: Wiley.

Mahrer, A. R. (1988). Discovery-oriented psychotherapy research: Rationale, aims, and methods. *American Psychologist, 43*, 694–702. doi:10.1037/0003-066X.43.9.694

May, R. (1958). The origins and significance of the existential movement in psychology. In R. May, E. Angel, H. F. Ellenberger, & F. Henri (Eds.), *Existence: A new dimension in psychiatry and psychology* (pp. 3–36). New York, NY: Basic Books. doi:10.1037/11321-001

McNeilly, C. I., & Howard, K. I. (1991). The effects of psychotherapy: A reevaluation based on dosage. *Psychotherapy Research, 1*, 74–78. doi:10.1080/10503309112331334081

Meltzoff, J., & Kornreich, M. (1970). *Research in psychotherapy*. New York, NY: Atherton.

Miller, N. K. (1991). *Getting personal: Feminist occasions and other autobiographical acts*. New York, NY: Routledge.

Muran, J. C. (2001a). Contemporary constructs and contexts. In J. C. Muran (Ed.), *Self-relations in the psychotherapy process* (pp. 3–44). Washington, DC: American Psychological Association. doi:10.1037/10391-001

Muran, J. C. (2001b). Meditations on Both/And. In J. C. Muran (Ed.), *Self-relations in the psychotherapy process* (pp. 347–372). Washington, DC: American Psychological Association. doi:10.1037/10391-000

Muran, J. C. (2002). A relational approach to understanding change: Plurality and contextualism in a psychotherapy research program. *Psychotherapy Research, 12*, 113–138. doi:10.1080/713664276

Norcross, J. C. (Ed.). (2002). *Psychotherapy relationships that work: Therapists contributions and responsiveness to patients*. New York, NY: Oxford University Press.

Orlinsky, D. E., & Russell, R. L. (1994). Tradition and change in psychotherapy research: Notes on the fourth generation. In R. L. Russell (Ed.), *Reassessing psychotherapy research* (pp. 185–214). New York, NY: Guilford Press.

Paul, G. L. (1967). Outcome research in psychotherapy. *Journal of Consulting Psychology, 31*, 109–118. doi:10.1037/h0024436

Rubinstein, E. A., & Parloff, M. B. (1959). *Research in psychotherapy*. Washington, DC: American Psychological Association. doi:10.1037/10036-000

Safran, J. D., & Muran, J. C. (1996). The resolution of ruptures in the therapeutic alliance. *Journal of Consulting and Clinical Psychology, 64*, 447–458.

Shlien, J. M., Hunt, H. F., Matarazzo, J. D., & Savage, C. (Eds.). (1968). *Research in psychotherapy*, Vol. 3. Washington, DC: American Psychological Association.

Sloan, R. B., Staples, F. R., Cristol, A. H., Yorkston, N. J., & Whipple, K. (1975). *Psychotherapy vs. behavior therapy*. Cambridge, MA: Harvard University Press.

Smith, M. L., Glass, G. V., & Miller, T. I. (1980). *The benefits of psychotherapy*. Baltimore, MD: Johns Hopkins University Press.

Strupp, H. H., & Howard, K. I. (1992). A brief history of psychotherapy research. In D. K. Freedheim, H. J. Freudenberger, J. W. Kessler, S. B. Messer, D. R. Peterson,

Strupp, H. H., & P. L. Wachtel (Eds.), *History of psychotherapy: A century of change* (pp. 309–334). Washington, DC: American Psychological Association.

Strupp, H. H., & Luborsky, L. (Eds.). (1962). *Research in psychotherapy* (Vol. II). Washington, DC: American Psychological Association.

Strupp, H. H., Horowitz, L. M., & Lambert, M. J. (Eds.). (1997). *Measuring patient changes in mood, anxiety, and personality disorders.* Washington, DC: American Psychological Association. doi:10.1037/10232-000

Toukmanian, S. G., & Rennie, D. L. (1992). *Psychotherapy process research: Paradigmatic and narrative approaches.* Thousand Oaks, CA: Sage Publications.

Wallerstein, R. S. (1986). *Forty-two lives in treatment: A study of psychoanalysis and psychotherapy.* New York, NY: Guilford Press.

Wampold, B. E. (2001). *The great psychotherapy debate: Model, methods, and findings.* Mahwah, NJ: Erlbaum.

Waskow, I. E., & Parloff, M. B. (1975). *Psychotherapy change measures.* Washington, DC: Department of Health, Education, and Welfare.

I

ESTABLISHING THE
FOUNDATION FOR
THE SCIENTIFIC STUDY
OF PSYCHOTHERAPY

2

CARL ROGERS: IDEALISTIC PRAGMATIST AND PSYCHOTHERAPY RESEARCH PIONEER

ROBERT ELLIOTT AND BARRY A. FARBER

In many ways, Carl Rogers was and continues to be a figure of contradictions. He was a dreamy idealist who was also a hard-headed pragmatist; a humanist grounded in positivism; a shy, somewhat stiff Midwesterner who ended up advocating openness, disclosure, and intimacy; a persuasive advocate for empathic and respectful listening raised in a judgmental, non-expressive home; the founder of a major school of therapy who discouraged followers, training institutes, and professional organizations; an academic who rebelled against almost all of the trappings of academia; and a key figure in the origins and development of psychotherapy research who at a crucial moment gave it all up to move to California to pursue encounter groups, educational reform, and peace-making. What are we to make of these contradictions? Do they detract from his contributions? Or are they essential to what drove him and what continues to inspire his supporters more than 20 years after his death in 1987?

Rogers's contributions to both practice and research are extensive. His filmed interview with Gloria (Shostrom, 1965) is almost certainly the most widely viewed clinical training recording ever made. His clinical career included work with adults and children, small and large groups, and even warring political entities. He wrote prolifically and compellingly about applying client-centered (later person-centered) approaches to problems related to education, marriage, racism, and geopolitical disputes. More generally, his emphasis on the mutative aspects of the relationship per se has been accepted by virtually all contemporary schools of psychotherapy, including those aligned with cognitive behavior therapy and psychodynamically-oriented approaches (Farber, 2007).

MAJOR CONTRIBUTIONS

Often obscured by the importance and far-reaching effects of his clinical innovations are Rogers's seminal contributions to psychotherapy research. Arguably, he was the first major psychotherapeutic figure who insisted on testing the validity of his clinical ideas. He was committed to making his clinical material available to all interested parties so that others could analyze and evaluate the process and outcome of his work. His 1942 book, *Counseling and Psychotherapy*, contains the first fully transcribed psychotherapy case ever published, "The Case of Herbert Bryan." He was proud of his research program and understood its significance for changing the field:

> These phonographic accounts, and the typescripts which have been made from them, have exposed the processes of counseling and therapy to an objective and microscopic examination which has illuminated the principles and problems of counseling in significant ways which thus far have only been partially utilized. This procedure holds much promise for the future." (Rogers, 1942, p. ix)

Rogers was not the first to conduct psychotherapy research. Crude outcome studies, most consisting of simple tallies of therapist-perceived improvement of heterogeneous samples of patients, can be traced back to the 1920s and 1930s (Bergin, 1971). What Rogers and his colleagues did was to change dramatically the methods and focus of psychotherapy research. In the course of his career, Rogers pioneered or foreshadowed most of the major genres of psychotherapy research: process research; systematic, controlled outcome research; process-outcome research; and finally, surprisingly, qualitative research. For example, while retaining an interest in outcome, Rogers began to examine the process of psychotherapy. His awareness that the words and actions of the therapist as well as the patient contribute substantially to the effectiveness of therapy was well ahead of its time. He traced client thematic patterns across sessions, looking for changes in clients' sense of self (e.g., greater congruence between their perceptions of real and ideal selves) and also looking for what we would now call "ruptures in the therapeutic alliance." He also investigated the ingredients underlying therapists' effectiveness, famously hypothesizing that therapists' provision of genuineness, positive regard, and empathy—in conjunction with the client's ability to experience, to at least a minimum degree, these last two attitudes—were the necessary and sufficient conditions for client change (Rogers, 1957). This work set the stage for the field's current emphasis on the overarching importance of the therapeutic alliance in facilitating positive outcome. Rogers was also the first major psychotherapeutic figure to analyze a "failure" case (Rogers & Dymond, 1954), expecting to learn as much from dissecting what went wrong as from analyzing the details of what, in other circumstances, had gone right. More generally, Rogers recognized the complexity of the therapeutic process and the need to investigate empirically the many variables involved. He asked, "What happens? What goes on during a period of contacts? What does the counselor do? The client?" (Rogers, 1942, p. 30). He was aware that research—what he termed "experimental study" (Rogers, 1942, p. 240)—should serve as a guide to answer clinical questions.

It is also noteworthy that as early as 1942 Rogers was advocating for the inclusion of research methods courses within professional training programs. A counselor, he wrote, should have "adequate techniques for evaluating his own work and that of others, and thus a sound basis for progress" (Rogers, 1942, p. 257). The radical nature of Rogers's position is apparent in the contrast with Freud's oft-quoted response in the 1930s to a researcher's attempts to investigate the concept of repression: "I have examined your experimental studies for the verification of the psychoanalytic assertions with interest. I cannot put much value on these confirmations because the wealth of reliable observations on which these assertions rest make them independent of experimental verification" (cited by MacKinnon & Dukes, 1962). Moreover, his research contributions to the field were so extensive and influential that in 1984 the Society of Psychotherapy Research (SPR) awarded him (along with Lester Luborsky) an SPR Senior Career Award.

EARLY BEGINNINGS

Kirschenbaum's (2007) biography of Rogers provides more information than ever before about Rogers's life and allows us to comprehend the full impact of Rogers's extensive accomplishments. Much of what follows is drawn from this account.

Carl Rogers was born in 1902, the fourth of six children, in a suburb of Chicago. Both his father, a successful businessman and college graduate, and his mother were Christian fundamentalists, subscribing to the virtues of a close family, hard work, and piety (i.e., no alcohol, dancing, theater attendance, or even card games). As a boy, Rogers was seen—and even teased—by his family as a reserved and oversensitive child who often retreated to the comfort of his books.

Motivated by his father's wish to pursue farming as a side interest (which soon grew into an early agribusiness venture), and by both parents' wish to protect their children from the temptations of living near a big city, the family moved to a farm outside Chicago when Carl was 12. There, Rogers developed a great interest in moths, rearing caterpillars and watching their development. Moreover, encouraged by his father, Rogers studied scientific agriculture, becoming familiar with experimental methods that emphasized the need for hypothesis testing, control groups, and random assignment.

Given these influences, it is not surprising that, at the University of Wisconsin, Rogers first turned his attention to scientific agriculture, and then to the ministry. Shortly after graduation, he married a young woman he had known since childhood, Helen, and the two of them moved to New York, where Carl began his studies at Union Theological Seminary. He soon became disenchanted with the doctrinaire nature of religious training, and during his second year of studies he began taking courses in psychology at Teachers College, Columbia University. Soon, he became a full-time student there, studying clinical and educational psychology in an academic culture marked by fairly strict adherence to research, statistics, and measurement. For his doctoral dissertation he developed a test for measuring adjustment in young adolescents.

ACCOMPLISHMENTS

Following graduation, Rogers accepted a position with the Child Study Department of the Rochester (New York) Society for the Prevention of Cruelty to Children. During his 12 years in Rochester, he carried out a search for an approach that made sense to him and could be proven effective. However, in this search he found himself severely hampered by two gaps in the existing literature: the absence of verbatim records of therapy and the lack of research on different therapeutic approaches. These limitations compelled him to spend most of these years experimenting with different approaches to therapy. His search was documented in his first book, *The Clinical Treatment of the Problem Child* (Rogers, 1939), in which he argued that the conduct of psychotherapy needed to be grounded in the principles of scientific inquiry so that it could be measured and objectified. This book, with its critique of directive approaches to child therapy, also contains the seeds of the nondirective approach, which he adapted primarily from the work of the psychoanalyst Otto Rank (considered by some a maverick) and the social worker Jessie Taft.

Therapy Process Research

Rogers's academic career began at Ohio State University in 1939, where he developed his formative ideas about client-centered therapy. These ideas culminated in his book *Counseling and Psychotherapy* (1942). In 1940, he had been able to obtain phonographic recording equipment and had begun recording therapy sessions. (A complex process: two phonographs were required so that while one was ending its few minutes of recording, the other would begin.) This led to several further developments. First, he and his students developed client consent procedures for recording and methods for transcribing sessions. Next, they began figuring out what to do with these data, in the process inventing therapy process research. As a first step, they classified the different types of therapist responses (e.g., questions, giving information, persuading, interpreting), in some studies (e.g., Porter, 1941) categorizing each therapist response as "directive" or "nondirective." Under Rogers's supervision, Snyder (1945) carried out the first sequential process research paradigm study in which client and therapist responses were both rated to identify which therapist responses led to which client responses; for example, Snyder found that asking questions and making interpretations did not lead to client insight, whereas simple acceptance and clarification of feelings did.

Systematic, Controlled Outcome Research

In 1945, Rogers moved to the University of Chicago to establish a counseling center there. The Chicago Counseling Center became a home for the development and expansion of client-centered therapy, and a place where research was strongly encouraged. He obtained his greatest scientific and professional recognition during this period: In 1947, he became the president of the American Psychological Association (APA). In 1951, *Client-Centered Therapy* was published; in 1954, a book of research studies, *Psychotherapy and Personality Change* (coedited by Rosalind Dymond) came out; and in 1956, Rogers received the Distinguished Scientific Contribution Award from APA.

Rogers's move to the University of Chicago also led to the development of the genre of large, systematic, controlled therapy research. At this time, he began moving away from his earlier interest in therapist technique, toward a more attitudinal–relational view that made outcome research more appealing. At first, Rogers and his students contented themselves with simple pre–post studies to document the nature and extent of client change over the course of therapy. These studies used then-standard psychological measures, such as the Thematic Apperception Test (TAT) and the Rorschach, with small samples of clients and no experimental controls. However, they subsequently obtained a series of grants for a larger study, the first large ($N = 25$) controlled investigation of psychotherapy outcome. This study used two different nonrandom no-treatment controls (Rogers & Dymond, 1954): One was a silent control group of nontreatment-seeking individuals matched to the treatment sample (a design that would be used 20 years later by Strupp and colleagues for the first Vanderbilt Psychotherapy Project); the other was a waiting-list control group of clients whose therapy was delayed for 2 months. While this study was later criticized for failing to randomize clients to treatment (less distressed clients were assigned to the waiting-list condition), it was an important step forward in the development of what is today considered the definitive group design for treatment research, the randomized clinical trial.

Measures for Person-Centered/Experiential Therapies

A key element of systematic psychotherapy research is the use of theory-relevant measures of outcome and process. Where these do not exist, as is so often the case, they must be invented. Thus, to support their increasingly sophisticated outcome studies and to assess the validity of their emerging theory, Rogers and his colleagues found that they needed measures for key client-centered concepts, such as congruence/incongruence, therapist facilitative attitudes, and client level of process or experiencing. (Actually, measure development is a consistent theme in Rogers's scientific career, from his dissertation to the early therapy process measures to the Chicago and Wisconsin studies.)

Among the first of these instruments to be developed to support the Chicago Counseling Center research was the Butler-Haig Q-Sort measure of self-concept congruence/incongruence, which measured discrepancies in ratings of actual and ideal self, with reduction in discrepancy seen as an indicator of positive change (Rogers & Dymond, 1954). After this came measures of therapist facilitative attitudes, including the Barrett-Lennard Relationship Inventory (Barrett-Lennard, 1962), a client and therapist self-report measure of accurate empathy, congruence, warmth and nonpossessiveness, and the most widely used measure of the therapeutic relationship prior to the advent of therapeutic alliance measures in the 1980s. Then, after Rogers and part of his team moved to Wisconsin to carry out the Schizophrenia Project, work began on developing observational process measures of therapist facilitative conditions and client experiencing (Rogers, Gendlin, Kiesler, & Truax, 1967), instruments that became the paradigmatic therapy process measures for a generation of psychotherapy research.

Process–Outcome Research

In 1957, Rogers decided returned to his alma mater, the University of Wisconsin, a decision largely influenced by his desire to broaden the impact of his ideas by training psychiatrists along with psychologists. His new Wisconsin research group employed their new observational measures in an ambitious study applying client-centered therapy in the treatment of schizophrenia (Rogers et al, 1967). These measures were necessary for establishing another new genre of research that Rogers and his team invented: the process–outcome paradigm, in which key therapy processes are sampled from therapy sessions and used to predict posttherapy outcome.

To be effective, process–outcome research needs to be guided by an explicit, detailed theoretical formulation. This was supplied by Rogers's classic 1957 paper, "The Necessary and Sufficient Conditions for Change in Therapeutic Personality Change," which launched hundreds of psychotherapy studies (see Orlinsky, Ronnestad, & Willutski, 2004). In this article, Rogers made the radical and somewhat outrageous claim that therapist warmth, empathy, and genuineness account completely for client posttherapy change. Moreover, he went beyond bold prediction to propose ways in which the key variables could be measured and the hypothesis tested.

Today, the Wisconsin Project is regarded as a noble failure: Its results were ambiguous and failed to support many of the key hypotheses; in addition, the study has passed into psychotherapy research folklore for the level of interpersonal conflict among team members, which featured threatened lawsuits and delayed its publication for years, so that the study was seen as outdated by the time it was finally published (see Kirschenbaum, 2007, for some of the juicy details). Nevertheless, this study influenced the field indirectly via the measures developed for it and through its clear implementation of the process–outcome research paradigm.

Qualitative Inklings

Rogers's major success during his years at Wisconsin was not in the research realm but rather with an immensely popular book, *On Becoming a Person* (1961). He had never been particularly at home in academia—among other grievances, he detested academic politics and power struggles—and had long harbored deep-seated doubts about conventional understandings of human nature and science. It appears likely that his experiences in Wisconsin permanently soured him on both academia and quantitative psychotherapy research (Kirschenbaum, 2007). He left full-time university life in 1963 to become a member of a new, nonprofit institution, the Western Behavioral Sciences Institute (La Jolla, California), dedicated to humanistically oriented research in the field of human relations. His final organizational home was in another newly created institution, the Center for Studies of the Person, formed in 1968. During his years in California, he published a number of popular books, including those that focused on encounter groups, education, politics, and marriage. His last years were devoted primarily to issues of international and group relations, and world peace.

Beginning in 1966 at Western Behavioral Sciences Institute, however, Rogers began a search for alternatives to traditional positivist approaches to studying people, hosting a series of dialogues among leading philosophers (Kirschenbaum & Henderson, 1989). By the mid-1980s, shortly before his death, he had aligned himself instead with more experience-based and inter-personal approaches to study and understanding, preferring to think in terms of research partners or coresearchers. He was interested in the kind of infor-mation that could be gleaned from mutual understanding, an undertaking not unlike that emphasized by contemporary relationally oriented psychoanalytic thinkers as well as qualitative methodologists.

These efforts are almost totally unknown today, but they contain within them the unmistakable first stirrings of the antipositivist revolution in the social sciences that emerged in the 1980s and eventually gave rise in the 1990s to modern qualitative research methods. As Kirschenbaum (2007) noted, the most likely explanation for the obscurity of this final research con-tribution by Rogers is that he was unable to provide a specific alternative to traditional quantitative research methods. Rogers's strength had always been his ability to link ideals to practice via concrete examples. However, in the mid-1960s there was nothing concrete yet to draw on, and it was not until shortly before his death in 1987 that the field caught up enough with Carl Rogers for him to be able to point to specific nonpositivist methods. Never-theless, it is our view that Rogers's final contribution to psychotherapy research lies precisely in his having helped create the initial conditions that, 25 years later, led to the rapid emergence and dissemination of qualitative psychother-apy research (e.g., Rennie, Phillips, & Quartaro, 1988), like the legendary butterfly of chaos theory flapping its wings in Asia.

CONCLUSION

We have tried to make the case for Carl Rogers's having founded or pio-neered nearly all the major genres of psychotherapy research, including, indi-rectly, qualitative research. At first, he did this through his own personal efforts, but increasingly over the years his influence was mediated through the students and colleagues he mentored and encouraged. Some of these, like Gene Gendlin, Laura Rice, and Natalie Rogers, his daughter, went on to develop their own unique person-centered forms of individual therapy and theory, while others became important as psychotherapy researchers in their own right, including (to name just a few) Marjorie Klein, Donald Kiesler, Allen Bergin, Irene Elkin, Godfrey Barrett-Lennard, Germain Lietaer, and (again) Laura Rice. An outstanding example is Irene Elkin, whose role in the design and conduct of the National Institute of Mental Health Collaborative Study of Treatments of Depression shows the unmistakable influence of the Chicago and Wisconsin studies. Others who did not work directly with Rogers but were nevertheless inspired by his work included William Miller (founder of motivational interviewing). Still others, too many to even try to list, became his intellectual grandchildren by virtue of having been mentored by former students of Rogers (e.g., Michael Lambert, Les Greenberg, Robert Elliott).

For humanistically oriented psychotherapy researchers, Rogers's departure from academia is today regarded as (to quote Don McLean) "the day the music died"; that is, the beginning of the long decline in the person-centered/ experiential/humanistic therapy tradition, leading to its near eclipse in the 1980s and eventually to recent hard-fought attempts to revive its standing through reinvigorated theory, research, and practice. For 20 years, a predominant view (e.g., Lietaer, 1990) has been that it all went wrong when Rogers, disillusioned with the intransigence of his academic colleagues at the University of Wisconsin, frustrated with the infighting of his research team, and longing for new challenges, left for more convivial company and climate in San Diego. Without research and significant new theory development, the person-centered approach (as it now came to be called) lost respectability and began to be pushed out of academia and mental health practice. If only Rogers had stayed in academia and continued to encourage research, the complaint goes, the approach would have fared much better over the ensuing decades, and we wouldn't have such an uphill battle today.

This narrative has a certain amount of credibility: Clearly, when we, as psychologists, compare the impact of Rogers's original evidence-based work on individual therapy to his later nonresearch-based applications of person-centered principles to small and large groups, education, couple relationships, multicultural communication, intergroup conflict and peace-making, it does appear to us that the earlier work has had a greater impact. However, several arguments can be made to counter this claim: First, important research on person-centered therapy continued in Europe through the supposed dry period. Second, although the main line of Rogerian thought as it applies to individual therapy appears to have gone into stasis in the mid-1960s, Rogers's departure encouraged important theoretical offshoots to develop in the 1970s and 1980s, including focusing and process–experiential therapy (Kirschenbaum, 2007). Third, the "dark ages" narrative reflects the rather narrow view of the traditional mental health professions and academics, who never fully embraced Rogers's iconoclastic views. Fourth, although the person-centered school of therapy appears to have gone into decline, at least in North America, it is also quite clear that during Rogers's last 20 years, his ideas about the important role of the therapeutic relationship in effective psychotherapy were absorbed into all the major approaches, suggesting "infusion" as a better metaphor than "decline" (Farber, 2007).

Today, the person-centered and experiential approaches are enjoying a lively revival and are expanding their applicability; moreover, research on these newer client-centered models, especially on humanistic–experiential therapies, is proliferating (e.g., Elliott et al., 2004). The central contradiction between idealism and pragmatism that drove Rogers has been assimilated by his intellectual progeny as a creative tension that continues to inspire contemporary theory, research, and practice on humanistic and related therapies. Rogers's legacy, as a pioneer in both the clinical and research realms, lives on.

REFERENCES

Barrett-Lennard, G. T. (1962). Dimensions of therapist response as causal factors in therapeutic change. *Psychological Monographs, 75* (43, Whole No. 562).

Bergin, A. E. (1971). The evaluation of therapeutic outcomes. In A. E. Bergin & S. L. Garfield (Eds.), *Handbook of psychotherapy and behavior change: An empirical analysis* (pp. 217–270). New York, NY: Wiley.

Elliott, R., Greenberg, L. S., & Lietaer, G. (2004). Research on Experiential Psychotherapies. In M. J. Lambert (Ed.), *Bergin & Garfield's handbook of psychotherapy and behavior change* (5th ed., pp. 493–539). New York, NY: Wiley.

Farber, B. A. (2007). On the enduring and substantial influence of Rogers' not-quite necessary nor sufficient conditions. *Psychotherapy: Theory, Research, Practice, Training, 44.* 289–294.

Kirschenbaum, H. (2007). *The life and work of Carl Rogers*. Ross-on-Wye, England: PCCS Books.

Kirschenbaum, H., & Henderson, V. L. (Eds.). (1989). *Carl Rogers: Dialogues*. Boston, MA: Houghton Mifflin.

Lietaer, G. (1990). The client-centered approach after the Wisconsin Project: A personal view on its evolution. In G. Lietaer, J. Rombauts, & R. Van Balen (Eds.), *Client-centered and experiential psychotherapy in the nineties* (pp.19–45). Leuven, Belgium: Leuven University Press.

MacKinnon, D., & Dukes, W. F. (1962). Repression. In L. Postman (Ed.), *Psychology in the making* (pp. 662–744). New York, NY: Knopf.

Orlinsky, D. E., Rønnestad, M. H., & Willutski, U. (2004). Fifty years of psychotherapy process and outcome research: Continuity and change. In M. Lambert (Ed.), *Bergin and Garfield's handbook of psychotherapy and behavior change* (5th ed., pp. 307–389). New York, NY: Wiley.

Porter, E. H. (1941). *The development and evaluation of a measure of counseling interview procedures*. Columbus: Ohio State University (Unpublished thesis).

Rennie, D. L., Phillips, J. R., & Quartaro, G. K. (1988). Grounded theory: A promising approach to conceptualization in psychology? *Canadian Psychology, 29*, 139–150. doi:10.1037/h0079765

Rogers, C. R. (1939). *The clinical treatment of the problem child*. Boston, MA: Houghton Mifflin.

Rogers, C. R. (1942). *Counseling and psychotherapy*. Boston, MA: Houghton Mifflin.

Rogers, C. R. (1951). *Client-centered therapy*. Boston, MA: Houghton Mifflin.

Rogers, C. R. (1957). The necessary and sufficient conditions of therapeutic personality change. *Journal of Consulting Psychology, 21*, 95–103. doi:10.1037/h0045357

Rogers, C. R. (1961). *On becoming a person*. Boston, MA: Houghton Mifflin.

Rogers, C. R., & Dymond, R. F. (Eds.). (1954). *Psychotherapy and personality change: Coordinated research studies in the client-centered approach*. Chicago, IL: University of Chicago Press.

Rogers, C. R., Gendlin, E. T., Kiesler, D. J., & Truax, C. B. (Eds.). (1967). *The therapeutic relationship and its impact: A study of psychotherapy with schizophrenics*. Madison, WI: University of Wisconsin Press.

Shostrom, E. L. (Producer) (1965). *Three approaches to psychotherapy (Part 1)* [Film]. Orange, CA: Psychological Films.

Snyder, W. U. (1945). An investigation of the nature of nondirective psychotherapy. *Journal of Genetic Psychology, 33*, 193–223.

3

JEROME D. FRANK: PSYCHOTHERAPY RESEARCHER AND HUMANITARIAN

BRUCE E. WAMPOLD AND JOEL WEINBERGER

The professional contributions of Jerome D. Frank, PhD, MD, or "Jerry," as he was known to family and friends, exemplify two major themes. First, Frank was committed to using evidence to reveal the essence of phenomena and abhorred dogmatism. Second, he was dedicated to improving society and establishing peace in a troubled world. These two strands led to significant contributions to the understanding of psychotherapy, the focus of this volume, but also to a psychological understanding of national leaders in a nuclear age.

EARLY BEGINNINGS

Frank was born in 1909 in New York City. He died in Baltimore at age 95, living through a period that spanned two world wars and two post–world war Asian conflicts (Korea and Vietnam), the industrialization of the Western world, and the spawning of globalization in the context of computers and technology. He earned his bachelor's degree at Harvard College in 1930, during which time he became acquainted with the work of Kurt Lewin. He worked with Lewin in Berlin (1930–1931) before earning his PhD at Harvard in 1934 and while a postdoc at Cornell. The experience in Berlin with Lewin was important intellectually and socially. Throughout his career, Frank subscribed to Lewin's thesis that cognition, behavior, and emotion are largely determined by the current social environment. This piqued Frank's interest in motivation. Lewin's emphasis on "action research," which suggested that the best way to understand a phenomenon was to attempt to change it, fueled Frank's interest in psychotherapy (Frank, 1992). As well, Frank was present in Germany when the Nazi party won its first significant election; Lewin's belief that psychologists should be involved in social issues elicited Frank's interest in promoting social justice, which had been nurtured by the Frank family's involvement in the ethical culture movement (Julia Frank, personal communication, Oct. 5, 2007). He was soon involved in political issues in Berlin (American Psychological Association, 1986).

Having completed his doctorate in psychology, Frank satisfied what was for some time a latent desire to be a physician by enrolling in the Harvard Medical School, where he received his MD in 1939. He began psychiatry residency at Johns Hopkins after completing an internship at New York Hospital. Immediately after residency, he spent several years in the United States armed forces. He was serving in the Far East when the two atomic bombs were detonated in Japan.

MAJOR ACCOMPLISHMENTS

Frank contributed to the field of psychology in two major areas: (a) the psychological issues of nuclear weapons and war and (b) the process and outcomes of psychotherapy. Although the focus of this volume is on the latter, it would be remiss to ignore his contributions to the former, which clearly intertwined with his perspectives on psychotherapy.

Psychological Issues of Nuclear Weapons

Frank's military experience and deep commitment to social issues created a desire to understand the psychological aspects of nuclear weapons and to advocate for policies that fostered peaceful relations among countries. He wrote an influential article in the *Atlantic Monthly* (Frank, 1954), served on the board of National Committee for a Sane Nuclear Policy (SANE), and published *Sanity and Survival: Psychological Aspects of War and Peace* (1967, reissued 1982). For these efforts, he was honored by the American Psychological Association in 1985 with the Award for Distinguished Contributions to Psychology in the Public Interest, for which he wrote another influential article, titled "The Drive for Power and the Nuclear Arms Race" (Frank, 1987).

Psychotherapy Process and Outcome

Frank began his studies of psychotherapy after his discharge from the armed services, first with the Veterans Administration, where he investigated group therapy, and then at Johns Hopkins, where he headed a psychiatric outpatient department. He was uniquely poised to make a contribution because of his training and his empirical inclinations. At the time (i.e., the 1950s), the practice of psychotherapy was mostly restricted to psychiatrists. Psychologists were involved with research design, data collection, and analysis. Because Frank was both a psychiatrist and a psychologist, he understood the practice of psychotherapy, research design and statistics, and psychological principles related to pathology and change processes. This is a unique set of skills for any period, but particularly so during the infancy of psychotherapy research.

In Search of Specificity and the Road to Common Factors

Trained in the medical model, Frank initially conceptualized treatment in terms of specificity. In 1956, he and David Rosenthal (1956) discussed designing research in psychotherapy to disentangle specific from placebo effects:

> It is concluded that improvement under a special form of psychotherapy cannot be taken as evidence for: (a) correctness of the theory on which it is based; or (b) efficacy of the specific technique used, unless improvement can be shown to be greater than or qualitatively different from that produced by the patients' faith in the efficacy of the therapist and his technique—"the placebo effect." This effect may be thought of as a nonspecific form of psychotherapy and it may be quite powerful in that it may produce end-organ changes and relief from distress of considerable duration. (p. 300).

This was cutting-edge thinking. Randomized placebo control group designs were just emerging in the United Kingdom and the United States and would not be generally accepted and required for the approval of drugs until the early 1980s (see Wampold, 2001).

Rosenthal and Frank (1956) noted that comparisons with no-treatment controls produced ambiguous results because all therapies seemed to work with some patients and that these benefits could be attributed neither to theory-specific ingredients nor to nonspecific effects such as expectancy of change. They concluded,

> The only adequate control would be another form of therapy in which patients had equal faith, so that the placebo effect operated equally in

both, but which would not be expected by the theory of therapy being studied to produce the same effects. (Rosenthal & Frank, 1956, p. 300)

In the early studies at Johns Hopkins, Frank and his colleagues set out to do exactly this: compare various approaches. The obstacles were immense, as there were no standard treatments (i.e., treatment manuals did not exist and psychotherapy was learned from one's supervisor) or outcome measures. So, the team set about to standardize treatments and use the best outcome measures that they could cobble together, and they designed a fair comparison between group therapy (1.5 hr per week for 6 months), individual therapy (1 hr per week for 6 months), and minimal therapy (.5 hr every 2 weeks for 6 months). As noted by Frank (1992), "To our astonishment and chagrin, despite obvious differences in therapies" only one variable, among many, showed any difference, and the research team was "forced to conclude that features shared by all three must have been responsible for much of patients' improvement" (p. 393). And thus was born Frank's interest in the common factors! Although he was not the first to discuss common factors (see Rosenzweig, 1936), Frank's thinking and research formed the core of the common factors school of thought for decades to come, culminating in publication of two editions of *Persuasion and Healing* (1961, 1973), and another edition (Frank & Frank, 1991) with his daughter, Julia B. Frank, MD, a tradition carried forth by such luminaries as Arthur Kleinman (e.g., Kleinman & Sung, 1979), Judd Marmor (e.g., 1962), Sol Garfield (e.g., 1995), and E. Fuller Torrey (1972).

We should not gloss over the courage that it took to abandon the medical model and embrace what turned into a model embedded in cultural healing practices, a journey that in many ways took Frank down a path far from the mainstream. The decision to pursue this line of research and thinking appears to have emanated from Frank's commitment to evidence foremost and his dedicated desire to improve lives, personal values that saturated his work. Over the years he attributed these values to his training and association with colleagues. For example,

> Psychiatric training at the Johns Hopkins Hospital under Adolf Meyer and John C. Whiteborn instilled a nondogmatic outlook, a respect for facts, and a conviction that systematic observation of individuals in their social context could yield worthwhile insights into human functioning. (Frank & Frank, 1991, p. 296)

We suspect that although colleagues may have nurtured these characteristics, Frank's fierce belief in evidence and his gentle respect for his fellow humans were intrinsic characteristics. Parloff and Shapiro (2005), in their *American Psychologist* obituary for Frank, quoted Paul McHugh, director of the Department of Psychiatry at the Johns Hopkins School of Medicine:

Jerome Frank combined two virtues that you don't usually find together: The vigorous virtue of being brave and the gentler virtue of being kind. He didn't hesitate to share his views, whether on nuclear war or psychotherapy. He did so with clarity, coherence, and with grace (p. 727).

The Common Factor Model

As mentioned previously, Frank was both an empiricist and a theorist, both a practitioner and a researcher. He followed his data and created a model of psychotherapy based on the data. For example, Frank extended the idea that placebo treatments have effects by conducting a study that found improvement in patient functioning to be due to simply being offered treatment (Frank, Gliedman, Imber, Stone, & Nash, 1959). In this study, minimal contact produced effects similar to group therapy and individual therapy. Following up on this, Frank, Nash, Stone, and Imber (1963) administered pretreatment symptom and mood measures. After some further testing, they readministered these measures. They then administered a placebo pill. Patients showed improved scores on the measures before they took the placebo. These effects were largely maintained when the patients returned for second and third visits 1 and 2 weeks later. Even more surprising, there were still measurable effects 3 years later. Frank therefore discovered that it is possible to get a placebo effect without a placebo. This finding was subsequently replicated many times (Friedman, 1963; Kellner & Sheffield, 1971; Piper & Wogan, 1970; Shapiro, Stuening, & Shapiro, 1980).

This kind of finding is not restricted to therapies practiced decades ago. It still seems that effects begin before what are thought to be the effective components of psychotherapy are applied to treatment. For example, Ilardi and Craighead (1994) looked at studies that followed the temporal course of improvement in cognitive therapy for depression. They reported that most positive change had occurred by the 3rd or 4th week of treatment. The specific techniques targeting depressive thought are not introduced into the treatment until a few sessions later, however. Moreover, the effects of these techniques are not presumed to be instantaneous but to develop with time. Thus, the cognitive techniques of cognitive therapy cannot account for these positive changes. This is Frank's finding all over again, this time with a modern and well-researched treatment that purports to be able to identify the relevant change agents underlying its effects. Whatever else is going on, some, perhaps most, change in this kind of therapy is not due to the usually identified factors. Based on these kinds of findings (although the Ilardi & Craighead, 1994, findings came later), Frank (1978) came to the conclusion that positive expectations are an important factor in psychotherapy. Having taken this step, he was on his way to his innovative common factors approach. (For more recent common factors approaches as well as rejoinders to critiques of such approaches, see Imel & Wampold, 2008; Wampold, 2007; Weinberger, 1995; Weinberger & Rasco, 2007.)

The common factors model Frank developed diverged radically from his initial belief that specific factors unique to specific treatments underlay the effectiveness of psychotherapy. He ended up arguing that radically diverse forms of psychotherapy have underlying similarities and that their effectiveness is due to these similarities (Frank, 1973). But his model was richer and more innovative than merely asserting common factors. He detailed what he thought those factors were. According to Frank's model (1973, 1978, 1982; Frank & Frank, 1991), patients have concluded that they are unable to deal with issues of importance to them. As a result, they feel incompetent and suffer for it. In Frank's terminology (e.g., Frank, 1974), they become *demoralized*. They hope and expect that psychotherapy can help them overcome these heretofore insurmountable issues. Once these hopes and positive expectations are in place, the demoralized state improves.

Although the mere intention to seek help results in some improvement, the elements of the treatment itself may enhance and solidify positive change. Additionally, the improvement based on positive expectation and hope needs to be maintained or it will dissipate over the course of treatment. Through certain practices, psychotherapy can improve morale beyond the effects of initial expectations and hopes. All effective psychotherapies, according to Frank (1973, 1978, 1982), employ four factors that function to mobilize hope and restore morale. The most important of these is an *emotionally charged, confiding relationship with a helping person*. Frank averred that such a relationship is absolutely essential to therapeutic improvement. Recent evidence has supported Frank's views on this matter (see, e.g., Weinberger & Rasco, 2007). A recent task force commissioned by Division 29 (Psychotherapy) of the American Psychological Association conducted a comprehensive review of the extant data and concluded that the relationship was a (in fact, the) critical factor in psychotherapy (Norcross, Beutler, & Levant, 2006).

Frank's second factor was a *healing setting*. Therapy has to take place somewhere. The therapeutic setting can and usually does symbolize the therapist's role as a healer. The setting can be a prestigious hospital or an impressive office, although even the most humble of settings will usually contain diplomas and impressive-looking books. Whatever the specifics, the setting provides a cultural context that communicates authority, expertise, and healing to the patient. All of this helps to enhance the patient's expectations and hope that the therapist knows what he or she is doing and can help. It sets the stage for the therapy and actively affects it. The setting also is a haven. The patient can feel safe and therefore more open in his or her communications to the therapist and to the therapist's interventions.

The third factor is a *rationale or myth* that plausibly explains the patient's difficulties and offers a sensible solution to them. Frank used the term *myth* purposely to denote a shared belief system that may or may not be scientifically true. What is important is that therapist and patient share a belief in this understanding of psychopathology and treatment. This can range from deep psychological conflicts originating in early childhood (e.g., Freud, 1917), to maladaptive ways of thinking (e.g., Beck, 1976), to a reinforcement history that has conditioned the person to behave maladaptively (Emmelkamp, 1994), to a lack of necessary skills (Lewinson & Hoberman, 1982), to possession by demons (Thong, 1976). As long as the myth can be shared, it can function effectively.

The fourth factor is a *believable treatment or ritual* for restoring emotional health. Again, Frank was very conscious of his terms. He referred to a *ritual* to highlight the idea that whatever takes place need not be scientifically valid but that something formal must occur in the course of treatment. A ritual involves the performance of actions or procedures in a set, ordered (often ceremonial) manner. Defined this way, the ritual can be described in a treatment manual or in the ceremonial treatment of a traditional shaman. In Frank's model, these are not different. What is important is that there be a logical connection between the rituals and the myth that explains the problem. Thus, lying on the psychoanalytic couch fosters regression to more primitive states (Freud, 1917), recording of "automatic thoughts" fosters the identification of maladaptive thought processes (Beck, 1976), and flooding or systematic desensitization extinguishes a maladaptive reinforcement history (Stampfl & Levis, 1967). This is no different in principle from drinking special potions and being ministered to by a shaman so that evil spirits can be exorcized (Peters, 1978). To Frank, the key was that the ritual be believable and clearly tied to the myth.

The equivalence of different forms of therapy flows naturally from Frank's model. After all, what makes therapy work is not the specific methods of the individual schools but what they all have in common, namely, Frank's four factors. One implication of this view is that the treatment manuals now required for clinical trial research do not actually contain within them the elements of therapeutic success (cf. Weinberger & Rasco, 2007). Rather, they are an example of a ritual that follows from the myth that one must proceed in a systematic manner and adhere to a theoretical approach if treatment is to work. Another implication that flows from Frank's model is that the therapeutic relationship is critical. Although few dispute this any more, it does not always garner the attention it should. Some schools of treatment do not accord it enough importance, if Frank is correct (cf. Weinberger, 1995; Weinberger & Rasco, 2007). The data seem to support the predictions of Frank's model. Outcome equivalence is the rule in psychotherapy outcome research (Wampold, 2001; Weinberger & Rasco, 2007), and when it does not appear, brand loyalty seems to account for the differences (Luborsky et al., 1999; Wampold, 2001).

CONCLUSION

Jerome Frank was a pioneer in psychotherapy research. His journeys were guided by critical thinking and empirical results, two hallmarks of rigorous science. His common factors model has stood as a viable alternative to the dedication to single theories and to the identification of treatments that purportedly are superior to others. A rereading of his and his Johns Hopkins' colleagues reminds us that innovative, creative, and rigorous research were the characteristics of this research program.

REFERENCES

American Psychological Association. (1986). Awards for distinguished contributions to psychology in the public interest: 1985, Jerome Frank. *American Psychologist, 41,* 398–405. doi: 10.1037/h0092128

Beck, A. T. (1976). *Cognitive therapy and the emotional disorders.* New York, NY: International Universities Press.

Emmelkamp, P. M. G. (1994). Behavior therapy with adults. In A. E. Bergin & S. L. Garfield (Eds.), *Handbook of psychotherapy and behavior change* (4th ed., pp. 379–427). New York, NY: Wiley.

Frank, J. D. (1958, November). The great antagonisms. *Atlantic Monthly, 202,* 58–62.

Frank, J. D. (1967). *Sanity and survival: Psychological aspects of war and peace.* New York, NY: Random House.

Frank, J. D. (1973). *Persuasion and healing.* Baltimore, MD: Johns Hopkins University Press. (Originally published in 1961)

Frank, J. D. (1974). Psychotherapy: The restoration of morale. *American Journal of Psychiatry, 131,* 271–274.

Frank, J. D. (1978). Expectation and therapeutic outcome: the placebo effect and the role induction interview. In J. D. Frank, R. Hoehn-Saric, S. D. Imber, B. L. Liberman, & A. R. Stone (Eds.), *Effective ingredients of successful psychotherapy* (pp. 1–34). New York, NY: Brunner/Mazel.

Frank, J. D. (1982). Therapeutic components shared by all psychotherapies. In J. H. Harvey & M. M. Parks (Eds.), *The Master Lecture Series: Vol. 1. Psychotherapy research and behavior change* (pp. 5–38). Washington, DC: American Psychological Association.

Frank, J. D. (1987). The drive for power and the nuclear arms race. *American Psychologist, 42,* 337–344. doi:10.1037/0003-066X.42.4.337

Frank, J. D., & Frank, J. B. (1991). *Persuasion and healing: A comparative study of psychotherapy* (3rd ed.). Baltimore, MD: Johns Hopkins Univesity Press.

Frank, J. D. (1992). The Johns Hopkins psychotherapy research project. In D. K. Freedheim (Ed.), *A history of psychotherapy: A century of change* (pp. 392–396). Washington, DC: American Psychological Association.

Frank, J. D., & Frank, J. B. (1991). *Persuasion and healing: A comparative study of psychotherapy* (3rd ed.). Baltimore: Johns Hopkins University Press.

Frank, J. D., Gliedman, L. H., Imber, S. D., Stone, A. R., & Nash, E. H. (1959). Patient's expectancies and relearning as factors determining improvement in psychotherapy. *American Journal of Psychiatry,, 115,* 961–968.

Frank, J. D., Nash, E. H., Stone, A. R., & Imber, S. D. (1963). Immediate and long-term symptomatic course of psychiatric outpatients. *American Journal of Psychiatry, 120,* 429–439.

Freud, S. (1917). Introductory lectures on psychoanalysis: Lecture XXVIII: Analytic therapy. In J. Strachey (Ed.), *The standard edition of the complete psychological work of Sigmund Freud* (Vol. 16, pp. 448–477). London, England: Hogarth Press.

Friedman, H. J. (1963). Patient expectancy and symptom reduction. *Archives of General Psychiatry, 8,* 61–67.

Garfield, S. L. (1995). *Psychotherapy: An eclectic-integrative approach.* New York, NY: Wiley.

Ilardi, S. S., & Craighead, W. E. (1994). The role of nonspecific factors in cognitive-behavior therapy for depression. *Clinical Psychology, 1,* 138–156.

Imel, Z. E., & Wampold, B. E. (2008). The common factors of psychotherapy. In S. D. Brown & R. W. Lent (Eds.), *Handbook of counseling psychology* (4th ed., pp. 249–66). New York, NY: Wiley.

Kellner, R., & Sheffield, B. F. (1971). The relief of distress following attendance at a clinic. *British Journal of Psychiatry, 118,* 195–198. doi:10.1192/bjp.118.543.195

Kleinman, A., & Sung, L. H. (1979). Why do indigenous practitioners successfully heal? *Social Science & Medicine, 13B,* 7–26.

Lewinson, P. M., & Hoberman, H. M. (1982). Depression. In A. S. Bellack, M. Hersen, & A. E. Kazdin (Eds.), *International handbook of behavior modification and therapy* (pp. 397–431). New York, NY: Plenum.

Luborsky, L., Diguer, L., Seligman, D. A., Rosenthal, R., Johnson, S., Halperin, G., . . . Schweizer, E. (1999). The researcher's own therapeutic allegiances: A "wild card" in the comparisons of treatment efficacy. *Clinical Psychology: Science and Practice, 6,* 95–106. doi:10.1093/clipsy/6.1.95

Marmor, J. (1962). Psychoanalytic therapy as an educational process. In J. H. Masserman (Ed.), *Science and psychoanalysis* (Vol. 5, pp. 286–299). New York, NY: Grune & Stratton.

Norcross, J. C., Beutler, L. E., & Levant, R. F. (2006). *Evidence-based practices in mental health*. Washington, DC: American Psychological Association.

Parloff, M. B., & Shapiro, D. L. (2005). Jerome D. Frank (1910–2005). *American Psychologist, 60*, 727. doi:10.1037/0003-066X.60.7.727

Peters, L. (1978). Psychotherapy in Tamang shamanism. *Ethos, 6*, 63–91.

Piper, W. E., & Wogan, M. (1970). Placebo effect in psychotherapy: An extension of earlier findings. *Journal of Consulting and Clinical Psychology, 34*, 447. doi:10.1037/h0029345

Rosenthal, D., & Frank, J. D. (1956). Psychotherapy and the placebo effect. *Psychological Bulletin, 53*, 294–302. doi:10.1037/h0044068

Rosenzweig, S. (1936). Some implicit common factors in diverse methods of psychotherapy: "At last the Dodo said, 'Everybody has won and all must have prizes.'" *American Journal of Orthopsychiatry, 6*, 412–415.

Shapiro, A. K., Struening, E., & Shapiro, E. (1980). The reliability and validity of a placebo test. *Journal of Psychiatric Research, 15*, 253–290. doi:10.1016/0022-3956(79)90016-5

Stampfl, T. G., & Levis, D. J. (1967). The essentials of implosive therapy: A learning-theory-based psychodynamic behavioral therapy. *Journal of Abnormal Psychology, 72*, 496–503. doi:10.1037/h0025238

Thong, D. (1976). Psychiatry in Bali. *Australian and New Zealand Journal of Psychiatry, 10*, 95–97.

Torrey, E. F. (1972). What Western psychotherapists can learn from witch doctors. *American Journal of Orthopsychiatry, 42*, 69–76.

Wampold, B. E. (2001). *The great psychotherapy debate: Model, methods, and findings*. Mahwah, NJ: Erlbaum.

Wampold, B. E. (2007). Psychotherapy: *The* humanistic (and effective) treatment. *American Psychologist, 62*, 857–873. doi: 10.1037/0003-066X.62.8.857

Weinberger, J. (1995). Common factors aren't so common: The common factors dilemma. *Clinical Psychology: Science and Practice, 2*, 45–69.

Weinberger, J., & Rasco, C. (2007). Empirically supported common factors. In S. G. Hofmann & J. Weinberger (Eds.), *The art and science of psychotherapy* (pp. 103–129). New York, NY: Routledge.

4

LESTER LUBORSKY: A TRAILBLAZER IN EMPIRICAL RESEARCH ON PSYCHOANALYTIC THERAPY

PAUL CRITS-CHRISTOPH, JACQUES P. BARBER,
BRIN F. S. GRENYER, AND LOUIS DIGUER

Lester Luborsky, who died in October 2009 at the age of 89, was one of the pioneers of psychotherapy research. His career began in the 1950s and only ended with his retirement in 2006. We are lucky to be intimately familiar with Lester's ideas and contributions throughout his career through our long-standing collaborations with him. We have benefited enormously from Lester's productivity, creativity, and perseverance in completing studies and projects. In this chapter we hope to provide a sense of his contributions to the field of psychotherapy research, not only in terms of his publications but also his personal influences on others.

MAJOR CONTRIBUTIONS

Lester Luborsky contributed in a variety of ways to many aspects of current psychotherapy research. His major contributions can be summarized in terms of the following broad themes.

Articulation of a Theory of Symptom Formation

A major theme in Luborsky's early research, but also continuing up to his retirement, was a focus on understanding the onset conditions for the appearance of both psychological and somatic symptoms during therapy sessions. His method, which he called the *symptom-context method*, involved the comparison of the material that had preceded the appearance of symptoms to sections of a session preceding a *control* event (i.e., a randomly selected event that was not describing the appearance of symptom). This work is summarized in his *Symptom-Context Method: Symptoms as Opportunities in Psychotherapy*, published in 1996.

Studies of Central Relationship Patterns

Perhaps Luborsky's most influential contribution later in his career was the quantitative study of relationship patterns in psychotherapy. The method Luborsky invented—the core conflictual relationship theme (CCRT) method—was a breakthrough in the operationalization of clinical psychodynamic concepts.

Studies of the Patient–Therapist Relationship

Luborsky developed one of the first scales to measure the therapeutic alliance in psychotherapy. This area of research went on to become perhaps the most highly researched aspect of the process of psychotherapy.

Development of a Treatment Manual for Brief Psychodynamic Therapy

Luborsky published one of the first psychodynamic treatment manuals. This contribution set the stage for the evaluation of the efficacy of this common form of psychotherapy.

Studies of Predictors of Therapeutic Outcome

Many of Luborsky's publications dealt with attempts to predict treatment outcome from patient, therapist, or process variables. The Penn Psychotherapy Project was a large-scale study conducted by Luborsky and colleagues designed to broadly assess the full range of potential predictors of outcome.

Studies of the Efficacy of Supportive–Expressive Psychotherapy

Early on, Luborsky collaborated with George Woody, Thomas McLellan, and Charles O'Brien on two studies of supportive–expressive therapy for patients with opiate dependence. In fact, this work is one of the few where a dynamic therapy for a specific disorder was replicated. This work led to additional studies of Luborsky and his colleagues looking at supportive–expressive therapy for major depressive disorder, generalized anxiety disorder, personality disorders, and cocaine dependence.

An Influential Review of the Literature on the Comparative Efficacy of Different Psychotherapies

In a widely cited classic publication, Luborsky, Singer, and Luborsky (1975) concluded from a qualitative review of about a hundred comparative treatment studies that all active treatments were equally effective. This convinced Luborsky of the importance of common factors across different psychotherapy.

EARLY BEGINNINGS

Lester Luborsky was born in 1920 and grew up during the Great Depression in Philadelphia, where he played in fields that disappeared as what was a town became a sprawling city. His family originated from Eastern Europe. After high school graduation, Luborsky took a research assistant job at Penn State to pursue his passion, botany. But while at Penn State he came across some of the works of Freud in his landlady's bookcase, and these books—together with a desire to work with people rather than plants—set the course of his future career. Luborsky then attended college at Temple University and graduated at the age of 22 with a bachelor of arts degree. He then proceeded to Duke University in North Carolina for his master's and PhD in psychology.

Even after turning to psychology and psychotherapy as his vocation, the theme of botany continued to be apparent throughout Luborsky's life and career. His passion for botany stemmed from a delight in what he termed "watching things grow"—which he later used as a natural basis for studying patients' growth and change over the course of psychotherapy. This theme was also placed by Luborsky on the last page (1984, p. 180) of his psychodynamic psychotherapy manual through an illustration showing the watering of a plant alongside a magnifying glass. These two symbols convey how the therapist provides the conditions and nutrients for growth and also provides a close examination of the thoughts, feelings, desires, and behaviors of the patient. One relevant memorable anecdote regarding botany was when, during Luborsky's training, he was discussing an idea with Eric Erikson. There was some contention between Luborsky and Erikson, but Erikson diplomatically replied that Luborsky's ideas "needed some watering." Also linked with Luborsky's interest in botany and gardening was that of rearranging stones and rocks within a natural setting (in the style of Japanese Zen rock gardens), an activity he pursued both in terms of the features in his own garden (which he tended religiously) and in miniature at his work desk. Luborsky's portrait, which hangs in the University of Pennsylvania Medical School, shows him with some rocks, an intentional reference to this aspect of his life and its influence on his other thinking.

Luborsky's PhD thesis, completed in 1945 and developed in the context of World War II, was on the topic of visual perception of aircraft recognition. Around this time his work for Raymond Cattell spurred his interest in psychological measurement. Following several positions at Duke and then the University of Illinois, Luborsky cemented his interest in Freud and psychoanalysis when he obtained a research post in 1946 at the world-renowned Menninger Foundation. The Menninger Foundation over the course of Luborsky's years there was a hotbed of influential psychoanalytic thinkers and researchers, including David Rapaport, Karl Menninger, George Klein, Roy Schafer, Philip Holzman, Herbert Schlesinger, Howard Shevrin, Merton Gill, Otto Kernberg, Robert Holt, and Robert Wallerstein. These individuals had an enormous influence on Luborsky's clinical training and research ideas. While working within the Menninger clinic research program, he was offered and accepted full psychoanalytic training with the affiliated Topeka Psychoanalytic Institute. This was at the time a rare opportunity, as psychologists generally were unable to obtain psychoanalytic training, and he was able to integrate his analysis with his paid work, making his analytic training affordable and possible.

His 13 years (1946–959) in Kansas at the Menninger Foundation were critical to shaping much of the direction of Luborsky's future research, for it was here that he worked on one of the first empirical studies of psychoanalytic psychotherapy, the Menninger Foundation Psychotherapy Research Project. In those years, research on psychotherapy and psychoanalytic was in its infancy. Important researchers at the time who were influences included Henry Murray and Christina Morgan at Harvard. Components of their work with the Thematic Apperception Test were probably influential in the later development of the tripartite structure of Luborsky's CCRT method.

Luborsky was offered, and accepted, a post at the University of Pennsylvania in 1959. Aaron Beck was on the panel that supported his professorship. The move "back home" to Philadelphia was his last career move, and he was highly productive at Penn until his retirement in 2006. The move to Penn allowed him to take leadership of projects and ideas that had been germinating in Kansas, and major projects began to emerge, including the Penn Psychotherapy Research project. Throughout most of his years at Penn, he was not only a researcher but actively involved as a clinical psychotherapist and a teacher of psychotherapy. He was highly sought after as a clinical supervisor and won an award within the Department of Psychiatry for his teaching of psychiatric residents and postdoctoral fellows.

ACCOMPLISHMENTS

In regard to specific contributions, we focus our brief review of Lester Luborsky's research accomplishments around a selection of some of his more influential and classic papers, taking them in historical order and placing them within the context of the science of psychotherapy, and his personal odyssey, of the time.

How does a career in psychotherapy research begin? For Luborsky, it began with a challenge that motivated him through much of his career. This challenge came in the form of a paper published in 1952 by the famous British psychologist Hans Eysenck. In this paper, Eysenck claimed that psychotherapy produced changes no larger than what is evident from the passage of time. Luborsky wrote a rebuttal to Eysenck's paper (Luborsky, 1954) arguing that Eysenck's control group (insurance company data) was flawed, as was the assessment of outcome. Eighteen years later, Luborsky (1972) again wrote a response to Eysenck, reiterating and extending some of his earlier points. For much of the rest of his career, he often spoke about the impact that Eysenck's paper had on him. The extensive research on psychotherapy outcome that was generated in the 1970s, 1980s, and 1990s, leading to the widespread consensus that Eysenck was wrong and that psychotherapy was effective, gave Luborsky satisfaction that the debate had been settled in Luborsky's favour.

Once you have decided to devote your career to the study of psychotherapy, what do you do first? The first step is to create valid ways of measuring the outcome of treatment. So this is where Luborsky began. One particular task he had within the context of the Menninger Foundation Psychotherapy Research Project was to help develop a measure of psychological health–sickness. Before the publication of the *Diagnostic and Statistical Manual of Mental Disorders* (*DSM*; 1952) and the current focus on syndromes and symptoms, psychotherapy was applied to the broad range of patients appropriate for outpatient treatment. Luborsky's work in this area led to the development of the Health–Sickness Rating Scale (HRSR; Luborsky, 1962). Although simple, this rating scale has been extremely useful in clinical research. With minor changes, the HRSR became the basis for the widely used Global Assessment of Functioning scale in the *DSM*.

Like any fledgling field of study, an early step in the development of the evolving field of psychotherapy research was to hold a consensus conference to map out the primary issues and problems that needed to be addressed. An initial consensus conference was held in 1958. The second, and more significant, consensus conference was held in 1961. Luborsky was prominently involved in the planning and implementation of this consensus conference, and participated as an editor of a book that summarized the conference findings (Strupp & Luborsky, 1962). His collaboration with Hans Strupp on this volume marked the beginnings of a lifelong friendship and friendly competition with Strupp. As Strupp remarked to a Vanderbilt graduate student who had worked in Luborsky's research program, he and Luborsky were the "Macy's and Gimbels" (an allusion to the department stores' legendary rivalry) of psychodynamic psychotherapy research—often pursuing similar research agendas and each keeping a close eye on what the other was doing.

After coming to the University of Pennsylvania, Luborsky obtained a major grant, in 1968, from the National Institute of Mental Health (NIMH) to conduct a 5-year comprehensive study of the factors that influence the outcome of psychotherapy. This study, later named by Luborsky the "Penn Psychotherapy Project," was the primary source of data and transcripts for a large number of his subsequent papers, chapters, and books for the rest of his career. At the same time he received the NIMH grant to conduct the Penn Psychotherapy Project, Luborsky applied for and received a Research Scientist grant (K-award) from NIMH (1968–1973). He would obtain renewals of this Research Scientist grant from NIMH from 1973 to 1992, and he then received similar awards from 1992 to 2000 from the National Institute on Drug Abuse.

Luborsky's interest in examining predictors of therapy outcome originated from his experiences working at the Menninger Foundation before coming to the University of Pennsylvania. The Menninger Foundation Psychotherapy Research Project also had the goal, among other goals, of examining predictors of treatment outcome. However, he left the Menninger Foundation before the study came to fruition. This seemed to motivate him, as he described in the acknowledgment section of the 1988 book, *Who Will Benefit From Psychotherapy? Predicting Therapeutic Outcomes*, to conduct his own study that would make use of the strengths but rectify the weaknesses of the Menninger study. Another input to his interest in examining predictors of therapy outcome was his previous work at Menninger's with Robert Holt on predictors of which physicians would make good psychiatrists (Holt & Luborsky, 1958). The difficult issues in the work with Holt regarding the assessment of outcome and how to manage a large number of predictors helped

Luborsky address similar methodological concerns when working on a comprehensive study of predictors of therapy outcome.

In preparation for conducting the Penn Psychotherapy Project, Luborsky and colleagues published in the *Psychological Bulletin* a review of all previous studies examining predictors of therapy outcome. This review (Luborsky et al., 1971) became highly influential, eventually receiving recognition as a "citation classic" by the Science Citation Index in 1981.

In 1975, Luborsky and colleagues published another highly cited and influential paper reviewing the literature to date on comparative studies of psychotherapies. The subtitle of the paper, "Everyone Has Won and All Must Have Prizes," was taken from the verdict of the dodo bird commenting on a race in Lewis Carroll's famous *Alice's Adventures in Wonderland*. Originally applied by Rosenzweig (1936) in a clinical analysis to convey the sense that diverse psychotherapies achieve comparable success owing to common factors, Luborsky's borrowing of the dodo's verdict to summarize his seminal review of the comparative effects of different psychotherapies has had a lasting impact on psychotherapy research. Since the publication of his paper, it is actually rare to see a paper that addresses comparative effects of psychotherapies that does not make reference to the "dodo bird verdict" and Luborsky's paper, either in support of his conclusion or attempting to refute it.

The primary results of the Penn Psychotherapy Project took several years to appear in print, with the full set of results published in book form later (Luborsky et al., 1988). The delay in publishing the results of the Penn Psychotherapy Project (data collection was finished in 1973, but the first primary paper giving results appeared in 1979) was probably due to a number of factors. One was that the funding for the study had ended and Luborsky's primary collaborator, Jim Mintz, who had provided the methodological and statistical expertise for the study, had moved on to another job. A second factor is that the results of the study were largely negative: The outcomes of psychotherapy were not very predictable from pretreatment information on patients or therapists. Luborsky always preferred to tell a positive message about his research studies, commenting once (to Paul Crits-Christoph) that "there are two types of researchers, those that say there is nothing in the data and those that say there is something in the data." The lack of findings left Luborsky searching for something to say. This then eventually spurred him to attack the question anew: If pretreatment factors mattered little, what determined the outcome of psychotherapy?

The answer, of course, was that aspects of the process of psychotherapy were particularly important to treatment outcome. The immediate stimulus for Luborsky's turning to creating new measures for studying the process of psychotherapy was his participation in a panel at the Society for Psychotherapy Research meetings in 1975. It was at this panel that Ed Bordin introduced his influential ideas on the concept of the working alliance. In preparation for the meeting, Luborsky began looking closely at transcripts of sessions from the Penn Psychotherapy Study to see if he could devise a way of measuring the alliance. The result was the creation of observer-rated scales to measure the *helping alliance* (Luborsky's term for what others referred to as the *therapeutic alliance* or *working alliance*), which he first published in a book chapter (Luborsky, 1976). He subsequently published on the development of an alliance questionnaire and conducted a variety of studies looking at the role of the alliance in psychotherapy.

In many ways it appears as though Luborsky's success at inventing a scale to measure the alliance unleashed his creativity and energies that set the stage for the rest of his career. Much of his research on psychotherapy up to this point (1975) was atheoretical in nature. The breakthrough of seeing that a central clinical notion like the alliance could be measured allowed him and others to ask further theoretically and clinically important questions about the process and outcome of psychotherapy, particularly psychodynamic psychotherapy. This shift in creative energies is evident in Luborsky's productivity: From 1945 to 1975 he published 87 publications and from 1975 to 2005 he published over 300 more.

Immediately after developing a measure of the alliance, Luborsky turned his attention to another key aspect of clinical psychodynamic psychotherapy: the assessment of the patient's central relationship theme. The concept of the CCRT was initially formulated in 1977 (Luborsky, 1977). With the CCRT, Luborsky wished to reach with empirical tools the deepest roots of clinical psychodynamic practice, that is, the transference, which is regarded as the keystone and the most specific characteristic of psychoanalytic and psychodynamic treatments. His efforts at measuring this element of psychotherapy were very productive. Numerous studies used the CCRT in a variety of contexts (summarized in Luborsky & Crits-Christoph, 1998). Further, the work on the CCRT fostered the emergence of other measures and methodologies that aim at exploring psychotherapy processes that were thought before to be too difficult to approach empirically.

The CCRT was also an important component of one of Luborsky's other most influential contributions: the codification of supportive–expressive psychodynamic psychotherapy in a treatment manual (Luborsky, 1984). After emerging from a period of "generic" or atheoretical psychotherapy research, Luborsky had now turned back completely to his psychoanalytic roots that were nurtured at the Menninger Foundation. The concept of a treatment manual—a guide to assist in the training of therapists and the standardization of treatment—was new to psychotherapy research. As part of his clinical teaching of therapy, Luborsky had developed in 1976 a rough unpublished guide to training psychodynamic psychotherapists called *The Task of the Psy-*

chotherapist. Sensing that a more formal treatment manual would help move the scientific study of psychodynamic therapy forward, he embarked on a systematic description of how to do what he felt was typical psychodynamic therapy. His model for the treatment was the supportive–expressive therapy taught at the Menninger Foundation. A further impetus for Luborsky's moving quickly on publishing his manual was the knowledge that Hans Strupp was also working on a guide to psychodynamic therapy. Both treatment manuals were published in 1984 with the same publisher (Strupp & Binder, 1984; Luborsky, 1984).

Luborsky's supportive–expressive treatment manual became a major success both clinically and in research circles. The manual was frequently used as a training device in graduate programs and psychiatric residencies. The manual, together with more specific addendums tailoring the treatment to specific patient population, served as the basis for studies of supportive–expressive therapy for generalized anxiety disorder, chronic depression, cocaine dependence, personality disorders, opiate dependence, and cannabis dependence.

Beyond his publications, Luborsky influenced psychotherapy research in many other ways. He was the fourth president (1973–1974) of the Society for Psychotherapy Research (SPR), the only professional conference that he regularly attended. Across a span of 32 years (from the first meeting in 1970 to 2002), we are aware of only one annual SPR meeting that he did not attend, presenting a paper at each and every meeting he attended.

Not being in a psychology department, Lester did not work directly with graduate students as an advisor. However, within the Department of Psychiatry at the University of Pennsylvania, his influence as a clinical teacher of psychiatric residents and postdoctoral fellows was enormous. His model of clinical supervision was a group one. This group supervision was a sought-after aspect of the psychiatric residency—with four to five residents or postdoctoral fellows participating every year for the more than 25 years that he offered this group. While other psychodynamic supervisors relied on the overwhelmingly large and diverse psychoanalytic literature as the base for their teaching, Luborsky's approach to psychodynamic therapy, anchored in his supportive–expressive therapy manual and the CCRT formulation, provided an understandable entry into the complex psychoanalytic arena. Thus, Luborsky was typically the first supervisor who made a generation of clinical trainees at the University of Pennsylvania comfortable with the ambiguous task of being a therapist.

Within the research domain, Luborsky had a major influence on a number of young PhDs or MDs who were junior faculty at the University of Pennsylvania and went on to have careers in psychotherapy research. Art Auerbach joined Luborsky at the beginning of the Penn Psychotherapy Project and continued working closely with him for about a decade. Jim Mintz was the project director of the Penn Psychotherapy Project. Paul Crits-Christoph and

Jacques Barber were also hired by Luborsky as junior faculty in the Department of Psychiatry. All four of these investigators went on to become presidents of SPR. By this metric, Luborsky mentored significantly more future presidents of SPR than did any other senior psychotherapy researcher in history. Other significant collaborators at the University of Pennsylvania were Tom McLellan, George Woody, and Charles O'Brien. Luborsky also had an influence internationally, developing strong collaborations with investigators and clinicians in Germany (Horst Kächele), Canada (Louis Diguer, Howard Book), and Australia (Brín Grenyer), among others.

CONCLUSION

Luborsky's work—particularly his writings on predictors of outcome, the CCRT, supportive–expressive therapy, comparative studies of psychotherapies, and the alliance—has had a broad influence on the field of psychotherapy and beyond. From the broadest perspective, perhaps his lasting legacy is in demonstrating that highly sophisticated clinical concepts about psychotherapy could be measured and validated. When a large faction of the field viewed psychotherapy as more of an art form that could not be rigorously studied, Luborsky was determined to show otherwise. Although he valued and respected the work of Sigmund Freud enormously, Luborsky's career was focused in a direction different from Freud's. In fact, in the 1930s, after receiving a letter from Saul Rosenzweig that described the results of experimental studies of some psychoanalytic concepts, Freud said that psychoanalysis had no need of such studies, because clinical observation was sufficient to establish the usefulness of the psychoanalytic concepts. In contrast to Freud, Luborsky was doggedly determined to show that quantitative studies of psychoanalytic concepts and therapy were useful and could more rigorously validate such constructs. To the extent that he succeeded in this agenda in multiple ways, the practice of psychotherapy and the scientific study of psychotherapy have both benefited enormously from Luborsky's career.

REFERENCES

American Psychiatric Association. (1952). *Diagnostic and statistical manual of mental disorders*. Washington, DC: Author.

Eysenck, H. J. (1952). The effects of psychotherapy: An evaluation. *Journal of Consulting Psychology, 16*, 319–324. doi:10.1037/h0063633

Holt, R. R., & Luborsky, L. (1958). *Personality patterns of psychiatrists: A study in selection techniques* (Vol. 1). New York, NY: Basic Books.

Luborsky, L., & Crits-Christoph, P. (Eds.). (1998). *Understanding transference: The core conflictual relationship theme method* (2nd ed.). Washington, DC: American Psychological Association.

Luborsky, L. B. (1954). A note on Eysenck's article: The effects of psychotherapy: An evaluation. *British Journal of Psychology, 45,* 129–131.

Luborsky, L. (1962). Clinician's judgments of mental health: A proposed scale. *Archives of General Psychiatry, 7,* 407–417.

Luborsky, L. (1972). Another reply to Eysenck. *Psychological Bulletin, 78,* 406–408. doi:10.1037/h0020022

Luborsky, L. (1976). Helping alliances in psychotherapy: The groundwork for a study of their relationship to its outcome. In J. L. Claghorn (Ed.), *Successful psychotherapy* (pp. 92–116). New York, NY: Brunner/Mazel.

Luborsky, L. (1977). Measuring a pervasive psychic structure in psychotherapy: The core conflictual relationship theme. In N. Freedman & S. Grand (Eds.), *Communicative structures and psychic structures* (pp. 367–395). New York, NY: Plenum Press.

Luborsky, L. (1984). *Principles of psychoanalytic therapy. A manual for supportive-expressive treatment.* New York, NY: Basic Books.

Luborsky, L., Chandler, M., Auerbach, A. H., Cohen, J., & Bachrach, H. M. (1971). Factors influencing the outcome of psychotherapy: A review of quantitative research. *Psychological Bulletin, 75,* 145–185. doi:10.1037/h0030480

Luborsky, L. (1996). (Ed). *Symptom-Context Method—Symptoms as opportunities in psychotherapy.* Washington: American Psychological Association.

Luborsky, L., Crits-Christoph, P., Mintz, J., & Auerbach, A. (1988). *Who will benefit from psychotherapy? Predicting therapeutic outcomes.* New York, NY: Basic Books.

Luborsky, L., Singer, B., & Luborsky, Lise. (1975). Comparative studies of psychotherapies: Is it true that "Everyone has won and all must have prizes"? *Archives of General Psychiatry, 32,* 995–1008.

Rosenzweig, S. (1936). Some implicit common factors in diverse methods of psychotherapy. *The American Journal of Orthopsychiatry, 6,* 412–415.

Strupp, H. H., & Binder, J. L. (1984). *Psychotherapy in a new key: A guide to time-limited dynamic psychotherapy.* New York, NY: Basic Books.

Strupp, H. H., & Luborsky, L. B. (Eds.). (1962). *Research in psychotherapy.* [Proceedings of a conference held in Chapel Hill, NC, May 1961.] Washington, DC: American Psychological Association.

5

HANS STRUPP: A FOUNDER'S CONTRIBUTIONS TO A SCIENTIFIC BASIS FOR PSYCHOTHERAPY PRACTICE

KARLA MORAS, TIMOTHY ANDERSON, AND WILLIAM E. PIPER

Hans Hermann Strupp's passion for psychotherapy practice and research fueled pioneering contributions to both and brought international influence and acclaim to this famously modest man. He stands among the most widely read, thoughtful, ecumenical, and avid scholar–scientist–clinicians in psychotherapy and therapy research during the latter half of the 20th century. Even his early writings and therapy research remain broadly cited and influential.

Beginning with his dissertation proposal in 1953, Hans Strupp's contributions coincided with and helped shape the coalescence of therapy research into a bona fide field in the United States. An auxiliary but key role was to serve both research and practice as a bridge builder. For example, he supported Goldfried's proposal that the power of psychotherapy might be increased by integrating theoretically diverse, and often warring, schools of therapy that dominated the emerging scene into the 1980s (e.g., Goldfried, 1982). Strupp continually pursued a variety of ways to close the refractory gap between practice and research (e.g., Strupp, 1989). As a researcher, he applied rigorous scientific methodology with a master practitioner's sensibilities for understanding the complexity of both psychotherapy and therapy research data. Two of his particularly well-known studies, popularly referred to as "Vanderbilt I" and "Vanderbilt II," illustrate the point. Both were conducted during the 3rd and

4th decades of his career while he was a Distinguished Professor at Vanderbilt University (Bein et al., 2000; Henry, Strupp, Butler, Schacht, & Binder, 1993; Strupp, 1993; Strupp & Hadley, 1979).

Hans Strupp remained an active, leading figure until about the year 2000, when his eloquent and incisive clinical–theoretical and research writing (e.g., Strupp, 1977) was increasingly challenged by Parkinson's disease. Hans's sonorous voice and charming, subtle wit stayed with us longer. His impact as mentor, colleague, and model for conducting one's life in ways that honor being human are as legendary as they are enduring.

MAJOR CONTRIBUTIONS

Hans Strupp is recognized for numerous major contributions. Perhaps most crucial, given the vulnerable, nascent periods of psychotherapy research and clinical psychology during which Strupp entered both fields, was his stalwart advocacy of a fundamental—yet often controversial—principle: A scientific basis for clinical practice is required. Although Strupp remained profoundly influenced by Freud's writings, he departed fundamentally from Freud by insisting on the need for scientific testing of efficacy and other claims about all forms of psychotherapy, including psychoanalysis (Bergin, 2007; Strupp, 1976b). More broadly, Strupp remained a resolute, even courageous, voice for excellence and responsible professionalism in all aspects of clinical psychology (training, practice, research) when anti-intellectual, antiscientific, and related ideas gained popularity both within the field of clinical psychology and as sociopolitical forces in the United States (Strupp, 1976a).

Strupp's contributions advanced knowledge on several core practice-relevant questions, notably: What are the key mechanisms of action of psychotherapy as a generic treatment modality? What are the implications for evaluating psychotherapies of the recurrent finding that interested parties, such as patient, therapist, and society's representatives, often do not closely agree on outcomes (Strupp & Hadley, 1977)? What is the therapist's contribution? and, importantly, What are the impacts of therapists' negative reactions to patients, and how can such reactions be managed to avoid compromising the potential benefits of therapy or, worse, promoting negative effects?

What might Strupp cite as his major contributions? He emphasized two conclusions near the close of his career on questions that were both central to the field and lifelong foci of his research (e.g., Henry & Strupp, 1992; Strupp, 1993, 1995).

- Conclusion 1. The nonspecific vs. specific factors model of therapeutic influence is fatally flawed as a general model of the action of psychotherapy and cannot productively guide research (Strupp, 1995).

- Conclusion 2. *"The quality of the interpersonal context* is the sine qua non in all forms of psychotherapy" (Strupp, 1995, p. 70, italics in original). Further, a major barrier to optimal therapeutic benefits is inadequate therapist skill in managing the interpersonal context of psychotherapy, particularly therapists' negative attitudes and behaviors toward patients. Therapeutic work carries with it a ubiquitous vulnerability to problems in the interpersonal context, which merits being *the* core focus of professional therapist training (Henry & Strupp, 1992; Strupp, 1995).

EARLY BEGINNINGS

The path to Hans Strupp's prodigiously successful career was neither easy nor obvious. He was born in Frankfurt am Main, Germany (August 25, 1921), less than 3 years after World War I. When he was 9 years old, Strupp was sent away to live briefly with an uncle because his father was ill. He was unaware of the gravity of his father's condition until he was told that his father had died, whereupon, he vividly recalled, he was whisked away to a local religious leader and declared head of the family.

Hans's early education was interrupted when Nazi influences made public schools problematic for Jewish students. When he was about 16, Hans's mother decided that he had best leave the school system. His education continued via private language lessons and work as an apprentice, focused on basic office skills and translation—to enhance the family's chances to immigrate to the United States. After a close encounter with the anti-Semitic fury of the Kristallnacht, he fled at age 17 from Nazi Germany to the United States with his mother and only sibling, a younger brother. They landed in New York City, where Hans worked as a bookkeeper but soon was offered a job transfer with higher salary in the Washington, DC, area. There, the family lived in an apartment from about 1940 to 1951 in an arrangement that Strupp described with affectionate wit as a "folie-à-trois." Into adulthood, Hans's prescribed role and sense of duty as head of the family endured: His advanced education was delayed and prolonged by working as a bookkeeper to provide for his mother. In 1951, his home situation changed when he married Lottie Metzger, who became the mother of their three children and his lifelong partner.

Strupp completed bachelor's and master's degrees at George Washington University via night school. His choice of an undergraduate major in

psychology was primarily due to pragmatic postdegree employability considerations, rather than to the field's intrinsic appeal to him, at least as it was
taught at the time. The same was not true of Freud's writings. In Strupp's
(n.d.) words:

> Freud's writings captivated me and opened horizons of unimaginable pro-
> portions. Untutored as I was in psychoanalysis, much of what I read
> escaped me but what I did comprehend left a deep impression. No other
> writer had a comparable effect on my life. Freud has remained one of my
> great heroes, the other being Mozart.

A fellow student, also a German refugee, serendipitously introduced
Strupp to Freud's works in about 1940. By 1946, Strupp pursued clinically oriented experiences, including a personal psychoanalysis, at the Washington
School of Psychiatry (WSP). The WSP was renowned for the interpersonal
model of one of its founders, Harry Stack Sullivan (Sullivan, 1953). Hans's
decision to apply to the WSP was likely bolstered in 1945 by a chance meeting with Frieda Fromm-Reichman, also a German refugee, who taught at
WSP and was a prominent psychiatrist at the famous Chestnut Lodge in
Maryland. Strupp never forgot "her indelible injunction: *The therapist listens*"
(Strupp, n.d., italics in original). He seemed to agree that "it is the crux of
all psychotherapy."

The completion of his doctorate in 1954, when Strupp was 32 years
old, launched his psychotherapy research career. Although his doctoral sub-
specialty was social psychology, his dissertation project was psychotherapy
research. Strupp received instant and strong reinforcement for the effort. His
dissertation yielded three articles, all published in 1955 and in the most prestigious, then and now, clinical research journal of the American Psychological Association (e.g., Strupp, 1955), the *Journal of Consulting and Clinical
Psychology*.[1]

Strupp's "heart's desire" became "to become a clinical psychologist," but
he encountered difficulty because his educational background was not the
accepted route to the profession (Strupp, n.d.). A hurdle he could not clear
even with doctorate in hand was the lack of a predoctoral internship. Unsuccessful applications for clinical positions and his signature persistence culminated in 1955 with a success—a grant from the National Institute of Mental
Health (NIMH) for a therapy research project. Strupp always believed that
Jerome Frank, a reviewer of the grant application (Strupp's first) with whom
he met during the review process, was integrally responsible. To Strupp, the
grant was "one of the greatest strokes of luck in [his] professional career"
(Strupp, n.d.).

---

[1]Formerly, *Journal of Consulting Psychology*.

ACCOMPLISHMENTS AND HONORS

Strupp published on or otherwise contributed to most, if not all, of the core issues and questions in therapy research and practice from the 1950s into the new millennium. Also, and important, his primary allegiance was always to advancing the potential effectiveness of psychotherapy as a treatment modality. Thus, while his sentiments remained closest to the psychodynamic perspective, he carefully evaluated the potential of other theoretical models, such as learning theory, to inform the effort. He both contributed to efforts to identify therapeutically potent elements of, and commonalities between, theoretically different forms of therapy (e.g., Strupp, 1973) and encouraged the efforts of others (Paul Wachtel, Marvin Goldfried) to do so.

Strupp received many prestigious awards, including the American Psychological Association's (APA) Distinguished Professional Contributions to Knowledge Award, the Society for Psychotherapy Research's (SPR) Distinguished Research Career Award, and an honorary Doctor of Medicine from the University of Ulm. Strupp treasured SPR, an organization of which he was a founding member and third president. In 1998, the American Psychoanalytic Association awarded him honorary membership

> . . . in recognition for his exploration of psychoanalytic science over many decades in academic settings rife with skepticism about psychoanalysis and his contributions toward legitimizing psychoanalytic thought and investigation in graduate and postgraduate education in psychology (Strupp, n.d.).

The award carried some irony: Around 1960, Strupp had been denied a deeply cherished goal—to receive psychoanalytic training at an officially recognized psychoanalytic institute. Full psychoanalytic training was closed to non-MDs despite Freud's explicit statements that psychoanalysis was distinct from medicine and properly separated from it.

Only a few accomplishments are highlighted in this short chapter. They are described mostly in chronological order to convey milestones that led to Strupp's two major conclusions, previously noted.

From Serendipitous Early Findings to Scientific, Practice, and Training Foci

In Strupp's view, his most constant goal was to elucidate how therapists can purposefully and consistently potentiate beneficial effects—and also avoid the opposite. The latter came to be a primary focus as his career progressed. His keen interest in the therapist's contribution is traceable to his first therapy study, his dissertation (e.g., Strupp, 1955). It and other of his early studies led to what Strupp called a "serendipitous finding" that became a central, guiding thread (Henry & Strupp, 1992):

> I adduced evidence that negative attitudes toward a patient tended to be associated with unempathic therapist communications and unfavorable clinical judgments, whereas the opposite was true of respondents who felt more positively toward the patient. I considered this a serendipitous finding whose implications for research, training, and practice I have been trying to explore ever since. (p. 437)

Any review of Strupp's major accomplishments requires noting that even his early research was characterized by rigorous scientific methods and thinking—and at a time when few therapy research studies existed and when most of them exhibited weak designs. Further, Strupp knew that it was crucial to determine if psychotherapy can work: Does it potentiate more rapid and/or more extensive benefits than the simple passage of time or informal, naturally occurring sources of help, such as caring, wise friends? He also viewed evidence that therapy can work as preliminary knowledge for both practice and science. If therapies work, then the next main practice-relevant challenge is to discover why and how they work: Do they work for theoretically posited reasons? Knowledge of mechanisms will enable practitioners to conduct treatments systematically and efficiently. Vanderbilt I was among Strupp's contributions to a fundamental mechanism question of his, and contemporary, times.

Frank's Common Factors Model and Vanderbilt I

Jerome Frank (1961, 1971) proffered his now classic common factors model of how psychotherapies work in the early 1960s. The model partially explained surprising but recurrent, then and now, findings of few if any statistically significant differences between the outcomes of theoretically different forms of psychotherapy. (More recent evidence indicates that the same often is true for psychotherapy vs. medication.) The common factors model logically attributes equivalent outcomes to variables that must be common to, that is, shared by, different therapy approaches rather than to their unique, theory-driven specific techniques. (Frank was aware of an alternative explanation: Outcome measurement methods could be a key cause of no difference findings.)

Frank's model, also cast as "nonspecific vs. specific factors," became a preoccupation for Strupp during groundbreaking NIMH-funded projects on which he and Allen Bergin collaborated. One fruit of their effort was a diligently crafted set of research questions and proposed experiments to answer them. The questions and experiments appear in *Changing Frontiers in the Science of Psychotherapy* (Bergin & Strupp, 1972), along with working papers in which Strupp began to sketch out what became a classic experiment on nonspecific versus specific factors, Vanderbilt I. The very influential book emphasized the need for experimentally controlled, well-designed psychotherapy research; Vanderbilt I later became a marker for the first of Strupp's aforementioned two major conclusions.

Vanderbilt I was designed to test hypothesized added contributions to outcomes of specific techniques that professional therapists are trained to use, beyond benefits that might be potentiated by nonspecific factors such as a confiding relationship with a trustworthy person who possesses socially sanctioned credentials (credentials such as those of professional therapists). Male college students who had clinically significant problems with depression, anxiety, and shyness were randomly assigned to receive up to 25 sessions of "therapy" twice a week from either professional psychotherapists or college professors who were reputed to be sought out by students for advice. Two experimental control conditions were included: minimal contact and waiting-list. No difference was found between the outcomes of professional therapists and college professors (Strupp & Hadley, 1979), another finding of the times that belied widespread assumptions.[2]

Within the next 10 years, Strupp concluded that the dichotomous conceptualization of nonspecific versus specific factors itself was misguided—"a pseudo problem that is not amenable to solution"—as a general model of the mechanisms of action of psychotherapy (Strupp, 1995, p. 70). He advised that it be abandoned. He came to believe that any curative effects of specific techniques could not be isolated from qualities of the relationship between patient and therapist in which techniques necessarily are embedded (Butler & Strupp, 1986; Strupp, 1995). He also sought to "move beyond simple notions of therapist warmth and genuineness to describe more precisely the important aspects of the therapist's personal contribution to the therapeutic process" (Strupp, Butler & Rosser, 1988, p. 693). Strupp's final conclusion was that a theory of therapeutic action that guided one of his major studies was an unproductive heuristic to (a) frame experimental investigation of how psychotherapies work, (b) strengthen psychotherapy as a generic treatment modality, or (c) guide clinical thinking. He searched elsewhere and differently after Vanderbilt I.

Vanderbilt I Toward Vanderbilt II: Process–Outcome Studies, Varieties of Scientific Method, Scientific Teamwork, and Negative Effects

The period after Vanderbilt I's launch was filled with intensive process–outcome studies (e.g., Gomes-Schwartz, 1978) and innovative research. For

---

[2]Strupp (1993; Strupp & Hadley, 1979) knew that the finding could be challenged due to the semianalogue nature of the sample, which consisted of randomly selected male undergraduate students recruited by mail, many of whom were not independently seeking treatment. The limitation contributed to the Vanderbilt II design in which treated adults were recruited by advertisement for low-cost therapy.

example, Strupp, in the scientific tradition of systematically exploring data to better understand surprising monothetic (aggregated group level) findings and develop new hypotheses, conducted a series of post hoc, within-therapist, case study comparisons of four Vanderbilt I therapists' good- and poor-outcome patients (e.g., Strupp, 1980). He concluded that patient characteristics and also weaknesses in some therapists' responses to interpersonally challenging patient features contributed to poorer outcomes. Additionally, Strupp and his research team surveyed relevant experts' views on the critical but neglected, then and now, topic of potential negative effects of psychotherapy (Strupp, Hadley, & Gomes-Schwartz, 1977). The team also developed an observer-rated process measure to identify predictors and potential causes of negative outcomes (Suh, Strupp & O'Malley, 1986).

Research of the foregoing type helped solidify Hans's conclusion that the common factors model, which supported the ongoing nonspecific vs. specific factors debate, was fatally flawed. The work also paved the way to both Vanderbilt II and to what ultimately became his aforementioned second major conclusion.

Vanderbilt II: The Therapist's Contribution, "Difficult" Patients, and Toward Advances in Therapist Training

Vanderbilt II was designed to determine (a) if experienced therapists could be trained to use intervention principles and techniques that were specifically developed to better manage problematic, albeit frequent, interpersonal processes in therapy sessions, and (b) if (a) was possible, whether outcomes were better after the training. The centerpiece of Vanderbilt II was a form of psychodynamically oriented psychotherapy that Strupp developed with Jeffrey Binder, time-limited dynamic psychotherapy (TLDP; Strupp & Binder, 1984). TLDP reflects the enduring impact of both Freud and Sullivan on Strupp's clinical understanding and research. Importantly, it also merged nonspecific "relationship factors" and specific technique by "stress[ing] the careful monitoring, exploration, and use of the therapeutic relationship as a technical strategy in its own right" (Strupp, 1993, p. 432).

A key aim of TLDP was to help therapists successfully avoid or otherwise manage limits to therapeutic progress potentially created by their negative attitudes and behaviors toward patients. TLDP also was intended to extend the reach of therapists to patients often referred to as "difficult" and "resistant." Strupp realized that they were most likely in need of something that professional, highly trained psychotherapists should be able to provide, rather than patients who, according to decades of outcome findings, improve no matter what form of therapy or placebo treatment they receive.

Observations from therapist training and supervision session material and other Vanderbilt II data revealed "the pronounced inability of therapists to avoid countertherapeutic processes with difficult patients" (Henry & Strupp, 1992, p. 440), even though pre- to post- TDLP training differences were obtained. Concern about potential countertherapeutic impacts of therapists' negative reactions to patients also was supported by process–outcome analyses of Vanderbilt I data that suggested that even small amounts of therapist blame and criticism were associated with poor outcome (Henry, Schacht, & Strupp, 1986). A next step that Strupp deemed essential was to

> develop training programs that are aimed at imparting fundamental interpersonal skills as a point of departure for other forms of training. . . . By developing new instructional approaches, we hope to narrow the gap between basic psychotherapy research and its application to clinical practice and training. (Henry & Strupp, 1992, p. 441)

The last sentence describes an unrealized goal and also a master's insight on a productive focus for contemporary psychotherapy research. Strupp's guiding suggestion after career-long investigation of the therapist's contribution was to refocus attention on training—a pivotal activity that remained mostly unstudied in the era when he completed his work.

CONCLUSION

Hans Strupp's later writings suggest that his strongest recommendation to contemporary and future researchers is to attend to the complexity of managing the therapeutic relationship and to the training of therapists. Both are key to meeting the ongoing practice-relevant challenge to extend the efficacy, effectiveness, and efficiency of psychotherapies as routinely provided. Notably, Strupp also left the field with an explicit challenge to a currently prominent view that nonspecific (common) relationship factors are the primary agent of psychotherapeutic change.

Strupp indeed concluded that qualities of the relationship between therapist and patient are core determinants of therapeutic action. However, he added two crucial caveats: (a) that one of the most "common" features of therapy relationships is problematic interpersonal processes, and (b) that such processes often are either cued or maintained by the therapist. Based on findings and clinical observations that support (a) and (b), Strupp came to strongly advocate research on developing therapist training methods that will enable therapists to manage well the typical and ubiquitous traps and snags of therapy relationships. Such developments are needed, Strupp would argue, because most psychotherapists' best intentions and natural relationship skills are inadequate to optimally serve individuals who stand most to benefit from what psychotherapy, as a unique treatment modality, might offer.

REFERENCES

Bein, E., Anderson, T., Strupp, H. H., Henry, W. P., Schacht, T. E., Binder, J. L., & Butler, S. (2000). The effects of training in time-limited dynamic psychotherapy: Changes in therapeutic outcome. *Psychotherapy Research, 10,* 119–132. doi:10.1080/713663669

Bergin, A. E. (2007). Hans H. Strupp (1921–2006). *American Psychologist, 62,* 249. doi:10.1037/0003-066X.62.3.249

Bergin, A. E., & Strupp, H. H. (1972). *Changing frontiers in the science of psychotherapy.* Chicago, IL: Aldine-Atherton.

Butler, S. F., & Strupp, H. H. (1986). "Specific" and "nonspecific" factors in psychotherapy: A problematic paradigm for psychotherapy research. *Psychotherapy, 23,* 30–40. doi:10.1037/h0085590

Frank, J. D. (1961). *Persuasion and healing: A comparative study of psychotherapy.* Baltimore, MD: Johns Hopkins Press.

Frank, J. D. (1971). Therapeutic factors in psychotherapy. *American Journal of Psychotherapy, 25,* 350–361.

Goldfried, M. R. (Ed.). (1982). *Converging themes in psychotherapy: Trends in psychodynamic, humanistic, and behavioral practice.* New York, NY: Springer.

Gomes-Schwartz, B. (1978). Effective ingredients in psychotherapy: Prediction of outcome from process variables. *Journal of Consulting and Clinical Psychology, 46,* 1023–1035. doi:10.1037/0022-006X.46.5.1023

Henry, W. P., Schacht, T. E., & Strupp, H. H. (1986). Structural analysis of social behavior: Application to a study of interpersonal process in differential psychotherapeutic outcome. *Journal of Consulting and Clinical Psychology, 54,* 27–31. doi:10.1037/0022-006X.54.1.27

Henry, W. P., & Strupp, H. H. (1992). The Vanderbilt Center for Psychotherapy Research. In D. K. Freedheim (Ed.), *History of psychotherapy: A century of change* (pp. 436–442). Washington, DC: American Psychological Association.

Henry, W. P., Strupp, H. H., Butler, S. F., Schacht, T. E., & Binder, J. L. (1993). Effects of training in Time-Limited Dynamic Psychotherapy: Changes in therapist behavior. *Journal of Consulting and Clinical Psychology, 61,* 434–440. doi:10.1037/0022-006X.61.3.434

Strupp, H. H. (1955). An objective comparison of Rogerian and psychoanalytic techniques. *Journal of Consulting Psychology, 19,* 1–7. doi:10.1037/h0045910

Strupp, H. H. (1973). On the basic ingredients of psychotherapy. *Journal of Consulting and Clinical Psychology, 41,* 1–8. doi:10.1037/h0035619

Strupp, H. H. (1976a). Clinical psychology, irrationalism, and the erosion of excellence. *American Psychologist, 31*, 561–571. doi:10.1037/0003-066X.31.8.561

Strupp, H. H. (1976b). Some critical comments on the future of psychoanalystic therapy. *Bulletin of the Menninger Clinic, 40*, 238–247.

Strupp, H. H. (1977). A reformulation of the dynamics of the therapist's contribution. In A. S. Gurman & A. M. Razin (Eds.), *Effective psychotherapy: A handbook of research* (pp. 1–22). Oxford, England: Pergamon Press.

Strupp, H. H. (1980). Success and failure in time-limited psychotherapy: A systematic comparison of two cases (Comparison 1). *Archives of General Psychiatry, 37*, 595–603.

Strupp, H. H. (1989). Psychotherapy: Can the practitioner learn from the researcher? *American Psychologist, 44*, 717–724. doi:10.1037/0003-066X.44.4.717

Strupp, H. H. (1993). The Vanderbilt psychotherapy studies: Synopsis. *Journal of Consulting and Clinical Psychology, 61*, 431–433. doi:10.1037/0022-006X.61.3.431

Strupp, H. H. (1995). The psychotherapist's skills revisited. *Clinical Psychology: Science and Practice, 2*, 70–74.

Strupp, H. H. (n.d., circa 1988–2003). Unpublished manuscript.

Strupp, H. H., & Binder, J. L. (1984). *Psychotherapy in a new key: A guide to time-limited dynamic psychotherapy.* New York, NY: Basic Books.

Strupp, H. H., Butler, S. F., & Rosser, C. L. (1988). Training in psychodynamic psychotherapy. *Journal of Consulting and Clinical Psychology, 56*, 689–695. doi:10.1037/0022-006X.56.5.689

Strupp, H. H., & Hadley, S. W. (1977). A tripartite model of mental health and therapeutic outcomes with special reference to negative effects in psychotherapy. *American Psychologist, 32*, 187–196. doi:10.1037/0003-066X.32.3.187

Strupp, H. H., & Hadley, S. W. (1979). Specific vs. nonspecific factors in psychotherapy: A controlled outcome study. *Archives of General Psychiatry, 36*, 1125–1136.

Strupp, H. H., Hadley, S. W., & Gomes-Schwartz, B. (1977). *Psychotherapy for better or worse: the problem of negative effects.* New York, NY: Jason Aronson.

Suh, C. S., Strupp, H. H., & O'Malley, S. S. (1986). The Vanderbilt process measures: The Psychotherapy Process Scale (VPPS) and the Negative Indicators Scale (VNIS). In L. S. Greenberg & William M. Pinsof (Eds.), *The psychotherapeutic process: A research handbook* (pp. 285–323). New York, NY: Guilford Press.

Sullivan, H. S. (1953). *The interpersonal theory of psychiatry.* New York, NY: Norton.

6

AARON T. BECK: THE COGNITIVE REVOLUTION IN THEORY AND THERAPY

STEVEN D. HOLLON

Aaron T. Beck is one of the leading clinical theorists of the last half century. Coming of age at a time when dynamic theory was monolithic and psychoanalysis the dominant method of treatment, he began his career by seeking to confirm the primacy of unconscious motivations and ended up formulating a theory of disorder that emphasized the role of inaccurate beliefs and errors in thinking that were largely accessible to conscious introspection. This novel cognitive theory led him to formulate principles of change that he codified into a cognitive therapy that has become one of the most widely practiced and best empirically supported interventions in the field today (DeRubeis & Crits-Christoph, 1998). Beck has been the recipient of numerous honors and is the only psychiatrist to have received research awards from the American Psychological Association, the American Psychological Society, the American Psychiatric Association, and the Institute of Medicine. He has lectured throughout the world and was named one of the most influential psychotherapists of all time by the *American Psychologist* (July 1989). Perhaps the capstone of his career came when he received the Lasker Award, the nation's most prestigious medical prize (*New York Times*, September 17, 2006). In announcing the award, Dr. Joseph L. Goldstein, the chairman of the Lasker

63

jury, called cognitive therapy "one of the most important advances—if not the most important advance—in the treatment of mental diseases in the last 50 years."

MAJOR CONTRIBUTIONS

Beck was trained in the psychodynamic model (like most psychiatrists in the middle part of the last century) and embarked on an ambitious program of research designed to test Freud's notion that depression was a consequence of unconscious anger directed against the self. In a series of experimental and clinical studies, he found little evidence of the retroflected anger posited by dynamic theory in the behavioral performance of his depressed patients or in their dreams and free associations; what he found instead were consistent themes of loss and personal failing. Rather than letting existing theories drive his interpretations, he proposed a major reformulation that held that the core problem in depression was not a product of unconscious drives and defenses but, rather, the consequence of unduly negative beliefs and biased information processing. In so doing he emphasized the causal role of one class of symptoms of depression, a causal role that had been largely overlooked by the major theoretical perspectives of the day.

In retrospect, it is easy to forget just how revolutionary this perspective was or how controversial it proved to be. Psychodynamic theory dating from Freud held that the causes of depression and other types of psychopathology lay in unconscious motivations that could not be directly addressed without triggering defenses in the patient that led them to resist efforts at change and required, instead, years of careful and indirect exploration. Conversely, behavior theory, its major competitor at the time, held that psychopathology was a consequence of outside forces and could best be resolved by reordering the external environment. Neither put much stock in the notion that the things a patient believed, what he or she thought or expected, played a role in the generation of distress and problems in coping. Beck's cognitive reformulation of psychopathology was truly revolutionary, and his cognitive theory of change paved the way for some of the most efficacious treatments of the modern era. It also was actively resisted at the time, and the larger psychodynamic community regarded his views as heretical at best.

Beck's monograph on depression, published in 1967, summarized this work and became a classic in the field. In it he proposed that depression was in part a consequence of a systematic tendency to perceive things in a negative and biased fashion. He introduced his concept of the negative cognitive triad—negative views about the self, the world, and the future—and explicated the role of schema, clusters of beliefs, and proclivities with respect to information processing that serve to warp the way that information is processed in the direction of existing beliefs. He also introduced the rudiments of an approach to treatment in which he laid out basic strategies for teaching patients how to explore the accuracy of their own beliefs and how to protect themselves from the biasing effects of schema-driven processing. In so doing, he drew heavily on recent advances in cognitive psychology that emphasized the way in which existing beliefs could bias information processing and developed a sophisticated set of clinical procedures to offset those proclivities.

By the early 1970s he had developed a coherent approach to treatment based on the principles that he called *cognitive therapy*. At this time, there was no evidence that any psychosocial intervention was as efficacious as medications in the treatment of depression or even superior to pill-placebo controls. Before the end of the decade, he and colleagues at the University of Pennsylvania published a randomized controlled trial in which cognitive therapy outperformed medications, the current standard of treatment (Rush, Beck, Kovacs, & Hollon, 1977). Patients in that trial were not only as likely to respond to cognitive therapy as to medications, but they also were considerably more likely to stay well after treatment termination. This was not only the first time that any psychosocial treatment had held its own with medication in the treatment of depression but also the first clear evidence of an enduring effect for psychotherapy, something that had long been claimed but never before demonstrated.

Thirty years of subsequent research have fully supported these early claims. Cognitive therapy is now widely recognized as an empirically supported psychosocial treatment for depression, and the proposition that it has enduring effects not found for medications is well supported in the literature (Hollon, Stewart, & Strunk, 2006). Moreover, evidence of its efficacy is not limited to depression; he has taken the lead in extending the approach to other disorders and many others have followed. There now is clear evidence for its efficacy and enduring effects for nearly all of the nonpsychotic disorders (including panic and the anxiety disorders, somatic disorders such as hypochondriasis, eating disorders such as anorexia and bulimia, substance abuse and addiction, marital distress, and a variety of both internalizing and externalizing childhood disorders), as well as emerging work in the personality disorders (including borderline personality disorder and antisocial personality) and the psychoses (including bipolar disorder and the schizophrenias; Butler, Chapman, Forman, & Beck, 2006).

Beck has been committed to the empirical evaluation of his theories and the therapy that developed from them. He viewed his theories as provisional only and sought to subject them to empirical disconfirmation in as timely a manner as possible. His empirical studies have consistently pitted his preferred intervention against the best existing treatments in the field, and he has shown a keen awareness of the need to balance investigator allegiance to be sure that each modality tested has a fair chance at success. The quality and impartiality of these investigations have contributed greatly to his impact on the field, and the ease with which they have been replicated speaks to the generalizability of the approach. Cognitive theory has evolved over the years, and cognitive therapy has been revised on the basis of both experimental findings and clinical insights, allowing it to be generalized to numerous other disorders across a variety of clinical situations. There is even evidence that cognitive therapy can be taught to persons at risk in the service of preventing the emergence of subsequent distress. His commitment to the principles of science and his willingness to subject his beliefs to potential disconfirmation have contributed both to shaping the approach and to the success it has enjoyed.

EARLY BEGINNINGS

Aaron T. Beck was the youngest of five children of parents who both emigrated from Russia (see Weishaar, 1993, for a detailed description of his early life). His father was a printer by trade and an intellectual by nature who was a strong supporter of socialistic principles. His mother was a strong-willed woman who gave up her dream of going to medical school to care for her younger siblings after the untimely death of her own mother. There are indications that his mother became depressed herself following the loss of a daughter during the great influenza epidemic of 1919 and that her distress remitted only after the birth of her youngest son, Aaron (perhaps his first successful cure).

Beck himself nearly died at age seven after a broken bone in his arm became infected and he developed septicemia, an infection of the blood that was nearly always fatal at that time. The surgery itself was traumatic. He was separated from his mother without warning and put under the knife before the anesthetic had taken effect. This experience led to fears of abandonment and health-related phobias that he only mastered later in life by thinking through their cognitive antecedents and testing their accuracy by exposing himself to the situations that he feared (one of his reasons for later going into medicine). Moreover, he missed so much time from school that he was held back a grade, leading him to think of himself as "dumb and stupid," but he sought help from his older brothers and came to excel in school, leading him to believe that he could overcome misfortune through hard work and use a "never say die" attitude to turn "a disadvantage adversity into an advantage" (Weishaar, 1993, p. 10). In many respects, In many respects, the seeds of his later theoretical innovations were sown by his own early life experiences; his initial response to these traumatic life events was to develop exaggerated beliefs (reasonable under the circumstances) that overestimated the risk inherent in health-related or educational situations and that underestimated his own capacity to cope—beliefs he overcame by thinking them through and forcing himself to engage in what he feared, to test their accuracy.

He graduated first in his high school class and followed his older brothers to Brown University. Although he majored in English and political science, he decided to pursue a career in medicine, only to be discouraged by a professor from applying to medical school because of the anti-Semitism of the time. He pursued extra premed course work nonetheless and graduated magna cum laude in 1942, having been elected to Phi Beta Kappa. He applied to only three or four medical schools and was admitted to Yale, in part because he shared an interest in the works of Aldous Huxley with the professor of pediatrics who conducted his admissions interview.

He was not originally interested in psychiatry or psychotherapy and embarked on a residency in neurology after completing medical school. He was attracted to neurology by its disciplined diagnostic procedures and its capacity to pinpoint the precise location of lesions in the nervous system on the basis of careful clinical observation. It was during the course of a mandatory 6-month rotation in psychiatry that he became fascinated with its subject matter and with psychoanalysis in particular, which he thought would reveal the inner workings of the human mind. He completed a 2-year fellowship at Austin Riggs Center in Stockbridge Massachusetts (supervised by Erik Erikson) before volunteering to serve at the Valley Forge General Hospital, an army hospital near Philadelphia. He was board certified in psychiatry in 1953 and became an instructor in psychiatry at the University of Pennsylvania the following year. He graduated from the Philadelphia Psychoanalytic Institute in 1958 and became an assistant professor at Penn the following year, receiving his first research grant (to study dreams) in the process.

It was during his internship that he met his wife, Phyllis. She was a journalist by training who wrote for *Time* magazine and the *Berkshire Eagle* (Pittsfield, MA) before taking a master's degree in social work and ultimately going on to law school while raising four children. She enjoyed a long and successful career in the law and became the first woman to be elected a superior court judge in Pennsylvania. Retired from the bench, she is now the chief counsel for the Barnes Foundation.

ACCOMPLISHMENTS

From the Exploration of Dreams to the Identification of Beliefs

Although Beck became deeply interested in psychodynamic principles, he initially approached them with some ambivalence. He had always had a rebellious streak intellectually, and he found that his pragmatic nature sometimes made psychoanalytic principles seem counterintuitive. Nonetheless, he decided to suspend his initial disbelief and threw himself into his analysis. He remained troubled by its lack of a scientific basis and came to believe that empirical evidence was necessary to convince the hard-headed skeptic. He came to view psychological research as a way to validate psychoanalytic concepts and make them acceptable to the scientific community.

He decided to focus on depression, the most frequent disorder in his practice, and began a series of studies designed to show that depression was a consequence of unconscious rage against others that became repressed and turned against the self. Adhering to the notion that dreams represented the "royal road to the unconscious," he began to study the dreams of his depressed patients and to compare them with the dreams of patients who were not depressed. What he found, to his dismay, was that the dreams of his depressed patients actually contained less hostility than those of his nondepressed controls. What they did contain were the same themes of rejection and failure that patients expressed in their waking conscious verbalizations. He considered other more complex interpretations that preserved the primacy of the unconscious (none supported by the data) before coming to what he termed the "simple-minded hypothesis" that the negative way in which patients see themselves is actually the basic process, rather than the derivative of unconscious forces (Beck, 2006, p. 1139). The essence of this formulation was that there was no need to go deeper; a model based on his patients' internal representations of themselves, their experiences, and their future could account for both their dreams and their symptoms.

Experimental work was crucial to this paradigmatic shift. In an effort to test between the competing interpretations, Beck and colleagues put depressed and nondepressed patients in controlled performance situations and manipulated their success or failure. In opposition to psychodynamic theory, which would have predicted a masochistic worsening of mood in reaction to positive feedback, what he found is that both the mood and performance of his depressed patients improved when they experienced instances of success (Loeb, Beck, & Diggory, 1971; Loeb, Feshbach, Beck, & Wolf, 1964). These studies not only contradicted predictions generated from psychodynamic theory but also pointed to the kind of clear and pragmatic strategies that could be used clinically to disconfirm the patients' negative beliefs.

Over the next several years, he began to experiment with helping patients recognize their own internal dialogue (often in the form of fleeting negative "automatic thoughts" that consisted of demeaning self-evaluations and distorted misinterpretations of innocuous events) and found that he could guide them to examine the validity of their own beliefs through a process of Socratic questioning and the use of behavioral experiments. He described his approach, which he called cognitive therapy, in a series of case reports that he presented at the Association for the Advancement of Behavior Therapy (Beck, 1970). John Rush, one of his residents at the time, encouraged him to conduct a randomized controlled trial that found that cognitive therapy was both superior to and longer lasting than medication (Rush et al., 1977).

Role of Beliefs in the Etiology and Treatment of Psychopathology

While Beck was developing his cognitive theory and therapy of depression, he also began to ask whether cognitive processes played a role in other disorders and whether he could identify a specific profile of distortions and beliefs that was associated with each. In order to carry out this work, he organized a clinic, called first the Mood Clinic and later the Center for Cognitive Therapy, that enabled him to study individuals with a variety of disorders and to use their clinical materials to probe the nature of their distress and to explore methods of intervention with his colleagues and his students. His treatise on the *Cognitive Therapy of the Emotional Disorders* provided an early road map to this approach (Beck, 1976). The basic strategy that he followed was to collect a large number of clinical observations for a specific disorder (focusing on the automatic thoughts and underlying beliefs), derive a formulation for the particular disorder, and devise inventories and rating scales to measure the specific clinical variables. Then, on the basis of the cognitive profile, he would adapt the generic cognitive model to fit the specific characteristics of the disorder.

He and his colleagues and students would then generate clinical interventions based on these principles and observations that were collated into treatment manuals that could be used in randomized controlled intervention trials. This basic research strategy, first developed in his work on depression (Beck, Rush, Shaw, & Emery, 1979), was subsequently applied to the study and treatment of panic and the anxiety disorders (Beck, Emery, & Greenberg, 1985), personality disorders (Beck, Freeman, & Associates, 1990), and substance abuse (Beck, Wright, Newman, & Liese, 1993).

Beck has had a long-standing interest in suicide and its prevention. Early in his career he and his colleagues constructed a new classification system and developed instruments to validate it (Beck, Resnik, & Lettieri, 1974). He found, for example, that persons with elevated levels of hopelessness were at significant risk of ultimate suicide and that predictors of subsequent risk among suicide attempters included expressions of regret over the failure of their attempt(s) and increasing intensity of ideation across attempts (Beck, Morris, & Beck, 1974). This work culminated in the development of a brief cognitive therapy for suicide that has been shown to cut the frequency of subsequent attempts in half among high-risk patients with a recent history of attempts (Brown et al., 2005).

During the 1970s and 1980s, Beck made a series of extended visits to Britain and particularly Oxford University, where the chairman of psychiatry, Michael Gelder, was strongly supportive of the cognitive therapy approach. There he met with John Teasdale and Mark Williams (joined by Zindel Segal of Toronto) who added meditation to develop a mindfulness-based approach to cognitive therapy. He had a strong influence on David M. Clark and Paul Salkovskis (later joined by Anke Ehlers), who used the systematic approach he applied to depression to adapt cognitive therapy to the treatment of a variety of anxiety disorders, including panic, social phobia, hypochondrias, posttraumatic stress disorder, and obsessive–compulsive disorder, among others. This latter group (who subsequently moved to the Institute of Psychiatry in London) has done some of the most elegant translational work in the field today. Dominic Lam, another former trainee, adapted the approach to the prevention of recurrence in bipolar disorder, and Christopher Fairburn at Oxford and Kelly Bemis Vitousek in Hawaii have been strongly influenced by cognitive therapy in their respective work with eating disorders. David Kingdon and Douglas Turkington in England applied the basic framework to successfully adapt cognitive therapy to the treatment of residual symptoms in schizophrenia (Kingdon & Turkington, 1994). Other research groups in the United Kingdom have found similarly promising results in the treatment of both acute and chronic patients. This work has been slow to be adopted in the United States (where clinical lore has long presumed that you cannot reason with someone who is psychotic) but is beginning to make its way across the Atlantic (Beck & Rector, 2005). In addition to his work on mindfulness, Zindel Segal in Toronto has investigated the neural processes underlying change in treatment in cognitive therapy versus medications, and David A. Clark in Nova Scotia has explored the cognitive process underpinning depression and related anxiety disorders. Much of the work in the United States has focused on depression (including that by Robert J. DeRubeis and Steven D. Hollon), and Martin Seligman at the University of Pennsylvania and Judy Garber at Vanderbilt have each investigated the role of cognitive interventions in the prevention of depression in at-risk children and adolescents.

Other Contributions

Beck was a driving force in establishing the journal *Cognitive Therapy and Research*. He served on its executive board for many years and published his classic comparison of cognitive therapy versus medication in the treatment of depression in its inaugural issue (Rush et al., 1977). He is an active participant in and regularly attends the Association for Behavior and Cognitive Therapies (ABCT), the Society for Psychopathology Research, and the Society for Psychotherapy Research. He was the driving force in establishing the Academy of Cognitive Therapy, an organization that certifies competence in cognitive therapy based on actual tape ratings, and has founded both the Center for Cognitive Therapy at the University of Pennsylvania and the Beck Institute in nearby Bala Cynwyd.

Dr. Beck has authored over 450 articles in peer-reviewed journals and 17 books and treatment manuals. Many of these publications (on depression, anxiety, personality disorders, and other clinical problems) have become classics in the field (e.g., Beck, 1967, 1976; Beck et al., 1979, 1985; Beck, Freeman, & Associates, 1990). In addition, Beck and his colleagues and students have written a number of treaties and self-help manuals for the public (Beck, 1988; Burns, 1980; Greenberger & Padesky, 1995). Beck has developed a number of major self-report and clinical rating instruments. The Beck Depression Inventory (Beck, Ward, Mendelson, Mock, & Erbaugh, 1961) is the most widely used self-report instrument in the field and the Hopelessness Scale (Beck, Weissman, Lester, & Trexler, 1974) has been shown to be a better predictor of risk of suicide than depression (Beck, Brown, Berchick, Stewart, & Steer, 1990). The Dysfunctional Attitudes Scale is widely used as a measure of beliefs and attitudes conferring risk for depression (Weissman & Beck, 1978) and the Cognitive Therapy Scale is widely used as a measure of competence with cognitive therapy (Young & Beck, 1980). He also developed the Suicide Intent Scale (Beck, Morris, & Beck, 1974) and the Scale for Suicide Ideation for work in the assessment of suicide and the prediction of risk (Beck, Brown, & Steer, 1997).

INFLUENCES

Beck was strongly influenced by Freudian theory in his early professional years, although he was restless and dissatisfied with its lack of scientific basis (Weishaar, 1993). He longed to provide the kind of empirical evidence necessary to convince a hard-headed scientist, and he numbered Seymour Feshbach and Marvin Hurvich, experimental psychologists on faculty in the Department of Psychology at Penn, among his early collaborators. His personal analyst, Leon Saul, who wrote about conscious processes, strongly influenced his interest in dream research. He also was greatly influenced by the writings of George Kelly and Albert Ellis, who were starting to challenge the dominance of psychodynamic thought in psychotherapy and were subsequently joined by colleagues like Donald Meichenbaum and Michael Mahoney, who introduced cognitive principles into conventional behavior therapy. Beck has mentored a number of students and junior collaborators, many of whom have gone on to distinguish themselves in independent careers. These include A. John Rush, one of the preeminent biological psychiatrists in the field today; Marika Kovacs, a noted developmental psychopathologist who does longitudinal research on the development of risk for depression in children; and David M. Clark, one of the most innovative and highly regarded anxiety researchers of his generation. Others greatly influenced by Beck include his daughter, Judith Beck (a major theorist in her own right), David Burns, Robert J. DeRubeis, Arthur Freeman, Steven D. Hollon, Christine Padesky, Jackie Persons, Brian F. Shaw, Kelly Bemis Vitousek, and Jeffrey Young, among others, three of whom have gone on themselves to become presidents of ABCT.

CONCLUSION

Aaron T. Beck has had a major impact on what the field thinks about psychopathology and the nature of treatment for the mental disorders. He is the architect of one of the most widely used and efficacious psychotherapies in the field today. His work has been prodigious and his influence profound, in part because of his insistence on subjecting his ideas to the stiffest possible empirical tests. His theoretical notions about the role of cognition in the etiology and maintenance of psychopathology have revolutionized the field, and the clinical innovations he developed have coalesced into one of the most widely practiced and best empirically supported interventions of the day. He is truly a giant in the field.

REFERENCES

Beck, A. T. (1967). *Depression: Clinical, experimental, and theoretical aspects*. New York, NY: Hoeber.

Beck, A. T. (1970). Cognitive therapy: Nature and relation to behavior therapy. *Behavior Therapy, 1*, 184–200. doi:10.1016/S0005-7894(70)80030-2

Beck, A. T. (1976). *Cognitive therapy and the emotional disorders*. New York, NY: Meridian.

Beck, A. T. (1988). *Love is never enough*. New York, NY: Harper & Row.

Beck, A. T. (2006). How an anomalous finding led to a new system of psychotherapy. *Nature Medicine, 12*, 1139–1141. doi:10.1038/nm1006-1139

Beck, A. T., Brown, G. K., & Steer, R. A. (1997). Psychometric characteristics of the Scale for Suicide Ideation with psychiatric outpatients. *Behaviour Research and Therapy, 35*, 1039–1046. doi:10.1016/S0005-7967(97)00073-9

Beck, A. T., Brown, G. K., Berchick, R. J., Stewart, B. L., & Steer, R. A. (1990). Relationship between hopelessness and ultimate suicide: A replication with psychiatric outpatients. *American Journal of Psychiatry, 147*, 190–195.

Beck, A. T., Emery, G., & Greenberg, R. (1985). *Anxiety disorders and phobias: A cognitive perspective*. New York, NY: Basic Books.

Beck, A. T., Freeman, A., & Associates. (1990). *Cognitive therapy of personality disorders*. New York, NY: Guilford Press.

Beck, A. T., & Rector, N. (2005). Cognitive approaches to schizophrenia: Theory and therapy. *Annual Review of Clinical Psychology, 1*, 577–606. doi:10.1146/annurev.clinpsy.1.102803.144205

Beck, A. T., Resnik, H. L. P., & Lettieri, D. (1974). *The prediction of suicide*. Bowie, MD: Charles Press.

Beck, A. T., Rush, A. J., Shaw, B. F., & Emery, G. (1979). *The cognitive therapy of depression*. New York, NY: Guilford Press.

Beck, A. T., Ward, C. H., Mendelson, M., Mock, J. E., & Erbaugh, J. K. (1961). An inventory for measuring depression. *Archives of General Psychiatry, 4*, 561–571.

Beck, A. T., Weissman, A., Lester, D., & Trexler, L. (1974). The measurement of pessimism: The Hopelessness Scale. *Journal of Consulting and Clinical Psychology, 42*, 861–865. doi:10.1037/h0037562

Beck, A. T., Wright, F. D., Newman, C. F., & Liese, B. S. (1993). *Cognitive therapy of substance abuse*. New York, NY: Guilford Press.

Beck, R. W., Morris, J. B., & Beck, A. T. (1974). Cross-validation of the Suicidal Intent Scale. *Psychological Reports, 34*, 445–446.

Brown, G. K., Have, T. T., Henriques, G. R., Xie, S. X., Hollander, J. E., & Beck, A. T. (2005). Cognitive therapy for the prevention of suicide attempts: A randomized controlled trial. *JAMA, 294*, 563–570. doi:10.1001/jama.294.5.563

Burns, D. D. (1980). *Feeling good: The new mood therapy*. New York, NY: William Morrow.

Butler, A. C., Chapman, J. E., Forman, E. M., & Beck, A. T. (2006). The empirical status of cognitive-behavioral therapy: A review of meta-analyses. *Clinical Psychology Review, 26*, 17–31. doi:10.1016/j.cpr.2005.07.003

DeRubeis, R. J., & Crits-Christoph, P. (1998). Empirically supported individual and group psychological treatments for adult mental disorders. *Journal of Consulting and Clinical Psychology, 66*, 37–52. doi:10.1037/0022-006X.66.1.37

Greenberger, D., & Padesky, C. A. (1995). *Mind over mood*. New York, NY: Guilford Press.

Hollon, S. D., Stewart, M. O., & Strunk, D. (2006). Cognitive behavior therapy has enduring effects in the treatment of depression and anxiety. *Annual Review of Psychology, 57*, 285–315. doi:10.1146/annurev.psych.57.102904.190044

Kingdon, D. G., & Turkington, D. (1994). *Cognitive-behavioral therapy of schizophrenia*. New York, NY: Guilford Press.

Loeb, A., Beck, A. T., & Diggory, J. (1971). Differential effects of success and failure on depressed and nondepressed patients. *The Journal of Nervous and Mental Disease, 152*, 106–114. doi:10.1097/00005053-197102000-00003

Loeb, A., Feshbach, S., Beck, A. T., & Wolf, A. (1964). Some effects of reward upon the social perception and motivation of psychiatric patients varying in depression. *Journal of Abnormal and Social Psychology, 68,* 609–616. doi:10.1037/h0044260

Rush, A. J., Beck, A. T., Kovacs, M., & Hollon, S. (1977). Comparative efficacy of cognitive therapy and pharmacotherapy in the treatment of depressed outpatients. *Cognitive Therapy and Research, 1*(1), 17–37. doi:10.1007/BF01173502

Weishaar, M. E. (1993). *Aaron T. Beck.* Thousand Oaks, CA: Sage Publications.

Weissman, A. N., & Beck, A. T. (1978, November). *Development and validation of the dysfunctional attitude scale: A preliminary investigation.* Paper presented at the meeting of the American Educational Research Association, Toronto, Canada.

Young, J., & Beck, A. T. (1980). Cognitive Therapy Scale: Rating manual. Unpublished manuscript, University of Pennsylvania, Philadelphia.

II

DOES PSYCHOTHERAPY WORK?

7

IRENE ELKIN: "THE DATA ARE ALWAYS FRIENDLY"

KARLA MORAS AND M. TRACIE SHEA

Clinical psychologist Irene Elkin[1] has had unique and profound influence on psychotherapy research since the early 1970s. Her career has shown her to be a consummate scientist, possessing a keen intellect and fund of knowledge, unassailable scientific integrity, and commitment to bringing the best science possible to research on psychotherapy. Elkin's achievements also document her commitment to balancing the tension between conducting rigorous experimental science and preserving the essentially human qualities of psychotherapy. Among her many contributions, Elkin is perhaps best known for spearheading a study that had a paradigm-shifting impact on the field during the last decades of the 20th century, the Treatment of Depression Collaborative Research Program (TDCRP; e.g., Elkin, 1994; Elkin et al., 1989, 1995; Parloff & Elkin, 1992) for the U.S. National Institute of Mental Health (NIMH). The TDCRP demonstrated the feasibility of several powerful scientific methods for use in psychotherapy outcome research. It thereby helped set new methodological standards for the field—standards that strengthened conclusions that could be drawn about a therapy's potential

---

[1]Elkin published some of her work as Irene Waskow, using her former husband's surname.

effects, its effects compared with those of other forms of therapy and also of medication, and related practice-relevant questions. More broadly, Elkin has brought conceptual and methodological clarity to many of the field's key questions.

MAJOR CONTRIBUTIONS

For this chapter, we organized Elkin's major contributions to therapy research into four main areas: conceptual and methodological clarity, increasing the rigor of the field's scientific standards and methods, promoting research on mechanisms of change (psychotherapy process research), and generativity. Elkin's contributions reflect the relatively unique trajectory of her career. Most of it was spent at NIMH, where her work focused on furthering the mental health mission of the institute and using its resources to advance the field of psychotherapy research. For example, early on she facilitated therapy research by providing expert consultation to those seeking NIMH funding, organized national conferences on key topics, and initiated and supported contracts in areas of specific need or interest.

In 1978, Elkin's main focus shifted dramatically when she took the reins of the TDCRP as its NIMH coordinator. She remained at NIMH for 12 more years, seeing the TDCRP through to completion and the write-up of major findings, before moving to academia as a tenured full professor at the University of Chicago in its School of Social Service Administration (SSA). There, Elkin revived the earliest phase of her career by pursuing her own therapy research interests, particularly process-based studies. In 1996, she received an NIMH Research Scientist Award grant for such work. She continued to examine crucial questions in therapy research (e.g., therapist effects) with SSA graduate students and other colleagues (e.g., Elkin, Falconnier, Martinovich, & Mahoney, 2006; Shaw et al., 1999) while teaching therapy research seminars, mentoring SSA students, directing an NIMH-funded training program in mental health services research for a number of years, and serving as the field's central resource for TDCRP data and other inquiries.

Elkin's enormous contributions have been recognized with many awards, including the Administrator's Award for Meritorious Achievement (1987) from the U.S. Alcohol, Drug Abuse, and Mental Health Administration for her work on the TDCRP; Research Career Award (1994) from the Society for Psychotherapy Research, and the American Association of Applied and Preventive Psychology's Distinguished Contributions to Applied Research in Psychology Award (1997).

EARLY BEGINNINGS

Irene Elkin was born on December 27, 1933, in Milwaukee, Wisconsin. She lived there with her parents and sister until 1951, when she moved to Madison to start college at the University of Wisconsin (UW). Valedictorian of her high school class, Elkin was the first in her family to complete college. At the time it was rare for students from the poor neighborhood in which she grew up to go to college, much less obtain a doctorate. After receiving a BS in psychology from UW, Elkin moved on to Indiana University in Bloomington, where she earned a master's degree in psychology (1957). She then returned to Madison and UW, where her husband was in graduate school. In 1960, Elkin received a PhD in clinical psychology from UW.

The two psychology departments in which Elkin completed her undergraduate and graduate education were often referred to as "hotbeds of empiricism." They were "mainly experimentally oriented, with stress on asking researchable questions about important aspects of human behavior" and "carrying out rigorous research with adequate statistical approaches to address them" (Elkin, personal communication, October 22, 2007). She internalized the scientific approach she learned. One of her career-long principles for therapy research was to "adapt the rigorous research approach to the realities and complexities of psychotherapy and [also to] the need to maintain the integrity of the clinical subject matter" (Elkin, personal communication, October 22, 2007). As Elkin's early UW colleague Eugene Gendlin recently observed at a celebration in her honor: A defining feature is her passionate interest in "the juncture of absolutely genuine research and absolutely genuine human phenomena."

How did Elkin choose psychotherapy research as a career focus? When starting college, she wanted to become a social worker. A friend's sister was a social worker, and Elkin was moved by the idea that social work would enable her to "do good things for people." However, once in college, Elkin was swiftly introduced to abnormal/clinical psychology by E. Earl Baughman, became hooked on research, and decided to pursue psychology because it placed a greater emphasis on research than did social work. As an undergraduate, while assisting UW professor Horace A. Page, Elkin observed the process of being able to ask an interesting question and then design and conduct a study to answer it. The experience sparked an enduring enthusiasm for research. Also formative was the work of the learning theorists, Miller and Dollard. Elkin was drawn to learning theory and specifically to how learning theory might elucidate the processes of therapy. Her dissertation, "Selective Reinforcement in a Therapy-Like Situation," was a psychotherapy study that also reflected the impact of learning theory on Elkin's thinking. In the study, published in the *Journal of Consulting Psychology* in 1962, she examined the effects of the therapist's behavior on the process of therapy, an enduring theme in her research (e.g., Elkin, 1999; Elkin et al., 2006). While completing her PhD at UW, Elkin worked closely with Carl Rogers and Gendlin on Rogers's famed study of psychotherapy with patients with schizophrenia. She identifies Rogers, Harry Stack Sullivan, and Miller and Dollard as major influences on her research career. Elkin's career-long research mantra, "the data are always friendly," likely was adapted from a similar statement that has been attributed to Rogers.

After graduate school, Elkin held a postdoctoral research fellowship at the NIMH intramural Psychology Laboratory, under the sponsorship of David Shakow. There she was exposed to a variety of psychotherapy approaches and researchers, learning about various therapeutic strategies from Paul Bergman and receiving training from Allen Dittmann in verbal and nonverbal emotional expression. A central, enriching, and lifelong colleagueship also began at the time: Elkin met Morris Parloff, then chief of the laboratory's section on personality, with whom she later worked closely on the conceptualization and initiation of the TDCRP, and other shared contributions to therapy research. In 1969, Elkin joined the Psychotherapy and Behavioral Intervention Section, marking the start of her many years of influence on the field of therapy research from NIMH.

ACCOMPLISHMENTS

Conceptual and Methodological Clarity

Elkin's career at NIMH illustrates how effectively a person can help advance a field by grasping its essential qualities and needs at a point in time, and then using public resources to guide and seed it. The preceding is exemplified in *Psychotherapy Change Measures: Report of the Clinical Research Branch Outcome Measures Project* (Waskow & Parloff, 1975). The book summarizes the Outcome Measures Project that was launched by Elkin (then Waskow) to improve the quality and impact of therapy outcome studies by providing reviews of various approaches to evaluating therapy outcome and by encouraging investigators to adopt a standard battery of outcome measures to include in their studies. A standard battery would allow direct, cross-study comparison of results, thereby enabling psychotherapy researchers to more quickly provide a cumulative body of knowledge on practice-relevant questions.

Elkin's conceptual and methodological clarity also contributed to the unique strengths of the TDCRP design and methods. She fully comprehended the field's primary practice-relevant questions at the time and also the scientific and methodological hurdles it faced to answer them when, in the late 1970s, Parloff and she proposed to NIMH administrators that the institute mount a therapy research study with the features of the TDCRP, unique to psychotherapy research at the time: a relatively large-sample, collaborative and multisite, controlled, comparative clinical trial design in which the therapies to be tested were clearly articulated in manuals that described their standard implementation.

Elkin also ensured that the advances in conceptual and methodological clarity that were a by-product of the TDCRP collaborators' painstaking attention to, and dialogue about, the study's scientific methods were made available to the entire field. For example, two articles elucidate core issues related to designing and interpreting comparative studies of the effects of psychotherapies and medication (Elkin, Pilkonis, Docherty, & Sotsky, 1988a, 1988b). Twenty years later, both articles still qualify as highly recommended reading for researchers and practitioners who want to deepen their understanding of comparative psychotherapy and psychopharmacology outcome studies.

A premier example of the clarity that Elkin brought to practice-relevant research questions is her analysis of the difficulties of distinguishing therapists' unique qualities from therapeutic techniques and other elements of therapies as possible effects on outcomes. Elkin's (1999) important article on "disentangling therapists from therapies" is a product of her career-long interest in the therapist's contribution to therapy processes and outcomes. It also serves as an update on a fundamental hurdle still facing therapy research, particularly if read in conjunction with Kiesler's (1966) classic, early articulation of conceptual and methodological issues in therapy research as it was typically done over 40 years ago.

Enhancing the Field's Scientific Standards and Methods

Through her work on the TDCRP, Elkin had a transformative impact on methodological standards for psychotherapy research. In short, many of the requirements currently taken for granted in designing and conducting psychotherapy outcome studies have become standards by virtue of the TDCRP. The most far-reaching contributions of the TDCRP might not ultimately be its substantive findings but, rather, its role in advancing psychotherapy research methods and also creating the opportunity via archived TDCRP data for non-TDCRP investigators to later examine additional questions about the process and outcomes of psychotherapies.

The two main aims of the TDCRP were to determine the feasibility of the multisite (collaborative) clinical trial design for psychotherapy research and to examine the efficacy of two forms of brief psychotherapy (16 weeks) for outpatient depression: cognitive therapy (Beck, Rush, Shaw & Emery, 1979) and interpersonal psychotherapy (Klerman, Weissman, Rounsaville, & Chevron, 1984). A pharmacological treatment (imipramine) served as a standard reference condition, and a pill placebo was included as a control for imipramine, to determine if imipramine was a valid standard reference condition in the study's sample of depressed patients. The placebo also served as control for the psychotherapies.

Elkin invested an enormous amount of time, energy, and passion in every aspect of the TDCRP throughout the many years covering its planning, implementation, and publication of findings. Her rigorous scientific standards and meticulous approach were crucial for such a large-scale, highly visible, and potentially influential—both on research and practice—study. At the inception of the TDCRP, the multisite, randomized controlled comparative clinical trial design had been widely used in psychopharmacology research but not psychotherapy research. Applying the design to test the efficacy of psychotherapies introduced new challenges. For example, in contrast to psychopharmacology studies, standardized delivery of psychotherapy could not be assumed. Ensuring adequate delivery of the putative "active ingredient" is far more complex in psychotherapy, requiring detailed articulation and assessment of specific therapist interventions. Development of manualized therapies and the assessment of therapist adherence to, and competence with, a specified form of therapy had begun, but they were in an early stage when the TDCRP was initiated. Elkin recognized the critical importance, for a comparative outcome study's internal validity, of being able to demonstrate that therapists administered the treatments as defined by their developers (adherence) and with an acceptable level of competency, and also to show that the treatments compared were distinct in their delivery. Through contracts, Elkin provided for the development and application of a reliable and comprehensive observer-based measure of therapist adherence to the TDCRP treatments, the Collaborative Study Psychotherapy Rating Scale (CSPRS; Hollon, Waskow, Evans, & Lowry, 1984). The CSPRS quickly became regarded as the "Cadillac" of such instruments. It was used to assess adherence to the theoretically key interventions of each therapy tested in the TDCRP and also to the clinical management component of the pharmacotherapy conditions (Hill, O'Grady, & Elkin, 1992). The use of such scales is now standard practice in the field.

One key aim of the TDCRP, to determine if the multisite clinical trial design was feasible for psychotherapy research, yielded a clear answer: Yes. Many such studies have been conducted since (e.g., Barlow, Gorman, Shear, & Woods, 2000). Further, the main TDCRP outcome paper (Elkin et al., 1989) alone has been cited more than 1,000 times to date, a sign of the study's huge impact. Although some controversy arose about interpretation of the main findings of the TDCRP (e.g., Elkin et al., 1989) and key others (e.g., Elkin et al., 1995), many of these findings have proved to be valuable and influential for both practice and further research. With respect to treatment effects, patients in all four conditions, including pill placebo plus clinical management, improved significantly. Furthermore, none of three specific treatments consistently differed significantly from the pill placebo condition in the main outcome analyses. Subsequent analyses yielded clinically relevant "customization" of the preceding—surprising—outcome findings. Pretreatment severity of depression and functional impairment were shown to be important clinical indicators of treatments of choice: For more severely depressed and functionally impaired patients, an antidepressant medication, and to a lesser extent, interpersonal therapy, may be particularly effective. In contrast, for less severely depressed patients, outcome in the condition of pill placebo plus clinical management was comparable with outcomes in the active treatment conditions, suggesting that for such patients "minimal supportive therapy in the hands of an experienced therapist might be sufficient to bring about a significant reduction of depressive symptomatology" within a brief, 3- to 4-month treatment (Elkin, 1994, p. 125). The reader is encouraged to review Elkin's (1994) summary of findings on the TDCRP's other key and highly practice-relevant questions, including examination of theoretically expected specific effects on areas targeted by each of the two specific forms of psychotherapy and how the treatments compared in rapidity of improvement.

Promoting Research on Mechanisms of Change

For several years while at NIMH, Elkin headed the Treatment Development and Process Research section of the Psychosocial Treatments Research Branch. She first began to master process research concepts and methods during her dissertation study and early work with Carl Rogers and others. Elkin's foundation in therapy process research no doubt highlighted, for her, the TDCRP's potential value beyond its implications for assessing the efficacy of psychotherapies. She knew that it also could serve the field as a psychotherapy process-outcome study, enabling many key theoretical and practice-relevant mechanisms of action questions to be investigated. Elkin worked to ensure that the TDCRP's potential in this regard was realized.

The TDCRP study design, methods, and other planning allowed for both the collection and archiving of data needed to conduct process-outcome analyses. For example, standardized instruments as well as measures developed specifically for the TDCRP were included to examine questions relating to (a) the effects of patient and therapist characteristics, (b) the therapeutic relationship, and (c) differential effects of different therapies. Data from such instruments have been used by a number of researchers as well as by Elkin to address a variety of questions. For example, based on data from the Attitudes and Expectations form developed in the TDCRP, Elkin and others found that congruence between a patient's assigned treatment and his or her pre-treatment predilections (patient–treatment fit) predicts early engagement in therapy (Elkin et al., 1999). Also, in one illustrative TDCRP process-outcome study, Krupnick et al. (1996) examined the relationship between the therapeutic alliance and overall treatment outcomes in both the psychotherapy and pharmacotherapy treatment conditions. The results were a valuable addition to existing findings that the strength of the patient–therapist alliance relates to therapy outcomes across treatments.

Generativity

Elkin's foresight about the TDCRP's potential to enable both the examination and heuristic exploration of fundamental mechanisms (process and process-outcome) questions is among her most generative accomplishments. Realization of this foresight required her perseverant effort to ensure that TDCRP data were archived and thereby made widely available to the field. Elkin oversaw the transfer of the main data to a TDCRP Public Access Data Tape that many non-TDCRP investigators have used. She also arranged, in collaboration with two of the TDCRP research sites and Paul Crits-Christoph at the University of Pennsylvania (UP), to have TDCRP assessment and treatment session audio- and videotapes archived for use by investigators at UP. The archives generated influential therapy process and other research (e.g., Tang & DeRubeis, 1999).

Also, as previously noted, Elkin worked to support and advance psychotherapy research for many years and in a variety of ways via resources available at NIMH. Her "Fantasied Dialogue" chapter (Waskow, 1975) is an early illustration of her mentoring via consultation to the field. Prominent and diverse contemporary investigators who have made major, practice-relevant contributions, such as Marsha Linehan and Leslie Greenberg, credit Elkin for nurturing them toward successful therapy research careers. While at NIMH, Elkin also helped guide the field by taking an active role in the annual conference of the Society for Psychotherapy Research (SPR). Aside from her own numerous panels and presentations, her informal, encouraging consultations to researchers remain among her trademarks at SPR conferences. In her last year at NIMH, Elkin and Ken Howard organized one of the first pre-SPR institutes on statistical methods useful for psychotherapy research. Elkin further served the field as an early president of SPR, 1978–1979. Most recently, Elkin's mentoring activities as a professor in the School of Social Service Administration at the University of Chicago helped to expand the role of research in clinical social work training—a full circle follow-up to her early decision to choose psychology over social work because of psychology's greater emphasis on research.

We have the good fortune to be able to testify from personal experience to Irene Elkin's talent as a mentor. One of us (Shea) began her career working with Irene as associate coordinator of the TDCRP, a position that had a tremendous impact on her subsequent career. Those years spent with Irene as mentor were filled with many wonderful experiences, personally and professionally. Many qualities made Irene a special mentor. Clearly, her intelligence and competence stand out. She has a tremendous ability to think through (and to help others think through) research issues. She was our gold standard. Another quality of hers is generosity in giving her time. You could walk into Irene's office with a question and she would let you sit down and discuss it, as often as not generating a long and stimulating discussion of all kinds of research issues and questions. (She and Shea once got so absorbed in such a discussion that they actually boarded the wrong plane while traveling back from an SPR meeting.) This giving of time is so rare these days that we have come to appreciate it even more as the years go on. It is from such informal discussions that we learned how to think about research.

CONCLUSION

Irene Elkin's contributions to date have had transformative impacts on the field of psychotherapy research and also on psychotherapy's viability as a socially sanctioned mental health treatment. In the 1960s, early in Elkin's career, psychotherapy research was handicapped by many methodological and conceptual weaknesses (Kiesler, 1966). The TDCRP, to which Elkin devoted enormous and persistent effort during the mid-phase of her career, constituted a major antidote to the weaknesses. The TDCRP and subsequent, similar collaborative, multisite, clinical trial types of studies in which the effects of medication and psychological treatments could be compared (e.g., Barlow et al., 2000) helped answer arguments that were made well into the 1990s that psychotherapeutic treatments, particularly compared with medications, had not been adequately tested and thus could not be assumed to be efficacious. In addition to the TDCRP's many influences on therapy research standards and methods described in this chapter, its successful completion also demonstrated that psychotherapeutic treatments could be tested on the same playing field used to test medications.

Aspiring psychotherapy researchers can well serve themselves and the field by studying closely Elkin's legacy thus far in (a) papers on basic methodological/conceptual issues (e.g., Elkin, 1994, 1999); (b) reports of study findings, because they provide models of clear and precise inductive and deductive scientific logic, as well as superb methodological and statistical sophistication (e.g., Elkin et al., 1989; Elkin et al., 2006); (c) rejoinders to challenges of TDCRP findings because the responses illustrate the strength of broad and deep scientific expertise, immutable scientific integrity, and the ability to maintain focus on the key scientific issues at hand (Elkin et al., 1990, 1996; Elkin, Falconnier & Martinovich, 2007).

We end on a personal note. In addition to her remarkable professional contributions, Irene has always remained a warm and engaging friend. She is honest and true and loyal. Her great sense of fun and energy for life can be heard in her laugh, which is one way to find Irene in a very crowded room. We are honored and proud to have been among her mentees.

REFERENCES

Barlow, D. H., Gorman, J. M., Shear, M. K., & Woods, S. W. (2000). Cognitive-behavioral therapy, imipramine, or their combination for panic disorder: A randomized controlled trial. *JAMA, 283*, 2529–2536. doi:10.1001/jama.283.19.2529

Beck, A. T., Rush, A. J., Shaw, B. F., & Emery, G. (1979). *Cognitive therapy of depression*. New York, NY: Guilford Press.

Elkin, I. (1994). The NIMH Treatment of Depression Collaborative Research Program: Where we began and where we are. In A. E. Bergin & S. L. Garfield (Eds.), *Handbook of psychotherapy and behavior change* (4th ed., pp. 114–139). New York, NY: Wiley.

Elkin, I. (1999). A major dilemma in psychotherapy outcome research: Disentangling therapists from therapies. *Clinical Psychology: Science and Practice, 6*, 10–32. doi:10.1093/clipsy/6.1.10

Elkin, I., Falconnier, L., & Martinovich, Z. (2007). Misrepresentations in Wampold and Bolt's critique of Elkin, Falconnier, Martinovich, and Mahoney's study of therapist effects. *Psychotherapy Research, 17*, 253–256.

Elkin, I., Falconnier, L., Martinovich, Z., & Mahoney, C. (2006). Therapist effects in the NIMH Treatment of Depression Collaborative Research Program. *Psychotherapy Research, 16*, 144–160. doi:10.1080/10503300500268540

Elkin, I., Gibbons, R. D., Shea, M. T., & Shaw, B. F. (1996). Science is not a trial (but it sometimes can be a tribulation). *Journal of Consulting and Clinical Psychology, 64*, 92–103. doi:10.1037/0022-006X.64.1.92

Elkin, I., Gibbons, R. D., Shea, M. T., Sotsky, S. M., Watkins, J. T., Pilkonis, P. A., . . . Hedeker, D. (1995). Initial severity and differential treatment outcome in the NIMH Treatment of Depression Collaborative Research Program. *Journal of Consulting and Clinical Psychology, 63*, 841–847. doi:10.1037/0022-006X.63.5.841

Elkin, I., Pilkonis, P. A., Docherty, J. P., & Sotsky, S. M. (1988a). Conceptual and methodological issues in comparative studies of psychotherapy and pharmacotherapy, I: Active ingredients and mechanisms of change. *American Journal of Psychiatry, 145,* 909–917.

Elkin, I., Pilkonis, P. A., Docherty, J. P., & Sotsky, S. M. (1988b). Conceptual and methodological issues in comparative studies of psychotherapy and pharmacotherapy, II: Nature and timing of treatment effects. *American Journal of Psychiatry, 145,* 1070–1076.

Elkin, I., Shea, M. T., Collins, J. F., Klett, C. J., Imber, S. D., Sotsky, S. M., . . . Parloff, M. B. (1990). NIMH Collaborative Research on Treatment of Depression [Letter to the editor]. *Archives of General Psychiatry, 47,* 684–685.

Elkin, I., Shea, M. T., Watkins, J. T., Imber, S. D., Sotsky, S. M., Collins, J. F., ... Parloff, M. B. (1989). National Institute of Mental Health Treatment of Depression Collaborative Research Program: General effectiveness of treatments. *Archives of General Psychiatry, 46,* 971–982.

Elkin, I., Yamaguchi, J. L., Arnkoff, D. B., Glass, C. R., Sotsky, S. M., & Krupnick, J. L. (1999). "Patient-treatment fit" and early engagement in therapy. *Psychotherapy Research, 9,* 437–451. doi:10.1093/ptr/9.4.437

Hill, C. E., O'Grady, K. E., & Elkin, I. (1992). Applying the Collaborative Study Psychotherapy Rating Scale to rate therapist adherence in Cognitive-Behavior Therapy, Interpersonal Therapy, and Clinical Management. *Journal of Consulting and Clinical Psychology, 60,* 73–79. doi:10.1037/0022-006X.60.1.73

Hollon, S. D., Waskow, I. E., Evans, M., & Lowry, H. A. (1984, May). *System for rating therapies for depression.* Paper presented at the annual meeting of the American Psychiatric Association, Los Angeles, CA.

Kiesler, D. J. (1966). Some myths of psychotherapy research and the search for a paradigm. *Psychological Bulletin, 65,* 110–136. doi:10.1037/h0022911

Klerman, G. L., Weissman, J. M., Rounsaville, B. J., & Chevron, E. S. (1984). *Interpersonal psychotherapy of depression.* New York, NY: Basic Books, Inc.

Krupnick, J. L., Sotsky, S. M., Simmens, S., Moyer, J., Elkin, I., Watkins, J. T., . . . Pilkonis, P. A. (1996). The role of the therapeutic alliance in psychotherapy and pharmacotherapy outcome: Findings in the NIMH Treatment of Depression Collaborative Research Program. *Journal of Consulting and Clinical Psychology, 64,* 532–539. doi:10.1037/0022-006X.64.3.532

Parloff, M. B., & Elkin, I. (1992). Historical developments in research centers: The NIMH Treatment of Depression Collaborative Research Program. In D. K. Freedheim (Ed.), *History of psychotherapy: A century of change* (pp. 442–449). Washington, DC: American Psychological Association.

Shaw, B. F., Elkin, I., Yamaguchi, J., Olmstead, M., Vallis, T. M., Dobson, D. S., . . . Imber, S. D. (1999). Therapist competence ratings in relation to clinical outcome in cognitive therapy of depression. *Journal of Consulting and Clinical Psychology, 67,* 837–846. doi:10.1037/0022-006X.67.6.837

Tang, T. Z., & DeRubeis, R. J. (1999). Sudden gains and critical sessions in cognitive-behavioral therapy for depression. *Journal of Consulting and Clinical Psychology, 67*, 894–904. doi:10.1037/0022-006X.67.6.894

Waskow, I. E. (1975). Fantasied dialogue with a researcher. In I. E. Waskow & M. B. Parloff (Eds.), *Psychotherapy change measures: Report of the Clinical Research Branch Outcome Measures Project* (pp. 273–327). Washington, DC: U.S. Government Printing Office.

Waskow, I. E., & Parloff, M. B. (Eds.). (1975). *Psychotherapy change measures: Report of the Clinical Research Branch Outcome Measures Project.* Washington, DC: U.S. Government Printing Office.

8

KENNETH I. HOWARD: THE BEST FRIEND THAT PSYCHOTHERAPY RESEARCH EVER HAD

DAVID E. ORLINSKY, MERTON S. KRAUSE, FREDRICK L. NEWMAN, ROBERT J. LUEGER, AND WOLFGANG LUTZ

Kenneth Irwin Howard was born in 1932 and died in 2000. He was a professor of psychology at Northwestern University in Evanston, Illinois, for 32 years, and before that was deputy director of research and chief of the program in measurement and evaluation at the Illinois Department of Mental Health's Institute for Juvenile Research. In these positions, he made major contributions to the field of psychotherapy research and also to research on adolescence and delinquency, psychometrics, and clinical research methodology. Howard coauthored six books and more than 175 book chapters, articles, and research instruments. He served as coeditor of the *Journal of Clinical Psychology* (1996–2000) and as consulting or associate editor for six other journals. He held a National Institute of Mental Health (NIMH) Senior Research Scientist Award and was a fellow of the American Psychological Association's (APA's) Divisions 5 (Evaluation, Measurement, and Statistics), 12 (Society of Clinical Psychology), and 29 (Psychotherapy), the American Psychological Society, the Association

The first four sections were prepared by David E. Orlinsky; the fifth section was prepared by Frederick L. Newman, Robert J. Lueger, and David E. Orlinsky; the sixth section was prepared by Robert J. Lueger; the seventh section was prepared by Wofgang Lutz; and the eighth and ninth sections were prepared by Fredrick L. Newman. All coathors shared in the final version.

for Clinical Psychosocial Research, and the American Association for the Advancement of Science. He cofounded and led the Society for Psychotherapy Research. His scientific and professional work has been recognized by many major groups, including APA.

EARLY INFLUENCES

Ken Howard began his graduate training in psychology at the University of Chicago in autumn of 1956, having been attracted both to the field of psychology and to the University of Chicago by a course he took as an undergraduate at the University of California–Berkeley from a visiting Chicago professor named Carl Rogers. The psychology department at Chicago in the 1950s presented a broad variety of intellectual influences with no one clearly dominant, which allowed students great leeway in choosing those that were most congenial to their talents. In this rich environment, Howard was not initially drawn to the study of psychotherapy—despite the presence of Rogers at the University of Chicago Counseling Center; instead he became intrigued with quantitative methods and discovered a special talent for research design, measurement, psychometrics, and statistics. Most influential for his development were methodologists like Campbell and Fiske, psychometricians like L. L. Thurstone, and factor analysts like Thurstone and Raymond Cattell (University of Illinois). Howard's early research focused on issues related to psychological assessment and included participation in a large-scale study of delinquency, street-corner youth, and, later on, adolescent development (with Daniel Offer). He also completed a clinical internship and worked at the clinic, where he began his research on psychotherapy.

PATIENTS' AND THERAPISTS' EXPERIENCES IN THERAPY

With a friend and fellow graduate student (D. Orlinsky) Howard in 1964 undertook a collaborative study of patients' and therapists' experiences during therapy sessions. Their Psychotherapy Session Project aimed to answer questions arising from their shared experiences as part-time staff therapists at a clinic. The instruments they developed to reflect and illuminate the "psychological interior of psychotherapy" were parallel patient and therapist versions of the Therapy Session Report (Orlinsky & Howard, 1975), one of the first in a long line of postsession questionnaires that researchers have used to explore and evaluate therapy process.

A stream of journal articles based on patients' and therapists' experiences appeared from the late 1960s (e.g., Howard, Krause, & Orlinsky, 1969) to the late 1970s (e.g., Howard, Orlinsky, & Perilstein, 1976), culminating in a book on the *Varieties of Psychotherapeutic Experience* (Orlinsky & Howard, 1975). These studies demonstrated the feasibility and the importance of methodologically objective research on subjective experience for understanding the process of therapy, going well beyond the clinical case history in rigor yet also correcting the overreliance of process researchers on audio recordings.

Ken Howard's most distinctive contribution to this project was his talent for psychological measurement and quantitative analysis and his singular perspective on clinical work. Through a deft strategy of multilevel factor and cluster analyses, Howard empirically defined the dimensions and types of patients' in-session experience, therapists' in-session experience, and their often oblique but clinically significant interdependence. The latter include several patterns of conjoint experience, such as therapeutic alliance vs. defensive impasse, healing magic vs. uncomfortable involvement, and sympathetic warmth vs. conflictual erotization, where the experiences of patient and therapist were statistically linked despite apparent differences in their manifest content (Orlinsky & Howard, 1975). These patterns provide clues for therapists about the nature of a patient's experience, not through observing the patient directly but rather by focusing on their own experiences during sessions.

PROCESS–OUTCOME RESEARCH REVIEWS AND THE GENERIC MODEL OF THERAPY

Because of his rising prominence, Howard was invited to write a review of psychotherapy process research for the 1972 issue of the *Annual Review of Psychology*. This was well received and brought an invitation from Bergin and Garfield to review research linking therapeutic processes to outcomes for the second edition of their esteemed *Handbook of Psychotherapy and Behavior Change* and, 8 years later, to the third edition as well. Work on the latter led to the formulation of a systematic, research-based model—the Generic Model of Psychotherapy—that integrated the cumulative findings of research in the field in a coherent conceptual framework and offered a way to integrate rival clinical theories as well (Orlinsky & Howard, 1986).

The Generic Model organized the variables that researchers have studied into three broad categories: input, process, and output. *Input* variables include conditions that are temporally prior and (potentially) causally related to the events of therapy: patients' and therapists' personal and professional characteristics and the institutional and cultural environments in which therapy takes place. *Output* variables include conditions that are temporal and (potentially) causal sequelae of the events of therapy, especially their consequences for the patient (clinical outcome) but also for the therapist (e.g., professional growth, burnout), for other persons in patients' and therapists' lives, and for the social and cultural environments in which therapy takes place. Research on both input and output variables were examined in relation to the varied facets of therapeutic *process* that researchers had studied. The latter included the therapeutic *contract* (e.g., goals, methods, schedule, fees), therapeutic *operations* (intervention procedures or techniques), the therapeutic *bond* (interpersonal rapport and compatibility), patient's and therapist's internal *self-relatedness* (openness, defensiveness), and *therapeutic realizations* (in-session impacts). The predictive value of the Generic Model was subsequently tested in several studies (e.g., Kolden & Howard, 1992; Saunders, Howard & Orlinsky, 1989).

NORTHWESTERN–CHICAGO STUDY

Inspired in part by their reviews of research on the relation of therapeutic process to outcome (as depicted in the Generic Model), Howard and Orlinsky and their collaborators in the mid-1980s established the Northwestern–Chicago Psychotherapy Research Program. This included in its aims "predicting treatment duration (service utilization) and treatment effectiveness by means of early therapy indicators, such as the quality of the early therapeutic bond or the initial level of symptomatic distress," and "interest in the relationships among length of treatment, phases of therapy, and treatment effectiveness" (Howard et al., 1991, pp. 65–66). Supported by NIMH grants, the project continued for nearly 8 years and produced many studies having measurement, process–outcome, and policy implications.

Most significant for the further development of Howard's work was his use of measures developed in the Northwestern–Chicago project to devise an outcome assessment battery for use by a managed care service delivery network (Howard, Lueger, & Kolden, 1997). This included a patient self-report inventory, therapist rating scales, a patient-rated measure of therapeutic alliance, and a survey of presenting problems. Data from over 16,000 patients established broad-based norms and made possible studies of patient change over time that led to the dose–effect model, the outcome phase model, and patient-focused research.

THE PROCESS OF OUTCOME: DOSE–EFFECT AND OUTCOME PHASE MODELS

To understand the relationship between the amount of psychotherapy and the benefit or outcome of that psychotherapy, Howard and colleagues had to address two problems. The first problem was how to measure a unit of treatment despite the diverse theories and processes of treatment. The solution to this problem was essential to solving the second problem—identifying a mathematical model that would describe the relationship between amount of treatment and amount of effect. The potential value of a mathematical model lay in its ability to predict the amount of benefit for selected durations of treatment and thus to identify those applicants for psychotherapy who are in need of treatment and to set rational limits on the duration of therapy.

Analyzing data on 2,431 patients from 15 studies conducted by themselves or others over a period of 30 years, Howard and his colleagues identified a log-linear relationship between the amount of therapy (dose) and the amount of improvement (effect) in which the outcome of interest was the proportion of patients achieving a dichotomously expressed result (improved or not improved). This has become known as the *dose–effect model* (Howard, Kopta, Krause, & Orlinsky, 1986). Improvement could be mathematically modeled by a negatively accelerating curve with a higher frequency of improvement earlier compared with later in treatment. The extrapolated curve did not reach zero at its origin but suggested that 10% to 18% (expressed in confidence intervals) of patients showed some improvement even before the first session of psychotherapy, possibly as a result on the patient's sense of efficacy in having made the appointment. With eight sessions of psychotherapy, 48% to 58% of the patients showed a measurable degree of improvement, and after a year of treatment, the improvement curve approached asymptote, with about 85% of patients having shown some improvement. By the common criterion of effective exposure used in pharmacological dosage studies, the amount of psychotherapy at which 50% of patients respond to treatment is about six to eight sessions. Analyses taking account of diagnosis at intake revealed that dosage estimates vary in relation to patient characteristics. Finally, the upper bound of responsiveness to psychotherapy, approximately 85% improvement, matched the results of earlier large meta-analyses of psychotherapy outcomes.

In the 20 years after its publication, the dose–effect paper was cited over 350 times in the psychological or medical literature, providing a measure of its influence on other researchers. The dose–effect relationship identified by Howard has been replicated by colleagues in his own group using larger samples and different self-report measures of improvement, and by other researchers with even larger sample sizes, different self-report measures, and alternative statistical analyses such as survival analysis.

Introduction of the *phase model* of outcome extended the dose–effect model to explore the differential response rates of diverse outcome domains (Howard, Lueger, Maling, & Martinovich, 1993). The phase model showed that three problem areas—general demoralization, symptoms, and deficits in life functioning—tend to change at different rates, and perhaps at different times, in the improvement trajectory. These changes define outcome phases defined as remoralization, remediation of symptoms, and rehabilitation of deficits.

The phase model proposes that these phases occur in a sequence suggesting a probable causal order. In the *remoralization* phase, clients begin to recover from feelings of powerlessness and hopelessness. This may start with the client taking steps to seek help, and it may continue in early sessions of therapy as symptoms and problems are clarified, some initial success in mastery of problems is realized, and clients gain hope that therapy will help in addressing their problems. In the *remediation* phase, therapy mobilizes the client's coping skills and continues to develop a sense of mastery or control, resulting in the reduction of symptomatic distress. In the *rehabilitation* phase, clients attempt to modify or control long-standing maladaptive patterns of thought and behavior, to develop more adaptive interpersonal and self-management skills, and to consolidate their ability to achieve positive change in their lives.

The value of the phase model for investigators is indicated by the many times it has been cited in the research literature. The basic precepts of the model—domains and probabilistic causal sequence—have been replicated in a large sample of patients using somewhat different measures of the same constructs. The value of the model for those who formulate service delivery policy is that it informs the stakeholders how much treatment will likely be required to produce improvement in various outcome domains.

PATIENT-FOCUSED RESEARCH AND EXPECTED TREATMENT RESPONSE

In 1996, Ken Howard and colleagues introduced the concept of *patient-focused research*, which has since become the standard term for a new paradigm in psychotherapy research (Howard, Moras, Brill, Martinovich, & Lutz, 1996). Patient-focused research involves the evaluation and outcomes management of psychological treatments in naturalistic service delivery settings, often while the therapy is in progress. Howard and colleagues drew a distinction between two traditions of outcome studies—efficacy research and effectiveness research—and proposed patient-focused research as an alternative strategy. Each strategy has strengths and weaknesses.

Efficacy research addresses the question of how well a treatment works under experimentally controlled conditions (i.e., whether the intervention produces better outcomes than a commonly used treatment or than a putatively inert placebo condition). However, it compares the average response of patients in different groups and says nothing about individual patients. Moreover, the effort to maintain experimental controls raises questions about the generalizability of results to uncontrolled real-world settings where internal validity often is compromised by treatment delivery conditions (Howard, Krause, & Orlinsky, 1986; Howard, Orlinsky, & Lueger, 1995).

Effectiveness research addresses the question of how well a treatment works as it is administered in actual clinical settings. These studies emphasize the generalizability of findings (external validity) and deal with the application of validated treatments to the circumstances of clinical practice. However, the quasi-experimental and systematic naturalistic designs of effectiveness research tend to sacrifice certainty of internal validity. Moreover, like efficacy research, effectiveness research says nothing about the progress of an individual patient.

Patient-focused research, by contrast, asks how well a particular treatment works for individual patients (i.e., whether the patient's condition is responding to the treatment). This model recognizes that patients differ in their expected outcomes or expected courses of treatment. To understand and evaluate the observed course of an individual's response to therapy, one needs to know the reasonable expected course of treatment for that patient, and a method for calculating an *expected treatment response* was developed using hierarchical linear modeling. This approach provides an individualized profile of each patient's progress in relation to the expected course of treatment response for that patient by modeling a patient's change over treatment as a log-linear function of session number and pretreatment clinical characteristics (Lutz, Martinovich, & Howard, 1999). The prediction weights of a patient's initial clinical status and the individual differences in growth curve characteristics allow the prediction of the course of treatment for individual patients once their intake information is available. Ongoing therapeutic effectiveness can be assessed for a single patient by tracking the patient's actual progress in comparison with expected progress based on pretreatment clinical characteristics.

In addition to many different research and outcomes management applications, the value of the model for clinical practice has been illustrated with many examples of successful and unsuccessful treatment cases. Further studies using this model have found (a) that predictions for change in later sessions are enhanced by incorporating information about the change that patients experienced during early sessions, (b) that initial predictions based on patient characteristics are reliable, (c) that predictions are useful for clinical case management, (d) that the model can be applied to different diagnostic groups and various symptom patterns, and (e) that a three-level hierarchical linear model can identify differential therapist influence on patient change.

Ken Howard recognized that the validity of growth curve prediction weights for any particular patient depends on the extent to which the study sample (reference group) is representative of the population of which that patient was a member and that most predictors work only for specific sub-sets of patients (Krause, Howard, & Lutz, 1998). To address this problem, an extended expected response model using nearest neighbor techniques was introduced. The nearest neighbor approach identifies those previously treated patients in the reference group who most closely match the target patient (hence "nearest neighbors") on intake variables. It then uses this homogeneous subgroup to generate predictions of treatment progress for the target patient.

The patient-focused model has been applied to large databases in the United Kingdom and the United States, and it has been used for continuous patient feedback into clinical practice to identify potential treatment failures early in the course of therapy. In this respect, patient-focused research has the potential to inform the clinical decisions of therapists in the course of treat-ment and thus to reduce the scientist–practitioner gap (Howard et al., 1996).

DEVELOPING AN EMPIRICAL BASIS FOR
MENTAL HEALTH SERVICE POLICY

For many years Howard and his colleagues argued that the random-ized clinical trial had only limited use in setting the standards and policies for what is now called *evidence-based practice* (Howard, Krause, & Lyons, 1993; Krause & Howard, 2003). They clarified issues, such as attrition and selection bias, that severely limited the inferences that can be drawn from randomized clinical trials, and they stressed the inadequacy of relying only on mean group differences and effect sizes to assess the value of treatments (Howard, Krause, & Vessey, 1994). They promoted the use of "systematic naturalistic" designs in studies, following a research protocol implemented in actual treatment settings with a minimum of intrusion on the clinical practice (Howard et al., 1996). In place of no-treatment and/or alternative-treatment control conditions, Howard argued for comparison of clinical samples with representative samples of "normal" persons in order to assess whether, and to what extent, patients progressed in a clinically significant direction, that is, toward behaviors statistically indistinguishable from those in a nonclinical population similar to those who entered treatment. Over a series of studies, they argued that one could provide an empirical basis for assessing the clinical significance of specific interventions as a function of a variety of moderator variables and thereby estimate what works best for whom (Howard, Krause, Caburnay, Noel, & Saunders, 2001; Howard, Krause, & Lyons, 1993; Lutz, Martinovich, & Howard, 1999; Lyons & Howard, 1991; Saunders, Howard, & Newman, 1988). Howard and his colleagues must be recognized as pioneers in the use of what is now called *practice-based evidence*, which became possible in large part through his example in the application of sound statistical methods and his leadership in encouraging others to depart from exclusive reliance on data from randomized clinical trials.

ADVANCES IN THE APPROPRIATE ANALYSES OF PSYCHOTHERAPY RESEARCH DATA

Howard's emphasis on the logical application of statistical methods and use of appropriate research designs should have a significant impact on mental health service practice and policy. At the level of statistical analysis, he advocated the collection of systematic quantitative data in naturalistic settings in order to focus on estimating "what works for whom." Howard's work in this area indicated that there are three questions that need to be answered by researchers to test for statistical equivalence or difference of patients' test scores from acceptable or "normal" psychological and social functioning:

1. *What are the relevant population characteristics and appropriate measures of outcome?* An explicit statement must be made of the characteristics of the sample and population and of the measures to be used in a comparison. Desired behavioral outcomes must be tailored to the "whom" in the question, "What works for whom?"
2. *How much difference makes a real difference?* The upper and lower limits of equivalence or difference must also be described a priori and defended on the basis of relevant theory or established empirical findings. Researchers and policymakers need to define the range of behaviors that are reliable and valid indicators of clinically appropriate ("normal") behaviors as distinct from those that would be considered "abnormal."
3. *What is an acceptable rate of being wrong (Type I error)?* The probability that the confidence interval falls outside of the boundaries of equivalence must be explicitly acknowledged if one is to follow the current scientific tradition of statistical decision making. This is essential for evaluating either a single study or a set of studies in a meta-analysis, as well as defining criteria for generating supervisory feedback to therapists and setting policy boundaries for acceptable evidence-based practice.

In addition to his own writing about the potential policy implications of research, Howard made strong and consistent efforts to support colleagues as they developed methods capable of providing data from naturalistic settings that could impact treatment guidelines and standards and influence evidence-based practice and policy (e.g., in special issues of the *Journal of Consulting and Clinical Psychology* that he instigated). The influence of Ken Howard's later research may be seen in the adaptation by several research groups of the clinical significance concept and community norms in their use of practice-based evidence and clinical progress feedback to the therapists as means of improving service outcomes in the United States, United Kingdom, Switzerland, and Germany; the development of new instrumentation for assessing outcomes of mental health services; and the development of practice-based research networks.

It is probably no accident that the research groups that have done most to develop and apply these concepts, methods, and statistical procedures had their intellectual home in the Society for Psychotherapy Research—a society that Howard cofounded and served as its first president and later as its first executive officer. In all his work, Ken Howard was known as a man of remarkable intelligence, unusual wit, and great personal charm. He is remembered by us and many others as a devoted friend and generous mentor.

REFERENCES

Howard, K. I., Kopta, S. M., Krause, M. S., & Orlinsky, D. E. (1986). The dose-effect relationship in psychotherapy. *American Psychologist, 41*, 159–164.doi:10.1037/0003-066X.41.2.159

Howard, K. I., Krause, M. S., Caburnay, C. A., Noel, S. B., & Saunders, S. M. (2001). Syzygy, science, and psychotherapy: The *Consumer Reports* study. *Journal of Clinical Psychology, 57*, 865–874. doi:10.1002/jclp.1055

Howard, K. I., Krause, M. S., & Lyons, J. S. (1993). When clinical trials fail: A guide to disaggregation. In L. S. Onken, J. D. Blaine, & J. J. Boren (Eds.), *Behavioral treatments for drug abuse and dependence* (NIDA Research Monograph No. 137, pp. 291–302). Washington, DC: National Institute for Drug Abuse.

Howard, K. I., Krause, M. S., & Orlinsky, D. E. (1969). Direction of affective influence in psychotherapy. *Journal of Consulting and Clinical Psychology, 33*,614–620. doi:10.1037/h0028299

Howard, K. I., Krause, M. S., & Orlinsky, D. E. (1986). The attrition dilemma: Toward a new strategy for psychotherapy research. *Journal of Consulting and Clinical Psychology, 54*, 106–110. doi:10.1037/0022-006X.54.1.106

Howard, K. I., Krause, M. S., & Vessey, J. (1994). Analyzing clinical trial data: The problem of outcome overlap. *Psychotherapy, 31*, 302–307. doi:10.1037/h0090213

Howard, K. I., Lueger, R. J., & Kolden, G. G. (1997). Measuring progress and outcome in the treatment of affective disorders. In L. M. Horowitz, M. J. Lambert,

& H. H. Strupp (Eds.), *Measuring patient change after treatment for mood, anxiety, and personality disorders: Toward a core battery* (pp. 263–281). Washington, DC: American Psychological Association.

Howard, K. I., Lueger, R. J., Maling, M. S., & Martinovich, Z. (1993). A Phase Model of psychotherapy: Causal mediation of change. *Journal of Consulting and Clinical Psychology, 61*, 678–685. doi:10.1037/0022-006X.61.4.678

Howard, K. I., Moras, K., Brill, P. L., Martinovich, Z., & Lutz, W. (1996). Evaluation of psychotherapy: Efficacy, effectiveness, and patient progress. *American Psychologist, 51*, 1059–1064. doi:10.1037/0003-066X.51.10.1059

Howard, K. I., & Orlinsky, D. E. (1972). Psychotherapeutic processes. In P. H. Mussen & M. R. Rosenzweig (Eds.), *Annual review of psychology* (Vol. 23, pp. 615–668). Palo Alto, CA: Annual Reviews.

Howard, K. I., Orlinsky, D. E., & Lueger, R. J. (1995). The design of clinically relevant outcome research: Some considerations and an example. In M. Aveline & D. A. Shapiro (Eds.), *Research foundations for psychotherapy practice* (pp. 3–47). Chichester, England: Wiley.

Howard, K. I., Orlinsky, D. E., & Perilstein, J. (1976). Contributions of therapists to patients' experiences in psychotherapy: A components of variance model for analyzing process data. *Journal of Consulting and Clinical Psychology, 44*, 520–526. doi:10.1037/0022-006X.44.4.520

Howard, K. I., Orlinsky, D. E., Saunders, S. M., Bankoff, E., Davidson, C., & O'Mahoney, M. (1991). Northwestern University–University of Chicago psychotherapy research program. In L. E. Beutler & M. Crago (Eds.), *Psychotherapy research: An international review of programmatic studies* (pp. 65–74). Washington, DC: American Psychological Association.

Kolden, G. G., & Howard, K. I. (1992). An empirical test of the Generic Model of Psychotherapy. *Journal of Psychotherapy Practice and Research, 1*, 225–236.

Krause, M. S., & Howard, K. I. (2003). What random assignment does and does not do. *Journal of Clinical Psychology, 59*, 751–766. doi:10.1002/jclp.10170

Krause, M. S., Howard, K. I., & Lutz, W. (1998). Exploring individual change. *Journal of Consulting and Clinical Psychology, 66*, 838–845. doi:10.1037/0022-006X.66.5.838

Lutz, W., Martinovich, Z., & Howard, K. I. (1999). Patient profiling: An application of random coefficient regression models to depicting the response of a patient to outpatient psychotherapy. *Journal of Consulting and Clinical Psychology, 67*, 571–577. doi:10.1037/0022-006X.67.4.571

Lyons, J. S., & Howard, K. I. (1991). Main effects analysis in clinical research: Statistical guidelines for disaggregating treatment groups. *Journal of Consulting and Clinical Psychology, 59*, 745–748. doi:10.1037/0022-006X.59.5.745

Orlinsky, D. E., & Howard, K. I. (1975). *Varieties of psychotherapeutic experience: Multivariate analyses of patients' and therapists' reports.* New York, NY: Teachers College Press.

Orlinsky, D. E., & Howard, K. I. (1978). The relation of process to outcome in psycho-therapy. In S. Garfield & A. Bergin (Eds.), *Handbook of psychotherapy and behavior change* (2nd ed., pp. 283–329). New York, NY: Wiley.

Orlinsky, D. E., & Howard, K. I. (1986). Process and outcome in psychotherapy. In S. L. Garfield & A. E. Bergin (Eds.), *Handbook of psychotherapy and behavior change* (3rd ed., 311–384). New York, NY: Wiley.

Saunders, S. M., Howard, K. I., & Newman, F. L. (1988). Evaluating the clinical significance of treatment effects: Norms and normality. *Behavioral Assessment, 10,* 207–218.

Saunders, S. M., Howard, K. I., & Orlinsky, D. E. (1989). The Therapeutic Bond Scale: Psychometric characteristics and relationship to treatment effectiveness. *Psychological Assessment, 1,* 323–330. doi:10.1037/1040-3590.1.4.323

9

ALLEN E. BERGIN: CONSUMMATE SCHOLAR AND CHARTER MEMBER OF THE SOCIETY FOR PSYCHOTHERAPY RESEARCH

MICHAEL J. LAMBERT, ALAN S. GURMAN, AND P. SCOTT RICHARDS

Allen E. Bergin has been a guiding light for the development and growth of psychotherapy by demonstrating that psychotherapy works for the majority of clients, pointing out the harm that psychotherapy can do, encouraging the use of a broad range of research methods that inform clinical practice, and integrating new dimensions of human functioning in our understanding and facilitation of change. These impressive contributions are noteworthy in scientific, clinical, and practice communities over a span of 40 years. At the center of Bergin's influence on the field is the publication of the seminal *Handbook of Psychotherapy and Behavior Change*, his outstanding scholarship on the general effects of psychotherapy, his inspirational effort to stimulate collaboration in psychotherapy research, his timely analysis of deterioration effects, his examination of the therapeutic effectiveness of paraprofessionals, and his opening up new horizons of scholarship and research on religious values and spirituality.

EARLY BEGINNINGS

Of special import with regard to Bergin's contributions to psychotherapy is the fact that he was trained first as a behavior therapist under the tutelage of Albert Bandura at Stanford University and, after receiving his PhD, did a postdoctoral fellowship focused on client-centered psychotherapy under Carl Rogers at the University of Wisconsin. Perhaps not at all ironically, after that postdoctoral year, Bergin joined the clinical psychology faculty at Columbia University (Teachers College [TC]), the program from which Rogers had received his PhD in 1931. The professional and intellectual atmosphere at the TC clinical psychology program could not have been better suited to Bergin's scholarly openness and natural inclination toward academic inclusiveness. Despite its location in the geographic center of psychoanalytic and psychodynamic ferment that was New York City, the TC program's faculty was diverse long before diversity became a household word. In the last few years of Bergin's tenure at TC (which he left in 1972 to move to Brigham Young University in Provo, Utah), the program's faculty included a Sullivanian psychoanalyst, a community psychologist, a "Tavistock"-style group therapist, a developmental psychopathologist, and a Rorschach researcher, in addition to Bergin's very empirically iconoclastic colleague and *Handbook* coeditor, Sol Garfield. Bergin highly valued a community of nonredundant ideas in his professional environment.

The same intellectual openness and searching that characterized Bergin's profoundly important writings also permeated his teaching at TC. For example, while demonstrating to his graduate student seminar on behavior therapy the actual conduct of systematic desensitization (very popular in 1968!), his authority-phobic client spontaneously reported a recent dream. The dream seemed to be speaking to the unconscious ways in which his experiencing therapeutic change regarding authority figures was evolving during his work with Bergin. Behavior therapist though he may have been, Bergin was clearly fascinated to hear the young man's account of his unconscious responding to such a direct behavioral intervention. He urged his students to appreciate the complexity and multidimensionality of human behavior and, thus, of the process of therapeutic change at a time when acrimonious debates between theoretical schools were more abundant than efforts toward integration and rapprochement.

It is not entirely clear if Bergin was able to provide such objective and balanced reviews of psychotherapy research because of his clinical training in learning theory and his early exposure to client-centered psychotherapy research or if he sought out this kind of diverse training because of his intellectual curiosity and openness. In any event, he was able to document what no one before him had been able to, that is, the existence of overwhelming evidence that people who are suffering with personal problems are better off seeing psychotherapists than going it on their own and hoping for their problems to abate.

MAJOR ACCOMPLISHMENTS

The *Handbook*

For most of its early history (extending into the 1930s) psychotherapy relied almost exclusively on clinical reports, case studies, and theoretical accounts of the effects of psychotherapy. Practice was based on theoretical allegiance with reference to authority figures or recourse to personal clinical experience. By 1970, a sufficient body of psychotherapy research existed to enable Allen Bergin and Columbia University (TC) colleague Sol Garfield to edit the first edition of the *Handbook of Psychotherapy and Behavior Change* (Bergin & Garfield, 1971). Their anticipation was that the exponential increase in empirical research would

> guide practice so that harmful and useless methods will be discarded and the best techniques (whether they be drugs, different methods of psychotherapy, or social intervention) will be used in the most efficient manner to help individuals overcome their problems. (Bergin & Garfield, 1971, p. xii)

Over its history, the *Handbook* became the primary reference on the critical review and integration of empirical investigations of all the major methods of psychotherapy. It rapidly ascended to the status of required reading for a majority of graduate programs in clinical and counseling psychology, and thereafter became a Science Citation Classic. It is not difficult to judge the importance of the first and subsequent editions of the *Handbook*. Generations of practitioners have been guided by the carefully integrated evidence for positive clinical practice and equally as important, it had a significant influence on the nature and types of questions that were being asked and the methodologies that guided psychotherapy researchers for decades.

Evaluation of Psychotherapy Outcome

Of considerable significance was Bergin's chapter in the first edition, "The Evaluation of Psychotherapy Outcomes," in which he addressed and almost put to rest one of the most resistant myths of the 20th century: that psychotherapy's impact on patients was no more helpful than the passage of time. This conclusion, prompted by a review of the existing research literature by Hans Eysenck (1952), had been hotly debated with strong invective, claims, and counterclaims over 2 decades. The traditional verbal therapies were under attack, but the research evidence Eysenck had relied on had been so ambiguous that it was open to numerous interpretations. Bergin was the first scholar in the field to approach the debate by carefully reexamining the evidence put forth by Eysenck. He documented numerous problems in the original studies that made them difficult to combine, and he found computational errors in both the original studies and in Eysenck's own calculations and tabulations of improvement rates based on those original studies, as well as a consistent tendency on Eysenck's part to interpret information about the results of psychodynamic psychotherapy in as negative a light as possible. The result was that Bergin's scholarship was so careful and clear that it illuminated the misinterpretations and cast serious doubt on the validity of Eysenck's original conclusions. As psychotherapy research methodology improved over the 35 years after that seminal analysis, and as quantitative reviewing techniques rose to prominence, Bergin's conclusions were substantiated, whereas Eysenck's have not been supported. We know that at the very least a wide variety of psychotherapies speed recovery even if their helpfulness does not ultimately surpass the natural healing effects of the passage of time. Bergin's tireless scholarship was without doubt the largest single reason the debate finally faded away. It is quite unfortunate that many of today's graduate students do not read this fine chapter, because it provides such a high standard of critical scholarship for anyone seriously interested in integrating research evidence into the ethical and effective practice of psychotherapy.

Changing the Frontiers of Psychotherapy Research

As compelling as Bergin's (1971) critiques of Eysenck's analyses were, and as defining of the world of psychotherapy research as the *Handbook* was, arguably his crowning written achievement in the field, and certainly the most creative and generative, was the extraordinary project he undertook with Hans Strupp of Vanderbilt University. Following the American Psychological Association Conference on Research in Psychotherapy in 1966, Bergin and Strupp undertook the massive joint project of attempting to stimulate collaborative research among independent psychotherapy investigators. The first product of this collaboration was "Some Empirical and Conceptual Bases for Coordinated Research in Psychotherapy," published as an entire issue of the *International Journal of Psychiatry* (Strupp & Bergin, 1969a). This groundbreaking call for collaborative therapy research was followed by Bergin and Strupp's joint preparation of another issue of that journal (Strupp & Bergin, 1969b), which consisted of commentaries by most of the world's leading therapy researchers on the earlier proposal to foster collaborative work on the central challenging issues and questions of the times (Strupp & Bergin, 1969a).

As innovative as those two publications were in the field, they could only be exceeded in their mind-expanding potential by the ultimate appearance of Bergin and Strupp's (1972) *Changing Frontiers in the Science of Psychotherapy*, probably the most visionary single published contribution to the evolution of psychotherapy research. In their quest to arouse a collaborative investigative spirit among like-minded clinical scholars, Bergin and Strupp obtained a federal research grant that allowed them to travel to visit and interview at length such conceptually diverse luminaries as Thomas Szasz, Kenneth Colby, Robert Wallerstein, Neal Miller, Peter Lang, and Gerald Davison. These interviews and Bergin and Strupp's reflections on these interviews constitute a truly unique contribution to the history of psychotherapy research. As Joseph Matarazzo wrote in his foreword to *Changing Frontiers*, Bergin and Strupp's commentaries and reflections illustrate and embody "the thoughts, hopes, aspirations, convictions, biases, frustrations, changes of heart and viewpoint, the excitement and despair experienced by every writer and scientist as he pursues his work" (p. vi).

Among Bergin's more important observations was that posttest scores on assessments of client functioning demonstrated greater variance than had been present at intake, and greater than in no-treatment controls. Bergin described this common occurrence as the *deterioration effect* and became the central figure in advocating the possibility that therapy was, on occasion, harmful as well as helpful. Bergin documented the presence of a deterioration effect as early as 1966 and pursued it in a large-scale review published in 1977 (Lambert, Bergin, & Collins, 1977) that attempted to examine the breadth of the findings across school-based psychotherapies and treatment modalities (e.g., group, family), actual deterioration rates, and the possible mechanisms responsible for such negative effects, including both client and therapist characteristics. His contributions inspired others to investigate and explore similar phenomena in areas of psychotherapy that had never before been subjected to empirical scrutiny, such as couple and family therapy (e.g., Gurman, 1973; Gurman & Kniskern, 1978).

After publishing his 1966 article, Bergin received considerable mail from patients as well as therapists, detailing injuries that seemed to have resulted from treatment and more specifically from the behavior and attitudes of therapists. Although cautious in his judgment about the reliability of such reports, Bergin noted that most came from clients who felt mistreated by their therapists but had found subsequent help and were functioning well at the time they contacted him. This anecdotal information, along with research accounts of the phenomenon, led Bergin to the conclusion that client deterioration was most closely linked to therapist attitudes and in-session interpersonal behaviors rather than the misuse of specific theory-based interventions, thereby presaging important contemporary work on therapist (vs. technique) factors in treatment outcome by about 3 decades. He also noted that negative therapist attitudes interacted with and were especially harmful with particularly vulnerable clients, a clinically important finding later corroborated in the realm of family therapy (Gurman & Kniskern, 1978).

Clearly, in his mind, the problem of deterioration was most likely a failure in the personal adjustment of, and lack of benevolence in, therapists. The problem this unmasked was, then, the common failure of graduate programs to select wise and goodhearted people and their failure to make difficult decisions about trainees who needed to be carefully monitored in their clinical work or perhaps even dismissed from their programs after accumulating evidence made it clear that they were responsible for an undue proportion of failed therapy cases, some with negative effects. With regard to deterioration, little evidence presented itself that failures in training for the technical aspects of interventions were an important area for concern.

Bergin was also an advocate of the importance of variability in a more general and statistical sense. He believed that what was hidden by a mean could be the most important information in need of assimilation. He at once advocated the necessity of reductionism:

> Some critics argue that to break down, isolate, and extract variables from the therapeutic context is to drastically modify and underestimate the complexity of the phenomena under study. I feel this is irrelevant and unnecessarily inhibiting because (a) no science or applied science has ever progressed without simplifying. (1971, p. 254)

and at the same time he advocated the experimental case study approach and said,

> For these reasons, I am generally distrustful of group-based multifactorial studies, and of statistical operations that are associated with them. The results are too often of no practical use because they amount to nothing more than abstractions on top of confusion. (1971, p. 255)

His early advocacy (4 decades ago) of both quantitative and qualitative methods foreshadowed current debates about the relative value of these divergent procedures.

As in many other ways, Bergin, when serving as students' dissertation advisor, eschewed "fancy" statistical techniques to reveal treatment effects that really mattered and maintained that simple line graphs should be able to show what he called "WOW!-effects." At TC, he strongly advocated for clinical students who had the courage to do "nontraditional" research, such as empirical single-case studies and theoretical dissertations, inevitably ending up as the primary advisor of students who wanted to break new dissertation ground.

The Effectiveness of Paraprofessionals

Reviews of the causes of client deterioration and the general effects of psychotherapy also led Bergin to examine the surprisingly positive outcomes that resulted when carefully selected laypeople offered treatments. This work left little doubt in his mind that the personal attributes of providers were central in whatever led to positive outcomes in clients, regardless of their theoretical orientation. His work certainly anticipated today's debates between those advocating evidence-based practices in the form of systems of psychotherapy, versus an emphasis on common curative factors.

While always remaining true to the data, whether they led to a conclusion about therapy's overall effectiveness or to a conclusion about the negative effects produced by some therapists, Bergin was hardly neutral in his view that proponents of therapy models are ethically obligated to show acceptable evidence of the efficacy and effectiveness of their preferred methods. About a decade after the publication of the first edition of the *Handbook*, Bergin remarked:

> It is one of the anomalies of the behavioral and psychiatric sciences that methods of intervention can still be invented, used and paid for by the public without a shred of standard empirical evidence to demonstrate efficacy and absence of harmful effects. This kind of proliferation is a professional scandal. (Personal communication, 1980, from Bergin to Gurman)

Religious Values, Psychotherapy, and Mental Health

Perhaps it is not surprising that during the latter half of his career, Bergin increasingly began to turn his professional attention to broader social issues that were pertinent to the science and practice of psychotherapy, including the topics of values and psychotherapy, religion and mental health, and spirituality and psychotherapy. Bergin had long been interested in such issues. As a young adult at the Massachusetts Institute of Technology and then at Reed College, in Portland, Oregon, Bergin considered himself agnostic regarding matters of faith. Although he respected the scientific enterprise and thrived on the rigor of empirical inquiry, Bergin found himself personally unsatisfied by the deterministic and reductionistic assumptions of the natural and behavioral sciences. After a couple of years of intense questioning and searching, Bergin's spiritual quest led him to enroll at Brigham Young University and to convert to the Church of Jesus Christ of Latter-day Saints

(LDS). During the remaining years of his undergraduate work at Brigham Young University, his graduate studies at Stanford University, and his post-doctoral experience with Carl Rogers at the University Wisconsin Medical School Psychiatric Institute, Bergin grew increasingly aware of and concerned about the alienation and conflicts that then existed between psychology and religious tradition. During his years as a professor at Columbia University, this awareness and concern continued to grow, and with increasing frequency he began to raise questions in professional contexts about value and moral issues as they pertained to psychotherapy (Bergin, 1991). While at Columbia University, Bergin served in various lay leadership positions within his church, including several years as the bishop of a local LDS congregation, where he frequently used the resources of his religious community to assist members of his congregation who were struggling with various emotional and relationship problems.

Bergin's first major publication about religion and psychotherapy, "Psychotherapy and Religious Values," was published in 1980 in the *Journal of Consulting and Clinical Psychology* (Bergin, 1980a) and previewed many of the scholarly themes he would pursue during the remainder of his career. In the article, Bergin documented the historical and philosophical alienation of religion and psychology and its effects on the practice of psychotherapy. He made a number of other points about psychotherapy and religious values. The majority of mainstream psychotherapists, he maintained, have adopted views of human nature (i.e., naturalistic and deterministic ones) that conflict with theistic, spiritual views. The values and therapeutic goals (i.e., clinical–humanistic ones) of most psychotherapists often conflict with those of their religious and spiritually oriented clients. He argued that by not being open about the values and goals that guide their therapeutic work, mainstream psychotherapists may implicitly impose alien values frameworks on their religious clients. As a result, he warned, many psychotherapists may be guilty of engaging in culturally biased and insensitive therapy with theistic religious clients by pursuing therapeutic goals that conflict with their clients' spiritual beliefs and values; not all clinical–humanistic beliefs and values are healthy and socially benevolent. Bergin maintained that there are many healthy and socially benevolent theistic religious values, and the psychotherapy profession would be enriched by the incorporation of these values into its theories and practices. Mainstream psychotherapists, he believed, have for too long been biased against religion and have excluded religious and spiritual perspectives from their theories and work.

The article, which became a citation classic, generated intense interest, enthusiasm, and controversy in the psychology profession. In the subsequent issue of the same journal, responses to Bergin's article by Albert Ellis (1980) and Gary Walls (1980) were published along with a rejoinder by Bergin

(1980b). Albert Ellis objected to Bergin's portrayal of the views of probabilistic atheist clinicians like himself and clarified his position on a number of value issues such as moral relativism, sexuality, and marriage and family. Ellis (1980) also hypothesized that "devout, orthodox, or dogmatic religion (or what might be called religiosity) is significantly correlated with emotional disturbance" (p. 637). In his rejoinder, Bergin (1980b) stated, "Although I believe that religion can be powerfully benevolent, I have to agree with Ellis and Walls that it is not always a positive influence. Religion is diverse and therefore its effects are diverse." Consistent with the commitment to empirical research that characterized his work on psychotherapy outcomes, Bergin also discussed the research literature concerning religion and mental health, characterizing it as "contradictory and ambiguous" (p. 643).

Following the publication of his 1980 article, Bergin launched a series of empirical studies concerning religion and mental health, including a meta-analysis of the existing research literature on this topic., During the next 2 decades, Bergin's scholarship increasingly focused on issues concerning religion and mental health and spirituality and psychotherapy, although he continued to make significant contributions to the literature concerning the outcomes of psychotherapy.

ADDITIONAL ACHIEVEMENTS

Bergin was among those who founded the Society for Psychotherapy Research (SPR), serving as its fifth president, 1974–1975, and he organized its first international meeting (London, 1975). SPR, like the *Handbook*, was dedicated to following the evidence wherever it led. Bergin's work always embodied and exemplified the attitude of his early mentor Rogers, who emphasized that "the facts are always friendly, every bit of evidence one can acquire . . . leads one that much closer to what is true" (Rogers, 1961, p. 26). Always eager to spread the word about the importance and excitement of investigating psychotherapy, Bergin attracted many of his 1971 clinical students to the Second International Annual Meeting of SPR in Saddle Brook, New Jersey, across the Hudson River from Manhattan. During the latter years of his career, despite significant health challenges, Bergin remained productive in scholarship, editing the fourth edition of the *Handbook of Psychotherapy and Behavior Change* and coauthoring and coediting two other volumes about spirituality and psychotherapy (Richards & Bergin, 1997, 2000) in which a variety of authors made suggestions for more effective, culturally sensitive practices for religious clients from a diversity of Western and Eastern spiritual traditions. Bergin remained open to diverse views.

REFERENCES

Bergin, A. E. (1966). Some implications of psychotherapy research for therapeutic practice. *Journal of Abnormal Psychology, 71,* 235–246. doi:10.1037/h0023577

Bergin, A. E. (1971). The evaluation of therapeutic outcomes. In A. E. Bergin & S. L. Garfield (Eds.), *Handbook of psychotherapy & behavior change* (pp. 217–270). New York, NY: Wiley.

Bergin, A. E. (1980a). Psychotherapy and religious values. *Journal of Consulting and Clinical Psychology, 48,* 95–105. doi:10.1037/0022-006X.48.1.95

Bergin, A. E. (1980b). Religious and humanistic values: A reply to Ellis and Walls. *Journal of Consulting and Clinical Psychology, 48,* 642–645. doi:10.1037/0022-006X.48.5.642

Bergin, A. E. (1991). Values and religious issues in psychotherapy and mental health. *American Psychologist, 46,* 394–403. doi:10.1037/0003-066X.46.4.394

Bergin, A. E., & Garfield, S. L. (1971). *Handbook of psychotherapy & behavior change.* New York, NY: Wiley.

Bergin, A. E., & Garfield, S. L. (Eds.). (1994). *Handbook of psychotherapy and behavior change* (4th ed.). New York, NY: Wiley.

Bergin, A. E., & Strupp, H. H. (1972). *Changing frontiers in the science of psychotherapy.* Chicago, IL: Aldine.

Ellis, A. (1980). Psychotherapy and atheistic values: A response to A. E. Bergin's "Psychotherapy and Religious Values." *Journal of Consulting and Clinical Psychology, 48,* 635–639. doi:10.1037/0022-006X.48.5.635

Eysenck, H. J. (1952). The effects of psychotherapy: An evaluation. *Journal of Consulting Psychology, 16,* 319–324. doi:10.1037/h0063633

Garfield, S. L., & Bergin, A. E. (1978). *Handbook of psychotherapy and behavior change* (2nd ed.). New York, NY: Wiley.

Gurman, A. S. (1973). The effects and effectiveness of marital therapy: A review of outcome research. *Family Process, 12,* 145–170. doi:10.1111/j.1545-5300.1973.00145.x

Gurman, A. S., & Kniskern, D. P. (1978). Deterioration in marital and family therapy: Empirical, clinical and conceptual issues. *Family Process, 17,* 3–20. doi:10.1111/j.1545-5300.1978.00003.x

Lambert, M. J., Bergin, A. E., & Collins, J. L. (1977). Therapist-induced deterioration. In A. S. Gurman & A. M. Razin (Eds.), *Effective psychotherapy: A handbook of research* (pp. 452–481). New York, NY: Pergamon.

Richards, P. S., & Bergin, A. E. (1997). *A spiritual strategy for counseling and psychotherapy.* Washington, DC: American Psychological Association.

Richards, P. S., & Bergin, A. E. (Eds.). (2000). *Handbook of psychotherapy and religious diversity.* Washington, DC: American Psychological Association.

Rogers, C. R. (1961). *On becoming a person.* Boston, MA: Houghton Mifflin.

Strupp, H. H., & Bergin, A. E. (1969a). Some empirical and conceptual bases for coordinated research in psychotherapy: A critical review of issues, trends and evidence. *International Journal of Psychiatry, 7,* 18–90.

Strupp, H. H., &, & Bergin, A. E. (1969b). Critical evaluations of: Some empirical and conceptual bases for coordinated research in psychotherapy: Critical review of issues, trends and evidence. *International Journal of Psychiatry, 7,* 116–121.

Walls, G. (1980). Values and psychotherapy: A comment on "Psychotherapy and Religious Values." *Journal of Consulting and Clinical Psychology, 48,* 640–641. doi:10.1037/0022-006X.48.5.640

10

KLAUS GRAWE: ON A CONSTANT QUEST FOR A TRULY INTEGRATIVE AND RESEARCH-BASED PSYCHOTHERAPY

FRANZ CASPAR AND MARTIN GROSSE HOLTFORTH

Klaus Grawe died unexpectedly from a heart attack, in Zürich in July 2005. He may be seen as the best-known and most influential psychotherapy researcher in Continental Europe. He had a unique way of being fascinated by psychotherapy and psychotherapy research, of using basic psychological and later neurobiological models to advance psychotherapy, and of conveying his concepts to colleagues in an engaging way. In line with developing concepts emphasizing the interpersonal aspects of psychotherapy, he was a very caring human being.

He was a fascinated reader of psychodynamic literature until he asked himself, "Where do they [the authors] know this from?" He then rigorously searched for empirically supported concepts, in an open way that emphasized their use for clinical practice. He was also always eager to argue with those who hindered scientific progress rather than contributing to it. Although not all colleagues were happy with the criticism he leveled against some claims by psychotherapy approaches that he considered empirically unjustified, European as well as international psychotherapy research has profited enormously from his unique spirit.

MAJOR CONTRIBUTIONS

Mindful of the inherent incompleteness of any summary of Klaus Grawe's contributions to psychotherapy research, we believe that his contribution reflects five major qualities as the expression of one spirit. First, Klaus Grawe was a *builder*, as demonstrated by the establishment of the clinics in Bern and Zurich, as well as a postgraduate program for psychotherapy training. Second, he was an *innovator* in various arenas. Empirically, he developed and tested new approaches to therapy (based on Plan Analysis and consistency theory). Conceptually, he enriched our understanding of the process of change via concepts borrowed from traditions as diverse as Piaget and neuroscience. Clinically, he was a pioneer on outcomes assessment and feedback of assessment results to therapists and patients. Third, he was also a *leader* in terms of policy (as demonstrated by his work for the German legislature) and a paradigm shift within research (as shown by his contribution to the second generation of approaches to psychotherapy). Fourth, he was also a *collaborator*, working with many people to change the way psychotherapy is investigated, practiced, conceived, and taught. Fifth, he was an outstanding *scholar*, having provided great summaries of the field (via meta-analysis; a handbook chapter on process–outcome research; and publication of two conceptual books, *Psychological Therapy* [2004] and *Neuropsychotherapy* [2006]) and fruitful heuristics for future conceptual and empirical developments (e.g., the identification of four mechanisms of change, in a presidential address in 1997). In sum, all his accomplishments were guided by an integrative spirit, which manifested itself in different forms:

- theoretical integration (as in his combination of learning and motivation principles in 1980, and his consistency theory later on);
- integration of process and outcome findings (as reflected, for example, in the trials published in 1990 and after his death; Grosse Holtforth, Grawe, Fries, & Znoj, 2008);
- integration of basic (psychopathology, cognitive, and neuroscience) and applied sciences;
- and, of course, integration of research and practice (as reflected in his Therapy Spectrum Analysis, as well as in the 2004 and 2007 books).

EARLY BEGINNINGS

Klaus Grawe was born in 1943 in Wilster (Northern Germany), during a time of evacuation, fleeing the bombs on his family's home town of Hamburg. He went to school in Hamburg and studied psychology in Hamburg and

Freiburg im Breisgau, receiving his diploma in 1968 in Hamburg. It was mainly his mother to whom he owed the firm belief that, although sometimes hard, life is fundamentally benign. After an accident that impaired one of his eyes at a young age, he had much time to reflect and to develop strength doing so. This did not hamper his amazingly energetic presence or his joie de vivre. On the contrary!

His dissertation on the differential effects of behavior and client-centered therapy with anxiety patients followed in 1976, and his habilitation, the German degree qualifying for a tenured position, in 1979. He cofounded the multiapproach psychotherapy ward at the Eppendorf University psychiatric hospital in Hamburg and worked there for 11 years. This was a decisive time for him: In the concrete everyday work with patients he experienced the limits of traditional behavior therapy in particular, and of traditional psychotherapy approaches in general. More specifically, he noticed that many patients were not able to concentrate on what they were supposed to do to reduce their symptoms. Instead, they were engaged in interactional struggles with their therapists and at times also with other therapy group members.

Although skillful in using traditional behavior analyses as a means for understanding the functioning of patients, Grawe was convinced that a different approach was needed to understand the often strange behavior of patients in the therapy session: One needed to understand the structure of patients' motives better. He found useful the "Plan" concept by Miller, Galanter, and Pribram (1960), which they had developed in the context of general psychology. The structure of Plans (written in the upper case, as suggested by Miller et al., to distinguish the term from its everyday meaning) is the total of instrumental strategies serving our basic needs. Individual Plan Analyses of patients allow a deeper understanding of how a reinforcer or punishment meet the individual motivational structure.

In 1979, he moved to Bern, along with with his young assistant Franz Caspar, to fill the newly installed position of the chair for clinical psychology, and he remained in this position until his death.

ACCOMPLISHMENTS

In Bern, a new era in his activities began, as he now had better resources for the realization of many of his ideas. A major postulate was to allow students to integrate practice with the theoretical knowledge acquired at the university, very much in the sense of the Boulder scientist–practitioner model. With his colleagues, Grawe installed an outpatient clinic in which qualified students had the opportunity to practice psychotherapy with patients. At this *Praxisstelle* he and his coworkers ran a comparative randomized study, in which treatments following different forms of case formulation were compared. Although the therapeutic procedure was not manualized, it was prescribed, in that it needed to be explicitly and logically derived from one of three forms of case formulations: (a) classical functional behavior analysis, (b) "vertical" behavior analysis, or (c) client-centered therapy (with no explicit form of case formulation). In a classical functional behavior analysis, stimuli, reactions, consequences, etc., are analyzed in the sense of temporal "horizontal" chains. Classical (i.e., Which stimulus triggers which reaction?) as well as instrumental/operant (i.e., Which reinforcer makes a behavior more frequent and/or intense?) conditioning, along with concepts such as model learning, are used to explain the development and maintenance or generalization of behavior. Vertical behavior analyses added a vertical dimension to the classical horizontal behavior analyses by analyzing patient motives following the Plan approach. *Vertical* refers to the hierarchical structure of Plans as proposed by Miller et al. (1960), in which concrete behaviors are allocated on the lowest level, general human needs on the top level, and the individual instrumental strategies in between. The criterion for the hierarchy is the instrumental function: Among connected elements, the higher represents the purpose or goal of the lower, which in turn represents the means for the higher element (Caspar, 2007).

In this project, the demand of specifying the therapeutic procedure was acknowledged, but instead of manualizing and measuring adherence, the therapists had more leeway for individualizing the procedure. By extensively describing the actual process from the perspectives of patient, therapist, and independent observers, the therapists made the procedure transparent. Findings of the trial were that the vertical behavior analysis condition outperformed the other conditions regarding outcome, but only in a subset of the criteria such as individually defined goals (goal attainment scaling; Kiresuk, Smith, & Cardillo, 1994). However in process measures, this form of therapy showed overwhelming superiority on a wide range of variables. Patients felt much better understood by their therapists, more motivated for change, etc. We were to some extent afraid that therapists engaged in reflecting the patients' Plan Structure could lose immediate contact with what the patient is experiencing or somehow convey that much of what they are thinking is being withheld from the patient. To be sure, we formulated items for the patient session questionnaire to assess exactly such potential side effects. As a matter of fact, and surprising to us, patients in the Plan Analysis condition felt even less than in the other conditions that their therapists were thinking things that they did not express, and they found even more that their therapists did justice to their emotions.

Grawe did not perceive the lack of strong superiority in outcome measures as just another "Dodo bird" result but felt motivated to trace many of the differential effects in detail. For example, submissive patients profited more from traditional behavior therapy, whereas more autonomy-seeking patients profited more from client-centered therapy. Empirically identifying such an aptitude–treatment interaction corresponds well with the frequently voiced need for selecting specific kinds of treatments for particular patients (Beutler & Clarkin, 1990; Beutler et al., 2003). The success of patients in the vertical behavior analysis condition depended much less on patient variables, suggesting that therapists in this condition were better able to adapt to the characteristics of specific patients (Grawe, Caspar, & Ambühl, 1990). This is much in line with what Bill Stiles (Stiles, Honos-Webb, & Surko, 1998) later designated *therapist responsiveness*. For example, with a patient deprived in his or her narcissistic needs, a therapist would invest much to satisfy such needs in a noncontingent way that does not reinforce problematic means used by the patient to force others to satisfy him narcissistically. A therapist would thus actively seek nonproblematic, positive patient properties and behaviors to which he or she can relate in a positive, acknowledging way. With a rather schizotypic patient, a therapist would rather avoid offering too much threatening closeness but would reassure the patient by giving him or her all the distance needed to feel safe. The idea is that a patient can engage much better in the process of change once he or she is convinced that the therapist represents no threat to his or her most important needs, but respects and furthers them.

Along with conducting this study and building the clinical psychology section at his department, Grawe represented psychotherapy research in a committee of the German government preparing the new psychotherapy law (Meyer, Richter, Grawe, Schulenburg, & Schulte, 1991). Unfortunately, against his clear intention, this cemented rather than challenged the school-oriented approach to psychotherapy. The new psychotherapy legislation sided with the efficacy of therapeutic techniques or approaches, although Grawe kept emphasizing the importance of other factors, such as the therapeutic relationship or a general orientation toward the patient's strengths (resources).

At the level of theoretical concepts, he elaborated his Schema Theory, a concept that referred to Piaget (1977) in several ways and offered elements related to the development of psychopathology as well as to the process of psychotherapy in a way independent from a specific school of psychotherapy. Influenced by developments in empirical psychology at the time, Klaus Grawe assimilated the schema concept with his motivation-based theoretical and therapeutic approach. By building this theoretical bridge Grawe hoped to make concepts and findings from various subdisciplines of psychology usable for the advancement of psychotherapy research and practice. Attractive features of the schema concept, according to Grawe, were that it is nonstatic, that is, it is well suited to describe therapeutic change, and that it addresses emotional aspects of patient functioning and change.

During this time, in the late 1980s, an intense cross-theoretical collaboration with the German psychoanalyst Horst Kächele (see Chapter 21, this volume) had been established. An important part of it took place in the framework of the PEP (Psychotherapeutisches Einzelfall (Single Case) Prozess Forschung) research group, in which two cases, one from Ulm and one from Bern, were intensely studied by a great number of colleagues engaged in process research in the German-speaking countries. Meetings among others in Bern and in Krattigen above the Lake of Thun are memorable in terms of research (of course!) but also in terms of personal encounters, landscape, and gastronomy.

In 1992, Klaus Grawe founded a postgraduate psychotherapy training program. The legal situation in Switzerland had changed in such a way that a 4-year postgraduate training was required to acquire the title of "psychotherapist" and the right to practice. Consequently, no training elements before and during master's level training in psychology counted, and students lost interest in psychotherapy practice during master's level training. Limited resources did not allow for engaging in both extensive introductions of master's students into practice, as well as running a new postgraduate training, so the former was terminated in favor of the latter. In 1999, Grawe added a training facility in Zürich, which was linked with an outpatient clinic codirected with his second wife since 1987, Mariann Grawe-Gerber.

While the aforementioned comparative study was running with a strong emphasis on process–outcome research, on which Grawe set his heart, he also engaged in a comparison of the outcomes of different psychotherapy approaches. In 1994, he published, along with his doctoral students Bernauer and Donati, his meta-analysis *Psychotherapie im Wandel. Von der Konfession zur Profession* [Psychotherapy in Transition: From Confession to Profession].

He experienced the compilation of such an immense body of material (which he largely did at night) as torture, but he felt an obligation to come up with a broad and fair comparison. While some therapeutic orientations failed completely in the empirical legitimization of their claims, psychoanalysis was credited for some evidence. Reactions from the psychodynamic camp were very strong, and his evidence was criticized for not supporting what members from this camp saw as the clearly superior and only sufficiently "deep" approach. In one incident at an event in Munich where he had been invited to present his book, Grawe (who was tall and never fearful) felt even physically threatened. He was deeply shocked by this experience and saw himself thrown back from the era of enlightenment to the medieval age. Although he did not consider conducting meta-analyses on psychotherapy outcome the most "thrilling" academic activity, he was strongly identified with this research by many colleagues who disliked his conclusions and did not know about his contributions in process research.

These strong reactions and the lack of an empirically informed, open search for the best procedure to help difficult patients stimulated articles postulating a "second generation" of approaches to psychotherapy (Grawe, 1995). These second-generation approaches would acknowledge the merits of the first-generation approaches, that is, the original approaches developed by the founders of the traditional schools of psychotherapy. In addition, second-generation approches would seek to overcome the limits of first-generation approaches by incorporating all relevant empirical findings related to the domain for which they claimed validity (such as the treatment of a particular disorder). At the same time, they would also incorporate findings incompatible with the conceptual point of departure. As empirical findings are developing continuously, the search for the most adequate concepts is by definition a never-ending process.

Anticipating empirical and clinical work that is predominant in the current field (Kraus, Wolf, & Castonguay, 2006; Lambert, 2007), Klaus Grawe also believed strongly in the value of ongoing feedback on the therapeutic process. To be realistic and meaningful, original data needed to be presented in a way that enabled therapists to see conspicuous information immediately. This applies equally to data from pretherapy assessments such as the Symptom Checklist-90-R or Beck Depression Inventory: Grawe's idea was to hold individual data against the background of a well-known reference group instead of an anonymous and abstract norm sample. For example, one might compare a client's SCL-90 scores with those of all patients who have been seen in the same outpatient clinic during the past 5 years. In this way, therapists can obtain immediately and concretely meaningful information if they know that on a particular criterion, a patient scores more than one standard deviation higher than the average of the reference group with which a therapist is familiar. To hold individual data against such a background was designated *figuration analysis* by Grawe. In addition, a representation in a graphic form instead of numbers in tables helps to screen out important information quickly and easily.

In his influential 1997 article based on his 1996 Society for Psychotherapy Research (SPR) presidential address, Klaus Grawe formulated a vision of a truly research-informed psychotherapy that would flexibly use all empirically validated mechanisms of change in psychotherapy. Based on available process and outcome research (Orlinsky, Grawe, & Parks, 1994), Grawe identified four such mechanisms of change: (a) mastery/coping, (b) clarification of meaning, (c) problem actuation, and (d) resource activation. These general change mechanisms were intended to cover the full spectrum of potential change processes in psychotherapy. To bridge the gap between psychotherapy process research and psychotherapy practice, Klaus Grawe and coworkers incrementally developed the Therapy Spectrum Analysis (TSA; German:

Wirkfaktorenanalyse [WIFA]; Smith & Grawe, 2003) as a standardized coding tool for the realization of these therapeutic change mechanisms within individual therapy sessions. In one example of productively using the TSA, Smith and Grawe (2005) analyzed the results of more than 700 therapy sessions with more than 100 patients. They formulated empirically validated heuristics that specified a mixture of resource- and problem-focused interventions suited to the different phases of therapy and guided the therapist's session-to-session decisions for the continual adaptation of treatment procedures. To give an example based on statistically derived rules predicting session productivity Smith and Grawe (2005) formulated the following recommendations:

> In the first few sessions of therapy, when the focus is on the analysis of the patient's problems, the therapist must pay special attention to acknowledging and encouraging the patient's resources and strengths. In the middle of therapy, when the focus is largely on the emotionally actuated problems of the patient, the therapist should encourage the patient to make an active contribution towards problem discussion. Towards the end of therapy, when the focus moves away from the discussion of emotionally actuated problems, the therapist should emphasize the resources of the patient and the achieved changes. (p. 121)

Further underscoring the importance of using the patient's strengths in a subsequent study, Gassmann and Grawe (2006) demonstrated that problem activation could unfold its therapeutic potential only when it was combined with thorough resource activation.

In 1998, Klaus Grawe summarized his current conception of psychotherapy in *Psychological Therapy* (published in English in 2004), written as a dialogue between a practicing therapist, a research psychologist, and a therapy researcher. After laying out the facets of therapeutic change, he related the mechanisms of action in psychotherapy to basic psychological concepts and formulated a psychological theory of psychotherapy (designated *consistency theory*) that should be continually developed and empirically updated. He gave suggestions as to how psychotherapy training and practice could be improved on the basis of consistency theory. On the basis of the central assumption that inconsistency in psychological functioning contributes to the development and maintenance of psychological disorders, he designed a randomized controlled trial that tested the hypothesis that the level of inconsistency differentially predicts the outcome in various forms of psychotherapy. In this trial, a condition that implemented the practical implications of consistency theory in an integrative psychotherapy was compared with a form of cognitive–behavioral therapy. At the level of change mechanisms, the integrative condition combined interventions fostering all four of the previously mentioned mechanisms of change on the basis of individual case formulations. While the two conditions demonstrated equal outcomes after 20 sessions, differential effects were observed for the level of avoidance motivation as a measure of inconsistency (i.e., patients with higher levels of avoidance goals fared better in the integrative condition; Grosse Holtforth, Grawe, Fries, & Znoj, 2008).

In his most recent work, Klaus Grawe focused on the integration of the fields of neurobiology and brain sciences with clinical psychology and psychotherapy and called this area "neuropsychotherapy" (Grawe, 2006). He attempted to bridge the gaps between the neurosciences, the understanding of psychological disorders outlined in consistency theory, and psychotherapy practice by providing necessary know-how for mental health professionals as it connects the findings of modern neuroscience to the insights of psychotherapy. Klaus Grawe was convinced that psychotherapy could be even more effective when it is grounded in a neuroscientific approach.

OTHER CONTRIBUTIONS

In addition to his scholastic and research contributions, Klaus Grawe contributed significantly to the growth of psychotherapy, by serving many roles in professional organizations and mentoring many generations of scientists and practitioners. Among his many professional activities he counted the executive committee and presidency of SPR and the executive committee of the German Society for Psychology (DGPs). He was editor of the *Zeitschrift für Klinische Psychologie und Psychotherapie* and *Psychotherapy Research*, inter alia, and cofounded a series (*Fortschritte der Psychotherapie* [Progress in Psychotherapy]) of state-of-the-art psychotherapy manuals.

His doctoral students are countless. The following researchers accomplished their habilitations with him (in alphabetical order): Franz Caspar, Martin Grosse Holtforth, Wolfgang Lutz, Wolfgang Tschacher, and Hansjörg Znoj.

CONCLUSION

Klaus Grawe was a prolific academic writer who published more than 150 articles and book chapters, as well as five books. Although he elaborated his view of mental problems and psychotherapy in many publications, his emphasis was on the continuous development of knowledge, rather than on the elucidation of particular concepts. For example, the approach of general psychotherapy that he developed remained for him a vehicle or template for research, rather than a specific theory in competition with the traditional schools of psychotherapy.

In his quest for better understanding psychotherapy, he continuously searched basic psychology and neighboring fields for useful, empirically grounded concepts, and he was in this sense grounded in empirical science. At the same time, he cultivated a solid sense for what is important in psychotherapy practice. He strongly advocated adapting research methods and designs to particular research questions instead of excluding practically important questions from research because of extrascientific considerations. This basic conviction contributed to an ongoing strong interest in his work among practitioners and to reducing the science–practice gap.

While he adhered to some principles, such as empirical grounding of psychotherapy practice and not limiting oneself by mind-stopping limitations of specific approaches (traditionally: the schools of psychotherapy), he used to question and revise concepts in a never-ending process. In this sense, perhaps his biggest legacy is to have conceptually opened our minds while remaining strictly empirical.

REFERENCES

Beutler, L. E., & Clarkin, J. (1990). *Systematic treatment selection: Toward targeted therapeutic interventions*. New York, NY: Brunner/Mazel.

Beutler, L. E., Moleiro, C., Malik, M., Harwood, T. M., Romanelli, R., Gallagher-Thompson, D., & Thompson, L. (2003). A comparison of the Dodo, EST, and ATI indicators among co-morbid stimulant dependent, depressed patients. *Clinical Psychology & Psychotherapy, 10*, 69–85. doi:10.1002/cpp.354

Caspar, F. (2007). Plan Analysis. In T. Eells (Ed.), *Handbook of psychotherapeutic case formulations* (2nd ed., pp. 251–289). New York, NY: Guilford.

Gassmann, D., & Grawe, D. (2006). General change mechanisms: The relation between problem activation and resource activation in successful and unsuccessful therapeutic interactions. *Clinical Psychology & Psychotherapy, 13*(1), 1–11. doi:10.1002/cpp.442

Grawe, K. (1995). Grundriss einer Allgemeinen Psychotherapie [Blueprint of a general psychotherapy]. *Psychotherapeut, 40*, 130–145.

Grawe, K. (1997). Research informed psychotherapy. *Psychotherapy Research, 1*, 1–19. doi:10.1080/10503309112331334001

Grawe, K. (2004). *Psychological therapy*. Toronto, ON: Hogrefe & Huber.

Grawe, K. (2006). *Neuropsychotherapy. How the neurosciences can inform effective psychotherapy*. Mahwah, NJ: Erlbaum.

Grawe, K., Donati, R., & Bernauer, F. (1994). *Psychotherapie im Wandel. Von der Konfession zur Profession* [Psychotherapy in transition. From confession to profession]. Göttingen, Germany: Hogrefe.

Grawe, K., Caspar, F., & Ambühl, H. (1990). Die Berner Therapievergleichsstudie [The Bern psychotherapy trial]. *Zeitschrift für Klinische Psychologie, 19*, 294–315.

Grosse Holtforth, M., Grawe, K., Fries, A., & Znoj, H. (2008). Inkonsistenz als differentielles Indikationskriterium in der Psychotherapie–eine randomisierte kontrollierte Studie [Inconsistency as a criterion for differential indication in psychotherapy]. *Zeitschrift für Klinische Psychologie und Psychotherapie, 37,* 103–111. doi:10.1026/1616-3443.37.2.103

Kiresuk, T. J., Smith, A., & Cardillo, J. E. (1994). *Goal attainment scaling: Applications, theory, and measurement.* Hillsdale, NJ: Erlbaum.

Kraus, D., Wolf, A., & Castonguay, L. G. (2006). The outcome assistant: A kinder philosophy to the management of outcome. *Psychotherapy Bulletin, 41,* 23–31.

Lambert, M. J. (2007). Presidential address: What we have learned from a decade of research aimed at improving psychotherapy outcome in routine care. *Psychotherapy Research, 17*(1), 1–14.

Meyer, A.-E., Richter, R., Grawe, K., Schulenburg, J.-M., & Schulte, B. (1991). *Forschungsgutachten zu Fragen eines Psychotherapeutengesetzes im Auftrag des Bundesministeriums für Gesundheit* [Experts' report for a psychotherapy law]. Universitätskrankenhaus Eppendorf, Hamburg, Germany.

Miller, G. A., Galanter, E., & Pribram, K. A. (1960). *Plans and the structure of behavior.* New York, NY: Holt, Rinehart &Winston. doi:10.1037/10039-000

Orlinsky, D. E., Grawe, K., & Parks, B. K. (1994). Process and outcome in psychotherapy—*noch einmal*. In A. E. Bergin & S. L. Garfield (Eds.), *Handbook of psychotherapy and behavior change.* New York, NY: Wiley.

Piaget, J. (1977). *The development of thought: Equilibration of cognitive structures.* Oxford, England: Viking.

Smith, E., & Grawe, K. (2003). What makes psychotherapy sessions productive? A new approach to bridging the gap between process research and practice. *Clinical Psychology & Psychotherapy, 10,* 275–285. doi:10.1002/cpp.377

Smith, E. C. & Grawe, K. (2005). Which therapeutic mechanisms work when? A step towards the formulation of empirically validated guidelines for therapists' session-to-session decisions. *Clinical Psychology & Psychotherapy, 12,* 112–123.

Stiles, W. B., Honos-Webb, L., & Surko, M. (1998). Responsiveness in psychotherapy. *Clinical Psychology: Science and Practice, 5,* 439–458.

III

HOW DOES
PSYCHOTHERAPY WORK?

A. THERAPIST CONTRIBUTIONS

11

MARVIN R. GOLDFRIED: PIONEERING SPIRIT AND INTEGRATIVE FORCE

LOUIS G. CASTONGUAY AND JOHN C. NORCROSS

Marvin R. Goldfried has continually advanced the science and practice of psychotherapy throughout his illustrious 30-year career as a psychotherapy process–outcome researcher and cognitive–behavior therapy (CBT) practitioner. To this end, he has originated or contributed to the development of at least four pivotal ideas that have significantly shaped the field of psychotherapy research. First, in the early 1970s, Goldfried became a highly regarded proponent of CBT and published widely in the psychotherapy research literature. Next, he played a key role in the establishment of psychotherapy integration during the 1980s. Continuing within the integrative tradition, he made a third, pivotal contribution to psychotherapy practice, research, and training when he spearheaded the integration of lesbian, gay, and bisexual (LGB) issues into mainstream psychology, in the early 2000s. And finally, throughout the course of his career, Goldfried has made significant contributions to the study of the therapy process by undertaking the difficult yet indispensable task of identifying key factors that facilitate client improvement.

EARLY BEGINNINGS

Marvin Goldfried was born in Brooklyn in 1936 to parents who had fled Eastern Europe in the early 1900s. As the first person in his family to go beyond high school, he attended Brooklyn College and majored in psychology. A number of faculty members in the Psychology Department were active, empirical researchers, and as an undergraduate he was encouraged by several professors to attend graduate school. Maintaining an active, empirically based research program would become a sustaining theme in his future academic career.

Goldfried received his graduate education in clinical psychology at the University of Buffalo, now known as the State University of New York at Buffalo. While projective testing and psychoanalytic theory were all the rage at the time, he found that much of what he read was speculative, with little or no research backing (Goldfried, 2001). By contrast, he also received a firm grounding in principles of learning and perception that were based on empirical research evidencebut which, at the time, seemed to have limited application for clinical practice. It was at an early point in his clinical graduate training that Goldfried experienced firsthand the gap between clinical practice and research.

While still in graduate school he also had the good fortune to meet and have dinner with Paul Meehl. This was an especially rare treat for Goldfried, as he had read virtually everything Meehl had written and had enormous respect for his insights on research, practice, and the philosophy of science. At one point during the evening, however, someone asked Meehl about the extent to which his clinical work was informed by research. Without any hesitation, he replied, "Not at all." As a clinical psychology graduate student, struggling to adopt the identity of a scientist–practitioner, Goldfriend found Meehl's response deeply disheartening and, as it turned out, impactful. Reflecting on this event in later years, he stated, "I don't think I *ever* fully recovered" (M. R. Goldfried, personal communication, January 2007). It is noteworthy that since his graduate school days—over 50 years ago—bridging the gap between research and clinical practice has become a defining theme that has shaped his many contributions to clinical psychology training, research, and practice.

A high point in his graduate career involved the completion of an internship at the Veterans Administration hospital in Palo Alto, California, in the late 1950s. It was truly a golden era, with Ullmann and Krasner laying the groundwork for behavior therapy at one end of the Psychology Department while, at the other end, Bateson, Haley, and Weakland developed systemic interventions for families. The exposure to a diverse range of theoretical, research, and therapy approaches during his internship placement may have planted the seeds for his later interest in psychotherapy integration.

After conducting research on projective techniques at the University of Rochester (Goldfried, Stricker, & Weiner, 1971), Goldfried joined the Psychology Department at the State University of New York at Stony Brook in 1964 (where he has remained since) and helped develop a clinical psychology doctoral program that was rooted in learning and experimental psychology. To this day, Goldfried's psychotherapy practice keeps him honest as a clinical researcher; his involvement in research keeps informing clinical practice; and his work with graduate students keeps him continually exploring how each activity can inform the other.

MAJOR CONTRIBUTIONS

Goldfried's scholarly efforts have all been directed toward creating a deeper, more integrative understanding of therapeutic change as it manifests itself in a diverse range of therapeutic approaches and clinical samples. In doing so, he has developed or contributed to four key ideas, discussed in detail in this section, that have led to better integration within the field of psychotherapy research and practice.

Cognitive–Behavior Therapy

After graduate training in the psychodynamic tradition (an approach, which at the time, dominated the field), Goldfried became an early and influential proponent of behavior therapy. He conducted an impressive number of studies that helped to establish the psychometric quality and clinical utility of behavioral assessment, as well as the effectiveness of behavioral interventions. As such, Goldfried's research helped behavior therapy gain credibility in the eyes of both clinicians and researchers. His work played a determinant role in establishing behavior therapy as a powerful approach that could effectively address complex and severe psychopathology—as opposed to an aggregation of mechanistic techniques dealing with relatively simple problems experienced by nonclinical populations (e.g., college students). In a very real sense, research conducted by Goldfried and his colleagues helped behavior therapy move from the ivory tower of academia to the reality of day-to-day clinical practice.

At the same time, Goldfried emerged as one of the pioneers of the cognitive revolution in behavior therapy. He agreed with the criticism of behavior therapy as exclusively focused on overt behavior and its reliance of classical and operant learning models with limited clinical value. Goldfried pursued several influential research studies demonstrating, among other critical constructs, the importance of self-control and cognitive coping skills in therapeutic change. He was actively involved with a number of colleagues (e.g., Beck, Davison, Ellis, Mahoney, Meichenbaum) in facilitating CBT within the field through workshops and conferences. These efforts eventually led to establishing the journal *Cognitive Therapy and Research*, for which he served as associate editor. Over the years, his numerous methodological (e.g., Goldfried & D'Zurilla, 1969), empirical (e.g., D'Zurilla & Goldfried, 1971), theoretical (e.g., Goldfried & Robins, 1982), and clinical (e.g., Goldfried & Davison, 1976, 1994) publications have become classics in the cognitive–behavioral literature.

In particular, Goldfried launched a seminal research program on cognitive–behavioral methods for coping with anxiety. He and his colleagues conducted outcome studies on the reduction of social anxiety, test anxiety, public speaking anxiety, and unassertiveness. The methods applied here were based on the premise that, in addition to using relaxation as a coping skill, individuals could reduce their anxiety by helping them more realistically reevaluate their perception of threat. Designed to help clients develop self-control or self-regulation, the coping skills training developed by Goldfried and his colleagues went a long way to counter the accusation (voiced by many humanistic and psychodynamic therapists in the 1960s and 1970s) that behavioral interventions undermined the client's autonomy and independence. As Marsha Linehan (personal communication, January 2007) has eloquently argued, Goldfried's notion that the core mechanism of many CBT treatments is the development of new behavior skills has led to the development of new treatments and the enhancement of existing CBT interventions.

One of these methods, problem solving training, has received particular attention over the last 20 years, having been shown to be helpful for problems such as depression, suicidal behavior, substance abuse, family conflict, childhood aggression, and mental retardation (Goldfried, Greenberg, & Marmar, 1990). Studies conducted in both naturalistic and controlled settings have shown that the resolution of specific problems is one of the helpful events most frequently identified by clients (Llewelyn, 1988; Llewelyn et al., 1988). Irrespective of their preferred theoretical orientation, therapists are likely to increase their ability to respond to their clients' needs by using strategies that Goldfried and his colleagues have developed to systematically and explicitly facilitate problem solving (i.e., problem definition, generation of alternatives, decision making, action taking, verification). A detailed description of these interventions, together with other cognitive–behavioral methods, appeared as *Clinical Behavior Therapy*, coauthored with Davison. Originally published in 1976, the book has been classified as a Social Science Citation Classic, was reissued in an expanded edition in 1994, and has sold over 35,000 copies.

Behavior therapy has successfully integrated cognition in recent decades, but emotional arousal has only recently been considered. In the past, emotion has typically been viewed as something that needs to be reduced, managed, or contained. Wiser and Goldfried (1993), for example, found that in treating depressed clients, cognitive–behavior therapists viewed lowering emotional experiencing as significantly contributing to the process of therapeutic change. By contrast, psychodynamic and experiential therapists considered increasing emotional experiencing to be clinically significant.

Interestingly, Goldfried and his colleagues have found that the client's level of experiencing predicts outcome in cognitive therapy (Castonguay et al., 1996). Clinically, these findings suggest that even though many CB therapists may not have been trained to foster emotional deepening, they should consider using methods that have been developed in other orientations to do so. These therapists will find in recent contributions from Goldfried (e.g., Samoilov & Goldfried, 2000) guidelines to assimilate such methods into their clinical repertoire, in what he has labeled *cognitive–affective behavior therapy*.

Psychotherapy Integration

While contributing to research and practice of CBT, Goldfried remained constantly open to the merits of diverse forms of psychotherapy. The notion of creating bridges among the different theoretical orientations dates back to the early 1930s and has been raised over the years by such luminaries as Franz Alexander, Thomas French, John Dollard, Neal Miller, and Jerome Frank. However, it remained a latent theme until the 1980s, when Goldfried and colleagues began working in this area. Some 30 years later, not only has integration or eclecticism emerged as a definite research area but it has also become the modal theoretical orientation among mental health professionals in North America and Western Europe (Norcross & Goldfried, 2005).

Goldfried was a pioneer in the psychotherapy integration movement. He has published some of the most influential work in this growing force in our field (e.g., Goldfried, 1982; Norcross & Goldfried, 2005) and is internationally recognized, along with a few others, as a leader of the integration movement—both organizationally and scientifically.

Recognizing that a network of professionals might facilitate a rapprochement across theoretical orientations, Goldfried and Paul Wachtel cofounded the Society for the Exploration of Psychotherapy Integration (SEPI) in 1983. This visionary organization and its journal, *Journal of Psychotherapy Integration*, has been a catalyst worldwide for the advancement of integrative approaches to psychotherapy research and practice. For psychotherapists whose practices are unencumbered by a single theory, SEPI has provided a forum to explore points of convergence and complementarity among differing systems of psychotherapy. And for therapists who have been accused of illegitimacy, heresy, or worse for their unwillingness to adopt a "purist" approach when confronting the complexity of clinical reality, SEPI is an important reference group that includes highly respected scholars who represent a wide range of theoretical orientations and therapy approaches.

In addition to cofounding SEPI, Goldfried has championed the need for empirical research studies evaluating the process and outcome of integrative therapeutic approaches. Not only has he been instrumental in identifying the agenda for researchers interested in integrative and eclectic therapy (see Wolfe & Goldfried, 1988), but he also is among a select group of psychotherapy researchers who have developed a productive research program in psychotherapy integration (Goldfried, 1991).

Psychotherapy Process

Across the decades and throughout his career, Goldfried has contributed significantly to the study of the psychotherapy process. His work on psychotherapy integration, in particular, took the form of comparative process and process–outcome research. Many practitioners are committed to going beyond the boundaries of a single theoretical orientation, but until recently there was little in the research literature to support doing so.

In a seminal 1980 article in *American Psychologist,* Goldfried persuasively argued that treatment methods prescribed by particular approaches are largely (though not entirely) idiosyncratic manifestations of a smaller number of change principles that cut across disparate psychotherapies. He described such *principles of change* as heuristics or guidelines at a middle-level of abstraction that exists somewhere between the specific treatment methods (e.g., interpretation, cognitive restructuring, two-chair) and the global theoretical systems (e.g., psychoanalytic, cognitive–behavioral, experiential). The delineation and identification of key principles of change (e.g., establishment of productive relationship, provision of a new view of self) in differing therapy approaches has offered the field a new integrative conceptualization of how client change happens in psychotherapy.

Although not the first to explicate common factors or to promote principles of change, Goldfried spurred a renewed interest in these matters and offered an explanation for a perplexing paradox in psychotherapy research, specifically, that diverse forms of psychotherapy tend to produce equivalent outcomes. The principles of change have guided Goldfried and his colleagues in their investigating of unique and common mechanisms of change across different forms of psychotherapy.

As part of their research program, they developed an instrument to measure the therapist's focus in attempting to offer the patient a new view of self (Goldfried, Newman, & Hayes, 1989). In one of the earliest studies, Goldfried and colleagues found that cognitive–behavioral (CB) and psychodynamic–interpersonal (PI) therapists placed a comparable focus on intrapersonal and interpersonal content, but that the intrapersonal focus (e.g., link between thoughts and emotions) was associated with improvement only in the CB therapy, whereas the interpersonal emphasis (e.g., maladaptive patterns of relating to self) was associated with change in only the PI condition (Kerr et al., 1992). Whereas the therapist's intrapersonal focus in CB predicted symptom change, the therapist's interpersonal focus in PI was associated with improvement in self-esteem and social functioning. These and related studies suggest that complementary mechanisms of change may be operating across different treatments.

Of particular significance in Goldfried's investigation of therapist's focus of interventions are the results of two studies that suggest that CBT and PI are much more similar when applied in a naturalistic clinical setting than when conducted as part of research clinical trials (Goldfried, Castonguay, Hayes, Drozd, & Shapiro, 1997; Goldfried, Raue, & Castonguay, 1998). These results added evidence to support a growing concern, shared by many researchers and clinicians, that RCTs may not necessarily reflect the way psychotherapy is conducted in actual clinical settings (Norcross, Beutler, & Levant, 2005).

Goldfried and students have also investigated another principle of change: the therapeutic alliance. A study conducted by Goldfried's research team was one of the first to demonstrate a positive relationship between the working alliance and patient outcome in CBT (Castonguay et al, 1996). Clinically speaking, psychotherapists—even those practicing within a tradition that has been slow to recognize the curative effect of the therapeutic relationship—should strive to establish and maintain a strong bond and active collaboration with their clients.

Lesbian, Gay, and Bisexual Issues

Goldfried has extended the theme of integration by incorporating LGB literature into mainstream psychology. He made a decision in 1999 to "come out" professionally not as a gay man but as the father of a gay son and then formed a network of family members within psychology who have gay, lesbian, or bisexual relatives (Goldfried, 2001). Members of AFFIRM: Psychologists Affirming Their Gay, Lesbian, and Bisexual Family are dedicated to supporting their own family members as well as to encouraging research in this area. Goldfried decided to establish AFFIRM after he attended a parade in support of gay rights, with his wife, and was told by many participants how much they regretted not receiving similar support from their parents and family. AFFIRM now counts more than 700 family members, including a large number of distinguished psychologists, two of whom are past presidents of the American Psychological Association. This organizational tour de force, born out of deep nurturing and sensitivity to painful experiences, conveys not only Goldfried's affiliative nature but also his vision and pioneering spirit.

His influential articles in *American Psychologist*, *Psychotherapy*, and *Clinical Psychology: Science and Practice* brought to the fore neglected research and practice questions on LGB issues. Insightfully, Goldfried has shown that while many of these matters remain "invisible" to psychotherapists, they have important implications for their practice. For example, his work urges clinicians to address the high prevalence of teenage suicideand substance abuse, as well as victimization and abuse, among LGB clients when constructing case formulations and making treatment recommendations.

His research team continues to carry out a number of studies on LGB issues, which are likely to improve our understanding of human functioning and the change process. These include investigations of bias in diagnosing LGB adolescents who are in the process of accepting their sexual orientation, what LGB individuals are looking for in a potential therapist, attitudes toward gender-atypical lesbians, and how the prevalence of social anxiety among gay men may vary with their acceptance of their sexual orientation.

OTHER ACCOMPLISHMENTS

In the mid-1990s, Goldfried created a unique journal aimed at bridging the divide between research and practice as well as the gap across different therapeutic orientations. The journal, *In Session: Psychotherapy in Practice*, was designed to feature clinical guidelines, case illustrations, and summaries of research findings for practicing therapists—not other researchers. Because the contributions reflected different orientations, all articles were written in theory-neutral, jargon-free English. In 2000, the quarterly journal became a branch of the *Journal of Clinical Psychology*, enabling wider circulation and greater practitioner impact. The *Journal of Clinical Psychology: In Session* now reaches more than 2,500 libraries around the world and literally tens of thousands of mental health professionals and those in training.

In addition to his editorial contributions, Goldfried has served on the National Institute of Mental Health (NIMH) study section dealing with psychosocial interventions and has participated in several NIMH workshops aimed at establishing guidelines for future research on issues such as process research, psychotherapy integration, and treatment development. As an organization leader, beyond SEPI, he served as the president of the Society for Psychotherapy Research, chaired the Research Committee of the APA Division of Psychotherapy, where he also was also a member of its Presidential Task Force on Empirically Supported Therapy Relationships.

In addition to these accomplishments, Goldfried has instilled an interest in and taught the skills of psychotherapy research to several generations of researchers. His mentoring began with the Stony Brook postdoctoral program in behavior therapy, and it has continued since the 1960s in his teaching and supervision of several generations of postdoctoral and graduate students in clinical psychology, many of whom have gone on to influential positions of their own. On a short list are Louis G. Castonguay, Adele M. Hayes, Cory F. Newman, Clive J. Robins, and Marsha Linehan. The mentoring did not stop with their postdoctoral or graduate education and has typically continued throughout their careers. He has also mentored junior faculty members at Stony Brook, as well as colleagues at other institutions (e.g., John Norcross, Jeremy Safran).

CONCLUSION

Marvin R. Goldfried has been a relentless pioneer in psychotherapy research and practice—charting new areas, pushing the frontiers, and expanding the terrain. In each of his seminal contributions, he has been an integrating force—bringing disparate, even conflicting, forces together and narrowing the practice–research gap. In many ways, his work has altered how researchers conceptualize, conduct, and investigate psychotherapy. He has raised awareness about the importance of cognition and emotion (especially in the minds of social-learning therapists). By delineating principles of change that cut across different orientations, he has brought clarity to basic, transtheoretical components of therapy and catalyzed the psychotherapy integration movement. He has increased therapists' clinical repertoire by developing behavioral methods of assessment and treatment, as well as by incorporating experiential methods into CBT. His process research has influenced many researchers to attend to the mechanisms of change in addition to treatment outcome. He has challenged the profession to recognize social and political biases, as reflected in his work on GLB issues. By all accounts, Dr. Goldfried's seminal contributions have been partly responsible for several of the most exciting and beneficial advancements in psychotherapy.

REFERENCES

Castonguay, L. G., Goldfried, M. R., Wiser, S., Raue, P. J., & Hayes, A. H. (1996). Predicting outcome in cognitive therapy for depression: A comparison of unique and common factors. *Journal of Consulting and Clinical Psychology, 64,* 497–504. doi:10.1037/0022-006X.64.3.497

D'Zurilla, T. J., & Goldfried, M. R. (1971). Problem solving and behavior modification. *Journal of Abnormal Psychology, 78*, 107–126. doi:10.1037/h0031360

Goldfried, M. R. (1980). Toward the delineation of therapeutic change principles. *American Psychologist, 35*, 991–999. doi:10.1037/0003-066X.35.11.991

Goldfried, M. R. (Ed.). (1982). *Converging themes in psychotherapy: Trends in psychodynamic, humanistic, and behavioral practice*. New York, NY: Springer.

Goldfried, M. R. (1991). Research issues in psychotherapy integration. *Journal of Psychotherapy Integration, 1*, 5–25.

Goldfried, M. R. (2001). Integrating gay, lesbian, and bisexual issues into mainstream psychology. *American Psychologist, 56*, 977–988. doi:10.1037/0003-066X.56.11.977

Goldfried, M. R., Castonguay, L. G., Hayes, A. H., Drozd, J. F., & Shapiro, D. A. (1997). A comparative analysis of the therapeutic focus in cognitive-behavioral and psychodynamic-interpersonal sessions. *Journal of Consulting and Clinical Psychology, 65*, 740–748. doi:10.1037/0022-006X.65.5.740

Goldfried, M. R., & Davison, G. C. (1976). *Clinical behavior therapy*. New York, NY: Holt, Rinehart & Winston.

Goldfried, M. R., & Davison, G. C. (1994). *Clinical behavior therapy* (Expanded ed.). New York, NY: Wiley-Interscience.

Goldfried, M. R., & D'Zurilla, T. J. (1969). A behavioral-analytic model for assessing competence. In C. D. Spielberger (Ed.), *Current topics in clinical and community psychology* (Vol. 1, pp. 151–196). New York, NY: Academic Press.

Goldfried, M. R., Greenberg, L. S., & Marmar, C. (1990). Individual psychotherapy: Process and outcome. *Annual Review of Psychology, 41*, 659–688. doi:10.1146/annurev.ps.41.020190.003303

Goldfried, M. R., Newman, C., & Hayes, A. M. (1989). *The coding system of therapist focus*. Unpublished manuscript, State University of New York at Stony Brook.

Goldfried, M. R., Raue, P. J., & Castonguay, L. G. (1998). The therapeutic focus in significant sessions of master therapists: A comparison of cognitive-behavioral and psychodynamic-interpersonal interventions. *Journal of Consulting and Clinical Psychology, 66*, 803–810. doi:10.1037/0022-006X.66.5.803

Goldfried, M. R., & Robins, C. (1982). On the facilitation of self-efficacy. *Cognitive Therapy and Research, 6*, 361–379. doi:10.1007/BF01184004

Goldfried, M. R., Stricker, G., & Weiner, I. B. (1971). *Rorschach handbook of clinical and research applications*. Englewood Cliffs, NJ: Prentice-Hall.

Kerr, S., Goldfried, M. R., Hayes, A. H., Castonguay, L. G., & Goldsamt, L. A. (1992). Interpersonal and intrapersonal focus in cognitive-behavioral and psychodynamic-interpersonal therapies: A preliminary analysis of the Sheffield Project. *Psychotherapy Research, 2*, 266–276.

Llewelyn, S. P. (1988). Psychological therapy as viewed by clients and therapists. *British Journal of Clinical Psychology, 27*, 223–237.

Llewelyn, S. P., Elliott, R., Shapiro, D. A., Hardy, G., & Firth-Cozens, J. (1988). Client perceptions of significant events in prescriptive and exploratory periods of individual therapy. *The British Journal of Clinical Psychology, 27*, 105–114.

Norcross, J. C., Beutler, L. E., & Levant, R. F. (2005). (Eds.). *Evidence-based practices in mental health: Debate and dialogue on the fundamental questions.* Washington, DC: American Psychological Association.

Norcross, J. C., & Goldfried, M. R. (Eds.). (2005). *Handbook of psychotherapy integration* (2nd ed.). New York, NY: Oxford University Press.

Samoilov, A., & Goldfried, M. R. (2000). Role of emotion in cognitive-behavior therapy. *Clinical Psychology: Science and Practice, 7*, 373–385. doi:10.1093/clipsy/7.4.373

Wiser, S. L., & Goldfried, M. R. (1993). A comparative study of emotional experiencing in psychodynamic-interpersonal and cognitive-behavioral therapies. *Journal of Consulting and Clinical Psychology, 61*, 892–895. doi:10.1037/0022-006X.61.5.892

Wolfe, B. E., & Goldfried, M. R. (1988). Research on psychotherapy integration: Recommendations and conclusions from an NIMH workshop. *Journal of Consulting and Clinical Psychology, 56*, 448–451. doi:10.1037/0022-006X.56.3.448

12

MICHAEL J. LAMBERT: BUILDING CONFIDENCE IN PSYCHOTHERAPY

BENJAMIN M. OGLES AND JEFFREY A. HAYES

Michael J. Lambert has been a leading voice for psychotherapy research and a key figure in bridging the gap between clinical research and practice for 4 decades. His early work began with his conducting comprehensive reviews and meta-analyses that made coherent arguments for the effectiveness of psychotherapy in the midst of a fierce debate regarding the potential influence of spontaneous remission on client improvement (Lambert, 1976). Since that early work, he has published numerous books, chapters, reviews, and primary studies that have made additional important contributions to clinical practice through addressing such questions as: Do measures of therapy outcome influence the perceived effect of psychotherapy? How much therapy is necessary to produce meaningful change? Is graduate training necessary to conduct effective psychotherapy? What are the essential ingredients of effective therapy? Do clients get worse during psychotherapy, and if so, what factors contribute to deterioration and how can deterioration be prevented? How can research methods be used in practice to inform the clinician regarding client progress during treatment? This chapter provides a brief overview of Dr. Lambert—not only his work, but also his personal background and characteristics and connections between the two.

MAJOR CONTRIBUTIONS

To a large degree, the focus of Michael J. Lambert's research has been a response to the most pressing questions facing the field during the course of his long and distinguished career. At the outset of his work, for example, Lambert's scholarship addressed questions regarding the helpfulness of client-centered variables and whether psychotherapy was more effective than either time alone or placebo conditions (e.g., Lambert, 1976). His research in these areas has advanced professional understanding about therapist interpersonal skills, spontaneous remission, and placebo effects. Throughout his career, Lambert also has been interested in whether psychotherapy might have harmful effects, and if so, what the contributing factors to patient deterioration were (Lambert, Bergin, & Collins, 1977). In addition, Lambert's work has contributed greatly to the field's knowledge about dose–response relationships, as well as the measurement of psychotherapy outcome (e.g., Lambert, 1992; Lambert, Christensen, & DeJulio, 1983). For example, Lambert conducted research and wrote literature reviews that deepened the field's understanding of clinically significant change and that helped establish cutoff scores for popular instruments such as the Beck Depression Inventory (Beck, Ward, Mendelson, Mock, & Erbaugh, 1961), Symptom Checklist-90 (Derogatis, 1994), Inventory of Interpersonal Problems (Horowitz, Rosenberg, Baer et al., 1988), and Hamilton Depression Rating Scale (Hamilton, 1967).

Lambert later developed the Outcome Questionnaire-45 (OQ-45; Lambert, Hansen, Umphress, et al., 1996), which has become a widely used measure of client distress in both clinical and research contexts (with translations into more than 15 languages). Lambert's own program of research with the OQ-45 used statistical modeling to predict patient treatment response, including treatment failure. With an ever-present eye toward integrating research and practice, Lambert developed and tested software that could quickly deliver information to therapists, demonstrably improving patient outcomes, especially in cases in which patients were progressing poorly or were in danger of deteriorating. This research led to the identification of common factors, such as the working alliance and patient motivation, to which therapists need to attend when patients are not progressing well in psychotherapy. Research on these interventions is being undertaken in settings across the globe, including China, Australia, the Middle East, and Europe, all places where the interventions are also being routinely used.

One of Lambert's most influential scholarly contributions to psychotherapy research involved his work on the multiple editions of the *Handbook of Psychotherapy and Behavior Change*. His early chapters, written with Allen Bergin, provided comprehensive overviews on the effects of psychotherapy and shaped the direction of many scholars' research programs. Of equal importance, these chapters were written in a clinically relevant manner so that research findings could be applied to the practice, supervision, and training of psychotherapy. Lambert eventually assumed an editorial role with the fifth edition of *Handbook of Psychotherapy and Behavior Change*, and his dual emphasis on scholarly excellence and clinical relevance continued to be apparent in his work as editor (Lambert, 2004).

EARLY BEGINNINGS

Mike Lambert was one of five children born and raised in Salt Lake City, Utah. His father was a small business owner who finished his career operating a successful travel agency. His mother stayed at home to raise the children. Lambert was part of a large and engaged extended family that worked, played, worshipped, and traveled together. He was an energetic youth who enjoyed outdoor activities. As a teenager, he was an avid sportsman who excelled in wrestling—he was the state champion in his weight class as a junior in high school. Later in life, he took up tennis and biking, but he also enjoyed basketball and other sports. When a young faculty member, he occasionally ended up in a wrestling match with a student or two when traveling to research conferences. Although the students were often bigger, Lambert was a formidable challenge who could never be pinned. Lambert has shared fond memories of his childhood with his students and displayed the interpersonal ease that is often typical of a child raised in a large family.

Lambert married his high school sweetheart soon after he graduated from high school. His responsibilities were increased when they had their first child before Lambert was 19 years old. As a result, he moved quickly into adulthood with family responsibilities while also working to gain an undergraduate and then graduate degrees. These were financially challenging years for the Lamberts, filled with many hours of work, class, study, and caring for family. By the time Lambert graduated with his PhD in counseling psychology from the University of Utah in 1971, he and his wife, Linda, had four children of their eventual five.

Lambert was first introduced to the field when he enrolled in a high school psychology class. While still in high school, he also stumbled on and read Karl Menninger's *The Human Mind* (1945). Its numerous case studies and in-depth analyses fascinated him, and he began to consider the possibility of becoming a practicing psychologist. He later enrolled in an educational psychology course taught by Ted Packard, at the same time he was working as an undergraduate research assistant for Ernst Beier. Both of these faculty members encouraged Lambert to consider applying for the doctoral program at the University of Utah.

During his graduate years, Lambert was drawn to the work of Carl Rogers, whose humanistic theory became the foundation of Lambert's research and practice throughout his career. He completed his internship at the University of Utah counseling center in a half-time appointment over 2 years. During that time, he also completed his dissertation, which involved the recording and analysis of parallel processes of therapy and supervision tapes. Thus, Lambert began his foray into therapy research.

After graduating from the University of Utah, Lambert accepted a job with joint appointments as a psychologist in the health center and faculty member in the psychology department at Brigham Young University. There, he became acquainted with Allen Bergin and began a successful collaboration that spanned decades. Lambert later moved into a full-time faculty position. His early work focused on documenting whether therapy was effective through critical reviews of the primary research literature. Several early themes evolved in his writing including methods used to evaluate treatment efficacy and especially the instruments used to assess outcome, the contribution of the therapist to treatment success, the degree to which specific versus common factors could account for treatment success, deterioration in treatment, and the increased variability in outcomes for treated versus control subjects, and the role of supervision in training. These early themes dominated his writing for more than 30 years.

ACCOMPLISHMENTS

Lambert has been an important contributor to psychology as a profession, the study of psychotherapy, and the practice of psychotherapy. It will not be possible to catalog all of his writing, mentoring, or service in this chapter, yet we review some of his most prominent and important accomplishments to date.

Research Studies

As mentioned earlier, Lambert's work reflected the profession's evolving theoretical and scientific questions of the day and increasingly addressed contemporary societal and practical issues. In the early 1970s, for example, the profession was concerned with issues related to spontaneous remission, Rogerian therapist-offered conditions, and the effects of psychotherapy. In response to these concerns, Lambert wrote critical and synthetic reviews of the literature in each of these areas that appeared in prestigious and influential outlets such as *Psychological Bulletin* and the *Journal of Consulting and Clinical Psychology*. Lambert's work helped establish that psychotherapy is superior to no treatment and placebo treatment conditions, that the positive effects of therapy are achieved fairly quickly and are relatively enduring, and that, whereas most patients do benefit from therapy, some patients deteriorate during the course of—and perhaps because of—sychotherapy. These same issues were important to Allen Bergin as well, as reflected in the attention he devoted to them in the first edition of the *Handbook of Psychotherapy and Behavior Change*. Lambert and Bergin both joined the faculty at Brigham Young University in 1971, the year the first edition of the *Handbook* was published, and their relationship had a considerable effect on Lambert's scholarly work, most notably in his long-standing association with the *Handbook*.

Lambert conducted meta-analyses and wrote integrative reviews on other highly pertinent topics as well, such as the effectiveness of time-limited dynamic therapy, the use of various instruments for measuring psychotherapy outcome, and the effectiveness of supervision. In addition, Lambert conducted meta-analyses that indicated that, whereas therapist training may help decrease patient dropout rates, on the whole, therapist experience demonstrates only a slight relationship with outcome. Not only did his scholarship continually address contemporary professional issues, he actually anticipated and helped the field begin to focus on significant concerns such as the use of therapy manuals (Lambert & Ogles, 1988) and the importance of individual therapist variables as opposed to techniques (Lambert, 1989).

When Lambert "left" graduate school in 1971 (his own typically modest words, which might erroneously suggest that he dropped out), his professional goals were to positively influence the practice of psychotherapy and to help clients feel and function better—both his own clients and, through his research, others' clients. Consequently, throughout his career, Lambert sought to make his research clinically relevant. His program of research was dedicated to enhancing patient outcome by providing feedback to therapists on patient progress. As mentioned previously, this line of research began with intensive and rigorous development of the OQ-45. The OQ-45 is a 45-item measure of outcome developed specifically to be brief enough, while maintaining sound psychometric properties, to administer repeatedly during treatment. The instrument has three subscales—symptom distress, interpersonal functioning, and social role performance—but the total score is most frequently used in both research and practice. Scores range from 0 to 225. The questionnaire correlates significantly with other outcome measures of symptomatic distress, such as the SCL-90-R and Beck Depression Inventory and has been extensively tested for reliability, validity, and sensitivity to change (e.g., Lambert et al., 1996; Vermeersch, Lambert, & Burlingame, 2000). Once the OQ-45 was developed, Lambert conducted a series of naturalistic studies that predicted outcome based on the patient's initial disturbance and early rate of progress and were used to provide feedback to therapists. This research established that providing feedback to therapists about patient progress reduced patient deterioration, increased clinically significant client change rates, and enhanced the cost-effectiveness of therapy (Lambert, 2007).

In one of the studies in this program of research, Lambert and his colleagues analyzed naturalistic data from more than 10,000 patients who received psychotherapy from a broad range of therapists in a wide variety of settings (e.g., university counseling centers, employee assistance programs, community mental health centers, managed care settings; Lambert, Hansen, & Finch, 2001). In this highly cited study, survival analyses determined that half of patients who were categorized as dysfunctional at the outset of treatment could be expected to achieve clinically significant change after 21 sessions of psychotherapy. That is, about 21 sessions are necessary for 50% of clients to meet two criteria that have been defined by Jacobson and Truax (1991) as *clinically significant change*. First, they make large enough changes that the pre- to posttreatment difference score could be considered a reliable change (reliable improvement) and, second, their posttreatment scores fall in the range of individuals in the general population (recovery). Using the less rigorous standard of reliable improvement (without recovery), half of dysfunctional patients could be expected to improve after seven sessions and 75% after 14 sessions. In addition, the data were used to develop growth curves based on patient initial disturbance and the degree to which patients varied from expected improvement at particular treatment sessions. This information was then used to alert therapists that a patient was a potential treatment failure so that corrective steps could be taken. Lambert's subsequent research suggested that these corrective steps might include assessing the client's social support and motivation, as well as the strength of the working alliance, to redirect the course of therapy. These three variables, collectively, were referred to as *clinical support tools* that could provide beneficial information to the therapist whose client was at risk of deterioration.

In a particularly impressive study investigating the effects of providing feedback to therapists, Lambert and his colleagues (Harmon et al., 2007) examined outcome data from 1,374 university counseling center clients who were randomly assigned to one of two treatment conditions. In the first condition, both the client and therapist received feedback about the client's progress, and in the second condition, only the therapist received feedback. In each of these two conditions, clients whose clinical progress suggested that they were at risk of deterioration were further randomly assigned to conditions in which their therapists did or did not receive feedback on clients' perceptions of the alliance, social support, and readiness for change (the clinical support tools). Outcome data on these 1,374 clients were compared with archival data from 1,445 university counseling center clients whose therapists did not receive any feedback on client progress. Results indicated that client outcome is enhanced by providing therapists with information on client progress, although outcome is not affected by also giving clients feedback on their progress. Furthermore, among clients whose early OQ-45 scores and trajectories indicated that they were in danger of deteriorating, 42% demonstrated reliable improvement when therapists received feedback that included data from both the OQ-45 and the clinical support tools. Only half as many clients demonstrated reliable improvement when therapists received no feedback. In fact, on average, at-risk clients showed essentially no improvement when therapists were not provided any feedback about their clients, whereas clients improved 14 points on the OQ-45 when therapists received feedback on client progress and clinical support tools.

In response to larger societal issues, later in his career, Lambert's meta-analytic and other scholarly work addressed broad concerns such as the extent to which psychotherapy reduces health care costs, quality management in diverse settings, accountability through outcome measurement, and the use of clinical significance markers to improve patient care (Chiles, Lambert, & Hatch, 1999). Lambert's scholarship in these areas carried policy implications in terms of managed care practices, and he engaged in consulting work to help translate his research findings into practice settings serving thousands of individuals.

OTHER CONTRIBUTIONS

In addition to a prolific research career, Lambert has also contributed to the field of psychotherapy research through his editorial work. He reviewed hundreds of journal articles as an ad hoc journal editor and served as the associate editor of the *Journal of Consulting and Clinical Psychology* for a 5-year term. He also served as the editor of several books, including the fifth edition of the *Handbook of Psychotherapy and Behavior Change*. He also served as the president of the Society for Psychotherapy Research and received the Distinguished Career Award from the same organization for lifelong contributions to psychotherapy research.

Lambert served on the State Licensing Board for the State of Utah and provided service through a small private practice for more than 30 years. As a faculty member, he also served as the director for many important dissertations that contributed to the psychotherapy literature. Clearly, Lambert's professional contributions extend far beyond his published studies.

INFLUENCES

Lambert made a clear distinction between those individuals who influenced his thinking about and research concerning psychotherapy and those who influenced his clinical practice. Although much of his research has had a direct influence on his own and others' practice, the individuals who played a foundational role in his thinking about practice tended to be a different group from those who influenced his writing and research.

As a clinician, Lambert was trained as a counseling psychologist in a department that was heavily steeped in Rogerian humanism. Although he met Carl Rogers only a couple of times for brief interactions, Lambert was profoundly influenced by Rogers's writing and thinking about the necessary conditions for successful therapy. This academic exposure was supplemented and eclectically expanded by the supervision he received in graduate school from Ted Packard, Addie Furhiman, Bob Finley, and Ernst Beier. He was also influenced by the interpersonal theories expressed in the writing of Harry Stack Sullivan.

This foundational Rogerian tradition matched well with Lambert's personal style. As a clinician, supervisor, researcher, and mentor, he displays an uncommon openness to ideas. He is genuinely curious about how each person views the world and almost eager to learn of the unique way in which each person interprets and negotiates interpersonal situations. This nonjudgmental attitude pervades his interactions and results in unusual and rare conversations with students and colleagues. For example, one of this chapter's authors has observed Mike Lambert listening intently to an inexperienced undergraduate's ideas about therapy research as though the student were a senior colleague who had just discovered the key to successful therapy. This same ability to engage in a genuine, open dialogue without judging forms the foundation of his therapeutic relationships.

Within the research domain, Lambert worked closely with Allen Bergin for many years. He was also drawn to the writing of Hans Strupp and Sol Garfield, in part because of their association with the writing of the *Handbook of Psychotherapy and Behavior Change*. He found the work of Jerome Frank to be especially persuasive. Indeed, threads of Frank's work can be clearly seen in Lambert's writing about the common factors contributing to therapeutic effectiveness across therapy orientations. Lambert's most recent and more practice-oriented work was influenced by simultaneously occurring research that was being conducted by Ken Howard. Indeed, Ken Howard, David Orlinsky, Allen Bergin, and others in the original group of psychotherapy researchers involved in the early years of the Society for Psychotherapy Research also contributed to Lambert's thinking through the open debate and lively discussion that typified the annual meetings.

CONCLUSIONS

When considering the broad range of Michael Lambert's productive research career, what might one conclude about his work in terms of its contribution to and influence on clinical research and practice? We have selected six central points that summarize the major contributions.

1. His early reviews and broad summaries of the therapy intervention literature helped to consolidate and confirm the field's confidence in the scientific finding that, on average, psychotherapy is effective.

2. In an era when most therapy researchers were interested in validating their intervention (the independent variable), Lambert highlighted the important contribution of the many measures of change (the dependent variables). These outcome measures play an important role in the determination of both the statistical and clinical significance of therapy effectiveness. Outcome measures also deserve to be studied in their own right as the science of therapeutic intervention evolves. Finally, Lambert developed a measure (OQ-45) and important methods for effectively integrating outcome measures into practice to evaluate ongoing change.

3. Some psychotherapy patients deteriorate. Lambert's early work attempted to highlight this fact, to get a sense for how prevalent such declines were, and he began to propose potential predictors of deterioration (including the possible negative effects of therapy). His later work focused on developing and validating early warning systems for therapists through tracking therapy progress in order to help intervene with clients and prevent ultimate deterioration.

4. Lambert's reviews of the therapy literature persuaded him that common and relationship factors played the most significant role in producing therapeutic change during psychotherapy, especially as compared to technical variables. He remained an important voice in the ongoing debate regarding the key ingredients of change throughout his career.

5. Perhaps Lambert's most significant practical or applied contribution to psychotherapy was the development of feedback systems using the OQ-45 to alert therapists regarding ongoing client progress. Embedded in this naturalistic research was the concurrent reinforcement of the fact that client outcome may be more related to the person of the therapist than to his or her theoretical orientation or specific interventions and techniques.

6. Beginning with his dissertation, Lambert had an interest in the effects of supervision. In contrast to the typical study that investigates the influence of supervision on the supervisee, he maintained an interest in the potential influence of supervision on the supervisee's client (Lambert & Ogles, 1997). As a result, the early warning systems developed to inform the therapist of potential deterioration are also available for informing supervision.

As can be readily seen, Michael J. Lambert has had and continues to have a broad and important influence on the practice of psychotherapy. In addition, he leads scientific advances in both primary research and syntheses of the literature with his prolific and insightful research. Perhaps most important, he is helping to bridge the gap that is so often seen between research and practice through the development of scientifically rigorous methods for informing practice.

REFERENCES

Chiles, J. A., Lambert, M. J., & Hatch, A. L. (1999). The impact of psychological interventions on medical cost offset: A meta-analytic review. *Clinical Psychology: Science and Practice, 6,* 204–220. doi:10.1093/clipsy/6.2.204

Derogatis, L. R. (1994). SCL-90-R: Administration, scoring, and procedures manual. Minneapolis, MN: National Computer Systems.

Hamilton, M. (1967). Development of a rating scale for primary depressive illness. *British Journal of Social and Clinical Psychology, 6,* 278-296.

Harmon, S. C., Lambert, M. J., Smart, D. M., Hawkins, E., Nielsen, S. L., Slade, K., & Lutz, W. (2007). Enhancing outcome for potential treatment failures: Therapist-client feedback and clinical support tools. *Psychotherapy Research, 17,* 379–392. doi:10.1080/10503300600702331

Horowitz, L. M., Rosenberg, S. E., Baer, B. A., Ureno, G., & Villesenor, V. S. (1988). Inventory of Interpersonal Problems: Psychometric properties and clinical applications. *Journal of Consulting and Clinical Psychology, 56,* 885–892.

Jacobson, N. S., & Truax, P. (1991). Clinical significance: A statistical approach to defining meaningful change in psychotherapy research. *Journal of Consulting and Clinical Psychology, 59,* 12–19. doi:10.1037/0022-006X.59.1.12

Lambert, M. J. (1976). Spontaneous remission in adult neurotic disorders: A revision and summary. *Psychological Bulletin, 83,* 107–119. doi:10.1037/0033-2909.83.1.107

Lambert, M. J. (1989). The individual therapist's contribution to psychotherapy process and outcome. *Clinical Psychology Review, 9,* 469–485. doi:10.1016/0272-7358(89)90004-4

Lambert, M. J. (1992). Psychotherapy outcome research: Implications for integrative and eclectic therapists. In J. C. Norcross & M. R. Goldfried (Eds.), *Handbook of psychotherapy integration* (pp. 94–129). New York, NY: Basic Books.

Lambert, M. J. (Ed.). (2004). *Bergin & Garfield's handbook of psychotherapy and behavior change* (5th ed.). New York, NY: Wiley.

Lambert, M. J. (2007). Presidential address: A program of research aimed at improving psychotherapy outcome in routine care: What we have learned from a decade of research. *Psychotherapy Research, 17,* 1–14. doi:10.1080/10503300601032506

Lambert, M. J., Bergin, A. E., & Collins, J. L. (1977). Therapist induced deterioration in psychotherapy patients. In A. S. Gurman & A. M. Razin (Eds.), *Effective psychotherapy: A handbook of research* (pp. 452–481). New York, NY: Pergamon Press.

Lambert, M. J., Burlingame, G. M., Umphress, V., Hansen, N. B., Vermeersch, D. A., Clouse, G. C., & Yanchar, S. C. (1996). The reliability and validity of the Outcome Questionnaire. *Clinical Psychology & Psychotherapy, 3,* 249–258. doi:10.1002/(SICI)1099-0879(199612)3:4<249::AID-CPP106>3.0.CO;2-S

Lambert, M. J., Christensen, E. R., & DeJulio, S. S. (Eds.). (1983). *The assessment of psychotherapy outcome.* New York, NY: Wiley-Interscience.

Lambert, M. J., Hansen, N. B., & Finch, A. E. (2001). Patient-focused research: Using patient outcome to enhance treatment effects. *Journal of Consulting and Clinical Psychology, 69,* 159–172. doi:10.1037/0022-006X.69.2.159

Lambert, M. J., Hansen, N.B., Umphress, V., Lunnen, K., Okiishi, J., Burlingame, G., . . . Reisinger, C.W. (1996). *Administration and Scoring Manual for the Outcome Questionnaire (OQ 45.2).* Wilmington, DE: American Professional Credentialing Services.

Lambert, M. J., & Ogles, B. M. (1988). Treatment manuals: Problems and promise. *Journal of Integrative and Eclectic Psychotherapy, 7,* 187–204.

Lambert, M. J., & Ogles, B. M. (1997). The effectiveness of psychotherapy supervision. In C. E. Watkins (Ed.), *Handbook of psychotherapy supervision* (pp. 421–446). New York, NY: Wiley.

Menninger, K. A. (1945). *The human mind* (3rd ed.). New York, NY: Knopf.

Vermeersch, D. A., Lambert, M. J., & Burlingame, G. M. (2000). Outcome Questionnaire: Item sensitivity to change. *Journal of Personality Assessment, 74,* 242–261. doi:10.1207/S15327752JPA7402_6

13

CLARA E. HILL: A REBEL WITH SEVERAL CAUSES

SARAH KNOX

Rare is the individual who has not only contributed to her or his profession's accumulated knowledge but has also created new research methods through which that very knowledge is gained. Perhaps rarer still is the researcher who has selflessly shared her accumulated wisdom with colleagues and students and, in so doing, has both enriched the experiences of all in her profession and planted the seeds for its continued growth. Clara E. Hill is that rare individual. This chapter, after briefly summarizing her major contributions and describing her early beginnings, will then more closely examine her accomplishments in a variety of areas.

MAJOR CONTRIBUTIONS

Clara Hill's contributions to her profession have indeed been profound. Her work on therapeutic processes not only transformed how therapy process research is performed but also added significantly to our understanding of the experiences, both overt and covert, of therapists and clients during the therapy endeavor. Building on her ever-increasing understanding of such therapy processes, as well as her experiences training therapists, Hill also developed an empirically and theoretically grounded, integrated approach to teaching helping skills, one that is clearly articulated and accessible to helpers of all developmental stages, and one that has become a central resource in many training programs. In addition, she applied the same level of theoretical and empirical thoroughness to her work with dreams and here, too, developed an extremely useful model for working with clients' dreams in therapy, a model that has shaped research in this area. An additional, and no less remarkable, contribution was her development of an intensely rigorous qualitative method that has enabled researchers to examine new questions, in new ways, and thereby further our understanding of therapy phenomena. Finally, she has contributed powerfully to her profession through several leadership positions. In each of these areas, Clara Hill's passion and enthusiasm for psychotherapy, whether in learning more about how psychotherapy works or in helping to train psychotherapists, have been extraordinary.

EARLY BEGINNINGS

Clara Edith Hill was born on September 13, 1948, in Shivers, Mississippi, the fourth of her parents' five children (a younger sister died in infancy). Her father, trained as a Baptist minister, had moved his family to Mississippi to be a preacher in a small church. When he could not make enough money to support his family, he tried being a teacher; the income afforded by that profession was also insufficient, so he moved the family to Rockford, Illinois, where he worked in a factory and Clara's mother became a social worker. Given her father's training, religion was a constant presence in Clara's early life, with nightly Bible meetings and church all day Saturday and Sunday, as well as Wednesday evenings. The Hills were also avid readers, through which Clara learned to think for herself and discover a world beyond the religiously confining environment of her home. Clara also played the flute from fifth grade through her first year in college, and it was from band that she learned her work ethic—"results, not excuses." An eagerness to examine fundamental questions and not necessarily conform to established dicta found its roots early in Clara Hill's life, and also carried through to her professional career. As an adolescent, for example, Clara questioned her father regarding Christian tenets, remaining unsatisfied with his response. "You just have to believe." Since that time, she has remained skeptical of and resistant to any force (whether religious, psychotherapeutic, or political) that tries to use persuasion or coercion to convert others or impose its views.

Hill's first year as an undergraduate at Southern Illinois University (SIU) was difficult—both her religious upbringing and her uncertainty regarding what she wanted to study left her on the outside. Once she decided to major in psychology, began working in a vision lab in the psychology department, and made friends, she finally began to thrive. During one college summer, Hill worked as a recreational assistant at a state hospital for adolescents in Chicago. It was here that she realized that she wanted to work with relatively healthy people (rather than with institutionalized patients)—an early step on her eventual path to counseling psychology. As an undergrad, Hill also took a class and did her honor's thesis (later published) with Dr. John Snyder, a counseling psychologist who supported her application to graduate school and eventually became her doctoral advisor.

Hill started her doctoral program in 1970 and loved those years, for she felt passionate about psychology and enjoyed her cohort of fellow students (and married one of them, Jim Gormally). She found the counseling psychology faculty at SIU open and supportive; they believed their students had worthwhile things to say and allowed them to freely pursue their own interests. The training she received in helping skills (based on Carkhuff, 1969) was invaluable both professionally and personally, and she experienced several early successes, with her research appearing in top-tier journals. From her graduate school years alone, in fact, Hill had 11 refereed publications. Her strongest influences in graduate school (primarily of humanistic and behavioral orientations) were John Snyder, Bill Anthony, Vince Harren, Jim O'Donnell, Dave Rimm, and Paul Schauble.

Clara Hill finished her doctorate in 4 years (including a year-long internship at the University of Florida) and initially planned to seek a clinical position. After a conversation with John Snyder, however, she decided to pursue an academic track, for doing so would provide her more professional options. She took a position as an assistant professor in the counseling psychology program in the Department of Psychology at the University of Maryland, and she has remained there ever since. Throughout her time at Maryland, Clara Hill has been highly involved in research, teaching, mentoring students, and administration. In the early years, she also maintained a small private practice.

ACCOMPLISHMENTS

Therapy Process

Hill's most abiding interest over the years has been in the investigation of therapist techniques, following her conviction that what therapists do in sessions indeed makes a difference. In examining therapist intentions, for example, she found that clients were not very accurate in identifying such intentions. Intriguingly, though, she also found that they need not be, for therapy to be successful. Through her exploration of therapist response modes, Hill discovered that although they do significantly affect the therapy process, they do not account for a large proportion of the variance. A few specific response modes, however, were found to be most helpful: interpretation, self-disclosure, paraphrase, and approval. As a complement to her work on therapist response modes, Hill also investigated client reactions, developing a coding system that enabled researchers to capture covert client experiences, particularly clients' hidden negative reactions. Continued research using her client behavior coding system revealed that clients responded differently to specific therapist interventions. After therapist interpretation, for instance, clients' levels of experiencing and exploration of the therapy relationship increased.

Hill continued to pursue her fascination with the therapy process in her later efforts, for she firmly believed that looking at specific interventions within the context of clinical cases allowed for a better understanding of how these interventions operate at specific times for specific clients than did examining the overall effects of therapist interventions across all of therapy and all clients. In this work, for example, she examined self-disclosure (Hill, Mahalik, & Thompson, 1989; Knox, Hess, Petersen, & Hill, 1997), silence (Hill, Thompson, & Ladany, 2003; Ladany, Hill, Thompson, & O'Brien, 2004), and immediacy (Hill, Sim, et al., 2008; Kasper, Hill, & Kivlighan, 2008). Using therapist self-disclosure as an illustration (see the review in Hill & Knox, 2002), Hill found that although such disclosures were rare, their frequency varied by theoretical orientation (e.g., humanistic/experiential therapists disclosed more than did psychoanalytic therapists) and they were perceived by clients as helpful in the short-term, although the longer term effects remained unclear.

In addition to looking at specific therapist interventions, Hill also examined client insight (see Castonguay & Hill, 2007), a line of research arising from her interest in how clients achieve these deeper understandings that she considers central to therapy. In a series of studies exploring the development of client insight within single sessions using Hill's model of dream work, Hill and colleagues (Hill et al., 2007; Knox, Hill, Hess, & Crook-Lyon, 2008) found that insight developed when clients discussed moderately salient dreams in the context of a solid therapy relationship, had positive attitudes toward dreams, were ready for dream work and remained motivated throughout the dream session, and were not overwhelmed by affect when discussing the dream. Insight was also facilitated when therapists were competent with the dream model, successfully managed their countertransference, and used probes for insight.

Clara Hill's plans for the near future involve integrating many of her previous interests in studying ongoing therapy. She will investigate, for example, the role of therapist interventions for working actively with the therapeutic relationship (immediacy, probes for insight, and interpretation) in fostering insight and corrective relational experiences.

Teaching Helping Skills

Given her career-long research interest in therapist techniques, as well as her years of training therapists, Hill wrote a text on helping skills, now in its second edition (Hill, 2004b; Hill & O'Brien, 1999), with the third edition expected in 2009. Hill had been frustrated by the lack of helping skills texts that integrated affect, cognition, and behavior as equally crucial elements in the change process. Nor had she found texts that incorporated both theoretical and empirical grounding for helping skills. Furthermore, Hill based *Helping Skills* on her conceptualization of the helping process "as comprising moment-by-moment interactional sequences":

> [A]t any moment in the helping process, helpers develop intentions for how they want to help clients. . . . With these intentions in mind, helpers select verbal and nonverbal skills with which to intervene. In turn, clients react to the interventions in ways that influence how they then choose to behave with helpers. Thus, helping involves not only the overt behaviors but also the cognitive processes of helpers (i.e., intentions) and clients (i.e., reactions). (Hill, 2004b, p. xviii)

The bulk of *Helping Skills* is devoted to the three stages of Hill's integrated helping skills model. Exploration, the first stage, is rooted in client-centered theory; insight, the second stage, is based on psychoanalytic and interpersonal theories; action, stage three, is built upon behavioral and cognitive theories. For each stage, Hill presents helping skills appropriate for that stage (e.g., open questions and restatements in exploration, challenges and interpretation in insight, process advisement in action) and not only defines and provides examples of each skill but also addresses therapist intentions for the skill, possible client reactions and behaviors evoked by the skill, and potential difficulties encountered when using the skill. Each skill-based chapter closes with helpful hints for using the skill, written exercises, and a practice activity through which students' mastery of the skills may be enhanced. Thus, *Helping Skills* not only provides excellent theoretical and empirical grounding for Hill's conceptualization of the helping process but also presents specific interventions appropriate for each stage, thereby enabling students to learn both the what and the how of counseling. Students find this text to be engaging and user-friendly, and they feel comfortable using it as a good primer for learning the basic skills and becoming empathic helpers.

Of course it was not enough just to propose a model of training. Hill next devoted considerable effort to understanding the effects of training (see Hill & Lent, 2006; Hill, Stahl, & Roffman, 2007). To facilitate this endeavor, she developed measures of helping skills usage (Hill & Kellems, 2002) and counselor self-efficacy (Lent, Hill, & Hoffman, 2003; Lent et al., 2006). Recent studies have suggested the effectiveness of helping skills training for under-graduates (Hill & Kellems, 2002; Hill, Roffman, et al., 2008), and another described the experiences of master's level students during their training (Hill, Sullivan, Knox, & Schlosser, 2007).

Dreams

Another of Hill's major accomplishments has been her work with dreams. Long interested in dreams, both her own and those of her clients, she also long believed that dreams hold important meanings that may be useful in therapy. When teaching an undergraduate seminar on dreams several years ago, Clara was especially drawn to Freudian, Jungian, and gestalt approaches to dream interpretation. To her dismay, she found little, if any, evidence in support of the various theories of dream interpretation. To pursue this area of research, Hill developed a model of dream interpretation so that therapists in her studies could follow a standard method.

In her two books in this area (Hill, 1996, 2004a), Hill explained her model of dream work in therapy, one that integrates client-centered, psycho-analytic, gestalt, and behavioral theories. As with her helping skills model, the Hill dream model involves three stages. In the exploration stage, the therapist helps the client explore several major images of the dream using four structured, client-centered steps (DRAW: description, re-experiencing, associations, and identifying waking life triggers). In the insight stage, the therapist builds on the foundation established in the exploration stage to help the client acquire insight into the dream. Finally, based on the understanding of the dream acquired through the first two steps, therapist and client work together in the action stage to develop ideas about how the client might introduce desired changes in waking life.

Reviews of the roughly 25 studies of this dream model (Hill, 1996; Hill & Goates, 2004; Hill & Spangler, 2007) clearly demonstrate the effectiveness of working with dreams in therapy. In a number of studies, clients rated the depth and working alliance of dream sessions more than a standard deviation higher than they rated sessions of regular therapy. In addition, clients reported gaining insight into their dreams, action ideas for what to do about problems in waking life, and resolution of target problems reflected in dreams. In addition, Hill and her colleagues found that clients with better attitudes toward dreams tended to volunteer for dream work and that clients preferred working with therapists to working alone on dreams. They have also found support for all of the components of the model, for client involvement, and for therapist adherence/competence in using the model. Hill's next challenge in this area is learning more about how therapists use dream work in ongoing therapy.

Qualitative Research

Feeling constrained by the type of understanding about inherently complex psychotherapy phenomena yielded by traditional quantitative approaches (see Hill & Gronsky, 1984), Hill began to explore qualitative approaches as a means of asking and answering questions about therapy. Because she found the descriptions of existing qualitative methods difficult both to understand and to implement, she and two colleagues (Hill, Thompson, & Williams, 1997) developed consensual qualitative research (CQR) to "integrate the best features of the existing methods and also be rigorous and easy to learn" (Hill et al., 2005, p. 196).

CQR is based on researchers asking open-ended questions via a semi-structured protocol (usually interviews), thereby allowing the collection of consistent verbal data across a relatively small number of participants, as well as the flexibility to deeply investigate individual experiences. The inductive data analysis process involves several judges collaborating to make all decisions about the data, thus promoting multiple perspectives on the data. All judges discuss their understanding of the data until they reach consensus, and at least one auditor reviews the work of the primary team of judges. The final results are presented in the form of domains (topic areas), core ideas (abstractions or paraphrases of participant data), and cross-analysis (common themes that emerge within a domain across all participants).

As a testament to the respect CQR has earned, 27 articles using this method were published in the profession's leading journals between 1994 and 2003 (the time span used by Hill et al., 2005, in their article reviewing the status of the method); more have appeared since that time, as well. Clearly, CQR answers a need for researchers seeking a clearly articulated, rigorous, appropriately flexible means of closely examining individuals' inner experiences—experiences that lie at the very heart of the therapy process.

Leadership Contributions

Clara Hill's mark on her profession has extended beyond the empirical, training, and methodological realms. She has served as editor of leading journals in her field (*Journal of Counseling Psychology*; *Psychotherapy Research*) and views this role as one in which she is afforded an opportunity to guide and shape her profession. Hill clearly enjoys her role as editor and firmly believes that she has an obligation to provide educational reviews that mentor authors in improving their manuscripts. Hill was also elected to serve as president of both the North American Chapter of the Society for Psychotherapy Research

(SPR) and the International Society for Psychotherapy Research and has been highly involved in SPR both before and since her presidential terms. As a more personal accomplishment, Clara notes that she and Jim have raised two children, of whom they are very proud.

INFLUENCES

Hill has acknowledged the influence of many individuals on her career. Notable colleagues have included those in the counseling psychology program at the University of Maryland (Bruce Fretz, Charlie Gelso, Mary Ann Hoffman, Bob Lent, and Karen O'Brien), as well as many colleagues from the Society for Psychotherapy Research (too many to list). Given her career stage, Clara now mentors others more often than she is mentored; many of these individuals have become frequent collaborators (again, too many to list).

CONCLUSION

The facts, summarized in this chapter, of Clara Hill's contributions to her profession are undeniably remarkable. No less remarkable, however, is the pattern that lies behind these observable accomplishments and their legacy. In each case, Hill identified a problem—a need to understand something in a new way, the lack of an existing research method to pursue that understanding, the limitations of extant tools for teaching the skills of therapy—and then sought to solve that problem, doing so with tremendous success. Her openness not only to being challenged by others but also to challenging herself has led to contributions noteworthy in both their quantity and quality. Her work is thus proactive, forward thinking, and forward moving, and in her demanding of herself that she continue to seek, to learn, and to create, she stimulates her colleagues to do the same. Though she has many a laurel upon which she could deservedly rest, Clara's unwillingness to do so is one of her greatest gifts to her profession.

REFERENCES

Carkhuff, R. R. (1969). *Human and helping relations* (2 vol.). New York, NY: Holt, Rinehart & Winston.

Castonguay, L., & Hill, C. E. (Eds.). (2007). *Insight in psychotherapy*. Washington, DC: American Psychological Association. doi:10.1037/11532-000

Hill, C. E. (1996). *Working with dreams in psychotherapy*. New York, NY: Guilford Press.

Hill, C. E. (Ed.). (2004a). *Dream work in therapy: Facilitating exploration, insight, and action*. Washington, DC: American Psychological Association. doi:10.1037/10624-000

Hill, C. E. (2004b). *Helping skills: Facilitating exploration, insight, and action* (2nd ed.). Washington, DC: American Psychological Association. doi:10.1037/10624-000

Hill, C. E., & Goates, M. K. (2004). Research on the Hill cognitive-experiential dream model. In C. E. Hill (Ed.), *Dream work in therapy: Facilitating exploration, insight, and action* (pp. 245–288). Washington, DC: American Psychological Association. doi:10.1037/10624-014

Hill, C. E., & Gronsky, B. (1984). Research: Why and how? In J. M. Whiteley, N. Kagan, L. W. Harmon, B. R. Fretz, & F. Tanney (Eds.), *The coming decade in counseling psychology* (pp. 149–159). Schenectady, NY: Character Research Press.

Hill, C. E., & Kellems, I. S. (2002). Development and use of the Helping Skills Measure to assess client perceptions of the effects of training and of helping skills in sessions. *Journal of Counseling Psychology, 49*, 264–272. doi:10.1037/0022-0167.49.2.264

Hill, C. E., & Knox, S. (2002). Self-disclosure. In J. C. Norcross (Ed.), *Psychotherapy relationships that work: Therapist contributions and responsiveness to patients* (pp. 255–265). Oxford, England: Oxford University Press.

Hill, C. E., Knox, S., Hess, S., Crook-Lyon, R., Goates-Jones, M., & Sim, W. (2007). The attainment of insight in the Hill dream model: A single case study. In L. Castonguay & C. E. Hill (Eds.), *Insight in psychotherapy* (pp. 207–230). Washington, DC: American Psychological Association. doi:10.1037/11532-010

Hill, C. E., Knox, S., Thompson, B. J., Williams, E. N., Hess, S., & Ladany, N. (2005). Consensual Qualitative Research: An update. *Journal of Counseling Psychology, 52*, 196–205.

Hill, C. E., & Lent, R. W. (2006). Training novice therapists: Skills plus. *Psychotherapy Bulletin, 41*, 11–16.

Hill, C. E., Mahalik, J. R., & Thompson, B. J. (1989). Therapist self-disclosure. *Psychotherapy: Theory, Research, Practice, Training, 26*, 290-295. doi: 10.1037/h0085438

Hill, C. E., & O'Brien, K. (1999). *Helping skills: Facilitating exploration, insight, and action* [Video included]. Washington, DC: American Psychological Association.

Hill, C. E., Roffman, M., Stahl, J., Friedman, S., Hummel, A., & Wallace, C. (2008). Helping skills training for undergraduates: Outcomes and predictors of outcomes. *Journal of Counseling Psychology, 55*, 359–370.

Hill, C. E., Sim, W., Spangler, P., Stahl, J., Sullivan, C., & Teyber, E. (2008). Therapist immediacy in brief psychotherapy: Case study II. *Psychotherapy: Theory, Research, Practice, Training, 45*, 298–315.

Hill, C. E., & Spangler, P. (2007). Dreams and psychotherapy. In D. Barrett & P. McNamara (Eds.), *The new science of dreaming* (pp. 159–186). Westport, CT: Greenwood.

Hill, C. E., Stahl, J., & Roffman, M. (2007). Training novice therapists: Helping skills and beyond. *Psychotherapy: Theory, Research, Practice, Training, 44*, 364–370.

Hill, C. E., Sullivan, C., Knox, S., & Schlosser, L. (2007). Becoming therapists: The experiences of pre-practicum trainees. *Psychotherapy: Theory, Research, Practice, Training, 44*, 434–449.

Hill, C. E., Thompson, B. J., & Ladany, N. (2003). Therapist use of silence in therapy: A survey. *Journal of Clinical Psychology, 59*, 513–524. doi:10.1002/jclp.10155

Hill, C. E., Thompson, B. J., & Williams, E. N. (1997). A guide to conducting consensual qualitative research. *The Counseling Psychologist, 25*, 517–572. doi:10.1177/0011000097254001

Kasper, L., Hill, C. E., & Kivlighan, D. (2008). Therapist immediacy in brief psychotherapy: Case study I. *Psychotherapy: Theory, Research, Practice, Training, 45*, 281–297.

Knox, S., Hess, S., Petersen, D., & Hill, C. E. (1997). A qualitative analysis of client perceptions of the effects of helpful therapist self-disclosure in long-term therapy. *Journal of Counseling Psychology, 44*, 274–283. doi:10.1037/0022-0167.44.3.274

Knox, S., Hill, C. E., Hess, S., & Crook-Lyon, R. (2008). The attainment of insight in the Hill dream model: Replication and extension. *Psychotherapy Research, 18*, 200–215.

Ladany, N., Hill, C. E., Thompson, B. J., & O'Brien, K. M. (2004). Therapist perspectives on using silence in therapy: A qualitative study. *Counselling & Psychotherapy Research, 4*, 80–89. doi:10.1080/14733140412331384088

Lent, R. W., Hill, C. E., & Hoffman, M. A. (2003). Development and validation of the Counselor Activity Self-Efficacy Scales. *Journal of Counseling Psychology, 50*, 97–108. doi:10.1037/0022-0167.50.1.97

Lent, R. L., Hoffman, M. A., Hill, C. E., Treistman, D., Mount, M., & Singley, D. (2006). Client-specific counselor self-efficacy in novice counselors: Relation to perceptions of session quality. *Journal of Counseling Psychology, 53*, 453–463. doi:10.1037/0022-0167.53.4.453

B. CLIENT CONTRIBUTIONS

14

EUGENE GENDLIN: EXPERIENTIAL PHILOSOPHY AND PSYCHOTHERAPY

DAVID L. RENNIE, ARTHUR C. BOHART, AND ALBERTA E. POS

Eugene Gendlin is one of the most influential thinkers in the person-centered/experiential psychotherapy world. Trained in philosophy, he turned to the field of psychotherapy early in his career and has participated in both fields since. Throughout, his interest has been the process of lived experience, or active experiencing. Upon his joining Carl Rogers's team at the Counseling Center of the University of Chicago, Gendlin's notion of experiencing enriched the Rogerian concept of therapeutic change. Subsequently, Gendlin contributed to the development of the Experiencing Scale, a much-used instrument in psychotherapy research. He also contributed substantially to psychotherapy process research. He directed and participated in Rogers's schizophrenia research project at the University of Wisconsin and did independent research on the relations between levels of experiencing and indicators of stress as well. He later developed a unique approach to therapy organized in terms of focusing on embodied experiencing, practiced around the world. He has also created a new philosophy based on embodied experiencing. In what follows, after attending to his early beginnings, we summarize this philosophy and Gendlin's contributions to psychotherapy theory, research, and practice.

EARLY BEGINNINGS

Gendlin was born in Vienna, Austria, in 1926. Being Jewish, the family fled the Nazis to the United States in 1939. Gendlin enrolled in the Department of Philosophy at the University of Chicago, where he developed a method of accepting a given system of thought in its entirety and then trying to formulate any point in terms of the ideas and symbols from within that system (see Gendlin, 1988). What interested him was that even though alternative systems entailed differing formulations and implications, there was nevertheless a sameness that cut across the systems. Meanwhile, he did his master's thesis on the philosophy of Wilhelm Dilthey (see, e.g., Makkreel, 1992), who challenged Enlightenment rationalist thought through his emphasis of the importance of *Erlebnis*, generally translated as "lived experience." This emphasis led Gendlin to the role of the body in felt experiencing of something, whence came the notion of an underlying sameness conceptualized as embodied experiencing, which became the linchpin of his thought.

Gendlin received his PhD in philosophy from the University of Chicago in 1958, under the mentorship of Richard McKeon. Around that time he became interested in psychotherapy because he saw it as involving the process of symbolizing experiencing freshly. He joined Rogers's team at the Counseling Center there, later moving with the team to the University of Wisconsin, where Gendlin directed the team's schizophrenia research project. Later he joined the Psychology Department at the University of Chicago, during which time he also founded the Focusing Institutes in Chicago and Spring Valley, New York, offering training in focusing and focusing-oriented psychotherapy.

ACCOMPLISHMENTS

Theory: Experiential Phenomenological Philosophy

Gendlin has developed a philosophy that he calls *experiential phenomenology*, formulated to take into account the body as a source of meaning. Gendlin first presented his philosophy in a seminal work, *Experiencing and the Creation of Meaning* (Gendlin, 1962), and has continued to develop it (e.g., Gendlin, 1997, 2001). His philosophy is too sophisticated to be depicted adequately here (for details, see, e.g., Levin, 1997; for brief interpretations by psychologists, see Pos, Greenberg, & Elliott, 2008; Rennie & Fergus, 2006). However, the gist of it is that, along with Heidegger and that minority of the contemporary philosophers who challenge the currently common emphasis on rationalism, Gendlin insists that the body plays an important role in how people create meaning out of experience. This is so because in any lived event, one's embodied experiencing is a consistent source of implicit knowing, in that bodily states reflect several overlapping processes (e.g., physiological, sensory-motor, relational); thus, implicit body-based meaning is full of potential implications and "may have countless organized aspects" (Gendlin, 1964, p. 140).

Accordingly, Gendlin proposes that bodily experiencing entails an implicit intricacy in any problematic situation. Although this implicit intricacy often seems vague—more like a felt sense of some kind—it is nevertheless a finely ordered complexity. If we attend to and symbolize (in words, images, etc.) this felt sense, its meaning will come to us. In this process, only the right symbols, those that fit the felt sense well, will do. When we come up with a fit that feels right, our experiencing changes; we move a step forward toward resolving the situation. The process usually proceeds through a series of steps. What the person turns to in each step usually is not a matter of logical deduction, although it logically makes sense in retrospect. Overall, experience is best thought of as *experiencing*—an ongoing process (Gendlin, 2001). Gendlin sees clients' working with their experiencing in psychotherapy as an excellent example of this process.

A word about Gendlin's philosophy of science: He maintains that philosophy is more abstract than science and operates on a different level. As a scientist, he endorses positivism, asserting that it can and should be improved by creating concepts through focusing on the implicit intricacy of phenomena, rather than by making the intricacy conform to concepts drawn from the externalizing logical order (Gendlin, 1962, 1991). His psychotherapy research has reflected this principle.

Psychotherapy Research

Two prominent research areas, on the process of clients' experiencing and on focusing as a therapeutic intervention, have emerged as a result of Gendlin's work.

Understanding and Working With Clients' Experiencing

Generally, conclusions from research on clients' experiencing suggest that (a) higher clients' experiencing predicts good session and overall outcome, and this has proved to apply to a number of therapy modalities and populations; (b) clients' early therapy experiencing levels often predict outcome; (c) improving clients' experiential processing during experiential therapy predicts outcome better than clients' beginning therapy levels of such processing; (d) other therapy processes, such as the therapeutic alliance in experiential therapy and good interpretations in dynamic therapy, contribute to deeper client experiencing; (e) focusing as an intervention increases clients' experiencing; and (f) some mixed results have been found.

Research on client experiencing began when Gendlin joined Rogers's team. Rogers's group had just completed a study on psychotherapy processes relating to positive therapeutic outcome. The hypothesis that clients' talking about the present rather than the past would relate to positive outcomes was not supported; however, *how* clients talked—whether they expressed their feelings or simply talked about them (Seeman, 1954)—did correlate with outcome. Gendlin, Jenney, and Shlien (1960) then redid the study, adding two psychotherapy process measures in an attempt to answer two new questions: (a) How important to the client is the relationship as a source of new experience? and (b) To what extent does the client express his or her feelings rather than talk about them? Both supplemental measures were found to correlate with positive outcome.

Gendlin and Berlin (1961) then tested whether focusing on experience would lead to tension reduction. One group of undergraduates received instructions to focus on their experiencing of strong, troublesome feelings, while other groups were instructed either to attend continuously to an external object or discontinuously to internal sensations different from troubling feelings. The group that focused on experiencing showed more tension reduction compared with the groups in other conditions. This study anticipated several others demonstrating a relationship between experiencing and physiological responsiveness (e.g., Don, 1977).

Under Gendlin's influence, the Process Scale developed by Walker, Rablen, and Rogers (1960) was refined into the Experiencing Scale (Klein, Mathieu, Gendlin, & Kiesler, 1969). The Experiencing Scale measures the degrees to which clients' in-session narratives demonstrate that they are orienting to and symbolizing their felt internal experiencing and using it in the solving of their problems. The scale measures seven levels of experiencing in terms of grammatical, expressive, paralinguistic, and content criteria. At Level 1 clients' narratives are objective and intellectual, showing no connection with or evidence of the personal significance of events described; at Level 7, as summarized by Gendlin (personal communication, October, 2007), clients tell very personal stories moving from "one direct experiential referent and speech to the next direct referent and speech."

Much discussion has gone on about what dimensions the Experiencing Scale actually measures. Lambert and Hill (1994) maintained that it is multidimensional, that it emphasizes emotional expressiveness rather than cognitive expression, and that it is unclear whether a high score on the scale indicates insight or involvement. In contrast, Wexler (1974) found that the scale correlated more with cognitive than with emotional factors, whereas Klein, Mathieu-Couglan, and Kiesler (1986) concluded that the Experiencing Scale is a measure of reflective style. Meanwhile, Gendlin has always held that experiencing is a felt sense much broader than emotion. Therefore, it may be supposed that from Gendlin's perspective the Experiencing Scale measures the degree of integration between clients' capacities both to experience embodied feeling states and to process cognitively (with awareness and conceptual symbolization) the personal information implicit within those states.

In 1968 Gendlin et al. evaluated extant research on the relationship between neurotics' and schizophrenics' experiencing and outcome and determined that the relationship was positive. Contrary to prediction, however, "half the clients were failure-predicted from the first interviews at .001 significance, which meant so much work, love, and money predictably was wasted" (E. Gendlin, personal communication, October, 2007). Also, on the whole, experiencing did not appear to increase over the course of psychotherapy. This finding was contrary to a key hypothesis held by the Rogerian group that psychotherapy helps clients move from a rigid, structure-bound manner of experiencing to a more fluid and internally congruent one.

Shifts from lower to higher levels of experiencing were expected to correlate with outcome in therapy. Kiesler, Klein, and Mathieu (1965) found some support for this hypothesis, finding an upward trend during a therapy hour with neurotics, although with schizophrenics the pattern was more irregular. On the whole, though, the team engaged in the Wisconsin Schizophrenia Project concluded that for both schizophrenics and neurotics, the level of experiencing changed only minimally over the course of therapy. The initial level of their experiencing was more important than change in the manner of it. Clients who benefited from therapy entered it already high in experiencing. Since then, more support for the original hypothesis has been established with respect to nonpsychotic clients. A series of studies of process–experiential therapy have demonstrated that increases in experiencing levels actually occur and better predict positive outcome than do clients' initial early therapy experiencing levels (Goldman, Greenberg, & Pos, 2005; Greenberg & Higgins, 1980; Pos et al., 2003; Pos, Greenberg, & Warwar, in press).

Meanwhile, other therapy processes appear to be related to client experiencing. Pos, Greenberg, and Warwar (in press) found that the therapy alliance contributes to the deepening of experiencing during emotion episodes in successful experiential treatment of depression. More generally, it has also been shown that good psychoanalytic interpretations, gestalt therapy, guided daydreams, encounter group training, and reevaluation counseling all increase clients' pre- and posttherapy experiencing compared with controls (Elliott,

Greenberg, & Lietaer, 2004), whereas Bohart (2001) has applied the concept of experiencing to self-healing.

Research has also shown mixed results, however. Hendricks (2002) found in a review of 29 studies entailing the Process Scale and the Experiencing Scale that 27 demonstrated positive correlations with outcome. In contrast, Orlinsky, Grawe, and Parks (1994) and Orlinsky, Rønnestad, and Willutzki (2004) gave a more mixed picture in which, among 39 effects distributed among a number of studies, 51% were positive.

Focusing and Focusing-Oriented Psychotherapy

The focusing technique and focusing-oriented psychotherapy are two major developments that came out of research on experiencing. To address the early research findings showing little evidence that experiencing level increases in therapy, Gendlin (1981) developed a technique for teaching clients to focus, the idea being that this would increase the probability of success in psychotherapy. The technique entails six basic steps, beginning with "Clearing a space. Focus attention inwardly and try to become receptively aware and welcome what is inside" and ending with "Receiving. Receive whatever arises in a friendly, accepting way." A number of studies have demonstrated that focusing can indeed be taught (Clark, 1980; Gendlin, 1981), although the effectiveness of the teaching (Durak, Bernstein, & Gendlin, 1997) and the durability of what was learned (Leijssen, 1996; Liejssen, Leitaer, Stevens, & Wels, 2000; see also Hendricks, 2002) were found to vary.

In addition to its application in individual (Gendlin, 1981, 1996b) and group (see http://www.focusing.org/gendlin/) therapy, self-help manuals, developed not only for psychotherapy clients but for anyone, have been based on the focusing technique (Gendlin, 1981). Moreover, it is used in other approaches, such as process–experiential therapy (Elliott, Greenberg, & Lietaer, 2004), discussed in the previous section, and eye movement desensitization and reprocessing (Francine Shapiro, personal communication to Art Bohart, 2000). Meanwhile, it has been shown that it is useful to train therapists to engage in focusing (e.g., Swaine, 1986). Moreover, it has been related to positive outcome in therapy, thus paralleling experiencing, as would be expected. It was found, for example, that learning to focus was related positively both to the effectiveness of client-centered therapy sessions and early, successful termination of therapy (Leijssen, 1996); to successful outcome with people with psychoses (Egendorf & Jacobson, 1982); to improved memory in older people (Sherman, 1987); and among patients with cancer currently in remission, to improved self-ratings of symptoms as well as improved scores on measures of personality (Katonah, 1991).

OTHER CONTRIBUTIONS

Gendlin published, in 1986, an influential article on the psychotherapy research agenda for the future, proposing 18 strategies. To give their flavor, his first suggestion is that therapists should routinely tape record their cases, measure variables before and after treatment, and send clearly successful cases to a data bank. In virtue of the increase in the present-day valuing of case history as method and the emphasizing of practice-based evidence, Gendlin was prescient. Another example is his fourth suggestion, that psychotherapy should be evaluated in terms of ongoing therapy process instead of through group-design research. He puts out a call to make it the order of the day to study how subprocesses work well, not just in therapy but in all aspects of life.

He was among the founders of both the journal of the Psychotherapy Division of the American Psychological Association (APA) and the group Psychologists for Social Responsibility. He also formed the International Focusing Society, which does training of focusing throughout the world. He is the author of several books that have become classics. He has influenced many theoreticians and researchers. For his contributions he has been presented with a Distinguished Professional Psychology Award by APA, a related award by APA's Society of Humanistic Psychology, and the Grand Award of the Victor Frankl Foundation by the city of Vienna.

CONCLUSION

Eugene Gendlin is a major founder of the general humanistic/experiential/person-centered approach to psychotherapy. Moreover, his lifelong work on experiencing and the creation of meaning is drawing increasing attention in philosophy (see Levin, 1997) and has played a central role in the conceptualization of the therapeutic process. The production of the Experiencing Scale, in expression of his theory of experiencing, continues to be used extensively. His technique of having clients engage in focusing in therapy has been incorporated into many approaches to therapy apart from Gendlin's particular use of it. Gendlin is a model of someone who can make a theory of the person work hand in hand with psychotherapy research and practice.

REFERENCES

Bohart, A. (2001). A meditation on the nature of self-healing and personality change in psychotherapy based on Gendlin's theory of experiencing. *Humanistic Psychologist, 29*, 249–279.

Clark, D. B. (1980). Effects of experiential focusing with psychotherapy patients. *Dissertation Abstracts International, 41*(2-B), 684. (University Microfilms No. 8017688).

Don, N.S. (1977). Transformation of conscious experience and its EEG correlates. *Journal of Altered States of Consciousness, 3*, 147–168.

Durak, G. M., Bernstein, R., & Gendlin, E. T. (1997). Effects of focusing training on therapy process and outcome. *Folio: A Journal for Focusing and Experiential Therapy, 15*(2), 7–14.

Egendorf, A., & Jacobson, L. (1982). Teaching the very confused how to make sense: An experiential approach to modular training with psychotics. *Psychiatry, 45*, 336–350.

Elliott, R., Greenberg, L. S., & Lietaer, G. (2004). Research on experiential psychotherapies. In M. J. Lambert (Ed.), *Bergin and Garfield's handbook of psychotherapy and behavior change* (5th ed., pp. 493–540). New York, NY: Wiley.

Gendlin, E. T. (1962). *Experiencing and the creation of meaning*. New York, NY: Free Press of Glencoe, Macmillan.

Gendlin, E. T. (1964). Personality change. In P. Worchel & D. Byrne (Eds.), *A theory of personality change* (pp. 102–148). New York, NY: Wiley.

Gendlin, E. T. (1981). *Focusing* (2nd ed.). New York, NY: Bantam.

Gendlin, E. T. (1986). What comes after traditional psychotherapy research? *American Psychologist, 41*, 131–136. doi:10.1037/0003-066X.41.2.131

Gendlin, E. T. (1988). Phenomenology as non-logical steps. In E. F. Kaelin & C. O. Schrag (Eds.), *Analecta Husserliana: The yearbook of phenomenological research: Vol. XXVI. American phenomenology: Origins and developments* (pp. 404–410). Dordrecht, Holland/Boston, MA: Kluwer.

Gendlin, E. T. (1991). Thinking beyond patterns: Body, language, and situations. In B. den Ouden & M. Moen (Eds.), *The presence of feeling in thought* (pp. 21–151). New York, NY: Peter Lang.

Gendlin, E. T. (1996). *Focusing-oriented psychotherapy*. New York, NY: Guilford.

Gendlin, E. T. (1997). How philosophy cannot appeal to experience, and how it can. In D. M. Levin (Ed.), *Language beyond postmodernism: Saying and thinking in Gendlin's philosophy* (pp. 3–41). Evanston, IL: Northwestern University Press.

Gendlin, E. T. (2001). A process model. http://www.focusing.org/postmod.htm.

Gendlin, E. T., & Berlin, J. I. (1961). Galvanic skin response correlates of different modes of experiencing. *Journal of Clinical Psychology, 17*, 73–77. doi:10.1002/1097-4679(196101)17:1<73::AID-JCLP2270170128>3.0.CO;2-Y

Gendlin, E. T., Jenney, R., & Shlien, J. M. (1960). Counselor ratings of process and outcome in client-centered therapy. *Journal of Clinical Psychology, 16*, 210–213. doi:10.1002/1097-4679(196004)16:2<210::AID-JCLP2270160228>3.0.CO;2-J

Goldman, R. N., Greenberg, L. S., & Pos, A. E. (2005). Depth of emotional experience and outcome. *Psychotherapy Research, 15*, 248–260. doi:10.1080/10503300512331385188

Greenberg, L. S., & Higgins, H. M. (1980). The differential effects of two-chair dialogue and focusing on conflict resolution. *Journal of Counseling Psychology, 27,* 221–224. doi:10.1037/0022-0167.27.3.221

Hendricks, M. N. (2002). Focusing-oriented/experiential psychotherapy. In D. Cain & J. Seeman (Eds.), *Humanistic psychotherapies: Handbook of research and practice* (pp. 221–251). Washington, DC: American Psychological Association. doi:10.1037/10439-007

Katonah, D. G. (1991). *Focusing and cancer: A psychological tool as an adjunct treatment for adaptive recovery.* Unpublished doctoral dissertation, Illinois School of Professional Psychology, Chicago, IL. Available at http://www.focusing.org/adjunct_treatment.html

Kiesler, D. J., Klein, M. H., & Mathieu, P. L. (1965). Sampling from the recorded therapy interview: The problem of segment location. *Journal of Consulting Psychology, 29,* 337–344. doi:10.1037/h0022422

Klein, M. H., Mathieu, P. L., Gendlin, E. T., & Kiesler, D. J. (1969). *The Experiencing Scale: A research training manual.* Madison, WI: University of Wisconsin Extension Bureau of Audiovisual Instruction.

Klein, M. H., Mathieu-Coughlan, P., & Kiesler, D. J. (1986). The Experiencing Scales. In L. S. Greenberg & W. Pinsof (Eds.), *The psychotherapeutic process: A research handbook* (pp. 21–71). New York, NY: Guilford.

Lambert, M. J., & Hill, C. E. (1994). Assessing psychotherapy outcomes and processes. In A. E. Bergin & S. L. Garfield (Eds.), *Handbook of psychotherapy and behavior change* (4th ed., pp. 72–113). New York, NY: Wiley.

Leijssen, M. (1996). Characteristics of a healing inner relationship. In R. Hutterer, G. Pawlowsky, P. F. Schmid, & R. Stipsits (Eds.), *Client-centered and experiential psychotherapy: A paradigm in motion* (pp. 427–438). Frankfurt am Main, Germany: Peter Lang.

Leijssen, M., Lietaer, G., Stevens, I., & Wels, G. (2000). Focusing training in stagnating clients: An analysis of four cases. In J. Marques-Teixeira & S. Antunes (Eds.), *Client-centered and experiential psychotherapy* (pp. 207–224). Linda a Velha, Portugal: Vale & Vale.

Levin, D. M. ((Ed.). 1997). *Language beyond postmodernism: Saying and thinking in Gendlin's philosophy.* Evanston, IL: Northwestern University Press.

Makkreel, R. A. (1992). *Dilthey: Philosopher of the human studies.* Princeton, NJ: Princeton University Press.

Orlinsky, D. E., Grawe, K., & Parks, B. K. (1994). Process and outcome in psychotherapy: Noch einmal. In A. E. Bergin & S. L. Garfield (Eds.), *Handbook of psychotherapy and behavior change* (4th ed., pp. 270–376). New York, NY: Wiley.

Orlinsky, D. E. Rønnestad, & Willutzki, U. (2004). Fifty years of psychotherapy process-outcome research: Continuity and change. In M. J. Lambert (Ed.), *Bergin and Garfield's handbook of psychotherapy and behavior change* (5th ed., pp. 307–390). New York, NY: Wiley.

Pos, A. E., Greenberg, L., & Elliott, R. (2008). Experiential therapy. In J. Lebow (Ed.), *Twenty-first century psychotherapies* (pp. 80–122). New York, NY: Wiley.

Pos, A. E., Greenberg, L. S., Goldman, R. N., & Korman, L. M. (2003). Emotional processing during experiential treatment of depression. *Journal of Consulting and Clinical Psychology, 71,* 1007–1016. doi:10.1037/0022-006X.71.6.1007

Pos, A. E., Greenberg, L. S., & Warwar, S. H. (2009). Testing a model of change in experiential treatment of depression. *Journal of Consulting and Clinical Psychology, 77,* 1055–1066.

Rennie, D. L., & Fergus, K. D. (2006). Embodied categorizing in the grounded theory method: Methodical hermeneutics in action. *Theory & Psychology, 16,* 483–503. doi:10.1177/0959354306066202

Seeman, J. (1954). Counselor judgments of therapeutic process and outcome. In C. R. Rogers & R. Dymond (Eds.), *Psychotherapy and personality change.* Chicago, IL: University of Chicago Press.

Sherman, E. (1987). Reminiscence groups for community elderly. *Gerontologist, 27,* 569–572.

Swaine, W. T. (1986). Counselor training in experiential focusing: Effects on empathy, perceived facilitativeness and self-actualization. *Dissertation Abstracts International,* 47(4-A), 1197.

Walker, A., Rablen, R. A., & Rogers, C. R. (1960). Development of a scale to measure process change in psychotherapy. *Journal of Clinical Psychology, 1,* 79–85. doi:10.1002/1097-4679(196001)16:1<79::AID-JCLP2270160129>3.0.CO;2-K

Wexler, D. A. (1974). A cognitive theory of experiencing, self-actualization, and therapeutic process. In D. A. Wexler & L. N. Rice (Eds.), *Innovations in client-centered therapy* (pp. 49–116). New York, NY: Wiley.

15

LAURA RICE: NATURAL OBSERVER OF PSYCHOTHERAPY PROCESS

JEANNE C. WATSON AND HADAS WISEMAN

Laura Rice was a pioneer of psychotherapy process research. With boundless curiosity, she was a keen observer of the natural world. Rice completed her doctoral studies at the University of Chicago in 1955, under the supervision of Jack Butler. It was in her work at the University of Chicago, with Carl Rogers and colleagues, that she brought together her passion for helping others with her curiosity and desire to do research. Schooled in client-centered therapy, she went on to develop the theory and practice of this approach based on cognitive science and her own understanding of psychotherapy process derived from her clinical experience as well as her research on patterns of change in psychotherapy. Subsequently, she developed process–experiential psychotherapy with Leslie Greenberg and Robert Elliott.

Laura Rice embodied the research clinician, successfully integrating theory, research, and practice to inspire her students and future generations to engage in psychotherapy process research. In the 1980s, Carl Rogers recognized her as a major contributor to research in client-centered therapy, and in 1988 the Society for Psychotherapy Research acknowledged her contributions to the field with the Distinguished Research Career Award.

MAJOR CONTRIBUTIONS

The primary focus of Rice's work was to identify the mechanisms of change and the active ingredients of client-centered therapy. She made important contributions to client-centered theory and practice: first, by conceptualizing change in terms of clients' cognitive–affective functioning; and second, by distinguishing between the relationship conditions and the task conditions (Rice, 1974, 1983). In terms of theory, Rice, in her work with Butler (Butler & Rice, 1963), proposed that stimulus hunger or adient motivation was a primary drive and the basis of organismic self-actualization, a central tenet of Rogers's theory of personality. They argued that adience or stimulus hunger, the basis of exploratory behavior and the organism's preference for complexity, facilitated development. Stimulus hunger was seen as stronger than the maintenance drives, such as those for food and water. According to these theorists, dysfunctional behavior reflected the organism's attempt to restrict experiences, thereby limiting its capacity for self-actualization (Butler, Rice, & Wagstaff, 1963). Thus the goal of therapy was to reduce anxiety and enable the organism to explore his or her environment to open up new possibilities and ways of being. Rice, like Rogers, believed that the individual's capacity for self-actualization could be activated in therapy so that clients could search for solutions to life problems with the support of their therapists (Rice, 1984).

Like many researchers today, Rice was disillusioned with psychotherapy outcome studies, because she did not see them as furthering understanding of client change. Instead, she turned her attention to identifying and understanding the resources that clients bring to therapy (Rice, 1992). She proposed a method of naturalistic observation, independent of theory, to identify client characteristics and resources, related to good and poor outcome. Then she examined how therapists' processes influenced clients' processes. These two foci resulted in the development of a number of therapist and client process measures, including client and therapist vocal quality and expressive stance (Rice & Kerr, 1986).

Rice's intense observation of the psychotherapy process enabled her to identify and explicate different types of change events in client-centered therapy (Rice & Greenberg, 1991). Using task analysis, she and Greenberg (1984) described and explicated the steps that therapists and clients engage in to resolve specific cognitive–affective problems in therapy, for example, helping clients to understand intense reactions or resolve states of intense vulnerability in a session. The primary objective of this work was to create microtheories of change that would enable therapists to intervene differentially at specific client markers to maximize the match between client and therapist resources. Another important contribution was Rice's distinction between primary and task-relevant relationship factors. While Rice saw the therapeutic conditions specified by Rogers as important in promoting client change, she thought therapists could do more to facilitate optimal conditions for certain kinds of client exploration (Rice, 1984). Her emphasis on therapist-directed process notwithstanding, Rice viewed the client as the expert on his or her own experiences.

Convinced that a common language was essential to advance the science of psychotherapy, Rice (1974, 1992) adopted a cognitive information-processing paradigm to understand and explain the complex processes of change. She criticized client-centered theory as focusing too much on the self concept and not enough on the individual's perceptions of and transactions with the world. Rice proposed that change in therapy occurred through alterations to clients' perceptual cognitive–affective frameworks and self-schemas. She suggested that client-centered therapy provided clients with the opportunity to become aware of their affective experiences and to explore them to create new experiences and ways of viewing self and other.

EARLY BEGINNINGS

Laura Rice was born in 1920, in New England, to parents of Puritan descent. Her father, whom Rice experienced as distant and critical, was a lawyer. Both her parents were intellectuals who home-schooled their children to ensure the quality of their education, so Laura was in her early teens before she attended public school. She later expressed regret that she had been cloistered at home as a child, as it left her with a sense of being out of step with her peers.

Rice's life was filled with personal tragedy. Both her brother and fiancé were killed during World War II, and she never quite recovered from those losses. More tragedy was to follow. As a close friend and companion to her sister throughout her life, Rice took much pride and pleasure in her role as aunt to her nephew and niece, who both died from cancer as young adults. Subsequently, Rice took comfort and found joy in her role as great-aunt to her nephew's son, with whom she spent vacations when he visited his grandparents during the summer.

Rice initially wanted to study botany; however, she switched to psychology and devoted her life to counseling others and to understanding and researching psychotherapy processes and outcomes, first at the University of Chicago and then at York University in Toronto. Prior to beginning her doctoral studies, Rice worked in human resources for an airline company conducting aptitude and cognitive assessments for pilots and other employees. She resigned from this position and returned to the University of Chicago to begin her doctoral studies in 1951. She gave two reasons for choosing the

University of Chicago: The Psychology Department offered, first, "an excellent program in theoretical psychology with a strong research focus," and, second, the presence on faculty of Carl Rogers, who was engaged in process research and whose book *Client-Centered Therapy* (Rogers, 1951) had just been published.

After graduating with her PhD from Chicago in 1955, Laura Rice worked at and later directed the Counselling Centre before moving to Toronto in 1970 to take up a faculty position at York University. She retained her early interest in plants and animals with a hobby farm just outside of Toronto, where she kept a horse and cultivated strawberries and other produce. On weekends the farm provided her with a retreat from the demands of the city, her clients at the University Counselling Centre, and students. Rice retired from York University in 1986; however, she stayed on as professor emeritus for another 6 years. In 1993, she returned to Massachusetts to be close to her sister and extended family. She died on July 18, 2004, at the age of 84.

ACCOMPLISHMENTS

Process Research Methods: Quantitative Naturalistic Research Program

Rice was an innovator of research methodologies (Rice, 1992). At the University of Chicago in the late 1950s and early 1960s, with Butler and Wagstaff, she began a research program, supported by the National Institute of Mental Health (NIMH), to investigate the psychotherapy process (Butler, Rice, & Wagstaff, 1963). They initiated a time-limited psychotherapy program to collect data and proposed the use of a quantitative naturalistic research methodology to generate groups of process categories to develop testable hypotheses that emerged from intense observation, independent of theory.

Initially, Rice (1965) attempted to classify the vocal and lexical aspects of therapists' styles of participation during the session (Duncan, Rice, & Butler, 1968; Rice & Wagstaff, 1967). She identified three aspects of therapist style: the type of language used, fresh and connotative or ordinary; vocal quality in terms of whether it was expressive, usual, or distorted; and the stance that therapists adopted toward the clients' experience in terms of whether it was focused on inner exploration, observation, or analysis. Interviews were then classified in terms of the frequency of these behaviors. Three different interview types were identified: Type 1 was characterized by commonplace language and an even, unexpressive vocal quality, with responses focused on client-self observation; Type 2 was characterized by little connotative language and distorted vocal quality; with a focus on client self-observation and few attempts to encourage inner exploration; Type 3, in contrast, was characterized by rich, connotative language and expressive voice, with therapists focusing on clients' inner self-exploration. Therapist behavior was then examined in relation to client outcome. As early as session two, Type 2 therapist behavior, characterized by distorted voice, little connotative language, and a focus on client self-observation, predicted poor outcome. In contrast, Type 3 therapist behavior in the second-to-last session predicted good client outcome.

Rice's objective of categorizing clients' behaviors led to the development of the Client Vocal Quality Measure (Rice, Koke, Greenberg, & Wagstaff, 1979) and the Expressive Stance Measure (Rice, Watson, & Greenberg, 1993). Client vocal quality was a feature of clients' style of participation that stood out as being most distinguishing of good therapy hours. Four different types of vocal quality were identified. *Externalizing* was characterized by the client's speaking in a rhythmical, chatty way that was focused on producing an effect on the other. *Focused* was characterized by high energy but with broken rhythm and a quality of the client's attention being turned inward and focused on inner exploration. *Limited* was characterized by low-energy, rhythmical speech with a breathless, brittle quality. Finally, *emotional* was characterized by clients' voices breaking up as they became overwhelmed by emotion (Rice & Kerr, 1986). The Expressive Stance Measure differentiated the way in which clients engaged with their experience. This measure consisted of four categories: objective analysis, labeling subjective reactions, static feeling descriptions, and differentiated exploration of feeling.

In a study conducted with Wagstaff, Rice observed that clients' performance in terms of their vocal quality and expressive stance in the second session predicted their outcome status at the end of therapy (Rice & Wagstaff, 1967). External vocal quality and objective analysis differentiated attrition clients from successful ones, whereas focused voice and a mix of subjective reaction and objective analysis distinguished the good outcome clients, and limited vocal quality and objective analysis distinguished the poor outcome group (Rice & Wagstaff, 1967). The authors suggested that client vocal quality could help identify which clients might benefit from different approaches to therapy. In a study of client resources, therapist style, and client process, the client resources, as measured by their Rorschach scores, were significantly related to client process in the second session, whereas therapist style of participation was not (Rice & Gaylin, 1973). However, by the 10th session, both client resources and therapist style of participation were predictive of client process, which in turn was predictive of outcome (Rice, 1973; 1992).

Process Research Methods: Task Analysis

Rice developed a method of identifying productive moments in psychotherapy and subjecting them to intensive analysis in order to model the steps necessary to specify resolution and improve client outcomes (Rice & Greenberg, 1984; Rice & Saperia, 1984). Rice was convinced that different approaches to psychotherapy fit some clients better than others and that, to understand the mechanisms of change and improve success rates research, clinicians needed to study productive and unproductive interactions in psychotherapy. She criticized an aggregate approach to studying change and instead advocated a bottom-up approach in which researchers examine clients' and therapists' behaviors and patterns of interaction in specific contexts, recognizing that specific behaviors have different meanings in different contexts.

Working with clients, Rice (1974; Rice & Saperia, 1984) observed a specific class of event that she called *problematic reaction points*, that is, client statements in which clients queried certain reactions as surprising, too intense, or otherwise problematic. The statements indicate that clients are becoming reflective about their own behavior and are potentially ready to turn inward to explore their experience more systematically. To help clients explore their reactions and come to a better understanding of their behavior, Rice developed *evocative unfolding*, which was an expansion of her technique of evocative reflections that facilitated clients' processing of painful experiences. With evocative unfolding, clients are encouraged to create vivid, graphic, and idiosyncratic descriptions of the situations in which problematic reactions occur, so as to identify the triggers for the reactions and to explore them so that clients can better understand their behavior and devise new ways of acting (Rice, 1974; Rice & Saperia, 1984; Watson & Greenberg, 1996). Subsequently Rice developed a performance model of the resolution of problematic reaction points and subjected it to verification (Watson & Rice, 1985; Wiseman & Rice, 1989; Wiseman, 1992). This work was expanded and carried forward by Leslie Greenberg and his students in their examination of two tasks from gestalt therapy (Rice & Greenberg, 1984).

Process–Experiential Psychotherapy

The joint program of research on task analysis led to the development of process–experiential psychotherapy (PE-EFT), an emotion-focused therapy for individuals (Greenberg, Rice, & Elliott, 1993; Rice, 1988; Rice & Greenberg, 1992). The authors integrated the client-centered relationship conditions and marker-guided empathy and focusing with gestalt interventions to develop a new approach to therapy. PE-EFT advocates that therapists be attentive to clients' moment-to-moment process and intervene differentially at specific client markers indicating that clients were wrestling with specific cognitive–affective problems such as self-criticisms, problematic reactions, difficulty identifying and labeling feelings, and so on. Today, PE-EFT is an empirically supported treatment that has numerous advocates and is taught around the world (Elliott, Watson, Goldman, & Greenberg, 2004; Greenberg & Watson, 2005; Watson, Gordon, Stermac, Steckley, & Kalogerakos, 2003).

CONCLUSION

Laura Rice made significant contributions to both theory and practice. She was a therapist of exquisite sensitivity and attunement to her clients' processes. The privilege of receiving clinical training from Laura on how to listen to moment-by-moment client process still resonates in us as we hear her voice on how we can help clients explore their inner experiences and achieve new self-understanding. As a researcher, Laura's journey from naturalistic observation led to the development of microtheories of change and finally an extension of person-centered and experiential psychotherapy with the development of PE-EFT.

One of her major contributions to the field was her mentorship of a generation of psychotherapy process researchers that led to a major shift in the intellectual climate of the Society for Psychotherapy Research (SPR) with the recognition of the importance of process research. Rice's mentoring of Leslie Greenberg, Jeanne Watson, Hadas Wiseman, Catherine Klaasen, Bill Pinsoff, and other psychotherapy researchers at York University, including Shake Toukmanian, David Rennie, and Lynne Angus, as well as her support of researchers at SPR, including Jeremy Safran and Robert Elliott, laid much of the groundwork for later developments in the field of psychotherapy change process research. Some innovative developments in different psychotherapy orientations show Rice's ongoing influence, including experiential, person-centered, and emotion-focused approaches (Elliott, et al., 2004; Greenberg & Watson, 2006), and ruptures in the alliance in relational therapy (Safran & Muran, 2000) and attachment-based family therapy (Diamond, Diamond, & Hogue, 2007). These research programs embody Rice's legacy of the importance of observation to the construction of models of change and her passion for the kind of psychotherapy research that would make valid contributions to practicing clinicians.

REFERENCES

Butler, J. M., & Rice, L. N. (1963). Audience, self-actualization, and drive theory. In J. M. Wepman, & R. W. Heine, R. W. (Eds.), *Concepts of personality* (pp. 79–110). Hawthorne, NY: Aldine.

Butler, J. M., Rice, L. N., & Wagstaff, A. K. (1963). *Quantitative naturalistic research.* Englewood Cliffs, NJ: Prentice-Hall.

Diamond, G. M., Diamond, G. S., & Hogue, A. (2007). Attachment-based family therapy: Adherence and differentiation. *Journal of Marital and Family Therapy, 33,* 177–191. doi:10.1111/j.1752–0606.2007.00015.x

Duncan, S., Rice, L. N., & Butler, J. M. (1968). Therapists' paralanguage in peak and poor psychotherapy hours. *Journal of Abnormal Psychology, 73,* 566–570. doi:10.1037/h0026597

Elliott, R., Watson, J. C., Goldman, R., & Greenberg, L. (2004). *Learning emotion focused psychotherapy: The process-experiential approach to change.* Washington, DC: American Psychological Association. doi:10.1037/10725–000

Greenberg, L. S., Rice, L. N., & Elliott, R. (1993). *Facilitating emotional change: The moment-by-moment process.* New York, NY: Guilford.

Greenberg, L. S., & Watson, J. C. (2005). *Emotion-focused therapy for depression.* Washington, DC: American Psychological Association. doi:10.1037/11286–000

Rice, L. N. (1965). Therapist's style of participation and case outcome. *Journal of Consulting Psychology, 29,* 155–160. doi:10.1037/h0021926

Rice, L. N. (1973). Client behavior as a function of therapist style and client resources. *Journal of Counseling Psychology, 20,* 306–311. doi:10.1037/h0034805

Rice, L. N. (1974). The evocative function of the therapist. In D. A. Wexler & L. N. Rice (Eds.), *Innovations in client-centered therapy* (pp. 289–311). New York, NY: Wiley.

Rice, L. N. (1983). The relationship in client-centered therapy. In M. J. Lambert (Ed.), *Psychotherapy and patient relationships* (pp. 36–60). Homewood, IL: Dow Jones Irwin.

Rice, L. N. (1984). Client tasks in client-centered therapy. In R. Levant & J. Shlien (Eds.), *Client-centered therapy and the person-centered approach: New directions in theory, research and practice* (pp.182–202). New York, NY: Praeger.

Rice, L. N. (1988). Integration and the client-centered relationship. *Journal of Integrative and Eclectic Psychotherapy, 7,* 291–302.

Rice, L. N. (1992). From naturalistic observation of psychotherapy process to micro theories of change. In S. Toukmanian & D. Rennie (Eds.), *Psychotherapy process research: Paradigmatic and narrative approaches* (pp. 1–21). Newbury Park, CA: Sage.

Rice, L. N., & Gaylin, N. (1973). Personality processes reflected in client vocal style and Rorschach performance. *Journal of Counseling and Clinical Psychology, 40,* 133–138. doi:10.1037/h0034052

Rice, L. N., & Greenberg, L. S. (Eds.). (1984). *Patterns of change: Intensive analysis of psychotherapy process* (pp. 29–66). New York, NY: Guilford Press.

Rice, L. N., & Greenberg, L. S. (1991). Two affective change events in client-centered therapy. In J. Safran & L. Greenberg (Eds.), *Emotion, psychotherapy, and change* (pp. 197–226). New York: Guilford Press.

Rice, L. N., & Greenberg, L. S. (1992). Humanistic approaches to psychotherapy. In D. K. Freedheim, H. J. Freudenberger, J. W. Kessler, S. B. Messer, D. R Peterson, H. H. Strupp, & P. L Wachtel (Eds.), *History of psychotherapy: A century of change* (pp. 197–224). Washington, DC: American Psychological Association.

Rice, L. N., & Kerr, G. P. (1986). Measures of client and therapist vocal quality. In L. S. Greenberg & W. M. Pinsof (Eds.), *The psychotherapeutic process: A Research Handbook* (pp. 73–105). New York: Guilford Press.

Rice, L. N., Koke, C. J., Greenberg, L. S., & Wagstaff, A. K. (1979). *Manual for the client vocal quality classification system.* Toronto, Canada: York University Counseling and Development Center.

Rice, L. N., & Saperia, E. P. (1984). Task analysis and the resolution of problematic reactions. In L. N. Rice & L. S. Greenberg (Eds.), *Patterns of change: Intensive analysis of psychotherapy process* (pp. 29–66). New York< NY: Guilford Press.

Rice, L. N., & Wagstaff, A. K. (1967). Client vocal quality and expressive styles and indexes of productive psychotherapy. *Journal of Consulting and Clinical Psychology, 31,* 557<en>563.

Rice, L. N., Watson, J., & Greenberg, L. S. (1993). *A measure of clients' expressive stance.* Toronto, Ontario, Canada: York University.

Rogers, C. R. (1951). *Client-centered therapy: Its current practice, implications, and theory.* Boston, MA: Houghton-Mifflin.

Safran, J. D., & Muran, J. C. (2000). *Negotiating the therapeutic alliance: A relational treatment guide.* New York, NY: Guilford Press.

Watson, J. C., Gordon, L. B., Stermac, L., Steckley, P., & Kalogerakos, F. (2003). Comparing the effectiveness of process-experiential with cognitive-behavioral psychotherapy in the treatment of depression. *Journal of Consulting and Clinical Psychology, 71,* 773–781. doi:10.1037/0022–006X.71.4.773

Watson, J. C., & Greenberg, L. S. (1996). Pathways to change in the psychotherapy of depression: Relating process to session change and outcome. *Psychotherapy 33,* 262–274. doi:10.1037/0033–3204.33.2.262

Watson, J. C., & Rice, L. N. (1985, June) *A test of a model of problematic reaction points.* Paper presented to the Society for Psychotherapy Research, Evanston, IL.

Wiseman, H., & Rice, L. N. (1989). Sequential analyses of therapist-client interaction during change events: A task focused approach. *Journal of Consulting and Clinical Psychology, 57,* 281–286. doi:10.1037/0022–006X.57.2.281

Wiseman, H. (1992). Conceptually-based interpersonal process recall (IPR) of change events: What clients tell us about our microtheory of change. In S. Toukmanian & D. Rennie (Eds.), *Psychotherapy process research: Paradigmatic and narrative approaches* (pp. 51–76). Newbury Park, CA: Sage.

16

LESLIE GREENBERG: EMOTIONAL CHANGE LEADS TO POSITIVE OUTCOME

RHONDA N. GOLDMAN, LYNNE ANGUS, AND JEREMY D. SAFRAN

By implementing innovative research strategies that creatively address meaningful questions of central concern to researchers and clinicians alike, Leslie Greenberg has consistently kept the field of psychotherapy research on its intellectual edge.

MAJOR CONTRIBUTIONS

It is not an overstatement to suggest that over the course of his career as a psychotherapy researcher, Les Greenberg has significantly influenced paradigm shifts, particularly with respect to psychotherapy process–outcome research methodology. As a young academic, he questioned the primary focus of process–outcome research, suggesting that the key subject of inquiry for psychotherapy researchers should not be "What treatment for whom?" but "What *intervention* at *what time* for whom?" Not satisfied with simply challenging psychotherapy researchers to address the complexity of psychotherapy change processes, he and his mentor, Laura Rice, proceeded to develop and validate a highly innovative *events-based* research paradigm that was designed to precisely answer the question he had posed. The events-based approach introduced a new, rational–empirical method for the intensive analysis of psychotherapy events—task analysis—that held the promise of providing greater understanding and specification of productive client performances and the interventions that facilitate them. Over the next 20 years, events-based task analyses of specific emotion markers and therapy tasks would become an important line of research for Greenberg and his collaborators (Elliott, Watson, Goldman, & Greenberg, 2004; Greenberg & Pinsof, 1986; Greenberg, Rice, and Elliott, 1993), resulting in the development and refinement of a unique, integrative psychotherapy model.

In a series of publications, Greenberg and graduate student Jeremy Safran argued that emotional responses, not cognitions or beliefs, prompted primary evaluations of goal attainment success and signaled the personal significance of events for clients, and as such should be the focus of therapeutic intervention. In *Emotion in Psychotherapy* (1987), they began to articulate the principles of working with emotion. With another graduate student, Susan Johnson, Greenberg suggested that emotion as a primary communication system was of major importance for couple therapy (Greenberg & Johnson, 1988). Ultimately, this gave way to the development of two innovative, research-supported psychotherapy approaches—emotion-focused therapy (EFT) for individuals and couples. Emotion-focused psychotherapy integrates gestalt methods into a client-centered relationship and synthesizes emotional, systemic, and constructivist perspectives. Together with collaborators and authors Laura Rice and Robert Elliott, Greenberg first laid down the guiding principles of the individual approach in the book *Facilitating Emotional Change*.

Having articulated a theoretically grounded, integrative model of humanistic psychotherapy, Greenberg and his coauthors now found themselves challenged by fellow psychotherapy researchers and funding agencies to empirically demonstrate the efficacy of their new treatment approach to working with clients. Although psychotherapy process researchers at heart, he and his colleagues received a major grant in 1992 to compare the effects of client-centered and process–experiential therapy for depression and ultimately to relate process to both session and final outcome. Over the years, strong empirical support has also been established for the efficacy of the individual EFT approach for depression (Goldman, Greenberg, & Angus, 2006; Greenberg & Watson, 1998) for resolving unfinished business and promoting forgiveness to help resolve emotional injuries in individuals (Paivio & Greenberg, 1995) and for the emotion-focused couples approach (Johnson, Hunsley, Greenberg, &, Schindler, 1999; Goldman & Greenberg, 1992).

EARLY BEGINNINGS

Leslie Greenberg was born and raised in Johannesburg, South Africa, and he witnessed the brutal impact of apartheid policies throughout his childhood. Sensitized to the negative impact of religious and racial prejudice as a young man of Jewish heritage, he became actively involved with student organizations fighting to effect change in the racist policies of the South African government. His political activism was grounded in humanist values that held that all human beings—irrespective of religion, race, or gender—are worthy of respect and compassionate care. Importantly, it was in the charged political context of the South African apartheid government that Greenberg would became aware of the abusive impact of unchecked power in social interactions and the need to assertively challenge those abuses, to effect positive change. It is these formative experiences in South Africa that prepared Greenbverg, later in life, to take a leadership role in championing humanistic approaches to therapeutic practice that embrace the values of mutuality and egalitarianism in therapeutic relationships. Greenberg's commitment to questioning the received wisdom of dominant cultural norms and expectations—evidenced in political systems or scientific communities—and to developing innovative methodological, theoretical, and treatment alternatives to address those concerns would mark his evolution as an innovative psychotherapy researcher and consummate clinical practitioner.

After he finished his undergraduate studies in engineering at the University of Johannesburg, Les and his wife Brenda found themselves at a turning point. In the face of a growing sense of disillusionment about the possibility of effecting significant political change in South Africa during their lifetimes, they made the difficult decision to leave their beloved homeland and emigrate to Canada—a young country that shared their cherished values of social caring and egalitarianism.

Les Greenberg began a master's program in systems engineering at McMaster University in Hamilton, Ontario, in 1968. Toward the end of that program he first became aware of the work of Laura Rice—a client-centered therapist and psychotherapy process researcher at York University who was interested in the role of curiosity in human motivation. As Rice's research interests dovetailed with his growing interest in understanding the complexity of knowing human systems, rather than machines, Greenberg made the fateful decision to meet with Dr. Rice at York. It was the end of the 1960s, a time of radical social change and redefinition for the culture at large, and so it would be for him.

Laura Rice decided that she would like to sponsor Greenberg's admission to the doctoral program at York. Rice was a client-centered therapist trained by Carl Rogers. Steeped as he was in the existential views of Camus and Sartre, Greenberg saw that client-centered theory fit with his belief system. He also felt critical of behaviorist and psychodynamic authors who seemed to adopt an overly simplistic view toward the complexity and richness of human experience. He was much more attracted to the writings of Carl Rogers and Eugene Gendlin. It was in graduate school that Greenberg completed a 3-year training at the Gestalt Institute of Toronto with Harvey Freedman, a protégé of Fritz Perls. He was beginning to lay the groundwork for his integrative Experiential approach to therapy, although it was not coherent at the time. Under Rice's tutelage he completed his ground-breaking dissertation study and, in so doing, introduced an innovative approach to psychotherapy process research—events-based task analysis—that would significantly advance the field of psychotherapy research as a whole.

ACCOMPLISHMENTS

Psychotherapy Process–Outcome Methods

Greenberg's collaboration with Laura Rice and background in humanistic therapy, as well as an interest in philosophical views of science that saw humans as complex, whole systems, contributed to the repudiation of reductionistic research methods for understanding the complex process of psychotherapy. In their collaborative quest to understand the process of change in therapy, he and Rice recognized that much of the existing psychotherapy research assumed that people were similar on some individual difference variable and would react to specific treatments in a somewhat homogenous fashion. The assumption was contrary to their observation and had received little research confirmation. Greenberg began to focus on process research as a means to help him further refine his understanding of how therapy works. Rice and Greenberg (1984) were the first in the field of psychotherapy research to propose that researchers study groups of episodes or *events* drawn from therapy sessions, rather than studying groups of people. They argued that the criterion for forming samples in psychotherapy process–outcome research should be an observable process *marker* that indicates that a client is evidencing a particular state or problem space, at a specific moment in time. They also advocated the intensive analysis of contextual, in-session events performed at markers for discovering recurring moments of change.

Around this time he met Juan Pascual-Leone, a neo-Piagetian cognitive developmental psychologist at York University, who had a broad interest in the complexity of human development and growth. Pascual-Leone introduced Greenberg to task analysis—a method that integrates both theory and rigorous observation of specific in-situation performances, for the identification of heuristic performance models (Pascual-Leone, 1976). Greenberg promoted the implementation of the method for psychotherapy process research studies to build models of therapeutic events across therapy sessions, such as, for example, the two-chair dialogue for intrapsychic conflict, a therapeutic technique adapted from gestalt therapy. First generating a theoretical model of clients "performing" the event, researchers could then study multiple two-chair dialogue events across different therapies, successively comparing the existing theoretical model with observation, allowing the model to be continually influenced and thus refined. The final stage involves testing and validating the model, for example, measuring the process during task work and relating it to outcome.

In his dissertation study, published in 1975, Greenberg laid out the principles of an events-based approach to psychotherapy process-outcome research. *Patterns of Change* (1984), edited with Laura Rice, presented a series of studies that employed task analysis. The method has been used subsequently to model many other EFT tasks.

Over the past 20 years, the main focus of Greenberg's process–outcome research program has been to further understand the relationship between emotional processes and change in therapy. For instance, Goldman, Greenberg, and Pos (2005) looked at the relationship between theme-related depth of experiencing and outcome in experiential therapy with depressed clients. Analyses revealed that client level of experiencing (EXP) on core themes in the last half of therapy was a significant predictor of reduced symptom distress and increased self-esteem. Experiencing on core themes accounted for outcome variance over and above that accounted for by early EXP and alliance, demonstrating that an early emotional processing skill, although likely an advantage, appears not to be as important as the ability to acquire and/or increase depth of emotional processing throughout therapy. Studies that examined expressed arousal showed that a combination of visible emotional arousal and experiencing was a better predictor of outcome than either index alone, supporting the hypothesis that it is not only arousal of emotion but also reflection on aroused emotion that produces change (Missirlian, Toukmanian, Warwar, & Greenberg, 2005). Finally, a recent study showed that clients with better outcomes expressed significantly more productive, highly aroused emotions than did clients with poor outcomes, suggesting that it is productivity, especially of highly aroused emotions, that is important in facilitating change (Greenberg, Auszra, & Hermann, 2007).

Emotion-Focused Psychotherapy

After completing his PhD in clinical-counseling psychology at York in 1975, Greenberg began his academic career as a young faculty member in the

Department of Counselling at the University of British Columbia. A year earlier, while participating on a panel at the Society for Psychotherapy Research (SPR), Greenberg had been introduced to Bordin's model of the working alliance. He and his new graduate student, Adam Horvath, became intrigued with the idea of developing a client self-report measure that could capture the separate contributions of bonds, tasks, and goals for the development of productive therapeutic relationships. The Working Alliance Inventory (WAI)—one of the most widely used alliance measures in the psychotherapy research field—was the result of this highly productive research collaboration. *The Working Alliance* (Horvath & Greenberg, 1994) included seminal contributions from psychotherapy researchers representing a broad range of therapy treatment approaches.

Greenberg discovered, in the context of his own psychotherapy process research program—using the WAI—that task alliance was a stronger predictor of outcome than the bond component or empathy (Horvath & Greenberg, 1989). Although challenging basic assumptions of his client-centered training at York, this research finding provided Greenberg with empirical support for his growing sense that client involvement in therapeutic tasks was as important as empathic engagement, for productive therapeutic outcomes. In his clinical practice with individuals, he had become increasingly impressed with how gestalt therapy interventions could rapidly evoke active experiencing in clients. He also felt, however, that the gestalt approach neglected the importance of empathy and paid insufficient attention to the therapeutic relationship. Searching for a way to integrate the "active ingredients" of both approaches, Greenberg began to wonder if the art and skill of therapy might not involve a balance between "being" and "doing," or bond and task principles. Thus began his odyssey to integrate gestalt active interventions with client-centered relational conditions, a journey that would arrive at an innovative, integrative form of humanistic psychotherapy–EFT.

Serendipitously, around this time Greenberg began a highly generative collaboration with a young graduate student named Jeremy Safran. Informed by developments in the newly emerging fields of emotion theory and research, they set out to develop a systematic theoretical framework that addressed the contribution of emotion processes for productive therapeutic outcomes. They took issue with the cognitive therapy proposal that people need to bring troublesome emotions into line with reason's dictates. Specifically, they argued that the arousal and symbolization of primary emotion processes, and the activation of core emotion schemes and their attendant action tendencies, were the essential ground of new meaning making and sustained client change and should be the focus of therapeutic interventions. Their articulation of a coherent, theoretical model of client emotional processing in psychotherapy (Greenberg & Safran, 1987) would provide a conceptual framework for the development of a new, integrative emotion-focused approach to working with clients and couples.

Greenberg returned to York in 1986 as a full professor of clinical psychology. His career was soaring, and he was receiving increased recognition. At this time he became more active in SPR, serving as its president in 1989. Informed by recent developments in his approach to working with emotions in psychotherapy, Greenberg began actively collaborating with his mentor, Laura Rice, once again. Rice had become increasingly receptive to Greenberg's interest in gestalt methods, and an important collaboration had begun with Robert Elliott, who was interested in the client's perspective on the process of change. The stage was now set for Greenberg and his collaborators to fully articulate a new, integrative, research-supported treatment approach that would significantly advance the field of psychotherapy research and practice. They laid down the principles of their new, brief therapy approach in *Facilitating Emotional Change* (1993), which provided a theoretical background of the approach, articulated relationship and task principles, and provided step-by-step guides to working with six key markers and tasks in process–experiential therapy (now more commonly referred to as emotion-focused therapy). Drawing on a new conceptualization of the contribution of emotion processes for client change, they viewed emotional experience as influencing modes of processing, guiding attention, and enhancing memory and much behavior in the service of emotional regulation and attachment.

Although at heart a process researcher, Greenberg felt increasingly challenged to address the question of whether brief humanistic treatments—especially EFT—could demonstrate treatment efficacy with clinical samples that had been assessed on standardized treatment outcome measures. He also began to appreciate that by conducting randomized, controlled treatment trials, he and Rice could have an important impact on the field of psychotherapy research practice wherein humanistic approaches—such as emotion-focused and client-centered therapy—would once again be viewed as viable and efficacious. Greenberg also saw the completion of a clinical trial as an excellent opportunity to intensively investigate client change processes.

In 1992, with Laura Rice as his coinvestigator, Les Greenberg received a National Institute of Mental Health grant in support of a randomized, controlled trial comparing brief client-centered and brief process–experiential therapy for depression that proposed to relate key client process variables to both session and final outcomes. This was also the beginning of an important collaboration with Jeanne Watson, a student of Laura Rice who came on to direct the research study. Results showed that both client-centered and process–experiential therapy were effective treatments for alleviating depression, although process–experiential therapy was more effective in alleviating interpersonal problems and increasing self-esteem (Greenberg & Watson,

1998). This finding was based on a sample size of 34 clients (17 in each group), however, and was moderately powerful according to research criteria but perhaps not powerful enough to demonstrate differences. He and Lynne Angus then received a grant in 1998 from the Ontario Mental Health Foundation to conduct a replication study, and they brought on Rhonda Goldman to direct it. Results demonstrated that with a second sample of 38 clients (19 in each group), EFT (formerly known as process experiential therapy) was equally effective in alleviating interpersonal problems and increasing self-esteem but more effective in alleviating depressive symptoms. When the two samples were combined, providing sufficient power to find differences, EFT was found to be more effective on all indices of change (Goldman, Greenberg, & Angus, 2006). Significant differences among treatments were found at termination on all indices of change, and the differences were maintained at 6-month and 18-month follow-ups (Ellison, Greenberg, Goldman, & Angus, 2009). Given the number of research studies supporting it, EFT for depression was recently listed by Division 12 (Society of Clinical Psychology) of the American Psychological Association as an evidence-based treatment.

In addition to demonstrating the effectiveness of EFT for the treatment of depression, Greenberg and colleagues concurrently conducted research demonstrating the effectiveness of EFT for treating people with emotional injuries associated with developmentally significant others from their past (Paivio & Greenberg, 1995). By establishing substantive empirical support for the efficacy of client-centered and emotion-focused psychotherapy for depression, Les and his collaborators have been instrumental in keeping humanistic approaches in the mainstream of psychotherapy research, training, and practice.

In the past decade, Greenberg continued to develop and differentiate his theory of emotion in psychotherapy, publishing a book explicating how to work with emotions (Greenberg & Paivio, 1997), another titled *Emotion-Focused Therapy* (Greenberg, 2002), in which he described the main job of the therapist as being one of coaching people to become more emotionally intelligent, and yet another in 2007 (Greenberg & Watson), in which he spelled out the emotion-focused approach to depression. From an emotion-focused perspective, disorder is seen as resulting from failures in the dyadic regulation of affect, avoidance of affect, traumatic learning, and lack of processing of emotion. Awareness, regulation, and transformation through accessing an alternate emotion are offered as three empirically supported principles of emotional change.

Emotion-Focused Therapy for Couples

Upon returning from a sabbatical in 1980 at the Mental Research Institute in Palo Alto, California, where he learned about the psychotherapeutic treatment of couples and families, Greenberg was surprised at how impressed he was with the importance of power dynamics in relationships (given his political experiences in South Africa). Feeling also, however, that an effective therapeutic approach for couples needed to emphasize a strong relationship and a focus on underlying emotions, he and his graduate student Susan Johnson began to develop an approach to couples therapy that integrated systemic and experiential approaches. The result was an EFT approach for couples (EFT-C; Greenberg & Johnson, 1988). His interest in studying couples had evolved mainly from his research on resolving intrapsychic conflict, in which he found that softening of the critic led to resolution. The EFT-C process looked very much like interpersonal conflict resolution, in which a critical or blaming partner softens and a withdrawn partner reveals. It was for the purpose of studying how couples resolved conflict that the couple therapy manual and Greenberg's first outcome study were first developed. As we have said, at heart he was always a process researcher. After its initial development, Greenberg moved away from the promotion of EFT-C to concentrate on research on individual therapy, making room for Johnson to integrate attachment theory (Johnson & Whiffen, 2003) and successfully promote its development. Over the years strong empirical support has been established for the efficacy of EFT-C in reducing couples' distress (Johnson, Hunsley, Greenberg, & Schindler, 1999). Greenberg became more involved again in research on EFT-C only after he had developed a study of the process of forgiveness in both individuals and couples. Research evaluated the effects of EFT-C for couples when one member had an unresolved emotional injury resulting from the partner's actions (Greenberg, Warwar, & Malcolm, 2003) and demonstrated that couples scored significantly better than waiting-list controls on all indices of change.

Thus began the resurgence of his effort to develop EFT-C and investigate it further. In *Emotion-Focused Couples Therapy: The Dynamics of Emotion, Love, and Power*, Greenberg and Goldman (2008) further delineated the approach to couples that he originally inspired. The book expands the framework of the therapy, focusing more intently on the role of emotion in marital therapy and the importance of both self and system change through the promotion of both self-soothing and other-soothing. The book outlines explicitly how to work with anger, sadness, fear, and shame, as well as with positive emotions, and focuses on both the dominance dimension of couples interactions as well as the attachment dimension.

Les Greenberg has significantly influenced the field of psychotherapy research, beginning with the events-based paradigm that shifted the emphasis of psychotherapy research to a focus on the process and context of psychotherapy to understand how change occurs. While he may not have set out to create a new approach to psychotherapy, continued research efforts designed to articulate how therapy works eventually led to the development of an integrative approach that marries client-centered therapy and gestalt methods and integrates modern emotion theory to create EFT. This was further adapted for couples with an integration of systemic, interactional therapy theory. Research efforts have resulted in the establishment of empirical support for these therapies and further articulation of how emotional change leads to positive outcome in psychotherapy.

REFERENCES

Ellison, J. A., Greenberg, L. S., Goldman, R., & Angus, L. (2009). Maintenance of gains following experiential therapies for depression. *Journal of Consulting and Clinical Psychology, 77*(1), 103–112. doi:10.1037/a0014653

Elliott, R., Watson, J., Goldman, R. N., & Greenberg, L. S. (2004). *Learning emotion-focused therapy: The process-experiential approach to change.* Washington, DC: American Psychological Assocation. doi:10.1037/10725-000

Goldman, A., & Greenberg, L. (1992). Comparison of an integrated systemic and emotionally focused approach to couples therapy. *Journal of Consulting and Clinical Psychology, 60,* 962–969.

Goldman, R. N., Greenberg, L. S., & Angus, L. A. (2006). The effects of adding emotion-focused interventions to the client-centered relationship conditions in the treatment of depression. *Psychotherapy Research, 16,* 536–546. doi:10.1080/10503300600589456

Goldman, R., Greenberg, L., & Pos, A. (2005). Depth of emotional experience and outcome. *Psychotherapy Research, 15,* 248–260. doi:10.1080/10503300512331385188

Greenberg, L. S. (2002). *Emotion-focused therapy: Coaching clients to work through their feelings.* Washington, DC: American Psychological Assocation. doi:10.1037/10447-000

Greenberg, L. S., Auszra, L., & Hermann, I. R. (2007). The relationship among emotional productivity, emotional arousal and outcome in experiential therapy of depression. *Psychotherapy Research, 17,* 482–493. doi:10.1080/10503300600977800

Greenberg, L. S., & Goldman, R. N. (2008). *Emotion-focused couples therapy: the dynamics of emotion, love, and power.* Washington, DC: American Psychological Assocation. doi:10.1037/11750-000

Greenberg, L. S., & Johnson, S. M. (1988). *Emotionally focused therapy for couples.* New York, NY: Guilford Press.

Greenberg, L. S., & Paivio, S. C. (1997). *Working with emotions in psychotherapy.* New York, NY: Guilford Press.

Greenberg, L. S., & Pinsof, W. M. (1986). *The psychotherapeutic process: A research handbook.* New York, NY: Guilford Press.

Greenberg, L. S., Rice, L. N., & Elliott, R. (1993). *Facilitating emotional change: The moment by moment process.* New York, NY: Guilford Press.

Greenberg, L. S., & Safran, J. (1987). *Emotion in Psychotherapy*. New York, NY: Guilford.

Greenberg, L. S. Warwar, S., & Malcolm, W. (2003, June). The differential effects of emotion-focused therapy and psychoeducation, for the treatment of emotional injury: Letting go and forgiving. Paper presented for panel at a meeting of the Society for Psychotherapy Research, Weimar, Germany

Greenberg, L. S., & Watson, J. (1998). Experiential therapy of depression: Differential effects of client-centered relationship conditions and process experiential interventions. *Psychotherapy Research, 8*, 210–224. doi:10.1093/ptr/8.2.210

Horvath, A., & Greenberg, L. S. (1989). Development and validation of the Working Alliance Inventory. *Journal of Counseling Psychology, 36*, 223–233.

Horvath, A., & Greenberg, L. S. (Eds.). (1994). *The working alliance: Theory, research, and practice*. New York, NY: Wiley.

Johnson, S. M., Hunsley, J., Greenberg, G., & Schindler, D. (1999). Emotionally focused couples therapy: Status and challenges. *Clinical Psychology: Science and Practice, 6*(1), 67–69. doi:10.1093/clipsy/6.1.67

Johnson, S., & Whiffen, V. (Eds.). (2003). *Attachment theory: A perspective for couple and family therapy*. New York, NY: Guilford Press.

Missirlian, T. M., Toukmanian, S., Warwar, S., & Greenberg, L. (2005). Emotional arousal, client perceptual processing, and the working alliance in experiential psychotherapy for depression. *Journal of Consulting and Clinical Psychology, 73*, 861–871. doi:10.1037/0022-006X.73.5.861

Pascual-Leone, J. (1976). Metasubjective problems of constructive cognition: Forms of knowing and their psychological mechanisms. *Canadian Psychological Review, 17*, 110–125. doi:10.1037/h0081828

Paivio, S., & Greenberg, L. S. (1995). Resolving "unfinished business": Efficacy of experiential therapy using the empty-chair dialogue. *Journal of Consulting and Clinical Psychology, 63*, 419–425.

Rice, L. N., & Greenberg, L. S. (Eds). (1984). *Patterns of change: Intensive analysis of psychotherapy Practice*. New York, NY: Guilford Press.

C. RELATIONSHIP VARIABLES

17

EDWARD S. BORDIN: INNOVATIVE THINKER, INFLUENTIAL INVESTIGATOR, AND INSPIRING TEACHER

MICHAEL J. CONSTANTINO, NICHOLAS LADANY, AND THOMAS D. BORKOVEC

Those who knew Ed Bordin personally were touched by his humanity, integrity, and intellectual brilliance. Those who knew him only through his professional writing were touched in a similar fashion, a feat not easily attained. As authors of this chapter, we all have felt the ease and effortlessness that comes from reading and rereading Bordin's work. Moreover, whether through direct or indirect experience with Bordin, we all have been inspired by his vision and foresight, impressive scholarship, respect for others' ideas, and integrative spirit.

Irene Elkin (1993) noted in her Society for Psychotherapy Research (SPR) tribute to Bordin that he was "one of the most important figures in psychotherapy research, who made some of the most important contributions to our field." In fact, Bordin had a remarkable breadth of professional interests about which he wrote and studied. By his own account, Bordin (1987) had two "enduring preoccupations." The first focused on vocational choice and personal development, whereas the second focused on personal change process and a theory of working alliance as the cornerstone of counseling and psychotherapy. However, our informal "factor analysis" of Bordin's published work also revealed at least seven other broad and multifaceted factors: (a) dimensions of the psychotherapy and counseling process (including client, therapist, and relational factors); (b) psychotherapy integration; (c) psychometrics (as related to the measurement of such constructs as ambiguity, depth of interpretation, resistance, and client compliance with free association); (d) psychotherapy research and design (including laboratory and effectiveness studies); (e) statistical issues; (f) diagnosis; and (g) supervision. As a psychotherapy researcher, Bordin argued for situating the science of psychotherapy within a larger context of human behavior, thus championing the integration of basic and applied knowledge. And as an exemplary scientist–practitioner, Bordin also understood the inherent tensions in clinical and research motivations and agendas, as he eloquently discussed in his article "Curiosity, Compassion, and Doubt: The Dilemma of the Psychologist" (Bordin, 1966). With his keen understanding of this dilemma, devotion to both sides of this false dichotomy, and his genuine synthesizing character, Bordin's career personified the marriage of science and practice. In the remainder of this essay, we elaborate on Bordin's personal life and professional contributions, with particular attention to his pioneering working alliance theory.

EARLY BEGINNINGS

Edward Bordin was born in Pennsylvania on November 7, 1913, to Russian Jewish immigrant parents. He was the youngest of three boys. Bordin (1987) characterized his father as reflective and analytical and his mother as driven. Based on their influences and his birth order, he described himself as an outsider with a questioning attitude, an "analytical, oppositional character" (1987, p. 359). To us, this self-concept seems synonymous with our reflections of Bordin as a constructively critical, innovative, and forward thinker. Equipped with his analytical disposition, Bordin earned his bachelor's and master's degrees at Temple University. He earned his doctorate in 1942 at Ohio State, where he overlapped for several years with Carl Rogers, who was a professor at Ohio State from 1940 to 1945, and engaged in substantial intellectual discourse with J. R. Kantor, to whom he acknowledged owing an intellectual debt (Bordin, 1987). After 3 years in the armed forces, Bordin took his first academic positions at the University of Minnesota and then Washington State University. In 1948, he was hired at the University of Michigan as an associate professor of psychology and the director of the Counseling Division of the Bureau of Psychological Services (Galinsky, 1995). Bordin was promoted to full professor in 1955. During his long tenure at Michigan, Bordin made significant theoretical and empirical contributions, as well as significantly influencing students he taught and mentored. Galinsky (1995) described Bordin as a first-rate teacher not only because of his own enthusiasm for new ideas and his wish to stretch students' capacity to think about complex issues but also because of the richness and breadth of his knowledge, which spanned many areas of psychology. (p. 172)

Edward Bordin, with his low-key and respectful, yet dynamic and influential personality, died in La Jolla, California, on August 24, 1992.

MAJOR CONTRIBUTIONS

Bordin (1987), during his 1986 Leona Tyler Award Address (an honor bestowed on him by the Division of Counseling Psychology of the American Psychological Association [APA]), humbly described having two enduring preoccupations. However, one could view his early career focus on vocational decision-making and his later career focus on his working alliance theory as the end points on a continuum of influence tied together by related and reciprocal contributions in counseling and psychotherapy integration, process, and research. We use these categories as organizational heuristics in recounting Bordin's major contributions.

Vocational Decision-Making

Dissatisfied with and critical of the dominant psychological testing tradition, an attitude he shared with Carl Rogers (see Orlinsky & Rønnestad, 2000), Bordin became interested in his early career in moving beyond test scores to understanding personal context as a determinant of vocational choice and satisfaction. Drawing on psychoanalytic constructs such as resistance, repression, and conflict, as well as Eriksonian (1959) constructs such as self-identity, Bordin strived to broaden the field's understanding of the vocational choice process and its related anxieties, expectations, and behaviors by understanding the client personally, developmentally, and dynamically. In this vein, and consistent with Rogers (1942, 1951), Bordin rejected narrow rationalism and the counselor-as-expert perspective, instead promoting a dynamically based interpersonal model first applied to vocational counseling and later broadened to the counseling process in general (which he defined as almost any human condition inviting intervention by another; e.g., Bordin, 1948, 1955, 1980a). In his 1986 Leona Tyler Award Address, Bordin acknowledged that his early focus on personal development and personality as factors in vocational decision making generated his later working alliance theory. In particular, he likened the importance of realistic and compatible expectations for vocational counseling (e.g., a client understanding that such counseling is not simply a matter of having test results interpreted back to her or him) to the psychotherapy process (e.g., a client understanding that an expert therapist will not simply prescribe a uniform road map to recovery). However, before fully elaborating his alliance theory, Bordin's academic trajectory turned next to the notions of integration and process, both conceptually and empirically.

Counseling and Psychotherapy Integration, Process, and Research

Although Bordin agreed with Rogers's denunciation of rationalism and counselor-as-expert perspective and the latter's promotion of the therapeutic relationship, he also respectfully took issue with Rogers's dogmatic view of what separated directive from nondirective in therapeutic approach (Orlinsky & Rønnestad, 2000). As Bordin (1987) recounted, when he was at the University of Minnesota he was lumped by Rogerians into the directive camp. However, his same philosophies were viewed as nondirective by the psychoanalytic thinkers at the University of Michigan. Bordin discussed how it was through this tension, and his "analytical oppositional" character, that he began exploring in depth the values, virtues, and shortcomings of both the directive and nondirective camps and the psychoanalytic and client-centered philosophies. In the aforementioned 1986 address, he noted:

> I was saved from a chameleonlike eclecticism and led toward true integration. I assumed that each of the proponents was seeing and expressing an important point of view. I thought that each was concentrating on different aspects of persons as well as on different kinds of persons with different pathological states. Rather than choosing one approach, I selected aspects of how they helped another and developed understandings of how the situation and the disposition of the person being helped influenced response. (Bordin, 1987, p. 362)

It was perhaps at this stage of his career that Bordin's name started to become, from our perspective, synonymous with the notions of synthesis and integration within the counseling and psychotherapy fields. In fact, it was his integrationist thinking that led him to collaborate at Michigan with such colleagues as Harold Raush and Allen Dittman in examining the active ingredients of psychotherapeutic change. This quest for uncovering what makes psychotherapy work began with the careful development of psychometrically sound measures of ambiguity, depth of interpretation, client resistance, and client compliance with free association (all constructs that underscore his psychoanalytic background).

Through his focus on specific psychotherapeutic processes, Bordin was calling for a paradigm shift in treatment research that focused on the dismantling of treatment packages to isolate causative change factors, with such work guided by theories that cut across articulated treatment packages. In this call, one can see Bordin's responsiveness to and immense influence on the field of psychotherapy research, including ideas that have subsequently persisted and matured, such as the scientific value of component control designs (e.g., Behar & Borkovec, 2003) and the clinical and empirical value of uncovering and rigorously studying common treatment and change principles (e.g., Castonguay & Beutler, 2006). Bordin impressively attempted to reconcile the tension between proponents of the so-called common, or nonspecific, factors and proponents of theory-specific factors. He argued that although all therapies have in common the importance of a quality working alliance, they also possess diverse tasks or task sets. He advocated the use of both the clinical laboratory and the naturalistic clinical setting to isolate and test the influence of specific tasks on various kinds of clients. Again we see in Bordin's ideas the importance of understanding the influence of personal context and development on counseling and psychotherapy interventions. We also see a genuine attempt to integrate at all levels of analysis both science and practice, basic and applied. In her SPR tribute, Elkin (1993) noted that Bordin perhaps made the strongest and most elegant case for such integration and the necessary reciprocal influence between the lab and clinic. And in doing so, he also cautioned researchers against "oversimplification" in the lab and the danger of neglecting naturalistic phenomena related to the construct under study (Bordin, 1965).

To us, such forward thinking could be viewed as a precursor to important contemporary developments, such as the bringing together of scientists and practitioners to preserve the interests of both parties and to advance clinical knowledge through collaboration (see, e.g., Borkovec, Echemendia, Ragusea, & Ruiz, 2001), a prediction that Bordin made in his article "Counseling Psychology in the Year 2000: Prophecy of Wish Fulfillment?" (Bordin, 1980b). In fact, as Elkin noted in her tribute, Bordin remarkably anticipated many developments in three domains: clinical (e.g., the need for developing a foundational alliance with schizoid and borderline clients), statistical (e.g., the need for a reliable statistic that would take base rates into account), and research (e.g., the need for developing coding schemes to capture interpersonal process and to account for individual bias of coders within rating systems). Many such issues were addressed in his "masterful research blueprint" (Galinsky, 1995, p. 172), *Research Strategies in Psychotherapy* (Bordin, 1974). The timelessness of this celebrated contribution was underscored in its recent endorsement by several contributors to an SPR Web discussion list on classic psychotherapy process research references.

Working Alliance Theory

In articulating his thoughts on a new tack in psychotherapy theory and research, Bordin was convinced that it would be based in the working alliance construct (Bordin, 1987). Always interested in how dimensions of the counseling process interact with the personal attributes of the person seeking a certain type of help and change, Bordin refocused the field on the client–therapist relationship. Before his seminal working alliance addresses (Bordin, 1976, 1980c) and article (Bordin, 1979), research interest in the relationship construct had started to wane, likely as a function of inconsistent findings related to Rogers's (1957) necessary and sufficient conditions hypothesis. Although lauding Rogers's relationship focus, Bordin drew on his own psychoanalytic background to propose a novel conceptualization of the alliance that focused on the perpetual negotiation of therapeutic goals and tasks between client and therapist as a function of client and therapist characteristics and the related strain of the work. As he noted in his 1986 address:

> I do not find it credible that change goals are interchangeable and that all of the therapeutic tasks that are embedded in various treatment packages are alternate paths to the same goal. It seems more likely to me that each of many sensitive and creative therapists arrived at methods that were appropriate to the kinds of persons he or she was trying to help who were different from the persons who were being helped by another equally sensitive therapist. (Bordin, 1987, p. 363)

Clearly privileging integration in theory and practice, as well as the person of the client and therapist, Bordin (1979, 1980c) viewed the working alliance as differing in strength and kind. He was central in formulating the alliance as not only scaffolding for subsequent change but also as a change product in and of itself via a process of building and repairing alliance breaks. To Bordin, a central component in such relational negotiation stemmed from understanding individual differences in clients' differential abilities to work through different therapeutic tasks, depending on the specific problems for which they sought change. Embedded in the building and negotiating of working alliances, he argued, is a therapeutic opportunity to tap into and then disrupt self-defeating patterns of the client. As Bordin (1980c) discussed in his SPR presidential address, such working through with the therapist will allow the person to develop new ways of thinking, feeling, or acting with self and others, a process akin to an interpersonal corrective experience complementary to theories set forth by the two other influential theorists in this section of the volume, Donald Kiesler and Lorna Benjamin.

In his discussion of different types of alliances, Bordin (1979, 1980c) also made a distinction between bonds that reflect, to borrow Benjamin's

(2003) term, *regressive loyalty* to the past versus those that reflect, again to borrow Benjamin's term, *growth collaboration*. Bordin also differentiated bonds
that result from collaboration versus those that contribute to collaboration.
To Bordin, it was this latter type that was so central to therapeutic change.
With his clear articulation that the alliance can be both a by-product of collaborative success and a mechanism of subsequent change, Bordin in many
ways anticipated the subsequent standing debate on this issue, and his view
may perhaps still hold the most promise for reconciling these disparate view-
points and for explaining inconsistent findings related to alliance–outcome
associations when controlling for prior change (see, e.g., Barber, 2009). To
Bordin's way of thinking, whether the alliance is a by-product of improvement or a facilitator of it depends on the alliance being measured and who is
engaging in the relationship.

As a pathway to understanding change from different perspectives
under different conditions with different clients, Bordin's (1980c, 1979, 1994)
alliance theory did nothing less than rejuvenate the field of psychotherapy
process research (Elkin, 1993). His conceptualization of the alliance, which
was more easily testable than previous relationship constructs (Orlinsky &
Rønnestad, 2000), was the primary impetus for alliance-focused instrument
development (Horvath & Greenberg, 1989) and what has now been several
decades of rigorous and voluminous alliance research (see Horvath & Bedi,
2002; Castonguay, Constantino, & Grosse Holtforth, 2006). Furthermore,
Bordin was not content with simply measuring the resultant strength of the
working alliance and linking that with outcome. He was keenly interested in
how strong alliances are developed and change over time, an agenda that has
been taken up in a second generation of alliance research (Safran, Muran,
Samstag, & Stevens, 2002). Bordin himself focused on the importance of
client–therapist mutuality with regard to therapy goals and tasks based on the
person of the client and her or his personal paradigm for understanding
pathology and change. Bordin stressed that there will be differences in the
types of goals and tasks that will lend themselves to certain clients, based on
a complex combination of personal characteristics, diagnosis, and context.
Following this tradition, the second wave of alliance research has illuminated
several client characteristics that may help forecast the development of a
quality working alliance, such as expectations for improvement and interpersonal problems (e.g., Constantino, Arnow, Blasey, & Agras, 2005). Bordin
also posited the importance of making mutuality transparent, that is, translating change language in a way that fits a client's own paradigm of problem,
process, and change.

As perhaps one of the most significant barometers of the influence of
a theory, Bordin's (1979, 1994) working alliance theory has not only been
widely cited in relation to individual psychotherapy, but has also been

adapted for contexts outside of its original scope, such as family therapy (e.g., Johnson & Wright, 2002). Moreover, his model of the supervisory work alliance (Bordin, 1983) has been the most investigated variable in psychotherapy supervision and, similar to findings for the therapeutic working alliance, the supervisory working alliance has been recognized as the foundation upon which both effective and ineffective supervision are based (Ladany & Inman, in press).

OTHER ACCOMPLISHMENTS

Bordin had many accomplishments in his academic career. Among the most notable, he served as president of APA's Division of Counseling Psychology in 1955, as well as chair of its Education and Training Board in 1956 and as a member of its Board of Professional Affairs in 1964. As noted, he won the division's Leona Tyler Career Contribution Award in 1986. He was also president of SPR in 1979–1980 and awarded the SPR Senior Career Research Award in 1985. In recognition of his immense and lasting influence on SPR, the society also established an annual student travel award in his name. Bordin was the editor of the *Journal of Consulting Psychology* from 1959 to 1964, and he was an integral participant in the National Institute of Mental Health Outcome Measures Project, to which Elkin (1993) recalled his contributions as "profound." Finally, Bordin is credited with shaping the Counseling Center at the University of Michigan into a highly successful training, research, and student services center (Galinsky, 1995), where he seemed to be on the cutting edge with respect to more recently articulated calls for conducting research in training clinics (e.g., Borkovec, 2004).

CONCLUSION

As should be clear, we agree with Elkin that Bordin was one of the most important and influential figures in the fields of counseling and psychotherapy. He was an innovative thinker who used his creative, integrative, and pioneering character and spirit to both define (when the field of vocational counseling required new definitions) and to rejuvenate (when the field of psychotherapy required rejuvenation of the relationship construct). All the while, Bordin was a masterful scientist, inspirational mentor, and strong leader. As a testament to his influence, we offer the threefold lesson that Ed Bordin taught T. D. Borkovec during a dinner one evening—a lesson that we believe can prove inspirational to anyone who aspires to be a psychotherapy researcher:

1. It does not matter what we choose as a research topic or a theoretical perspective, as long as we go deeply into what we have chosen and do so with intrinsic devotion to the truth and its discovery.
2. The reason that the choice does not matter, as long as the quest is deep and honorable, is that everything is connected to everything else.
3. Differing theories contain differing relative truths at their specific level, but are the same at their metaphorical level, and it is at this level that we can best approximate (though never achieve) absolute truth.

REFERENCES

Barber, J. P. (2009). Toward a working through of some core conflicts in psychotherapy research. *Psychotherapy Research, 19*, 1–12. doi:10.1080/10503300802609680

Behar, E. S., & Borkovec, T. D. (2003). Psychotherapy outcome research. In J. A. Schinka & W. F. Velicer (Eds.), *Handbook of psychology: Research methods in psychology* (Vol. 2, pp. 213–240). New York, NY: Wiley.

Benjamin, L. S. (2003). *Interpersonal reconstructive therapy: Promoting change in nonsponders.* New York, NY: Guilford Press.

Bordin, E. S. (1948). Dimensions of the counseling process. *Journal of Clinical Psychology, 4*, 240–244. doi:10.1002/1097-4679(194807)4:3<240::AID-JCLP2270040306>3.0.CO;2-1

Bordin, E. S. (1955). *Psychological counseling.* East Norwalk, CT: Appleton-Century-Crofts. doi:10.1037/10642-000

Bordin, E. S. (1965). Simplification as a strategy for research in psychotherapy. *Journal of Consulting Psychology, 29*, 493–503. doi:10.1037/h0022760

Bordin, E. S. (1966). Curiosity, compassion, and doubt: The dilemma of the psychologist. *American Psychologist, 21*, 116–121. doi:10.1037/h0023187

Bordin, E. S. (1974). *Research strategies in psychotherapy.* New York, NY: Wiley.

Bordin, E. S. (1976, September). *The working alliance: Basis for a general theory of psychotherapy.* Paper presented at the 1976 American Psychological Association Convention, Washington, DC.

Bordin, E. S. (1979). The generalizability of the psychoanalytic concept of the working alliance. *Psychotherapy, 16*, 252–260. doi:10.1037/h0085885

Bordin, E. S. (1980a). A psychodynamic view of counseling psychology. *Counseling Psychologist, 9*, 62–70. doi:10.1177/001100008000900114

Bordin, E. S. (1980b). Counseling psychology in the year 2000: Prophecy of wish fulfillment? *Counseling Psychologist, 8*, 24–26. doi:10.1177/001100008000800410

Bordin, E. S. (1980c, June). *Of human bonds that bind or free*. Presidential address given at the 11th annual meeting of the Society for Psychotherapy Research, Pacific Grove, CA.

Bordin, E. S. (1983). Supervision in counseling: II. Contemporary models of supervision: A working alliance based model of supervision. *Counseling Psychologist, 11*, 35–42. doi:10.1177/0011000083111007

Bordin, E. S. (1987). 1986 Leona Tyler Address: Aim and trajectory. *Counseling Psychologist, 15*, 358–367. doi:10.1177/0011000087152018

Bordin, E. S. (1994). Theory and research on the therapeutic working alliance: New directions. In A. O. Horvath & L. S. Greenberg (Eds.), *The working alliance: Theory, research and practice* (pp. 13–37). New York, NY: Wiley.

Borkovec, T. D., Echemendia, R. J., Ragusea, S. A., & Ruiz, M. (2001). The Pennsylvania Practice Research Network and future possibilities for clinically meaningful and scientifically rigorous psychotherapy effectiveness research. *Clinical Psychology: Science and Practice, 8*, 155–167. doi:10.1093/clipsy/8.2.155

Borkovec, T. D. (2004). Research in training clinics and practice research networks: A route to the integration of science and practice. *Clinical Psychology: Science and Practice, 11*, 211–215. doi:10.1093/clipsy/bph073

Castonguay, L. G., & Beutler, L. E. (Eds.). (2006). *Principles of therapeutic change that work*. New York, NY: Oxford University Press.

Castonguay, L. G., Constantino, M. J., & Grosse Holtforth, M. (2006). The working alliance: Where are we and where should we go? *Psychotherapy, 43*, 271–279. doi:10.1037/0033-3204.43.3.271

Constantino, M. J., Arnow, B. A., Blasey, C., & Agras, W. S. (2005). The association between patient characteristics and the therapeutic alliance in cognitive–behavioral and interpersonal therapy for bulimia nervosa. *Journal of Consulting and Clinical Psychology, 73*, 203–211. doi:10.1037/0022-006X.73.2.203

Elkin, I. (1993, June). *Tribute to Ed Bordin*. Paper presented at the 24th annual meeting of the Society for Psychotherapy Research, Pittsburgh, PA.

Erikson, E. H. (1959). *Identity and the life cycle*. Oxford, England: International Universities Press.

Galinsky, M. (1995). Edward S. Bordin (1913–1992): Obituary. *American Psychologist, 50*, 172. doi:10.1037/0003-066X.50.3.172

Horvath, A. O., & Bedi, R. P. (2002). The alliance. In J. C. Norcross (Ed.), *Psychotherapy relationships that work: Therapist contributions and responsiveness to patients* (pp. 37–69). New York, NY: Oxford University Press.

Horvath, A. O., & Greenberg, L. S. (1989). Development and validation of the Working Alliance Inventory. *Journal of Counseling Psychology, 36*, 223–233. doi:10.1037/0022-0167.36.2.223

Johnson, L. N., & Wright, D. W. (2002). Revisiting Bordin's theory on the therapeutic alliance: Implications for family therapy. *Contemporary Family Therapy, 24*, 257–269. doi:10.1023/A:1015395223978

Ladany, N., & Inman, A. G. (in press). Training and supervision. In E. A. Altmaier & J. I. Hansen (Eds.), *Oxford handbook of counseling psychology*. New York, NY: Oxford University Press.

Orlinsky, D. E., & Rønnestad, M. H. (2000). Ironies in the history of psychotherapy research: Rogers, Bordin, and the shape of things that came. *Journal of Clinical Psychology, 56*, 841–851. doi:10.1002/1097-4679(200007)56:7<841:: AID-JCLP3>3.0.CO;2-V

Rogers, C. R. (1942). *Counseling and psychotherapy: New concepts in practice*. Boston, MA: Houghton Mifflin.

Rogers, C. R. (1951). *Client-centered therapy*. Boston, MA: Houghton Mifflin.

Rogers, C. R. (1957). The necessary and sufficient conditions of therapeutic personality change. *Journal of Consulting Psychology, 21*, 95–103. doi:10.1037/h0045357

Safran, J. D., Muran, J. C., Samstag, L. W., & Stevens, C. (2002). Repairing alliance ruptures. In J. C. Norcross (Ed.), *Psychotherapy relationships that work: Therapists contributions and responsiveness to patients* (pp. 235–254). New York, NY: Oxford University Press.

18

DONALD J. KIESLER:
INTERPERSONAL MANIFESTO

CHRISTOPHER C. WAGNER AND JEREMY D. SAFRAN

Donald J. Kiesler (1933–2007) was a clinical psychologist who focused on a variety of issues related to personality, psychopathology, and psychotherapy over a 45-year career. Although his direct empirical contributions to psychotherapy research left an important legacy in and of themselves, we believe that his conceptual, theoretical, and analytical contributions to the field were even more significant. In the 1960s, he identified several common myths that he believed were keeping the field of psychotherapy research from fulfilling its promise, and he developed a paradigm that helped move the field beyond the question, "Does psychotherapy work?" and on to the significantly more useful question, "What works, for whom?" Thus began the era of factorial psychotherapy outcomes research, which in many respects continues to define the structure of outcomes research today. Kiesler also furthered work in psychotherapy process research as research director of Carl Rogers's Wisconsin study of psychotherapy with schizophrenia patients, codeveloping some of the first process measurement instruments and later publishing an encyclopedic book cataloguing methodologies of psychotherapy process research. During the 1970s, he focused on nonverbal communication in dyadic relationships, leading him to his later focus on interpersonal theory and research and the development of his interpersonal communications psychotherapy model. His emeritus years found him focusing on biopsychosocial models of mental disorders and studying the role of health care interactions in medical patient outcomes.

EARLY BEGINNINGS

Donald Kiesler was raised in Louisville, Kentucky, the second of four boys in a German family. He attended parochial schools and a Catholic high school, played on school football and basketball teams through high school, and participated on his high school debate team. He attended a Catholic novitiate in Indiana, studying to become a priest, before deciding instead that he wanted to pursue a career as a high school counselor. During his pursuit of that goal, he was offered a job in a psychology department. Believing that this had better career potential, he chose psychology as his field. In later years he would laugh about how casual career entry was in those "innocent" days, when word of mouth from one professional to another could result in a telephone call offering one a job, and thus the beginning of a lifelong career.

He pursued his PhD at the University of Illinois, obtaining it in 1963. Like many in his field in that era, he was trained in psychodynamic therapy on the one hand and experimental research methods on the other, and he grew frustrated that the two were separate streams flowing through his professional life, parallel but ever disconnected. This early frustration provided the impetus for the following 45 years of work focused on integrating theory, research, and practice.

MAJOR ACCOMPLISHMENTS

Rogers's Wisconsin Psychotherapy Project

Shortly after completing his graduate education, Kiesler landed a promising opportunity as a postdoctoral researcher with Carl Rogers, on Rogers's innovative Wisconsin-based research project studying the effectiveness of client-centered therapy for individuals with schizophrenia. His excitement was to be short-lived, however, because within 3 weeks of his arrival in Madison, serious problems emerged with the project. This was the first major psychotherapy process research study of its kind, and all therapy sessions were recorded and the recordings coded by a team of researchers. One day, however, it was discovered that most of the coded data from the project had disappeared. Suspicion fell on a team member, based on circumstantial evidence, and 4 years of significant turmoil followed for all involved. As the new research director on the project, Kiesler led the effort to recode the recordings over the next year, but he was caught up (and actively participated) in a struggle of considerable proportions among team members, eventually escalating to hostile interactions, threats of lawsuits over authorship credit, and the ending of several professional relationships.

Kiesler believed that Rogers did not adequately address the apparent theft of data and that Rogers's nondirective leadership style exacerbated the problems among team members (D. Kiesler, personal communication, August 6, 1993). Kiesler came to feel that Rogers sacrificed congruence in favor of unconditional positive regard, both as a therapist and in communication with his research team. Eventually, the book summarizing the multiyear project appeared (Rogers, Gendlin, Kiesler, & Truax, 1967), but after years of anticipation, the mixed findings were received with relatively little enthusiasm by the field. This difficult period in Kiesler's personal and professional life played a role in his subsequent development of an interest in the role that incongruent communication plays in interpersonal problems and an interest in the use of therapeutic metacommunication as a vehicle for highlighting this type of incongruence in treatment and communicating congruently as a therapist.

Conceptual and Methodological Contributions to Psychotherapy Research

As the Wisconsin project wound down, Kiesler turned to the broad methodological question of how to move psychotherapy research in a more sophisticated direction that might yield results that could challenge Eysenck's (1952) highly publicized conclusion that research did not demonstrate the effectiveness of psychotherapy. In his landmark *Psychological Bulletin* article, "Some Myths of Psychotherapy Research and the Search for a Paradigm" (Kiesler, 1966), he synthesized previous rebuttals of Eysenck's position into a cogent position paper, and he charted the course for the type of research that would be needed to challenge Eysenck's negative conclusions.

In this article he examined a number of myths in psychotherapy research that he believed continually led psychotherapy researchers to reach the wrong (negative) conclusion about the value of psychotherapy. A key myth was the patient uniformity myth. Kiesler argued that it was inappropriate to lump patients with different types of problems in the same research sample, arguing instead that research samples should isolate patient groups by type. He also focused on the therapist uniformity myth—the assumption that "therapists are more alike than different and that whatever they do with their patients may be called 'psychotherapy'" (Kiesler, 1966, p. 112).

Kiesler thus dismissed the question "Does psychotherapy work?" as naive and reframed the field of psychotherapy research around the question "What works for whom?" His 1966 article became one of the most widely cited articles in psychotherapy research (later identified as one of 12 "classic" articles in clinical psychology by the journal *Clinician's Research Digest*) and helped unleash a flood of efforts to begin researching psychotherapy in a more nuanced fashion. It continues to exert a guiding influence on psychotherapy research to this day.

Kiesler's book, *The Process of Psychotherapy: Empirical Foundations and Systems of Analysis* (1973), constituted another landmark contribution to psychotherapy research methodology. He had previously contributed to methodological and measurement advances in psychotherapy process research, and his 1966 "Myths" article had decried the "misconception" that "process research is not outcome research and outcome research is not process research" (p. 126). The book attempted to remedy this lack of attention to process research by providing a conceptual and methodological framework that would serve to substantially guide the next generation of psychotherapy process researchers (Greenberg & Pinsof, 1986). In addition to providing a comprehensive review of the major psychotherapy process coding systems existing at the time, the book questioned the traditional distinction between process and outcome, arguing that this distinction had led to an almost exclusive (and unfortunate) focus on two measurement points: pretreatment and posttreatment. Instead, Kiesler argued for the importance of conceptualizing changes occurring throughout the course of treatment as "sub-outcomes"—a perspective that continues to guide contemporary psychotherapy researchers. The book also provided a vitally important discussion of a number of critical methodological issues, including the unit problem, sampling issues, training and clinical sophistication of judges, and assessment of interrater reliability.

Communications Analysis and Interpersonal Theory

One of the factors stimulating Kiesler's interest in communication analysis and interpersonal theory was a perception that the Wisconsin research team had developed that therapist congruence can play an important role in the treatment of schizophrenia. Another factor was his perception that incongruent communications within the Wisconsin research team exacerbated conflict that may have been resolvable had it been openly addressed. In this context, Kiesler turned to communications analysis, analyzing discrepancies between overt and covert communications and their influence on developing relationships. He focused on how nonverbal messages exerted strong influence in defining the developing relationship between two parties, often outside of their awareness, in ways that they could neither identify nor defend against. Investigation of the role that communication played in shaping relationships led him to the works of interpersonal psychologists such as Timothy Leary and the Kaiser team that he was a part of, as well as works by Bob Carson and Jerry Wiggins. Synthesizing interpersonal psychology with the communications focus of Ernst Beier (1966) and others, Kiesler concluded that individuals' psychological and behavioral patterns are largely created and sustained in interpersonal relationships through patterned interaction cycles.

Following Beier, Kiesler argued that individuals create stability in relationships through the use of unconscious *evoking messages* that function to constrain the others' reactions to those that are predictable and comfortable for the individual. He became interested in studying the "receiving" end of communications, and theorized a counterpart to the sender's evoking message in the form of a receiver's *impact message*. Kiesler theorized that covert impact messages included elements of feelings, action tendencies (impulses to respond in specific ways), fantasies, and attributions (about the evoking person's intent, character, etc.). He and his team developed the Impact Message Inventory (IMI) to measure impacts corresponding to the interpersonal circle categories. The IMI has been used in more than 100 studies of the propositions of interpersonal theory, the interpersonal elements of depression, personality disorders and other psychopathologies, and interpersonal processes in psychotherapeutic and other relationships (Kiesler, 2001b).

His work with the IMI spurred Kiesler to delve deeper into the interpersonal circle tradition, resulting in his intricate 1982 Interpersonal Circle taxonomy in which he integrated the numerous previous theoretical and empirical versions of the circle (Kiesler, 1983). The circumplex he constructed was highly detailed, included both normal and abnormal levels, and resulted in the publication of another instrument, the Checklist of Interpersonal Transactions (CLOIT), used in over 50 studies of interpersonal transactions in psychotherapy, including studies on countertransference, therapeutic alliance, patient–therapist matching, metacommunication, and group therapy interactions (Kiesler, 2001a).

Kiesler became intrigued by and expanded on Leary's (1957) notion of interpersonal reflexes and Carson's later (1969) circumplex-based propositions regarding the principle of interpersonal complementarity. The concept of complementarity suggests that individuals in ongoing relationships tend to mutually reinforce one another's behavior, emotions, perceptions, and perspectives. In regard to the interpersonal circle, the complementarity hypothesis is that friendly behaviors complement friendly behaviors (and hostile, hostile), and that dominant behaviors complement submissive behaviors (and vice versa). Relationships are hypothesized to be most stable and mutually reinforcing when two individuals' trait styles are complementary to one another. When their trait styles are not complementary, they rely on evoking messages that tend to pull for complementary responses as a means of trying to alter partners' behavior (and thus the relationship) toward behavior that is reinforcing to their own preferred style. Thus, if a person with high trait friendliness is in a relationship with a person whose base style is colder, each will try to evoke reactions that are more fitting with their preferred style—the friendly person will try to use warm, friendly, engaging, and agreeable behaviors to try to pull her partner toward a closer, more affiliative relationships, whereas the colder partner will likely use indifferent or hostile behaviors to try to establish greater relational distance between the two, consistent with that person's comfort zone.

In a burst of activity in the early 1980s, Kiesler synthesized concepts from communications analysis, the interpersonal circumplex assessment tradition, personality development theory, and behavioral, client-centered, and relational therapies into what he referred to as an *interpersonal manifesto* and a structured therapy—interpersonal communications psychotherapy. Across two chapters in the groundbreaking *Handbook of Interpersonal Psychotherapy* (Kiesler, 1982a, 198b), he laid the foundation for the work he would engage in for the remainder of his career. He first summarized the radical conceptual framework established by Harry Stack Sullivan (1953), in which the concept of "individuals" is seen as a Western cultural abstraction, and personality is seen primarily as "the relatively enduring pattern of recurrent interpersonal situations that characterize a human life" (pp. 110–111).

Kiesler went on to synthesize elements of what he saw as the four branches of post-Sullivanian development of interpersonal theory: (a) family communications theory and resultant family therapy approaches, (b) the study of nonverbal communication, (c) the study of interpersonal behavior, and (d) the social psychological study of interpersonal interactions. Kiesler's synthesis of these various branches resulted in directing psychological and psychotherapeutic study toward interactionism (with interpersonal transactions rather than individuals as the basic unit of study), circular causality rather than linear causality (interactants are simultaneously influencing and being influenced, and this context is required to examine individual behaviors of either), phenomenology (covert experiences are a central element of interactions and must be studied along with overt behavior), and use of the interpersonal circle model as a conceptual map for considering social behavior.

Part II of his interpersonal manifesto defined psychopathology from an interpersonal perspective and laid the foundation for psychotherapy that directly addresses clients' "disordered, inappropriate, or inadequate interpersonal communications" (Kiesler, 1982b, p. 13). Rather than focusing on internal factors such as maladaptive thoughts and feelings in an isolated manner, Kiesler focused on the interpersonal context in which those thoughts and feelings occur. Individual psychopathology is conceptualized in relation to *maladaptive transaction cycles* between the person and significant others that cause it, sustain it, and are shaped by it. Causality is not linear but circular. For example, an individual's depression may have roots in past experiences (e.g., others who treated the person poorly, thwarted the person's autonomy), but the depression also elicits characteristic reactions of others (e.g., to tell the person to "look on the bright side"), which then sustain and reinforce the depression (because the person can't simply "cheer up" and becomes frustrated by hearing this). Over time, others may lose patience and begin challenging the person (e.g., "You always seem to see the glass as half empty"), distancing or avoiding the person altogether. The person is likely to have negative reactions to this outcome and become more withdrawn and pessimistic as a result. From Kiesler's point of view, to conceptualize depression (or other psychopathologies) decontextualized from interpersonal interactions was to deprive the conceptualization of its most important elements.

Like Leary (1957), Kiesler emphasized that when a person interacts rigidly (with little variation in style across situations) or extremely (intensely displaying a particular style within a situation, beyond a level that would be appropriate to the situation at hand), that person's inflexible and intense behavior significantly constrains others' reactions. Thus, not only do social interactions serve as reinforcers for an individual's maladaptive behaviors, but the person's own interactional style unduly influences and shapes others' reactions directly toward those behaviors, which then sustain the pathology. Because the person consciously attends to his or her verbal behavior, and because the person's influential nonverbal behavior is often discrepant from his or her verbal behavior, the person "has little understanding of how he had come to or is responsible for this miserable state of affairs" (Kiesler, 1982b, p. 13). Kiesler concluded that "the culprit in disordered behavior, therefore, is duplicitous communication" (p. 14) that is in conflict with the person's conscious self-definition, and of which the person is largely unaware.

Interpersonal Communication Psychotherapy

Kiesler focused on the role of the therapist as another interactant in the person's social world. As another interactant, the therapist experiences *pulls* and reactions that are similar to those experienced by others having relationships with the client. Just as clients' rigid and extreme interpersonal patterns shape others' reactions toward complementary responses that reinforce the clients' own cognitive, emotional, and behavioral patterns and troubled self-identity, therapists are also shaped to react in these constrained and reinforcing ways. Thus, therapists can determine how they are being constrained and use this information to help clients change the patterns that constrain significant others, hopefully interrupting the cycle of mutual reinforcement that leads to sustenance of clients' pathology.

Kiesler developed his interpersonal communication psychotherapy out of this basic model and identified therapeutic tasks across two stages of therapy. In the first stage, labeled the *engaged* stage, the client intentionally and unintentionally shapes the therapist

> to respond to him from a restricted aspect of the therapist's own internal experience and behavior repertoire. . . . The therapist cannot *not* be hooked or sucked in by the client, because the client is more adept, more expert in his distinctive, rigid, and extreme game of interpersonal encounter. (Kiesler, 1982a, p.281)

Thus, to begin the second therapeutic stage, the *disengaged* stage, the therapist's first task is to identify how the client is constraining him or her. The therapist does this by noticing the experienced impact messages—the feelings, action tendencies, attributions, and fantasies that the therapist experiences while interacting with or imagining the client.

The therapist's second task is to interrupt his or her automatic responses to the client. If pulled to advise or comfort the client, the therapist notices this and begins to withhold advice or comfort to interrupt the pattern of reinforcement of the client's pathological style. The therapist then goes beyond withholding automatic complementary responses to the client's bids for reinforcement and begins engaging in asocial ways, intended to influence the client to act differently because old behaviors no longer elicit predictable and comforting reinforcement. Kiesler precisely defined these actions in relation to the interpersonal circle model, identifying acomplementary and anticomplementary responses that reject the client's bid for reinforcement in terms of either degree of affiliation or control in the relationship (or both).

As one particular type of asocial response, Kiesler focused extensively on the process of metacommunication, in which the therapist draws explicit attention to the verbal and nonverbal influencing behaviors of the client and the role that they play in shaping in-session interactions as well as the extratherapeutic social interactions that ultimately sustain the client's problematic self-definition and relationship difficulties. The therapist prioritizes client communications that directly refer to the therapist for feedback. The therapist carefully focuses on both positives and negatives, being careful to convey a supportive attitude and helpful intent. The therapist discloses the impacts the client makes upon him or her and ties these impacts to specific client actions to help the client understand how he or she influences others. Then therapy explores the ways in which the client uses communication to influence others besides the therapist, helping the client also explore how he or she is in turn influenced by significant others' communications.

Kiesler continued to develop this approach to psychotherapy over the remainder of his career and featured it in his encyclopedic book *Contemporary Interpersonal Theory and Research* (Kiesler, 1996). In this book, Kiesler made a compelling case for interpersonal theory as one of psychology's hallmark accomplishments, an underrecognized and underappreciated integrative theory that logically and empirically ties together personality, psychopathology, social interaction, assessment and diagnosis, psychotherapy, and clinical supervision. Kiesler saw interpersonal theory as bridging the subdisciplines of personality and social psychology with those of clinical and counseling psychology, with the potential to contribute toward the unification of psychology.

CONCLUSION

Donald Kiesler contributed significantly to the field of psychology over his 45-year career. From his early work on psychotherapy process research and linking process with outcomes, through his widely heralded work identifying uniformity myths in psychotherapy research and introducing a focus on "what works for whom" in place of the discarded question "Does psychotherapy work?" he helped set the stage for modern psychotherapy research. His synthesis of knowledge on process and outcomes research in the early 1970s laid a solid foundation for the next generation of psychotherapy researchers to build on. His synthesis of communications theory, early interpersonal theory, and social interactions research into a fully realized modern interpersonal theory left the field a complex system with strong empirical grounding that can be mined for years to come. His work on therapeutic metacommunication and interpersonal psychotherapy anticipated trends in the field of psychotherapy by many years (e.g., the relational tradition in contemporary psychoanalysis), and in this respect he was remarkably prescient.

Kiesler's work influenced and was influenced by other contemporary researchers, such as Hans Strupp, Paul Wachtel, and Jerry Wiggins. His work also significantly influenced (and in turn was influenced by) Jeremy Safran and colleagues' work on interpersonal process in psychotherapy and alliance ruptures (e.g., Safran & Muran, 2000; Safran & Segal, 1990), James McCullough's cognitive–behavioral analysis system of psychotherapy for chronic depression (McCullough, 2003), and a host of interpersonal personality and psychotherapy researchers (e.g., Lynn Alden, Timothy Anderson, Michael Gurtman, Anton Hafkenscheid, Leonard Horowitz, Stan Murrell, Aaron Pincus, Stan Strong, and Terry Tracey).

We believe it would be a mistake to conclude without at least mentioning the human aspects of his legacy. For many people Don Kiesler was a uniquely supportive and engaged mentor with an unparalleled ability to bring out the best in them. Regardless of what form his mentorship assumed, his personal qualities played an incalculably important role in transforming many people's professional lives.

REFERENCES

Beier, E. G. (1966). *The silent language of psychotherapy: Social reinforcement of unconscious processes.* Chicago, IL: Aldine.

Carson, R. C. (1969). *Interaction concepts of personality.* Chicago, IL: Aldine.

Eysenck, H. J. (1952). The effects of psychotherapy: An evaluation. *Journal of Consulting and Clinical Psychology, 16,* 319–324.

Greenberg, L., & Pinsof, W. (1986). *The psychotherapeutic process. A research handbook.* New York, NY: Guilford Press.

Kiesler, D. J. (1966). Some myths of psychotherapy research and the search for a paradigm. *Psychological Bulletin, 65,* 110–136. doi:10.1037/h0022911

Kiesler, D. J. (1973). *The process of psychotherapy: Empirical foundations and systems of analysis.* Chicago, IL: Aldine.

Kiesler, D. J. (1982a). Confronting the client–therapist relationship in psychotherapy. In J. C. Anchin & D. J. Kiesler (Eds.), *Handbook of interpersonal psychotherapy* (pp. 274–295). Elmsford, NY: Pergamon.

Kiesler, D. J. (1982b). Interpersonal theory for personality and psychotherapy. In J. C. Anchin & D. J. Kiesler (Eds.), *Handbook of interpersonal psychotherapy* (pp. 3–24). Elmsford, NY: Pergamon.

Kiesler, D. J. (1983). The 1982 Interpersonal Circle: A taxonomy for complementarity in human transactions. *Psychological Review, 90,* 185–214. doi:10.1037/0033-295X.90.3.185

Kiesler, D. J. (1996). *Contemporary interpersonal theory and research: Personality, psychopathology, and psychotherapy.* New York, NY: Wiley.

Kiesler, D. J. (2001a). Empirical studies that used the Checklist of Interpersonal/ Psychotherapy Transactions: An annotated bibliography. Retrieved from http://www.vcu.edu/sitar/cloit.pdf

Kiesler, D. J. (2001b). Empirical studies that used the Impact Message Inventory: An annotated bibliography. Retrieved from http://www.vcu.edu/sitar/imi.pdf

Leary, T. (1957). *Interpersonal diagnosis of personality.* New York, NY: Wiley.

McCullough, J. P. (2003). *Treatment for chronic depression: Cognitive behavioral analysis system of psychotherapy (CBASP).* New York, NY: Guilford Press.

Rogers, C. R., Gendlin, E. T., Kiesler, D. J., & Truax, C. B. (1967). *The therapeutic relationship and its impact: A study of psychotherapy with schizoprenics.* Madison: University of Wisconsin Press.

Safran, J. D., & Muran, J. C. (2000). *Negotiating the therapeutic alliance: A relational treatment guide.* New York, NY: Guilford Press.

Safran, J. D., & Segal, Z. V. (1990). *Interpersonal process in cognitive therapy.* New York, NY: Basic Books.

Sullivan, H. S. (1953). *The interpersonal theory of psychiatry.* New York, NY: Norton.

19

LORNA SMITH BENJAMIN: LOVE, LOYALTY, AND LEARNING IN CLOSE ATTACHMENT RELATIONSHIPS

KENNETH L. CRITCHFIELD

> I love to work with seriously troubled people who are driving everyone else crazy and have been unresponsive to many previous treatments. . . . I want to help relieve suffering. I want to see change in the patient's personal life. I want to see the patient rediscover delight and to thrive. I want patients to become fully engaged in their lives to the best of their abilities. The best reward for me is to see people who were once remarkable for causing trouble, for being almost nonexistent, or for other unhappy reasons, learn to fly.
> — (Benjamin, 2001, p. 27).

Lorna Smith Benjamin is a master clinician and preeminent scientist–practitioner known for her work to help people with severe and complex psychopathology. Her contributions have been far-reaching and profoundly influential in psychotherapy research. In her work as a researcher, Benjamin's quest has been to articulate psychodynamic clinical theory and make it amenable to empirical testing. As a theorist she provides a comprehensive view of psychopathology and a treatment approach based on attachment, interpersonal, and object relations theories. Her model of relational behavior has been applied transtheoretically by many research groups to study psychiatric disorder and its treatment, as well as normative patterns of interaction.

MAJOR CONTRIBUTIONS

Benjamin's primary accomplishments include the creation of the structural analysis of social behavior model (SASB; Benjamin, 1979, 1993/1996) and development of an associated treatment approach, interpersonal reconstructive therapy (IRT; Benjamin, 2003). She is an expert in the assessment and treatment of personality disorder (PD), elaborating an interpersonal approach to PD diagnosis (Benjamin, 1993/1996) and contributing substantially to other assessment methods, including the Structured Clinical Interview for the *DSM–IV* Personality Disorders (SCID-II; First, Gibbon, Spitzer, Williams, & Benjamin, 1996), and the Wisconsin Personality Inventory (WISPI; Klein et al., 1993).

Across her career, Benjamin has played many important roles, including as an advisor to the *DSM–IV* work group on Axis II. She also contributed to Fetzer Institute and National Institute of Mental Health–sponsored meetings to explore inclusion of relational disorder in future *Diagnostic and Statistical Manual of Mental Disorders* (*DSM*) systems (Benjamin, Wamboldt, & Critchfield, 2006). She is a past president of the Society for Psychotherapy Research (SPR) and was granted an honorary doctoral degree from the University of Umea, Sweden, for her work with SASB. She has received many awards, including the Society for Personality Assessment's Klopfer Award, for outstanding long-term professional contributions to personality assessment, and the Distinguished Research Career Award from SPR.

As a clinician, Benjamin is well-known for her work in treating patients for whom standard interventions have not been sufficient to prevent repeated hospitalizations and suicide attempts. IRT clinic trainees and hospital staff observe her consultations directly as she develops a case formulation that makes sense of patient pathology in light of the unique interpersonal history. Benjamin's approach uses SASB to identify repeating patterns in patient narratives and quickly narrow the focus to the most important themes. She views psychopathology as reflecting failed attempts at adaptation using previously internalized values and learning. In her view, maladaptive internalized patterns often persist because they are driven by love and loyalty to the attachment figures with whom they were first learned. In the introduction to the 2006 edition of *Interpersonal Reconstructive Therapy*, she called this "attachment gone awry" (Benjamin, 2003/2006, p. *v*) and had boldly asserted elsewhere that "every psychopathology is a gift of love" (Benjamin, 1993). Her treatment approach, IRT, directly addresses the relationship with these internalizations.

BEGINNINGS

Benjamin was born and raised in upstate New York, near Rochester. Her father was a research chemist who later became an executive for the Eastman Kodak Company. He was a major source of her lifelong fascination and respect for the sciences. Early socialization on the family farm instilled values of hard work, competence, and performance. It also brought early insight and attunement to how relationships work. She described how in childhood she trained and befriended an aggressive quarter horse that had been severely abused:

I learned more about not being easily scared and, once again, to take things slowly and with great patience. I also learned about the impossibility of controlling another creature. The most you can do is persuade and negotiate your mutual interests as you move with the other. (Benjamin, 2001, p. 29)

Having grown up studying music, Benjamin eventually attended the Eastman School of Music and Oberlin College before shifting course to the sciences. Her deep appreciation for practice, repetition, and attention to detail in conservatory learning is now reflected in her approach to therapy training. Her conviction is that the art of therapy can and should be grounded in a theory of fundamental principles and taught to high levels of proficiency.

Professional Training

Benjamin began her graduate training at the University of Wisconsin in 1956. In 1960, she received her PhD in experimental psychology with a minor emphasis in mathematical statistics. Her major professor was Harry Harlow. Benjamin contributed to the famous studies on contact comfort and maternal deprivation in rhesus monkeys. Her thesis and dissertation focused on the impacts of hunger, frustration, and type of mother surrogate on thumb-sucking in young primates. During her graduate training Benjamin met John Bowlby, who was then conversing with Harlow about attachment theory. Benjamin's work was profoundly influenced by both Harlow and Bowlby, especially in terms of the impact of early relationships on adult problems.

Benjamin would go on to receive clinical training with primary input from psychodynamic and client-centered perspectives, including a brief period of supervision by Carl Rogers. She also was influenced by Carl Whittaker's approach to family work and David Graham's demonstrations of precise connections between relational patterns and medical diseases (e.g., Graham et al., 1962).

Benjamin had not been long in clinical practice when she began applying her scientific training to the psychotherapy process itself:

To try to figure out what really goes on, I began to take notes in transcript form . . . . I wanted to have a record uncontaminated by my thoughts and interpretations of what happened—raw data, so to speak. I wanted to be able to look back at difficult sessions and track what happened the next time. (Benjamin, 2001, pp. 22–23)

Across her career Benjamin has repeatedly emphasized the need for well-articulated theory that can be tested directly with observable data. Like Harlow, her preference is for direct demonstrations of principle in well-designed experiments with few subjects. Reflecting her concern with the vital role of theory and method in testing clinical hypotheses, Benjamin's early publications included a mathematical defense of the use of covariance to adjust for the impact of the law of initial values in psychophysiology studies (Benjamin, 1967). In another article (Benjamin, 1965), she used modular algebra to defend the legitimacy of the allegedly fatal confounds in the Latin square design. That dispelled, she suggested that the Latin square is an ideal paradigm for using each subject as his or her own control in psychotherapy studies. Her careful self-study of psychotherapy process would eventually result in SASB, which she has referred to as a "periodic table of the elements for relating" (Benjamin, 2001), as well as her treatment approach, IRT.

ACHIEVEMENTS

Charting Relational Behavior With SASB

When first described in Westman's *Individual Differences in Children* (Benjamin, 1973), SASB was humbly referred to as a "chart" to organize the basic elements of social relating in primates. From a formal and theoretical perspective, however, SASB was a powerful integration of competing relational models developed by Leary (1957) for adults and by Schaefer (1965) for parent–child interactions. SASB organizes interpersonal and intrapsychic behavior with three basic dimensions: focus, affiliation, and interdependence. Each of these dimensions is seen as having evolved to enhance biological survival of primates. The model is represented as three circular, or "circumplex," arrangements of behavior. The focus distinction specifies which circle a behavior is located on according to whom a behavior is to, for, or about. Focus includes transitive focus on the other, intransitive focus on the self (in relation to the other), or introjective focus on the self by the self. For each focus, a horizontal dimension shows the degree of affiliation (love vs. hate) and a vertical dimension traces the degree of enmeshment (control/submit) versus differentiation (emancipate/separate). Labels are provided for behaviors around the perimeter of the model, each representing a precise combination of the three underlying dimensions. For example, the behavior "protect" involves focus on another person that involves moderate affiliation and moderate control. Since it is possible for behavior to be at once hostile and friendly, enmeshed and separate, or focused on both self and other, such "complex" behaviors are represented by more than one simultaneous position on the model.

SASB has been elaborated to varying degrees of specificity, from simple division into quadrants, to a full model with 36 points articulated for each focus (Benjamin, 1979). The octant model has a medium degree of specificity and is the most commonly used version (Benjamin, 1993/1996). In addition to the focus on behavior, Benjamin proposed parallel models of affect and cognition that involve the same basic structure (described in Benjamin, 2003/2006). As a descriptive framework for human interaction, SASB has obvious application to clinical work, including the study of therapy process, relational patterns associated with psychopathology, family dynamics, and much more.

SASB has undergone extensive validation and testing to confirm the structure and reliability of the model (reviews of validity and application in multiple settings are available in Benjamin, 1993/1996; Benjamin, Rothweiler, & Critchfield, 2006; Constantino, 2000). It has been used extensively in both research and clinical settings as an observational coding system (Benjamin & Cushing, 2000) and as a self-report questionnaire (Intrex; Benjamin, 2000). SASB has been translated into 14 languages and used by diverse research groups to test theories of clinical pathology, case formulation, patient and therapist attachment histories, and couples interactions. In psychotherapy research, SASB has been used to study relational outcomes and in-session processes in psychodynamic (e.g., Henry, Schacht & Strupp, 1990), cognitive–behavioral (e.g., Critchfield, Henry, Castonguay, & Borkovec, 2007; Shearin & Linehan, 1992; Vittengl, Clark, & Jarrett, 2004), and humanistic therapies (e.g., Paivio & Greenberg, 1995).

Defining Normal Interpersonal Relating and Specifying Common Interactional Patterns

Benjamin (2003/2006) used SASB to precisely define adaptive, normal relating as having a flexible baseline that is appropriate to context but primarily involves friendliness, moderate enmeshment, moderate differentiation, and a balance of focus on self and others. By contrast, psychopathology is characterized by baselines involving hostility, extremes of enmeshment or differentiation, imbalance of focus, or rigid responding that is not responsive to circumstance. Normative data on the SASB-based Intrex questionnaire support this definition for normal and patient samples, as do numerous studies associating interpersonal hostility with psychopathology. Benjamin proposed that relational disorder is diagnosable as any significant deviation from normative relating with significant others (Benjamin, Wamboldt, & Critchfield, 2006).

Benjamin uses SASB to specify the dyadic interaction patterns, or "predictive principles," of similarity, complementarity, introjection, opposition, and antithesis. Similarity is defined by identical positioning of two people on the model, such as in sequences of control and countercontrol. Complementary behaviors also share the same dimensionality, but they differ in terms of focus. For example, if one partner is controlling, it invites the other to complement with submission; as another example, affirmation (friendly autonomy-granting) invites open disclosure (friendly separateness). Complementary interactions are thought to be relatively stable because each behavior pulls for the other in self-reinforcing cycles.

The predictive principle of introjection is defined as self-treatment that reflects actions of another. For example, a student who may be feeling hopeful about academic pursuits is told by an important family member that she has always been a disappointment. If the student responds to this critical input with self-criticism and the belief that she will now fall short in her studies, it has been introjected. Opposites are behaviors that share behavioral focus but are positioned 180 degrees apart. Antitheses are maximally different on all three SASB dimensions. Opposition and antithesis also have clinical relevance. For example, if a patient begins a session by sulking and complaining about the therapist or therapy (hostile, self-focused enmeshment), the SASB-defined antithesis would be to nondefensively affirm the patient's point of view as important (friendly, other-focused autonomy-granting), and through the principle of complementarity invite open disclosure (the opposite of sulking: friendly focus on self that is moderately separate) to regain collaboration.

When complex codes are included along with SASB's predictive principles, it becomes possible to identify double binds, ambivalence, and mixed messages of many kinds, as well as to trace their impact on unfolding interactional sequences. A great deal of sophistication can thus be captured by SASB's three simple distinctions. Benjamin has written extensively on how to apply SASB to both research and clinical work in couples, families, and groups. In a novel application, she has even shown that diagnostic categories involving auditory hallucinations (schizophrenia, mania, psychotic depression, borderline personality) can be differentiated by the quality of the relationship with the voices (Benjamin, 1989). Beyond this, Benjamin (1986) has offered powerful statistical approaches for studying relational patterns, including sequential analysis with Markov chains. Vividly demonstrating the importance of sequence in psychotherapy sessions, Karpiak and Benjamin (2004) showed that therapist affirmation may have very different impacts on outcome, depending on whether it follows adaptive or maladaptive patient content.

Interpersonal Diagnosis of Personality Disorder

In 1993, Benjamin published a comprehensive interpersonal diagnostic framework for the *DSM* PDs, now in its second edition (1996). This book was a monumental achievement, contributing significantly to identification and treatment of PDs. Her method provided a concrete picture of prototypic relational patterns, interpersonal learning histories, wishes and fears, needed interpersonal learning, and expectable processes in the treatment of each PD. As an example, the prototypic interpersonal summary of obsessive–compulsive PD is:

> There is a fear of making a mistake or being accused of being imperfect. The quest for order yields a baseline interpersonal position of blaming and inconsiderate control of others. The OCD's control alternates with blind obedience to authority or principle. There is excessive self-discipline, as well as restraint of feelings, harsh self-criticism, and neglect of the self. (1993/1996, p. 247).

Each statement in the description occupies a precise location on the SASB model. Her method reduces diagnostic overlap between categories through clear specification of patterns plus the use of interpersonal necessary and exclusionary criteria. Early histories are described in parallel SASB terms and provide a bridge to the relational learning history. Tests of SASB-defined links between interpersonal history and adult pathology have held up well for PDs with adequate representation in study samples (Smith, Klein, & Benjamin, 2003).

Interpersonal Reconstructive Therapy (IRT)

In her first book (Benjamin, 1993/1996), Benjamin provided an outline for tailoring treatment to address each category of PD. She also offered an approach to treating less common personality patterns falling under the *not otherwise specified* label. Her method emphasized internalized relational patterns measurable with SASB. This individually tailored approach to psychotherapy would later be elaborated as IRT.

IRT is organized around two core ideas that grew directly out of work with the SASB model: copy process theory and the gift of love. *Copy processes* are imitative connections to important attachment figures such as parents, romantic partners, siblings, grandparents, teachers, religious leaders, and so on. Imitative repetition of internalized relationships is thought to reflect a normative process of attachment. It is also thought to be a powerful and ubiquitous influencer of perception and behavior. Copy processes become problematic when effective adaptation is compromised because a person is responding to internalizations of important persons more than to present-day reality. It is in this sense that Benjamin referred to psychopathology as "attachment gone awry" (Benjamin, 2003/2006, p. *v*).

Copy processes are detectable as repeating patterns of thought, feeling, and behavior that parallel those experienced with important others. The copying is measurable with SASB and takes three primary forms: identification (be like the other person), recapitulation (behave as if the other person is still present and in charge), and introjection (treat the self as he or she did). Critchfield and Benjamin (2008) provided evidence that the three primary forms of copy process are detectable in both normal and clinical samples, involve behavior from all around the SASB model, and show variability by clinical status, gender, and which early figures are copied.

The gift of love hypothesis states that copy processes are ultimately maintained, even when obviously maladaptive, by attachment-based desires to receive love and acceptance from the internalized figures. The gift is inherent in copy process repetitions. As Benjamin wrote, it is as if the message to the internalized loved one is "If I do this well enough, long enough, faithfully enough, *then* maybe you will love me" (2003/2006, p. 49). Understanding psychopathology as an ongoing, internalized, relationship process, IRT directly addresses conflict between the part of a patient loyal to the internalized rules and values (termed the *Regressive Loyalist*) and the part that seeks flexible, adaptive, healthy relating with self and others (the *Growth Collaborator*). Awareness of the repeating patterns, where they come from, and what they are for, enhances the patient's ability to choose a reworking of attachments, including grief over losses and unfulfilled wishes for reconciliation and acceptance. This in turn creates space for pursuit of more adaptive, fulfilling ways of experiencing and being.

Setbacks and conflicts in the change process of therapy are predictable as a result of what Benjamin recently described as IRT's "autoimmune theory of psychiatric disorder" (Benjamin, 2008). According to this theory, moves toward more healthy adaptation can be perceived as threatening the connection to internalized figures. A resulting pattern of self-attack in response to this threat is similar to autoimmune disorders in which healthy cells are destroyed when misidentified as dangerous. Significant regressions to self-destructive patterns are seen as reflecting attempts by the Regressive Loyalist part of the self to stay close to important attachment figures. This view is fundamentally interactive in nature, explicitly frames psychopathology as a misdirected attempt at adaptation, and stands in sharp contrast to what Benjamin called the "broken brain" theory of psychopathology (2008). In light of the autoimmune theory, IRT is a long-term approach that requires a strong therapeutic collaboration to both motivate and support patients through the difficult work of defying internalizations and developing healthier patterns and self-concepts.

Ongoing IRT Research

Benjamin remains very active in research activities to test the efficacy and proposed mechanisms of change in IRT at the University of Utah Neuropsychiatric Institute. Preliminary findings include that the SASB-based case formulation is reliable (Hawley, Critchfield, Dillinger, & Benjamin, 2005) and discriminates well among cases. Significant associations have been found between adherence to IRT principles and outcome, especially for interventions focused on the gift of love (Critchfield, Davis, Gunn, & Benjamin, 2008). Pre–post comparisons over 1 year with patients referred for chronic and severe psychopathology show significant reductions in suicidality, hospitalizations, and days hospitalized compared with the year before IRT (Critchfield, Benjamin, Hawley, & Dillinger, 2006). Ever pushing forward, Benjamin is now preparing a book geared toward helping clinicians engage a patient's will to change, based on empirical findings from the IRT clinic about the central importance of focus on the gift of love to change persistent psychopathology.

CONCLUSION

Benjamin's work brings together all of the early themes in her life, refined and enhanced through roughly 50 years of clinical experience and careful research. These themes most crucially involve attunement to relationship patterns or what she has referred to as "the harmonics of therapy" (Benjamin, 1993/1996), the importance of attachment as fundamental to our evolutionary heritage, and a sharp focus on empirical data organized by her periodic table of interpersonal relating. For Benjamin, psychopathology is about love, or more precisely about love gone wrong. Her theory offers a profoundly humanizing view of psychiatric disorder and is backed up with compelling data. She summarized her view succinctly: "Psychopathology is best attributed to broken hearts (attachment gone awry) rather than to broken brains" (Benjamin, 2008, p. 414). According to Benjamin, when the past is reckoned with and impossible wishes successfully grieved, patients can revise impacts of abuse, neglect, and other toxic patterns. They then have the opportunity to learn new, more adaptive skills, and in this respect "learn to fly."

REFERENCES

Benjamin, L. S. (1965). A special Latin Square for the use of each subject "as his own control." *Psychometrika, 30,* 499–513.

Benjamin, L. S. (1967). Facts and artifacts in using Analysis of Covariance to "undo" the Law of Initial Values. *Psychophysiology, 4,* 187–206.

Benjamin, L. S. (1973). A biological model for understanding the behavior of individuals. In J. Westman (Ed.), *Individual differences in children* (pp. 215–241). New York, NY: Wiley.

Benjamin, L. S. (1979). Structural analysis of differentiation failure. *Psychiatry, 42,* 1–23.

Benjamin, L. S. (1986). Operational definition and measurement of dynamics shown in the stream of free associations. *Psychiatry, 49,* 104–129.

Benjamin, L. S. (1989). Is chronicity a function of the relationship between the person and the auditory hallucination? *Schizophrenia Bulletin, 15,* 291–310.

Benjamin, L. S. (1993). Every psychopathology is a gift of love. *Psychotherapy Research, 3,* 1–24.

Benjamin, L. S. (1996). *Interpersonal diagnosis and treatment of personality disorders* (2nd ed.) New York, NY: Guilford Press. Originally published in 1993.

Benjamin, L. S. (2000). *Intrex user's manual.* Salt Lake City: University of Utah.

Benjamin, L. S. (2001). A developmental history of a believer in history. In M. R. Goldfried (Ed.), *How therapists change: Personal and professional reflections* (pp.19–35). Washington, DC: American Psychological Association. doi:10.1037/10392-002

Benjamin, L. S. (2006). *Interpersonal reconstructive therapy:* A personality-based treatment for complex cases. New York, NY: Guilford Press. Paperback with new subtitle and introduction. Originally published in 2003.

Benjamin, L. S. (2008). What is functional about functional autonomy? *Journal of Personality Assessment, 90,* 412–420. doi:10.1080/00223890802248596

Benjamin, L. S., & Cushing, G. (2000). *Reference manual for coding social interactions in terms of Structural Analysis of Social Behavior.* Salt Lake City: University of Utah.

Benjamin, L. S., Rothweiler, J. C., & Critchfield, K. L. (2006). The use of Structural Analysis of Social Behavior (SASB) as an assessment tool. *Annual Review of Clinical Psychology, 2,* 83–109. doi:10.1146/annurev.clinpsy.2.022305.095337

Benjamin, L. S., Wamboldt, M. Z., & Critchfield, K. L. (2006). Defining relational disorders and identifying their connections to Axes I and II. In D. J. Kupfer, M. B. First, & D. E. Regier (Eds.), *Relational processes and DSM-V: Neuroscience, assessment, prevention and intervention* (pp.157–173). Washington, DC: American Psychiatric Press.

Constantino, M. J. (2000). Interpersonal process in psychotherapy through the lens of the Structural Analysis of Social Behavior. *Applied & Preventive Psychology, 9,* 153–172. doi:10.1016/S0962-1849(05)80002-2

Critchfield, K. L., & Benjamin, L. S. (2008). Repetition of early interpersonal experiences in adult relationships: A test of copy process theory in clinical and nonclinical settings. *Psychiatry, 71,* 72–93.

Critchfield, K. L., Benjamin, L. S., Hawley, N., & Dillinger, R. J. (2006, June). Attempted replication of effectiveness for Interpersonal Reconstructive Therapy (IRT) to reduce hospitalizations and suicide attempts in "nonresponder" patients. Presented to the Society for Psychotherapy Research, Edinburgh, Scotland.

Critchfield, K. L., Davis, M. J., Gunn, H. E., & Benjamin, L. S. (2008, June). Measuring therapist adherence in Interpersonal Reconstructive Therapy: Conceptual framework, reliability, and validity. Presented to Society for Psychotherapy Research, Barcelona, Spain.

Critchfield, K. L., Henry, W. P., Castonguay, L. G., & Borkovec, T. D. (2007). Interpersonal process and outcome in variants of cognitive-behavioral psychotherapy. *Journal of Clinical Psychology, 63,* 31–51. doi:10.1002/jclp.20329

First, M. B., Gibbon, M., Spitzer, R. L., Williams, J. B. W., & Benjamin, L. S. (1996). *Structured Clinical Interview for the DSM-IV Axis II Personality Disorders (SCID-II)*. New York, NY: New York State Psychiatric Institute.

Graham, D. T., Lundy, R. M., Benjamin, L. S., Kabler, J. D., Lewis, W. C., Kunish, N. W., & Graham, F. K. (1962). Specific attitudes in initial interviews with patients having different "psychosomatic" diseases. *Psychosomatic Medicine, 25*, 260–266.

Hawley, N., Critchfield, K. L., Dillinger, R. J., & Benjamin, L. S. (2005, June). Case formulation in Interpersonal Reconstructive Therapy: Using SASB and copy process theory to reliably track repeating interpersonal themes. Poster presented to the Society for Interpersonal Theory and Research, Montreal, Canada.

Henry, W. P., Schacht, T. E., & Strupp, H. H. (1990). Patient and therapist introject, interpersonal process, and differential psychotherapy outcome. *Journal of Consulting and Clinical Psychology, 58*, 768–774. doi:10.1037/0022-006X.58.6.768

Karpiak, C. P., & Benjamin, L. S. (2004). Therapist affirmation and the process and outcome of psychotherapy: Two sequential analytic studies. *Journal of Clinical Psychology, 60*, 659–676. doi:10.1002/jclp.10248

Klein, M. H., Benjamin, L. S., Rosenfeld, R., Treece, C., Husted, J., & Greist, J. H. (1993). The Wisconsin Personality Disorders Inventory: I. Development, reliability, and validity. *Journal of Personality Disorders* (Suppl. 1), 18–33.

Leary, T. (1957). *Interpersonal diagnosis of personality: A functional theory and methodology for personality evaluation*. New York, NY: Ronald Press.

Paivio, S. C., & Greenberg, L. S. (1995). Resolving "unfinished business": Efficacy of experiential therapy using empty-chair dialogue. *Journal of Consulting and Clinical Psychology, 63*, 419–425. doi:10.1037/0022-006X.63.3.419

Schaefer, E. S. (1965). Configurational analysis of children's reports of parent behavior. *Journal of Consulting Psychology, 29*, 552–557. doi:10.1037/h0022702

Shearin, E. N., & Linehan, M. M. (1992). Patient-therapist ratings and relationship to progress in dialectical behavior therapy for borderline personality disorder. *Behavior Therapy, 23*, 730–741. doi:10.1016/S0005-7894(05)80232-1

Smith, T. L., Klein, M. H., & Benjamin, L. S. (2003). Validation of the Wisconsin Personality Disorders Inventory-IV with the SCID-II. *Journal of Personality Disorders, 17*, 173–187. doi:10.1521/pedi.17.3.173.22150

Vittengl, J. R., Clark, L. A., & Jarrett, R. B. (2004). Self-directed affiliation and autonomy across acute and continuation phase cognitive therapy for recurrent depression. *Journal of Personality Assessment, 83*, 235–247. doi:10.1207/s15327752jpa8303_07

20

DAVID E. ORLINSKY: DEVELOPING PSYCHOTHERAPY RESEARCH, RESEARCHING PSYCHOTHERAPIST DEVELOPMENT

MICHAEL HELGE RØNNESTAD, ULRIKE WILLUTZKI,
AND MARGARITA TARRAGONA

David E. Orlinsky has taught since 1960 at the University of Chicago, where he is a professor in the Department of Comparative Human Development. He has coauthored two books, *Varieties of Psychotherapeutic Experience* (Orlinsky & Howard, 1975) and *How Psychotherapists Develop* (Orlinsky & Rønnestad, 2005), and coedited *The Psychotherapist's Own Psychotherapy: Patient and Clinician Perspectives* (Geller, Norcross, & Orlinsky, 2005). He is the principal author of authoritative reviews of research on therapeutic process and outcome that have appeared as chapters in the *Handbook of Psychotherapy and Behavior Change* (Orlinsky & Howard, 1978; Orlinsky & Howard, 1986a; Orlinsky, Grawe, & Parks, 1994; Orlinsky, Rønnestad, & Willutzki, 2004). He has authored or coauthored more than 100 original journal articles and book chapters. He also practiced psychotherapy in Chicago for many years.

Orlinsky's contributions to psychotherapy research can be summarized under five headings: (a) pioneering empirical studies of patients' and therapists' experiences in sessions and in the intervals between sessions, as well as groundbreaking studies of psychotherapist development; (b) constructing comprehensive, conceptually informed research instruments; (c) advanced scholarship resulting in often-cited research reviews; (d) developing the integrative, research-based generic model of psychotherapy; and (e) cofounding and organizing the Society for Psychotherapy Research (SPR), which he continues to sustain as a vital community of researchers at the national, international, and local levels.

David Orlinsky has received formal recognition for distinguished scientific and professional contributions through awards from the American Psychological Association (APA) Division of Psychotherapy, the Illinois Psychological Association, and SPR, and he received an award for teaching excellence from the University of Chicago. For nearly 5 decades he has influenced generations of undergraduate and graduate students and has supervised, mentored, and inspired numerous doctoral students and younger colleagues nationally and internationally within the field of psychotherapy research.

EARLY BEGINNINGS

David Orlinsky was born in 1936 in New York City, the first child of his parents and the first grandchild and nephew in a large, close-knit, upwardly mobile working-class family of East European Jewish background. Looking back at his origins (Orlinsky, 2005), he noted that having parents who were also first-born meant that his youngest uncles and aunts were as close as or closer in age to him than to his parents, which effectively put him between generations. In relating "up" to his elders, he received much attention and affection but was clearly not one of them. In relating "down" to cousins and brother, he was naturally a leader, a "first among equals." In this early family environment, he learned to value close personal relationships and close-knit groups, and he gained an awareness of complexity and context, an ability to view questions from multiple perspectives, and a heightened sensitivity to issues of inclusion and exclusion—traits that we think have influenced his work in the field of psychotherapy.

Orlinsky received his elementary and secondary education at public schools in New York, where his interest and talent in science and poetry were nurtured. After high school, he attended the College of the University of Chicago (1953–1954) where a coherently organized curriculum and committed teachers introduced him to classical works in the fields of humanities, social science, and the physical and biological sciences. Next, he studied in the University of Chicago's master's program on the history of culture (1954–1955) and won an award for excellence in humanities and first prize in the university's poetry contest. Thereafter, he transferred to the University of Chicago's doctoral program in clinical psychology (1955–1962), where he met his classmate Kenneth Howard, who was to become his lifelong friend and research partner.

The friends trained and had internships together in clinical psychology but did not do psychotherapy research when they were students. It was not until after graduation, when they worked part-time as staff therapists at an outpatient clinic, that they started their first major study of psychotherapy, which they called the Psychotherapy Session Project. What finally brought them to do psychotherapy research? David wrote (Orlinsky, 2005, p. 1004): "We did that, I confess, mainly as an excuse to continue seeing each other after graduating."

They described the influence that their graduate school training had on their early work thus:

> We had been educated in a properly but not narrowly positivistic spirit in the graduate program. . . . We learned our Hull, Tolman, Guthrie, and Skinner; but we were also exposed to Freud, Allport, Murray, and Lewin, and the phenomenological, client-centered concerns of Carl Rogers and his colleagues at the University's Counseling Center. . . . [Rogers and his group] provided the strong assumption that experience could and should be made the subject of psychological science, even if they did not furnish a fully appropriate research methodology. Our approach to the latter was undoubtedly influenced by the work of another eminent Chicago psychologist, L. L. Thurstone, whose pioneering accomplishments in the psychometric scaling of subjective qualities and attitudes provided the basis for attempting the same sort of thing with participants' experiences in psychotherapeutic sessions [and whose pioneering work in factor analysis provided the basis for their approach to data analysis]. (Orlinsky & Howard, 1986b, pp. 478–479)

ACCOMPLISHMENTS

Therapy Session Project and the Study of Therapeutic Experience

The Psychotherapy Session Project began with the development of a postsession questionnaire for patients and therapists called the Therapy Session Reports (TSR). Orlinsky and Howard (1986b) described their approach as follows:

> We began by reflecting on our own experiences in psychotherapy, as therapists and as patients. We drew, of course, on our theoretical understanding of psychotherapy as a special kind of relationship, and more generally on our broader understanding of personality and social relationships. However, what we wanted were questions that were as purely descriptive and noninferential—as close to the experienced "surface" of events—as possible. We wanted questions about the most obvious features of the experiences . . . that could be answered . . . without lengthy reflection or calculation. (p. 479)

Steering clear of clinical theories in their quest to describe "the most obvious features" allowed Orlinsky and Howard to see the therapy session with fresh eyes and to think about it systematically and from multiple aspects. Consequently, the TSR explores patients' and therapists' experiences during sessions (a) in terms of a dialogue about topics that directly or indirectly express the patient's problematic concerns, (b) as a process of exchange in which patients seek certain benefits from their therapist and receive those (or other) benefits in varied measure, (c) as a relationship expressed in the manner that patient and therapist interact with one another, (d) as an encounter capable of evoking and transmuting the patient's (and therapist's) feelings, (e) as an experience whose quality depends on the patient's level of self-relatedness, and through all these (f) as an emergent, jointly constructed "social act"[1] that progresses sequentially over the course of the session toward its therapeutic goal. The TSR was designed to allow patients and therapists to report separately from their own perspectives on these multiple aspects of their sessions by using numerous but easily answered scales—a task that both the patients and therapists in their study found meaningful.

Through statistical analyses and interpretations of the data generated with the TSR, Orlinsky and Howard established that it was both possible and important to study the experiences of therapy as reported by patients and therapists—the "psychological interior of psychotherapy"—and not just their behaviors, seen from the limited perspective of external observers. This is now taken for granted, but it was somewhat revolutionary at the time because process researchers believed (naively) that reliance on audiotapes of sessions would allow them to observe "what *really* happens in therapy." The TSR also informed the development of some nonparticipant process measures like the Vanderbilt Psychotherapy Process Scale (VPPS), as acknowledged by Strupp, who noted that "the VPPS . . . conception owes much to the pioneering research of Orlinsky and Howard" (Suh, Strupp, & O'Malley, 1986, p. 286).

Using the TSR, data were collected on approximately 2,500 sessions from patients and 1,500 sessions from therapists between 1965 and 1967, enabling the investigators "to delineate the objective structure of its intersubjective reality" (Orlinsky & Howard, 1986b, p. 486). Factor and cluster analyses indicated the presence of 11 dimensions and four profiles or patterns of patient experience, which the investigators identified as helpful, stressful, dependent, and counterdependent experiences (Orlinsky & Howard, 1975). The data for therapists yielded 11 dimensions but only two patterns, which were identified as helping experience and stressful experience.

---

[1]In the sense defined by George Herbert Mead (1954).

Perhaps the least appreciated and theoretically most important of the findings were those of the five *conjoint experience* dimensions that were significantly loaded by both patient and therapist dimensions. Conjoint experience dimensions such as sympathetic warmth vs. conflictual erotization, therapeutic alliance vs. defensive impasse, and productive rapport vs. unproductive contact showed how patients' and therapists' experiences of the same therapy sessions can be manifestly different and yet powerfully interconnected.

Studies based on the TSR generated a series of other publications during the 1960s and 1970s, including the now classic article on "the good therapy hour" (Orlinsky & Howard, 1967). In addition to being valuable for researchers, this work can also assist therapists in connecting to the experiences of clients and can specifically sharpen therapists' focus on the great variability in how clients assess the therapy process.

Patients' and Therapists' Experiences Between Sessions

Another example of Orlinsky's interest in exploring obvious but excluded aspects of therapy, and in devising innovative instruments to study them, is the work on patients' and therapists' intersession experiences. It is common knowledge that patients and therapists recall and make use of their experiences of therapy in the intervals between sessions and imagine interacting with one another. Recognizing the importance of these phenomena for therapy, Orlinsky and his students developed parallel instruments called the Intersession Experience Questionnaires (IEQ) for patients and therapists (Orlinsky, Geller, Tarragona, & Farber, 1993).

The IEQ represents an attempt to understand how therapy "keeps working" between sessions, and it can be seen as complementing or expanding the TSR. The relationships between patients' in-session and intersession experiences were initially explored with this instrument (Tarragona & Orlinsky, 1988), and research on the topic was recently renewed (Zeeck, Hartmann, & Orlinsky, 2006). This work continues with large samples of intersession data collected in Chicago and Freiburg (Germany) currently being analyzed by Orlinsky and Hartmann.

Empirical Study of the Development of Psychotherapists

Traditionally, psychotherapy research has focused mainly on treatment methods and on clients' characteristics, in-session behaviors, and clinical outcome, whereas the psychotherapist has largely remained terra incognita. This aspect of therapy once more motivated Orlinsky to launch into a new area of research, and in 1989 he played a major role in cofounding the SPR Collaborative Research Network (CRN) to conduct an international study of the development of psychotherapists. Meeting intensively before and after SPR conferences, a group of colleagues from different countries, professional backgrounds, and theoretical orientations worked together to construct an instrument with which they could learn more about how psychotherapists work and develop over the course of their careers. Those who participated in these meetings recall countless revisions of questions after long, sometimes heated discussions, and then—after enjoying a fine meal together—when most went to rest, Orlinsky worked during the night and arrived with new, improved proposals the next morning. His commitment to thorough conceptual analysis and empathy with those to be studied significantly shaped the Development of Psychotherapists Common Core Questionnaire (DPCCQ).

The DPCCQ has been translated into 20 languages to date and has been used in more than two dozen countries to collect reports about their work experiences and professional development from nearly 9,000 psychotherapists. Details of the instrument and its findings have been published in journals (e.g., Orlinsky, Botermans, & Rønnestad, 2001) and in the book by Orlinsky and Rønnestad (2005), *How Psychotherapists Develop: A Study of Therapeutic Work and Professional Growth*. Grounded inductively in descriptive ratings by therapists of diverse professions and orientations, at all career levels and in many countries, this work traced four patterns of practice—effective, challenging, disengaged, and distressing—based on two factor-analytic dimensions of therapist work experience, identified as healing involvement and stressful involvement (resembling findings mentioned earlier based on use of the TSR to examine individual therapy sessions). These practice patterns in turn were differentially related to dimensions of current development (empirically identified as currently experienced growth and currently experienced depletion) and to measures of overall career development. These and other findings were integrated theoretically in a "cyclical-sequential model of psychotherapist development" and applied practically to make empirically grounded recommendations for clinical training, supervision, and therapeutic practice. Based on this, Orlinsky and Rønnestad (2005) constructed normed self-monitoring scales of work involvement and professional development for use by students, supervisors, and practicing psychotherapists. These scales may be used for many purposes, as described by Orlinsky and Rønnestad (2005).

Here, we would like to highlight the pragmatic purpose of having supervisors and supervisees identify the eroding consequences of experiencing therapeutic work as a stressful involvement, the elements of which are frequently experiencing difficulties in practice, in-session feelings of anxiety or boredom, and avoiding therapeutic engagement. Therapists and those responsible for therapist training and practice should be aware of the potentially deleterious effects of lack of work setting support and work satisfaction, and also the limitations of a narrow range of case experience. Conversely, because breadth and depth of case experience fuels overall career development and because theoretical breadth predicts healing involvement, therapists should ensure variety in their therapeutic work and seek theoretical inspiration from many sources. Orlinsky and his CRN colleagues are continuing their international study by expanding data collection in previously unstudied Western and non-Western countries; examining the distinctive characteristics shared by therapists of specific orientations (e.g., Elliott et al., 2003); and exploring aspects of therapists' personal lives, such as the nature and impact of their religious background and experiences (e.g., Smith & Orlinsky, 2004). The CRN project has become the largest study of psychotherapist development and one of the longest-lasting research projects ever conducted in the field of psychotherapy research.

Process–Outcome Research Reviews and Theoretical Contributions

David Orlinsky has written several major reviews of psychotherapy and psychotherapy research. The stage for his integrative contributions was set as early as 1972, when Ken Howard and he published a review of psychotherapy research in the prestigious *Annual Review of Psychology* (Howard & Orlinsky, 1972). This was followed by chapters on process–outcome psychotherapy research in four successive editions of the *Handbook of Psychotherapy and Behavior Change*. In addition to providing an invaluable bibliographic resource for researchers, work on these chapters led directly to the formulation of the empirically grounded conception of process and outcome known as the *generic model of psychotherapy* (Orlinsky & Howard, 1986a, 1987).

Drawing on knowledge from the social sciences in general, the generic model distinguishes therapy process as a system of action that affects and is affected by surrounding systems like patients' and therapists' personalities and their social and cultural environments. Six facets of process are differentiated on the basis of extant research: (a) the organizational aspect of therapy (therapeutic contract), (b) the technical aspects of therapy (therapeutic operations), (c) the interpersonal aspects of therapy (therapeutic bond), (d) the intrapersonal aspects of therapy (participants' self-relatedness), (e) clinical aspects of therapy (in-session impacts), and (f) sequential aspects of process (temporal patterns). The model provides a contextualized view of psychotherapy by delineating the relation of therapeutic process both to antecedent conditions in the psychological, cultural and social system environments (inputs) and to consequent conditions in those environments (outputs), which include the psychological consequences of therapeutic process for patients (clinical outcome).

The findings of more than 50 years of psychotherapy process–outcome research have been successfully synthesized in this framework (Orlinsky, Rønnestad, & Willutzki, 2004). The model has generated a number of empirical studies that also demonstrate its prospective utility (e.g., Kolden, 1991). The model also has served as a framework for integrating a variety of clinical theories and treatment approaches to help students "learn from many masters" (e.g. Orlinsky, 1994).

More recently, Orlinsky has worked to extend the generic model in ways that clarify and differentiate the contextual domains in which outcome is assessed (Orlinsky, 2004a, 2004b), that illuminate the widely accepted but largely unexplained power of the therapeutic relationship to change the patient's life and personality (Orlinsky, in press), and that elucidate the spiritual aspect of psychotherapeutic work.

Society for Psychotherapy Research

In addition to his research, Orlinsky has contributed much to psychotherapy research through his ongoing efforts to bring researchers together. In 1968–1969, David Orlinsky and Ken Howard founded SPR to serve as an open forum for all who are interested in the scientific study of psychotherapy. David has elsewhere told how he and Ken were motivated to do this when they were young researchers by being excluded in 1966 from attending a closed conference on therapy research sponsored jointly by APA and the National Institute of Mental Health, even though it was held on their home campus at the University of Chicago (Orlinsky, 1995). Ken Howard served SPR as its first president and David served as its first president-elect; they drafted the society's constitution and bylaws; they organized and hosted SPR meetings from 1968 through 1971, in 1985, and again in 2000. Orlinsky also served as the first president of the North American chapter of SPR; chaired the constitution and bylaws committee and the committee on international development; cofounded the SPR CRN; and, most recently, led in creating the SPR interest section on culture and psychotherapy. Nowhere is David Orlinsky's drive to make meaningful connections between ideas and people more evident than in his efforts to establish, organize, and sustain SPR.

CONCLUSION

We can summarize what has been said about David Orlinsky by highlighting some dominant characteristics of his work. One is a consistent focus on the scientific study of subjective experience, rooted in his early interests in science and poetry and brought to fruition by his undergraduate and graduate studies at the University of Chicago. Another is his attention to the contextual embeddedness of experience—including the experience of psychotherapy—reflecting his broad background in the social sciences and humanities. His interest in the nature of personal relationships (in psychotherapy, in friendship, and in love relationships) reflects early family experiences, as do his commitment to collaborative research, his efforts to create and sustain personal communities based on shared intellectual interest, and his inclination to find and study phenomena that others tended to overlook. His efforts to construct systematic conceptual models also subtly reflect his early family experience, as well as the interdisciplinary knowledge and intellectual discipline acquired through his long tenure at the University of Chicago.

In focusing on David's scientific and professional contributions, we have only been able to hint at some of his qualities as a person—his warmth, wit, and welcoming manner; the care and commitment he shows towards friends; the patience, intellectual stimulation, and support he extends to students and colleagues. If one phrase can capture the spirit of a man, for David it would probably be the words that E. M. Forster chose as the epigraph for his novel *Howards End:* "Only connect." Reflecting his background, values, and personality, David has sought to connect in many ways: to connect facts in ways that produce knowledge; to connect concepts in ways that produce theory; to connect and integrate different theoretical perspectives; and, not least, to connect persons.

REFERENCES

Elliott, R., Orlinsky, D., Klein, M., Amer, M., & Partyka, R. (2003). Professional characteristics of humanistic therapists: Analyses of the Collaborative Research Network Sample. *Person-Centered and Experiential Psychotherapies, 2,* 188–203.

Geller, J. D., Norcross, J. C., & Orlinsky, D. E. (Eds.). (2005). *The psychotherapist's own psychotherapy: Patient and clinician perspectives.* New York, NY: Oxford University Press.

Howard, K. I., & Orlinsky, D. E. (1972). Psychotherapeutic processes. *Annual Review of Psychology, 23,* 615–668. doi:10.1146/annurev.ps.23.020172.003151

Kolden, G. G. (1991). The Generic Model of Psychotherapy: An empirical investigation of process and outcome relationships. *Psychotherapy Research, 1,* 62–73. doi:10.1080/10503309112331334071

Mead, G. H. (1934). *Mind, self, and society from the perspective of a social behaviorist.* Chicago, IL: University of Chicago Press.

Orlinsky, D. E. (1994). Ansaetze zu einer wissenschaftlichen Integration psychotherapeutischer Behandlungsmethoden [Learning from many masters]. *Psychotherapeut, 1,* 2–9.

Orlinsky, D. E. (1995). The greying and greening of SPR: A personal memoir on forming the Society for Psychotherapy Research. *Psychotherapy Research, 5,* 343–350.

Orlinsky, D. E. (2004a). Der menschliche Kontext von Psychotherapien, Teil 1 [The human context of psychotherapy, part 1: Social and cultural contexts of psychotherapy]. *Psychotherapeut, 49*, 88–100. doi:10.1007/s00278-004-0360-7

Orlinsky, D. E. (2004b). Der menschliche Kontext von Psychotherapien, Teil 2 [The human context of psychotherapy, part 2: The individual context of psychotherapy]. *Psychotherapeut, 49*, 161–181.

Orlinsky, D. E. (2005). Becoming and being a psychotherapist: A psychodynamic memoir and meditation. *Journal of Clinical Psychology/In Session, 61*, 999–1007.

Orlinsky, D. E. (in press). Die psychotherapeutische Beziehung, Soziale Unterstützung und die Heilende Energie des Therapeuten: Eine Neo-Durkheim'sche Perspektive [The therapeutic relationship, social support, and the psychotherapist's healing energy: A neo-Durkheimian perspective]. In B. Röhrle & A.-R. Laireiter (Eds.), *Soziale Unterstützung und Psychotherapie*. Tübingen, Germany: dgvt-Verlag.

Orlinsky, D. E., Botermans, J.-F., & Rønnestad, M. H. (2001). Towards an empirically-grounded model of psychotherapy Training: Five thousand therapists rate influences on their development. *Australian Psychologist, 36*, 139–148. doi:10.1080/00050060108259646

Orlinsky, D. E., Geller, J., Tarragona, M., & Farber, B. (1993). Patients' representations of psychotherapy: A new focus for psychodynamic research. *Journal of Consulting and Clinical Psychology, 61*, 596–610. doi:10.1037/0022-006X.61.4.596

Orlinsky, D. E., Grawe, K., & Parks, B. K. (1994). Process and outcome in psychotherapy—noch einmal. In A. Bergin & S. Garfield (Eds.), *Handbook of psychotherapy and behavior change* (4th ed., pp. 270–376). New York, NY: Wiley.

Orlinsky, D. E., & Howard, K. I. (1967). The good therapy hour: Experiential correlates of patients' and therapists' evaluations of therapy sessions. *Archives of General Psychiatry, 16*, 621–632.

Orlinsky, D. E., & Howard, K. I. (1975). *Varieties of psychotherapeutic experience: Multivariate analyses of patients' and therapists' reports.* New York, NY: Teachers College Press.

Orlinsky, D. E., & Howard, K. I. (1978). The relation of process to outcome in psychotherapy. In S. Garfield & A. Bergin (Eds.), *Handbook of psychotherapy and behavior change* (2nd ed., pp. 283–329). New York, NY: Wiley.

Orlinsky, D. E., & Howard, K. I. (1986a). Process and outcome in psychotherapy. In S. Garfield & A. Bergin (Eds.), *Handbook of psychotherapy and behavior change* (3rd ed., pp. 311–381). New York, NY: Wiley.

Orlinsky, D. E., & Howard, K. I. (1986b). The psychological interior of psychotherapy: Explorations with the Therapy Session Reports. In L. Greenberg & W. Pinsof (Eds.), *The psychotherapeutic process: A research handbook* (pp. 477–501). New York, NY: Guilford Press.

Orlinsky, D. E. & Howard, K. I. (1987). A generic model of psychotherapy. *Journal of Integrative and Eclectic Psychotherapy, 6,* 1, 6–36.

Orlinsky, D. E., & Rønnestad, M. H. (2005). *How psychotherapists develop: A study of therapeutic work and professional growth*. Washington, DC: American Psychological Association. doi:10.1037/11157-000

Orlinsky, D. E., Rønnestad, M. H., & Willutzki, U. (2004). Fifty years of psychotherapy process-outcome research: Continuity and change. In M. J. Lambert (Ed.), *Garfield and Bergin's handbook of psychotherapy and behavior change* (5th ed., pp. 307–389). New York, NY: Wiley.

Smith, D. P., & Orlinsky, D. E. (2004). Religious and spiritual experience among psychotherapists. *Psychotherapy: Theory, Research, Practice, Training, 41*, 144–151.

Suh, C. S., Strupp, H. H., & O'Malley, S. S. (1986). The Vanderbilt process measures: The psychotherapy process scale (VPPS) and the negative indicators scale (VNIS). In L. S. Greenberg & W. M. Pinsof (Eds.), *The psychotherapeutic process: A research handbook* (pp. 285–323). New York, NY: Guilford.

Tarragona, M., & Orlinsky, D. E. (1988, June). *During and beyond the therapeutic hour: An exploration of the relationship between patients' experiences of therapy within and between sessions*. Paper presented at the 19th annual meeting of the Society for Psychotherapy Research, Santa Fe, NM.

Zeeck, A., Hartmann, A., & Orlinsky, D. E. (2006). Internalization of the therapeutic process: Differences between borderline and neurotic patients. *Journal of Personality Disorders, 20*, 22–41. doi:10.1521/pedi.2006.20.1.22

D. INTEGRATION OF MULTIPLE VARIABLES

21

HORST KÄCHELE: BRINGING RESEARCH, PRACTICE, AND PEOPLE TOGETHER

BERNHARD STRAUSS

It is almost self-evident that the German-speaking countries have a positive tradition of psychoanalytic psychotherapy and psychodynamic psychotherapy research. Otto Fenichel (1930) was one of the first to document the effectiveness of psychoanalysis in his systematic "Statistical Report About the Therapeutic Work of the Berlin Psychoanalytic Institute Between 1920 and 1930." More than 30 years later, an influential report by Annemarie Dührssen (Dührssen & Jorswieck, 1965) indicated positive long-term effects of psychoanalytic treatment in a follow-up study of 1,004 patients treated in Berlin. In retrospect, this study has had tremendous influence on the political decisions to include psychotherapeutic treatment as a standard benefit of both public and private insurance in the German health system (Kächele, 2001). Today, psychodynamic treatment (including long-term psychoanalysis) and cognitive behavior therapy are standard inclusions covered by the insurance system.

It is not surprising that such a positive environment has favored many activities of researchers in the field of psychotherapy in psychology and medicine. Today, there are many active research groups in international networks distributed over the entire country. This was not always the case: During the postwar decades German universities had only a few collaborations in psychoanalysis and psychotherapy research.

Subsequently, the research group at Ulm, where Horst Kächele has spent most of his professional life, holds specific importance among the German research groups in at least two respects. One is the intensive and ongoing effort to contribute to the development of psychoanalytic treatment based upon theory, clinical work, and empirical research, and the other is the early attempt of Horst Kächele and Helmut Thomä, the former head of the Department of Psychotherapy, to bring researchers and research approaches from around the world together through international collaboration and organization, especially within the Society for Psychotherapy Research (SPR).

This chapter is primarily aimed at describing how Horst Kächele achieved his two major contributions, namely, (a) advocating empirical process and outcome research within psychoanalysis and (b) developing international collaborations in psychotherapy research and professional practice.

MAJOR CONTRIBUTIONS

Having served as the head of the Ulm Department of Psychotherapy and Psychosomatic Medicine and as the chair of the Center for Psychotherapy Research in Stuttgart, Horst Kächele has always regarded psychoanalytic process research as his's primary passion. His work using qualitative and quantitative approaches to the understanding of psychodynamic treatment has been fundamental for the profile of the entire Ulm research group. His and Helmut Thomä's attempts to integrate these research findings into a teachable theory of psychoanalytic psychotherapy have been summarized in different editions of their textbook *Psychoanalytic Practice* (Thomä & Kächele, 1987, 1991; Kächele & Thomä, 1999). In addition to his work related to a model of process research to describe psychoanalytic treatment, Kächele was a very successful initiator and stimulator of research projects—in many specific fields of psychosomatic medicine and psychotherapy, motivating young researchers to establish and to continue scientific work in these fields.

Horst Kächele always has been a cosmopolitan in the psychotherapeutic world. Accordingly, he has been very active in trying to establish clinical and research cooperation with South American and Eastern European countries, and he considers himself one of the godfathers of the Latin American chapter of SPR.

EARLY BEGINNINGS

Born in 1944 in a peaceful Tyrolean village, where his father administered the production of motors for Heinkel airplanes until the end of World War II, Horst Kächele grew up in Stuttgart. His father worked as a public attorney in the postwar denazification campaign. This second career of his father's probably had an impact on Kächele's choice of his profession, which values empathy and social justice, and also on his continuous political activities that aimed at preserving memories of the dark chapters of German history (e.g., he was very active in a committee promoting a memorial for the Oberer Kuhberg concentration camp in Ulm, situated close to Kächele's department).

A salient feature of his life trajectory was a rather early imprint from meeting psychoanalysts of various convictions as a high school (gymnasium) student in Stuttgart. His idea to move in the direction of psychoanalysis as a career was set around the age of 17 or 18 because he thought that this profession could be a synthesis of art and science. However, a young man who already knows at the age of 18 that he wants to become a psychoanalyst has to suppress this drive for awhile. Horst Kächele decided to bridge the time until the start of his psychoanalytical training with a medical education (at the universities of Marburg, Leeds [UK], and Munich) instead of a psychological one, because of his affinity for the natural sciences. He received his MD in 1969 for a thesis titled "Psychogenic Death in the Medical Literature" (Kächele, 1970). His doctoral dissertation was related to an issue thatin psychoanalytic circles today would be called "conceptual research." He was screening the literature for the psychophysiological mechanisms involved, to explain this surprisingly common phenomenon.

When he finished his doctoral thesis, he chose Ulm University for his professional career. At that time, Ulm University was newly founded, and the medical faculty had been assembled in light of a number of reformist ideas, among them the inclusion of a department of psychosomatic medicine (chaired by Thure von Uexküll, one of the most influential mentors of this medical discipline in Germany) and a psychotherapy department led by Helmut Thomä, who already was a very well-known psychoanalyst at this time.

Between 1970 and 1975, Horst Kächele obtained a German Research Council–funded research position in Ulm. At the unusually young age of 33 he became *Privatdozent* following his postdoctoral lecture qualification (including a thesis, on "Computer- assisted Content Analysis in Psychoanalytic Process Research"). He was then appointed as an associate professor of psychotherapy, heading a section on psychoanalytic methodology for the next 13 years at the Ulm Department of Psychotherapy. During this time (1980–1989), his major achievements were to urge cooperation in creating a funded multidisciplinary research effort on the psychotherapeutic process and later to establish the "Ulm Textbank," together with the computer scientist and later SPR president Erhard Mergenthaler. This database enabled the administration and analysis of huge amounts of psychotherapy-related transcripts.

In 1990, Horst Kächele followed Helmut Thomä as the head of the entire department that, a few years later, was combined with the Department of Psychosomatic Medicine.

ACCOMPLISHMENTS

When Kächele was hired by Thomä at the psychotherapy department of Ulm University, it was for working to resolve the very specific problem of handling and analyzing tape recordings of psychotherapeutic sessions. Thomä became his mentor from that moment—it is said that Thomä handed a can opener to Kächele when he began to work to symbolize the wish that he would succeed in opening the many "canned goods" he had collected!

The relationship between the two was always complementary, sometimes controversial (especially when Thomä and Kächele talked about patients—many colleagues might remember brilliant disputes) but mostly friendly, and resulted in a large number of publications of which their textbook on psychoanalysis (see Thomä & Kächele, 1987, 1991; Kächele & Thomä, 1999) undoubtedly is the most important. A highlight of their cooperation was their joint receipt in 2002 of the Sigmund Freud Award from the City of Vienna. Even today, the two have a very productive friendship, and their collaboration is central to Kächele's research contributions.

Research Studies

When Horst Kächele was president of the SPR, he presented a programmatic presidential address that advocated for the intensive analysis of narratives generated in psychotherapy using qualitative and quantitative measures. His early clinical practice sharpened his view of salient research issues (e. g., the urgent need to overcome the "fairy-tale culture" of clinical reporting).

When the Ulm group began its systematic work on psychoanalytic processes in the early seventies, it first focused on the extensive analysis of single patient cases that were treated by H. Thomä. The rationale for intensive case studies was to bridge the gap between the clinical and the scientific approach and to keep qualitative and quantitative approaches combined. Therefore, this strategy first involved investigation into a single case in which narrative accounts of the therapists were available. Next, cases were aggregated when the research team felt safe enough not to violate the specifics of the single case:

> We comprehend the transference neurosis as an interactional representation in the therapeutic relationship of the patient's intrapsychic conflicts, the concrete arrangement of which is a function of the analytic process.

This is unique for each dyad, and thus psychoanalysis can legitimately be called a historical science; on the other hand, at a higher level of abstraction it permits the identification of typical patterns of the course of analysis. (Thomä & Kächele, 1987, p. 331)

Both Thomä and Kächele continually reflected on aspects of methodology and the philosophy of science related to psychoanalysis and intensively discussed critical arguments against psychoanalytic theory (e.g., Grünbaum, 1984) by demonstrating the usefulness of empirical research methods to support the validity of psychodynamic constructs. A basic essay on the philosophy of science in psychoanalysis from 1973 was recently reviewed and revised (Kächele & Thomä, 1999).

The leading idea of the Ulm research program on psychoanalysis was to use descriptive data of a different quality to examine clinical process hypotheses. The basic methodological conception was inspired by Helen Sargent's (1961) recommendations for the Topeka Project, consisting of a four-level approach; on each level, different methods with appropriate material representing different levels of conceptualization should be worked on:

I   Clinical case study
II   Systematic clinical descriptions
III Guided clinical judgment procedures
IV   Computer-assisted and linguistic text analysis

The long-term goal of Kächele's work has been to establish ways of systematically describing the various aspects and dimensions of the psychoanalytic processes. This has entailed the generation of general process hypotheses as well as the specification of single-case process assumptions:

Specifying *how* a psychoanalytic process should unfold must go beyond general clinical ideas by considering the kind of material brought forth by each patient and the strategic interventions most appropriate to achieving change in the dimensions of theoretical relevance specified for each particular case. Although our approach excluded the use of nonclinical measures to limit the intrusions on the clinical process, independent psychometric pre-post outcome data were used to assess the effectiveness of the psychoanalytic treatment, and have been published. (Thomä & Kächele, 1997, p. 458)

The first case to be treated by such comprehensive clinical description, the case of Christian Y, was a collaborative endeavour that included the treating analyst, a second psychoanalyst, and a clinical psychologist, in a group-discussion working style. Later, a similar description was prepared for a second research case, that of Amalie X, which has become a specimen case of psychoanalytical single-case research and still is the subject of intensive research (Kächele et al., 2006): Amalie X (born 1939) suffered from body image difficulties and was in psychoanalytic treatment (517 sessions) during the early 1970s with good results. Some years later she returned to her former therapist for a short period of analytic therapy because of problems with her lover, many years her junior. Twenty-five years later, her final separation from this partner was causing her unbearable difficulties, and she consulted a colleague for additional help.

The case of Amalie has been analyzed with a variety of objective and standardized methods that have been described in a series of publications (for a summary, see Kächele et al., 2006). The group studied (a) change of emotional insight, (b) change of self-esteem, (c) types of subjective suffering, (d) change in dreams, (e) the focal model of process assessed by the core conflictual relationship theme (CCRT) method, (f) breaks between sessions and the analytic process, (g) the "unconscious plan" in terms of control-mastery theory, and (h) psychoanalytic technique as assessed by the psychotherapy process Q-sort method.

At the next level of data analysis, computer-aided text analyses were used with the goal of extending the descriptive power of these observational methods toward narrative efforts that would bring enriched meaning to the lexical analyses from the textbank. The following list summarizes the single approaches developed in the Ulm Textbank to analyse verbal material from psychoanalysis and that have been comprehensively used in a variety of studies: verbal activity, long-term transference trends, personal pronouns, redundancy in patient's and therapist's language, classification of anxiety themes, emotive aspects of therapeutic language, change of body concepts, cognitive changes during psychoanalysis, changes of latent meaning structures, affective dictionary, parts of speech, and core conflictual words.

All results on psychoanalytic dialogues studied by these techniques underscore the dyadic nature of the process. "Whatever microsystem is analyzed, one finds dyadic dependencies and specifics within dyads. This has been one of the reasons why the Ulm research paradigm has been so intrigued by the study of singular cases" (Kächele, 1992b, p. 11). One of the fruits of Kächele's initiative that is closely linked with the Ulm Textbank is Erhard Mergenthaler's therapeutic cycle model describing the changing ratio between abstraction and emotion and their connection during the psychotherapeutic process.

Implications of Kächele's research on clinical practice can mostly be seen as the continuous attempt to sensitize therapists for specific aspects or variables of the therapeutic process, such as language, emotion, and conflict, and to relate these variables to an operational model or system. Although Horst Kächele was not directly involved in its development, it is not surprising that many of the authors of the operationalized psychodynamic diagnosis system (OPD Working Group, 2008) have their professional origin in the Ulm Department of Psychosomatic Medicine and Psychotherapy.

Stimulated by his visits to colleagues in the United States, such as Lester Luborsky, Hans H. Strupp, or Hartvig Dahl, Horst Kächele imported a variety of measures and approaches into German psychotherapy research, such as the CCRT, the frames of mind-method, plan-analysis, and others. Together with Klaus Grawe, he founded the PEP (*Psychotherapeutische Einzelfall Prozessforschung*, or, in English, Single-case Process Research [SPR]) project. The idea of PEP was to collect a large number of process researchers who were experts in a variety of measures/approaches and to initiate comparative research related to just two single cases. The verbatim transcripts of two short-term psychotherapies (one psychodynamic, the other one cognitive behavioral) provided the basis for PEP. Kächele and Grawe succeeded in bringing more than 40 different groups together, all working intensively with the material. This project resulted in a large number of publications describing the process of the two therapies on a linguistic level, using hermeneutic and specific (process) measures such as SASB, the Vanderbilt Scales, the CCRT, and many others (Kächele, 1992a).

OTHER CONTRIBUTIONS

Although process research, narration, and observation are Horst Kächele's primary interests, he also has initiated research in a wide variety of other fields within the disciplines of psychotherapy and psychosomatic medicine. In his function as the chair of the Stuttgart Center for Psychotherapy Research (between 1988 and 2003), he was successful in getting a huge grant from the German research ministry to run a 5-year research project consisting of a multisite study of the effectiveness of an inpatient psychodynamic treatment of eating disorders (e.g., Kächele, Kordy, & Richard, 2001). The study investigated factors determining the length of treatment and the effect of treatment duration on treatment outcome among patients with eating disorders (anorexia and bulimia nervosa). It consisted of an observation of the symptomatic status of 1,171 patients who were assessed for 2.5 years after their admission to one of 43 participating hospitals. Treatment modalities, especially length and intensity, varied considerably between and within hospitals but were related to patient characteristics to a very small degree. At 2.5-year follow-up, 33% of patients with anorexia and 25% of the patients with bulimia were symptom free. Length of treatment showed weak effects on outcome and interacted with other relevant patient characteristics, whereas treatment intensity was not clearly related to treatment outcome. This project (TR-EAT) initiated a similar study on a European level and has contributed to the implementation of patient-focused treatment research as one major field of Horst Kächele's team in Stuttgart, with Hans Kordy, another influential person in SPR, being the major representative (e.g. Puschner, Kraft, Kächele, & Kordy, 2007).

Horst Kächele also stimulated research on the screening and utilization of treatment in mothers suffering from postnatal depression (e.g., von Ballestrem, Strauss, & Kächele, 2002), a study that was part of his major research on perinatal medicine. In his Ulm group, a variety of well-funded projects dealt with the determinants and consequences of premature birth (e.g., Brisch et al., 2005; Buchheim et al., 1999). Research on attachment was part of these projects and also figured in his work with adults (cf. Strauss, Buchheim, & Kächele, 2002) and psychoanalytic single-case research (e.g., Buchheim & Kächele, 2003).

Among a wide variety of research fields (including music therapy, ethics in psychotherapy, psycho-politics, neurobiology, and service and training research; cf. http://www.la-vie-vecu.de), one important issue in Horst Kächele's work that deserves mention is psychooncology: Together with his colleagues Volker Tschuschke and Norbert Grulke, he succeeded in establishing a research group at Ulm University mainly dealing with research on coping and determinants of survival in patients undergoing bone marrow transplantation (e.g., Grulke, Bailer, Hertenstein et al., 2005).

INFLUENCES

Horst Kächele's primary mentor was Helmut Thomä, but there were several others who continuously worked with him and largely influenced his theoretical thinking and the way he conceptualized psychotherapy research. North American colleagues have already been mentioned (Luborsky, Strupp, Orlinsky, Howard, Dahl, among others). Within the German-speaking world, it was especially Adolf-Ernst Meyer, chair of the Department of Psychosomatic Medicine in Hamburg, with whom Horst was closely connected and who supported his scientific ideas. Meyer's conception of psychoanalytic research was very similar to Horst Kächele's, especially with respect to his request that psychoanalytical concepts (and treatments) always should to be empirically supported.

Conversely, Horst Kächele has mentored a variety of researchers in his departments in Ulm and Stuttgart—Hans Kordy, Erhard Mergenthaler, Michael Hölzer, Anna Buchheim, Reiner Dahlbender or Dan Pokorny, to mention just a few—and he has significantly contributed to the development of a well-functioning network of researchers and institutions active in psychodynamic psychotherapy research inside and outside of Germany.

Kächele and Thomä attended several early SPR meetings in the United States. After presenting at the first international conference on psychoanalytic process research at Ulm University in 1985 (see Dahl, Kächele, & Thomä, 1988), Horst Kächele and his team hosted the 18th International Meeting of the SPR in Ulm in 1987. This meeting was the first international SPR meeting in a non-English-speaking country, and the first ever in Continental Europe (many others, e.g., in Lyon, Geilo, Braga, Weimar, and Rome, were to follow). The Ulm meeting opened the gate to SPR for many Europeans (and people from other countries). Accordingly, this meeting also led to several Europeans' assuming responsible positions in SPR during the following years. It is not surprising that Horst Kächele himself became the first European to be president of SPR. Several other Europeans, namely, Klaus Grawe, Franz Caspar, Erhard Mergenthaler, and the author of this chapter, were able to follow him.

CONCLUSION

Although close to retirement, Horst Kächele is still a very active researcher, and he is still pursuing his idea of bringing psychoanalytical practice and empirical research more closely together. In one of his recent articles (Kächele et al., 2006) he summarized this work:

> We say this in order to encourage other psychoanalysts to open the privacy of their clinical work in the endeavour to improve clinical work by allowing others in the scientific community to carefully scrutinize their work. For this purpose, we recommend the training of researchers who are also trained as clinicians, and the training of clinicians who are also trained as researchers, so that they may learn to identify with both the clinical and research tasks. (p. 824)

Although Horst Kächele also has actively participated in mainstream psychotherapy research, as the variety of his projects in Ulm and Stuttgart reflects, his legacy will be predominantly his specific efforts and approaches to validate the process of psychoanalytic treatment. Horst Kächele's major interest was always directed to the empirically based development of psychoanalytic theory that can be used by practicing clinicians. This has found its condensation in his three-volume textbook *Psychoanalytic Practice*. This textbook, which was published in a German second edition in 1996, has meanwhile been translated into 11 languages (from Armenian to English to Spanish). The numerous translations of this textbook reflect Horst Kächele's ability to bring the psychotherapy world together.

Perhaps it was two specific traits of Horst Kächele that made an extraordinary psychotherapy researcher out of him. One is his ability to daydream. He once described himself as a daydreamer in the sense of Ernst Bloch, who conceptualized daydreaming as the anticipation of imagination instead of a regression to the past. Daydreams have undoubtedly quickened Horst Kächele's scientific imagination.

The other trait is described in an unpublished virtual dialogue with his mentor Helmut Thomä. In this dialogue, Horst Kächele cites himself with the statement: "Not to be counted among the conformists is the precondition of creative beginning for me. This is always connected with the risk of a failure!"

REFERENCES

Brisch, K., Bechinger, D., Betzler, S., Heinemann, H., Kächele, H., Pohlandt, F., . . . Buchheim, A. (2005). Attachment quality in very low birthweight premature infants in relation to maternal representations and neurological development. *Parenting: Science and Practice*, 5, 311–331. doi:10.1207/s15327922par0504_1

Buchheim, A., Brisch, K. H., & Kächele, H. (1999). Clinical significance of attachment research for the premature infant group: An overview of most recent research. *Zeitschrift für Kinder- und Jugendpsychiatrie und Psychotherapie*, 27, 125–138.

Buchheim, A., & Kächele, H. (2003). Adult attachment interview and psychoanalytic perspective: A single case study. *Psychoanalytic Inquiry*, 23, 81–101. doi:10.1080/07351692309349027

Dahl, H., Kächele, H., & Thomä, H. (Eds.). (1988). *Psychoanalytic process research strategies*. Berlin, Germany: Springer.

Dührssen, A. M., & Jorswieck, E. (1965). Eine empirisch-statistische Untersuchung zur Leistungsfähigkeit psychoanalytischer Behandlung [An empirical statistical study on the effectiveness of psychoanalytic long-term treatment]. *Der Nervenarzt*, 36, 166–169.

Fenichel, O. (1930). Statistischer Bericht über die therapeutische Tätigkeit 1920–1930. [Statistical report about therapeutic work 1920-1930] In S. Radó, O. Fenichel, & C. Müller-Braunschweig (Eds.), *Zehn Jahre Berliner Psychoanalytisches Institut* (pp. 13–19). Vienna, Austria: Int. Psychoanalytischer Verlag.

Grulke, N., Bailer, H., Hartenstein, B., Kächele, H., Arnold, B., Tschuschke, V., & Heimpel, H. (2005). Coping and survival in patients with leukaemia undergoing allogeneic bone marrow transplantation: Long-term follow-up of a prospective study. *Journal of Psychosomatic Research*, 59, 337–346.

Grünbaum, A. (1984). *The foundations of psychoanalysis*. Berkeley: University of California Press.

Kächele. H. (1970). Der Begriff "psychogener Tod" in der medizinischen Literatur [The term "psychogenic death" in the medical literature]. *Zeitschrift Psychosomatische Medizin und Psychoanalyse*, 16, 105–129/ 202–223.

Kächele, H. (1992a). Une nouvelle perspective de recherche en psychotherapie : Le projet PEP. *Psychothérapies 2*, 73–77.

Kächele, H. (1992b). Narration and observation in psychotherapy research. Reporting on a 20-year-long journey from qualitative case reports to quantitative studies on the psychoanalytic process. *Psychotherapy Research, 2*, 1–15.

Kächele, H. (2001). Psychotherapeutische Forschung über ein Jahrhundert [Psychotherapy research over one century]. In H. C. Deter (Ed.), *Psychosomatik am Beginn des 21. Jahrhunderts* [Psychosomatics in the beginning of the 21st century] (pp. 39–46). Bern, Switzerland: Huber.

Kächele, H., Albani, C., Buchheim, A., Hölzer, M., Hohage, R., Jiménez, J. P., . . . Thomä, H. (2006). The German specimen case Amalia X: Empirical studies. *International Journal of Psycho-Analysis, 87*, 809–826. doi:10.1516/17NN-M9HJ-U25A-YUU5

Kächele, H., Kordy, H., & Richard, M. (2001). Therapy amount and outcome of inpatient psychodynamic treatment of eating disorders in Germany: Data from a multicenter study. *Psychotherapy Research, 11*, 239–257.

Kächele, H., & Thomä, H. (1999). *Textbook of psychoanalytic therapy: Vol. III. Research.* http://sip.medizin.uni-ulm.de.

OPD working group (2008). *Operationalized psychodynamic diagnosis (OPD-2).* Bern, Switzerland: Huber.

Puschner, B., Kraft, S., Kächele, H., & Kordy, H. (2007). Course of improvement during two years in psychoanalytic and psychodynamic outpatient psychotherapy. *Psychology and Psychotherapy, 80*, 51–68.

Sargent, H. D. (1961). Intrapsychic change: Methodological problems in psychotherapy research. *Psychiatry, 24*, 93–108.

Sargent, H. D., Horwitz, L., Wallerstein, R. S., & Appelbaum, A. (1968). *Prediction in psychotherapy research. Method for the transformation of clinical judgments into testable hypothesis.* New York, NY: International Universities Press.

Strauss, B., Buchheim, A., & Kächele, H. (Eds) (2002) *Klinische Bindungsforschung* [Clinical attachment research]. Stuttgart, Germany: Schattauer.

Thomä, H., & Kächele, H. (1987). *Psychoanalytic Practice. Vol.1: Principles.* Berlin, Springer.

Thomä, H., & Kächele, H. (1991). *Psychoanalytic Practice. Vol.2: Clinical Studies.* Berlin, Germany: Springer.

von Ballestrem, C.-L., Strauss, M., & Kächele, H. (2002). Screening and utilization of treatment in mothers with postnatal depression. In D. Ebert, K. P. Ebmeier, & W. P. Kaschka (Eds.), *Perspectives in affective disorders* (pp. 25–34). Basel, Switzerland: Karger. doi:10.1159/000066874

22

ENRICO JONES: APPRECIATING COMPLEXITY

TAI KATZENSTEIN, PETER FONAGY, AND J. STUART ABLON

Enrico Jones had a unique capacity, both professionally and personally, for weaving multiple ideas, roles, and worlds together synergistically. As a psychotherapy researcher and practicing psychoanalyst, Enrico was committed to avoiding oversimplification, and that commitment laid the groundwork for some of his most outstanding achievements. He examined the psychotherapeutic and psychoanalytic treatment process in a way that allowed for the richness and depth of true clinical complexity, while holding firmly to the importance of empirical methodology as the mode for doing so.

MAJOR CONTRIBUTIONS

Enrico Jones's considerable and multifaceted scientific contributions stemmed from his attention to the social factors underlying both individual differences and psychotherapy, as well as his focus on elucidating key elements of psychotherapeutic process. In his efforts to identify sources of therapeutic action, Jones created his empirically derived instrument, the Psychotherapy Process Q-set (PQS). He also generated interaction structure theory, a theoretical and empirical model, to better understand the mutative elements in psychotherapy.

In the late 1970s, Jones's research focused on the psychological aspects of race. He actively challenged racial stereotypes present in the literature. He insisted that psychologists not accept simple answers. He warned against the dangers inherent in regarding African Americans as a homogeneous group. In keeping with the complex and subtle thinking for which he was so widely respected, he voiced his reservations about the construction of ethnically specific norms of measurement. On the one hand, culture-specific measures acknowledged a pluralism that had previously been disregarded. On the other hand, Jones believed that these measures could themselves strike an exclusionary note (by upholding a static view of society).

Enrico Jones was one of the earliest researchers to examine race and psychotherapy systematically. In a brief and wonderfully cogent critique of the field in the late 1980s, he argued that race was the wrong level of conceptualization for the individual differences among therapists (Jones, 1985). Presaging some of the most salient themes to emerge in discussions about cultural competence, Jones wrote succinctly: "The question is not how to treat *the* black client but how to treat *this* black client" (p. 175). Jones's emphasis on the individuality of the patient and of each therapy relationship became central to the second part of his career.

During the 1980s, Jones developed the PQS. His programmatic line of research using this measure established him as a leading psychotherapy process researcher. Whereas many researchers were pursuing the question of whether therapy worked, Jones found the question of how therapy worked more compelling. To this day, many regard the PQS as one of the most comprehensive and clinically relevant empirical measures of psychotherapy process.

Jones's research on psychotherapy process culminated in the publication of his book, *Therapeutic Action: A Guide to Psychoanalytic Theory* (Jones, 2000). This book details a conceptualization of therapeutic action that Jones termed *repetitive interaction structures*. His interaction structure theory provides an empirical method with which to deconstruct not only the essence of the therapy relationship but also the directions of influence that operate between patient and clinician. Jones's model of therapeutic action uses both a methodological paradigm and a theoretical frame to answer one of the field's most important questions: What is it about the nature of the therapy relationship that either facilitates or hinders change?

BEGINNINGS

Enrico Edison Jones was born in Munich, Germany, on November 25, 1947. Enrico's father was African American and served as a master sergeant in the U.S. Army. Enrico's mother was born in Germany and worked as an early-childhood educator. Enrico's parents met and fell in love when his father was deployed to Germany during World War II. He spent his early childhood living on military bases in Germany with his four siblings and parents. German was his first language. When Enrico was 2 years old, his family moved to the United States and eventually settled in Rochester, New York (after passing through Maine, New Jersey, Camp Kilmer, and Fort Dix). It is evident, even in this brief snapshot of Jones's early life, that the seeds of his unique capacity to bridge complexities were planted early as he negotiated the challenges of growing up as an African American in postwar Germany, on two different continents, and in two different societies. The opportunities and challenges that Jones no doubt encountered along the way played an important role in shaping his thoughts about race, psychology, and relationships.

Jones was recruited from his Catholic high school as a National Merit Scholar to attend Harvard. While he was growing up, his mother encouraged him to follow in the steps of her father, a well-known and widely respected physician. While Jones considered the option of pursuing medical school in his early college years, he ultimately decided to major in history. During this period, he attended a series of lectures delivered by Erik Erikson. He was intrigued by Erikson's developmental theory because of its attention to change across time. This exposure formed an important bridge between the world of psychology and Enrico's interest in history (in which actors and narratives also figure prominently).

In 1969, Jones graduated cum laude from Harvard. That same year, he decided to pursue psychology in graduate school. He earned his PhD from Berkeley in 1974 after completing his predoctoral internship at Mount Zion Hospital. He joined the faculty directly out of graduate school. This rare occurrence (the department did not typically hire from within) reflected the high esteem in which Jones was held as a researcher, teacher, and intellectual. He rose quickly through the ranks to full professor.

In 1981, Jones spent a sabbatical year in Paris as a member of the *Centre National de la Recherche Scientifique*. This year marked an important shift in the direction of his interests. Prior to his sabbatical, Jones's line of research had been in the field of ethnic minority health. In the years following his return from sabbatical, he became intrigued by psychoanalysis from both research and clinical perspectives. This new interest, combined with a long-held interest in studying psychotherapy, formed the foundation for the programmatic line of research that dominated the second phase of his career.

Displaying his remarkable talent for fully living both parts of the hyphenated identity of scientist–practitioner, in addition to holding an academic appointment as full professor at Berkeley, Jones maintained an active clinical practice from 1982 onward. He completed psychoanalytic training at the San Francisco Psychoanalytic Institute in 1992. Jones also held clinical appointments at the San Francisco Psychoanalytic Institute (1997–2000); the Department of Psychiatry and Langley Porter Psychiatric Institute, University of California–San Francisco (1982–1996); and Mount Zion Hospital (1976–1994).

ACCOMPLISHMENTS

Enrico Jones dedicated his research career to the following four domains (listed chronologically in the order in which they emerged): (a) social aspects of individual differences; (b) social factors in psychotherapy; (c) the study of the psychotherapy process using the PQS; and (d) interaction structures and therapeutic action.

Social Aspects of Individual Differences

Enrico Jones's research on the psychological aspects of race revealed that much of what psychologists were saying revolved around simplistic, untenable assumptions with disturbingly little validity. In an early paper (Jones, 1978a), Enrico challenged the racial stereotype propagated in the psychological literature of the period, namely, that blacks showed estrangement, distancing, or mistrust of society ("marks of past oppression"). Jones and Zoppel (1979) demonstrated that dichotomies such as internal and external locus of control did not translate cross-culturally or for different samples of the same population within the United States. Jones's pioneering work in the area of ethnic minority mental health culminated with the publication of the classic text *Minority Mental Health* (Jones & Korchin, 1982). This volume provided the field with a comprehensive theoretical and empirical overview of minority group differences in attitudes toward mental health, assessment of symptoms, and therapeutic intervention.

Social Factors in Psychotherapy

In its early days, the Berkeley Psychotherapy Research Project, which Enrico Jones founded, focused on the impact of demographic and social variables on psychotherapy. Jones was particularly interested in the effect on outcome of the patient–therapist match. In one study, White therapists rated both their Black and White—but particularly their Black—clients as psychologically more impaired than did Black therapists (Jones, 1982). Jones demonstrated that a substantial number of Black clients (50%) failed to return to their therapist after an initial consultation. Many of his writings in the 1970s addressed a cohort of clinicians who did not systematically think about race. Jones contributed the idea that Black clients' discussion of race with their white therapists was not resistance, and that the liberal pretence of "color blindness" was actually a denial of the uniqueness of the individual (points that, on account of writings like Enrico Jones's, are now assumed in the provision of culturally competent care).

Yet, once again, Jones found that the simple view fit poorly with the data. The Berkeley Psychotherapy Research Project found race to be a weak predictor of patient outcome (Jones, 1978b, 1982; Jones & Zoppel, 1982). The complex answer was that African and European American patients in psychotherapy were more alike than different (Jones, 1982). Furthermore, ethnic matching did not in and of itself affect the quality of the therapeutic alliance. For Jones, the answer to this conundrum lay in the importance of fully and thoroughly appreciating an individual's subjectivity. Jones believed that the way the field of psychology operationalized race was problematically ambiguous and nonspecific. His focus on subjectivity and his finding that the quality of the therapy alliance was not related to ethnic match led him down a new and fruitful research path.

The Study of Psychotherapy and the Q-Set

During the 1980s, Enrico Jones responded to the field's need for quantitative methods that preserved the depth and complexity of clinical material while conforming to the requirements of empirical science. In an effort to address this need, Jones spent more than a decade pioneering and developing the PQS; Jones, 2000). The Q-set instructs coders to sort its 100 items according to a normal distribution in terms of how well they describe a therapy session. The items concern (a) patients' attitudes, behavior, and experience; (b) therapists' actions and attitudes; and (c) the nature of the interaction of the dyad. The Q-set is designed to provide a basic language for the description and classification of treatment processes in a form suitable for quantitative analysis. This instrument captures the uniqueness of each treatment hour while also permitting the assessment of the similarities or dissimilarities between hours and patients. (See Jones, 2000, for a more detailed discussion of the instrument and its psychometric properties.)

The PQS has been used reliably for both group comparison and intensive single-case designs. It has been applied to study treatments as diverse as psychoanalysis, long- and short-term psychodynamic psychotherapy, cognitive behavior therapy (CBT), interpersonal therapy, rational emotive therapy, and gestalt therapy. The Q-set has also been used by panels of experts from different theoretical orientations to construct prototypes of ideal treatment hours instantiating their respective orientations. Use of the Q-set in this way (referred to as *prototype methodology*) facilitates examining differences between what clinicians and patients actually do in treatment and what experts and theories stipulate dyads should ideally be doing.

Using this measure, Jones and his colleagues contributed a series of remarkable findings to the psychotherapy process and outcome literature. In early studies, the Q-set demonstrated its value by empirically grounding commonly held clinical observations. For instance, one study (Jones, Cumming, & Horowitz, 1988) empirically substantiated the clinical claim that technique must be adjusted to the severity of presentation. In this study, patients with milder posttraumatic stress responses and pathological grief were observed to do relatively well when their memories were linked with current experience, their views of themselves were examined in relation to others, and they were exposed to transference interpretations. By contrast, those who suffered greater psychological distress did best when their therapist was more reassuring, offered advice about reality-based problems, and provided feedback about the patient's defenses. These findings, which make intuitive clinical sense, are not in and of themselves surprising. What is remarkable, however, is that they were demonstrated in an empirical study. The Q-set's capacity to tap a range of therapy techniques in a way that is highly relevant to one's work as a clinician is one of its unique and striking characteristics.

In several other studies, Enrico Jones applied the PQS empirically to capture subtle therapeutic shifts in the treatment process. In one study (Jones & Windholz, 1990), improvements were reflected in a shift from intellectualization and rationalization to seeking separation and increased access to the patient's thoughts and feelings. In another study (Jones, Parke, & Pulos, 1992), Jones and his colleagues determined that patients who experienced clinically significant changes manifested a gradual shift from external reality-oriented constructions of their difficulties to an emphasis on an inner self-reflective orientation.

In a unique and complex article (Jones, Ghannam, Nigg, & Dyer, 1993), Jones and his colleagues analyzed a two-and-a-half-year, twice-weekly, videotaped psychodynamic psychotherapeutic treatment of a depressed woman. They coded 53 hours of treatment and then identified four patterns (using factor analysis) characterizing the nature of the patient's and therapist's interactions: (a) the therapist was accepting/neutral (i.e., conveyed a sense of nonjudgmental acceptance); (b) the therapist was interactive (didactic, challenged the patient's views, was tactless); (c) the therapist used psychodynamic technique (e.g., interpreted warded-off/unconscious wishes); and (d) the patient experienced dysphoric affect (e.g., patient felt sad/depressed, anxious/tense). Jones innovatively applied time series methodology (later a central component of his methodological paradigm for examining the interaction patterns between patients and clinicians) to identify the regular cooccurrences as well as the lag effects between therapist and patient behavior.

He found that the patient's dysphoric affect regularly triggered high levels of acceptance and neutrality in the therapist. Interestingly, the therapist's supportive stance and reassurance triggered the patient's dysphoric affect. Jones identified a large number of bidirectional effects. For example, the therapist's interactive and somewhat controlling behavior was triggered by and, in turn, triggered the patient's dysphoric affect.

A powerful feature of the PQS is that it can be applied to study psychotherapeutic treatments across a broad range of theoretical perspectives. In a 1993 article with Steven Pulos, Jones reported that coders could use the PQS to distinguish psychodynamic from CBT. The process–outcome results suggested that in the 30 brief psychodynamic interventions, the score on the Psychodynamic factor strongly related to outcome. That is, the more psychodynamic process fostered, the better the outcome. Interestingly, this was not the case for CBT. The factor labeled CBT Technique did not relate to outcome for the 32 CBT treatments. Also, the higher the scores on the factor labeled Negative Affect, the better the outcome in the case of psychodynamic therapy. The opposite relationship held for CBT, which emphasizes regulation and control of negative affect. Strikingly, in the CBT treatments, improvement was associated with higher scores on the psychodynamic factor.

These findings might suggest that the mode of action in CBT has more in common with psychodynamic processes than has traditionally been assumed. But this would have been a simplification. Jones realized that there was a weakness in this study: Both the Psychodynamic and the Cognitive Behavioral factors were empirically derived and confounded with the material they were supposed to evaluate. In a programmatic line of work conducted with Stuart Ablon (Ablon & Jones, 1998, 1999, 2002), Jones used independent experts to define prototypes of CBT and psychodynamic therapy using the PQS. The degree to which treatments adhered to these theoretically derived prototypes was then measured and correlated with outcome.

The Q-prototypes were applied to two archived treatment samples of psychodynamic treatments ($N = 30$ and $N = 38$). Interestingly, in these data sets, psychodynamic therapy correlated with both the psychodynamic and the CBT prototypes, whereas CBT was only related to the CBT prototype. Similarity to the psychodynamic prototype predicted outcome in one of the two psychodynamic samples and the CBT sample. In this study, the CBT prototype was not significantly correlated with positive outcome (Ablon & Jones, 1998). The same technique was used to reanalyze tapes from the National Institute of Mental Health Treatment of Depression Collaborative Research Program. In this series of studies, both interpersonal psychotherapy and CBT sessions adhered most strongly to the ideal prototype of CBT. Positive outcome was associated with adherence to the CBT prototype (Ablon & Jones, 2002). The study shows just how misleading "brand-name" therapy can be; in particular, interpersonal psychotherapy was demonstrated in actual practice to be startlingly similar to CBT.

The results of this programmatic line of research contain a warning about the risks of oversimplification. Awarding the status of empirically supported treatments to particular brands of therapy without actually studying the contents of these brands is equivalent to the Food and Drug Administration approving the trade name of a drug without concerning itself with the generic substance on which it is based (Ablon & Jones, 2002). Ablon and Jones powerfully reminded us of this point in a 1999 article in which they demonstrated that for both interpersonal therapy and CBT, the process correlates of outcome at the individual item level were neither technique- nor orientation specific but patient-related.

Interaction Structures

Enrico Jones's psychotherapy process research culminated in the publication of his book *Therapeutic Action* (2000). Here, Jones advanced a methodological and theoretical paradigm for examining the way in which relationship representational structures could be observed in the therapeutic dyad and linked to treatment outcome. Jones defined interaction structures as the repetitive, mutually influencing patterns that emerge over time when patients and therapists engage in psychotherapy. According to Jones, interaction structures were the major source of therapeutic action in psychodynamic/analytic treatments. He stipulated that the repetitive, slow-to-change two-person patterns comprising interaction structures reflected the psychological architecture (e.g., character structure/personality and defenses/coping mechanisms) of both clinicians and patients. Interaction structures were, therefore, highly specific to the dyad in which they emerged. Instead of talking about individuals, Jones (2000) required that we have a language describing the dyad and its patterned interactions, again foreshadowing the field's relatively recent focus on intersubjectivity.

Jones's interaction structure theory brings together the polarities of insight and relationship. According to this theory, neither insight nor relationship alone brings about change. Instead, change is facilitated by the mutual exploration and shared understandings of patterns in the therapy relationship. Jones (2000) wrote: "Therapeutic action is located in the experience, recognition, and understanding by patient and therapist of these repetitive interactions" (p. 4). It is through interaction with the patient that the therapist tries to understand the patient's mind and the patient endeavors to understand his or her self. Through identifying the recurring themes in the way therapist and patient interact, the psychological structure that motivates both patient and therapist is thrown into relief.

Interaction structure is a bridging concept. It is also a construct that is open to empirical scrutiny through sophisticated statistical analyses of PQS ratings using factor analysis and time series analysis. The grouping of these three methodologies—the PQS, factor analysis, and time series analysis—into one unified paradigm reflected Jones's overarching view that psychotherapy process of all orientations, including longer term psychodynamic treatment, could be examined in a clinically relevant and methodologically rigorous way.

OTHER CONTRIBUTIONS

Enrico Jones was the first African American professor in the psychology department at Berkeley. Over the course of his career, he assumed a major leadership role in the education and training of ethnic minority students. He received the Kenneth and Mamie Clark Award for Outstanding Contributions to the Professional Development of Ethnic Minority Students. Jones also served on the editorial boards of several organizations, including the *Journal of Consulting and Clinical Psychology*, the *Journal of the American Psychoanalytic Association*, the *International Journal of Psychoanalysis*, and *Psychological Issues*. He was a member of the Society for Psychotherapy Research, the International Psychoanalytic Association, and the board for the Scientific Affairs of the American Psychoanalytic Association. He enjoyed a number of fruitful intellectual collaborations with both mentors and students (Robert Wallerstein, Sheldon Korchin, Jack Block, and Stuart Ablon).

CONCLUSION

A central theme throughout this chapter has been Enrico Jones's commitment to avoiding oversimplification. Yet, ultimately, his achievement was that of simplicity. He made the complexities of psychotherapeutic process, including psychoanalytic thought and technique, understandable and accessible. He mastered the dialectic of not succumbing to illusions generated by reductionism and simplification, while avoiding the trap of creating mystique and religion where the innocent questions can no longer be asked and the truth is buried under multiple layers of false sophistication.

Enrico Jones's legacies are considerable and multifaceted. His creation and application of the Psychotherapy Process Q-set originated in his strong belief that both process and outcome needed to be investigated in order to understand why certain treatments worked and certain others failed. Jones's commitment to identifying and examining the processes that were actually (as opposed to theoretically) unfolding and facilitating change in treatment has laid important groundwork for the field's newfound interest in identifying change processes. His inner conviction that it was possible to study psychodynamic and psychoanalytic treatments, even in an era in which funding from traditional agencies was draining away, communicates an important message to young researchers about the value of following what is most compelling, even when the logistical and external variables are formidable.

Looking back at Enrico Jones's 25 years of research, the tragedy of his premature death is felt deeply and sharply. It is evident that he could have continued and needed to continue for at least another quarter of a century to fulfill his mission. Those who knew Enrico and his work can take some solace in the realization that his work lives on in the current studies that use the measure he created and in the breadth and depth of his students' and colleagues' ongoing work, as well as in the continued efforts of the Research Committee of the International Psychoanalytic Association and the Psychotherapy Research Group at Massachusetts General Hospital.

REFERENCES

Ablon, J. S., & Jones, E. E. (1998). How expert clinicians' prototypes of an ideal treatment correlate with outcome in psychodynamic and cognitive-behavior therapy. *Psychotherapy Research, 8,* 71–83. doi:10.1093/ptr/8.1.71

Ablon, J. S., & Jones, E. E. (1999). Psychotherapy process in the National Institute of Mental Health Treatment of Depression Collaborative Research Program. *Journal of Consulting and Clinical Psychology, 67,* 64–75. doi:10.1037/0022-006X.67.1.64

Ablon, J. S., & Jones, E. E. (2002). Validity of controlled clinical trials of psychotherapy: findings from the NIMH Treatment of Depression Collaborative Research Program. *American Journal of Psychiatry, 159,* 775–783. doi:10.1176/appi.ajp.159.5.775

Jones, E. E. (1978a). Black–White personality differences: Another look. *Journal of Personality Assessment, 42,* 244–252.

Jones, E. E. (1978b). Effects of race on psychotherapy process and outcome: An exploratory investigation. *Psychotherapy: Theory, Research and Practice, 15,* 226–236.

Jones, E. E. (1982). Psychotherapists' impressions of treatment outcome as a function of race. *Journal of Clinical Psychology, 38,* 722–731.

Jones, E. E. (1985). Psychotherapy and counseling with Black clients. In P. Pedersen (Ed.), *Handbook of cross-cultural counseling and therapy* (pp. 173–179). Westport, CT: Greenwood Press.

Jones, E. E. (2000). *Therapeutic action: A guide to psychoanalytic therapy.* Northvale, NJ: Jason Aronson, Inc.

Jones, E. E., Cumming, J. D., & Horowitz, M. J. (1988). Another look at the non-specific hypothesis of therapeutic effectiveness. *Journal of Consulting and Clinical Psychology, 56,* 48–55. doi:10.1037/0022-006X.56.1.48

Jones, E. E., Ghannam, J., Nigg, J. T., & Dyer, J. F. (1993). A paradigm for single-case research: the time series study of a long-term psychotherapy for depression. *Journal of Consulting and Clinical Psychology, 61,* 381–394. doi:10.1037/0022-006X.61.3.381

Jones, E. E., & Korchin, S. J. (Eds.). (1982). *Minority mental health.* New York, NY: Praeger.

Jones, E. E., Parke, L. A., & Pulos, S. M. (1992). How therapy is conducted in the private consulting room: A multidimensional description of brief psychodynamic treatments. *Psychotherapy Research, 2,* 16–30.

Jones, E. E., & Pulos, S. M. (1993). Comparing the process in psychodynamic and cognitive behavioral therapies. *Journal of Consulting and Clinical Psychology, 61,* 306–316. doi:10.1037/0022-006X.61.2.306

Jones, E. E., & Windholz, M. (1990). The psychoanalytic case study: Toward a method for systematic inquiry. *Journal of the American Psychoanalytic Association, 38,* 985–1015. doi:10.1177/000306519003800405

Jones, E. E., & Zoppel, C. L. (1979). Personality differences among Blacks in Jamaica and the United States. *Journal of Cross-Cultural Psychology, 10,* 435–456. doi:10.1177/0022022179104003

Jones, E. E., & Zoppel, C. L. (1982). Impact of client and therapist gender on psychotherapy process and outcome. *Journal of Consulting and Clinical Psychology, 50,* 259–272. doi:10.1037/0022-006X.50.2.259

23

DAVID A. SHAPIRO: PSYCHOTHERAPEUTIC INVESTIGATIONS

MICHAEL BARKHAM, GLENYS PARRY, AND GILLIAN E. HARDY

David Shapiro has made a unique and enduring contribution to psychotherapy research over a period of 3 decades and was the first UK member—and the second non–North American—to be elected international president of the Society of Psychotherapy Research (SPR), for 1993–1994. The title of his presidential address—"Finding Out How Psychotherapies Help People Change" (1995)—encapsulates his classic scientist–practitioner approach to investigating the psychological therapies, an approach that Shapiro called *psychotherapeutic investigations* in reference to Wittgenstein's *Philosophical Investigations*, where insights are derived from examining the inextricable links between methods and findings. Shapiro has long been regarded as preeminent among psychotherapy researchers, a position acknowledged in 2000 when he was awarded both a Lifetime Achievement Award by the UK chapter of SPR and was the recipient of the M. B. Shapiro Award by the Division of Clinical Psychology of the British Psychological Society in recognition of his work in the field of psychotherapy research.

271

MAJOR CONTRIBUTIONS

In considering David Shapiro's major contributions to psychotherapy research, it is probably easiest to think in terms of research "episodes" across which runs a golden thread—that of applied science. His skill as a scientist derived from his ability to combine conceptual clarity with innovative and pluralistic research methodologies, whereas his skill as a practitioner drew heavily on a combination of his trust in, and willingness to test, the process and theoretical basis of any therapy model he was delivering. The vehicle for his delivery of applied science was the research clinic he established, in which all therapy was audiotaped (and some videotaped), open to peer-group supervision, and available as research data. A key axiom of his approach was that he and members of his team were both clinicians and researchers. Shapiro's approach fully embraced the role of the applied scientist. Moreover, although Shapiro was the research leader, there was always equity in terms of clinical caseload among members of the group, and he always placed himself under as much scrutiny as he placed others under.

In addition to combining both roles of scientist and practitioner, Shapiro and his team trained in contrasting forms of therapy—that is, cognitive behavioral (CB) therapy and psychodynamic interpersonal (PI) therapy—thereby enabling Shapiro to employ designs in which therapists were crossed with therapies rather than nesting them within treatments. This strategy enabled Shapiro to address two central research agendas: (a) ensuring delivery of high-quality research in contrasting psychological therapies and (b) providing a unique data set to address issues of common factors in the psychological therapies. Shapiro's approach to the research process encompassed deeply held personal values about the importance of providing an even playing field in the evaluation of differing psychological therapies and mechanisms of change, be they specific or common. These research themes remain central because many therapies still lack a high-quality research base and the loss of diversity in psychotherapeutic approaches is a potential loss to the mental health field and to the aspiration of giving clients a real choice of evidence-based treatments. In this context, the significance of Shapiro's contribution has been as much about the demonstration of the importance of understanding process in order to develop effective services as it has been about discovering specific change processes.

EARLY BEGINNINGS

David Shapiro was born in 1945 and grew up on the borders of South London and Kent, attending Eltham College and winning a Sacher Open Scholarship in Modern Studies to New College Oxford. There he gained first class honors in psychology and philosophy. His teachers included Richard Dawkins, Jeffrey Gray, Rom Harré, Niko Tinbergen, Gilbert Ryle, and Peter Strawson. He was named *proxime accessit* to the Henry Wilde Prize in philosophy and almost diverted from his planned career in psychology by the intellectual appeal of graduate work in that field. He then completed an MSc with distinction in clinical psychology at the Institute of Psychiatry, London. He stayed at the Institute of Psychiatry on a Medical Research Council (MRC) studentship to read for his PhD under the supervision of Robert F. Hobson.

Frustration with the limitations of the behavioral paradigm then predominant at the Institute of Psychiatry led Shapiro to work with Robert (Bob) Houston. This frustration had already led him to an interest in client-centered therapy research and to working on understanding and implementing the work of Truax and Carkhuff on therapeutic conditions. Therefore, a creative research partnership with Bob Hobson was a very attractive proposition for Shapiro's doctoral work. From that doctoral work, David Shapiro and Bob Hobson published a number of papers (e.g., Shapiro & Hobson, 1972) that addressed issues of methodology as well as of psychotherapeutic change processes. Substantive issues addressed included the possible role of short-term deterioration in the securing of longer term gains from sessions of psychodynamic therapy.

In 1973, Shapiro moved north to the University of Sheffield to take up a post as a lecturer in the psychology department, a move influenced by John Davis, a Sheffield faculty member with an American PhD, who had persuaded his department to meet students' dissatisfaction with the dryness of their curriculum by making an appointment in the then-fashionable area of humanistic psychology, for which Shapiro offered a scientifically acceptable face. In 1977, Peter Warr—director of the MRC's Social and Applied Psychology Unit at the University of Sheffield—took the initiative to add a clinical strand to his industrial/organizational (or work) psychology unit, and Shapiro was appointed as team leader, with the brief to set up a program of work focusing on psychological interventions to support people who were stressed at work. Shapiro formed a research team whose core members were qualified clinical psychologists serving as both clinicians and researchers. The psychotherapy program targeted clients meeting robust clinical criteria who were employed (typically in white-collar jobs, to minimize variability in occupational status) and whose mental health problems had an impact on their work.

Throughout this project the group's research was informed by Shapiro's fascination with the process of psychotherapy; his wish to see more thorough research attention to nonbehavioral therapies, including psychodynamic, interpersonal, and experiential approaches; and his commitment to pursuing rigorous psychotherapeutic investigations synthesizing a wide range of research methods to find out how psychotherapies help people change. The group's strategies and philosophy were intended to exemplify and inform the development of the scientist–practitioner model.

ACCOMPLISHMENTS

As a way of framing Shapiro's research achievements, we have grouped his work into five episodes: (a) research on client-centered conditions, (b) meta-analytic research, (c) conceptual and comparative outcome research, (d) process research, and (e) clinical and service delivery research.

Research on Client-Centered Conditions

Through the early and mid 1970s, Shapiro published a series of articles focusing on the theme, "What are the ingredients of change?" Shapiro carried out studies testing key Rogerian concepts, in particular that of empathy. In one study he evaluated the rating scales devised by Truax and Carkhuff for rating empathy, genuineness, and nonpossessive warmth and found supporting evidence for the use of the empathy scale but not for the other two conditions (Shapiro, 1973). He also employed innovative experimental designs using nonclinical participants with the aim of bringing precision to what had previously been considered somewhat vague concepts. An exemplar of such work was a study in which participants attempted to reconstruct the serial order of dialogues according to examples defining successive points on the Truax Accurate Empathy (AE) Scale (Shapiro, 1976). Contrary to expectations, findings showed a decrease in accuracy with higher AE ratings, suggesting that dialogue representing higher levels of AE indicated tacit understanding rather than an explicit structure identifiable to external raters.

Meta-Analytic Work

On his joining the MRC unit in 1977, Shapiro's focus moved to the question of comparative outcomes across therapeutic approaches, working with Diana Shapiro. Informed by Smith and Glass's (1977) classic meta-analytic study on the effects of psychotherapy—a watershed in outcomes research that had always impressed Shapiro—his work with Diana Shapiro provided him with a question to be addressed in terms of replicating and refining the Smith and Glass study. They refined Smith and Glass's study by implementing a number of amendments, primarily in response to criticisms made of it by Stanley Rachman and G. Terence Wilson. The resulting study comprised 143 outcome studies published between 1975 and 1979 in which two or more psychological treatments were compared with a control group (Shapiro & Shapiro, 1982).

They drew three primary conclusions from the study. First, the mean of the 1,828 effect size measures approached one standard deviation, a finding slightly larger than that reported by Smith and Glass. Second, the relatively modest differences between treatment methods were largely independent of other factors. Finally, they concluded that outcome research at that time was not representative of clinical practice. In a separate review of meta-analysis as applied to treatment outcomes research, Shapiro concluded that the most promising application for this methodology lay in "same experiment" data in which studies compared contrasting conditions within the same experiment. With typical pithiness, he highlighted the methodological problems of aggregating data collected under differing circumstances: "Between-study confounds are the enemy of disaggregation" (Shapiro, 1985, p. 33).

Conceptual and Comparative Outcome Studies

The meta-analytic research provided the basis for two parallel streams of work, each of which captures the clear strengths of Shapiro's research repertoire. One activity focused on a conceptual treatment of issues around evidence of equivalence of outcomes and its implications for research, in work carried out collaboratively with Bill Stiles and Robert Elliott. This arose from the meeting of like-minded scientist–practitioners during the SPR meetings of the early 1980s and yielded a watershed article titled "Are All Psychotherapies Equivalent?" in the *American Psychologist* (Stiles, Shapiro, & Elliott, 1986). The other activity focused on designing a comparative study of contrasting therapies that investigated the processes as well as the outcomes of therapies. Shapiro referred to this approach as a "comparative, content-impact-outcome research strategy."

David Shapiro was subsequently joined by Jenny Firth (later Firth-Cozens), Glenys Parry, and Chris Brewin. With Jenny Firth, Shapiro set about designing a trial to test whether delivering contrasting therapies in differing sequences might yield enhanced outcomes (Shapiro & Firth, 1987). Two therapies were selected in terms of their ability to represent broadly differing approaches: prescriptive (later to be renamed *cognitive behavioral* [CB]) and exploratory (later to be renamed *psychodynamic* interpersonal [PI]) therapy.

A driving concern behind this study, which became known as the (first) Sheffield Psychotherapy Project, was to generate an even playing field between contrasting therapies and, in particular, to deliver quality research on non-CBT approaches. Shapiro, informed by his father's priority of strategy over procedure, realized that the evidence base will always be incomplete; for example, he was always clear that there was no such thing as a "definitive" study—and its application to many clinical situations would be uncertain. Hence, the most compelling need for scientist–practitioner skills arises when the evidence is equivocal or lacking, and he saw a desperate need to evaluate the contribution of non-CBT models of psychological therapy. In this way, the focus and the means for testing it relied on building a team of scientist–practitioners.

Although clinical psychology training in the UK at the time was predominantly CB, the scientist–practitioners were recruited for an evenhanded approach to PI and CB therapies (as reflected in their training placements). This evenhandedness and openness to training in both therapy modalities enabled the studies to be designed with therapists delivering both treatment modalities. Hence, therapists were crossed with treatments, in contrast to most research studies, in which separate groups of trained therapists delivered only one therapy mode.

The Sheffield Psychotherapy Project and the Second Sheffield Psychotherapy Project were designed to compare the two treatment modalities—PI and CB—and to examine explanatory models and processes of change. The design of the Second Sheffield Psychotherapy Project was replicated in a smaller effectiveness study carried out in National Health Service (NHS) clinical settings across multiple sites to determine the extent to which the outcome results could be generalized to NHS outpatients. The final study in the series tested the two treatment modalities in a very brief format—two-plus-one sessions. While this quartet of studies held the comparison between PI and CB therapy constant, they variously used differing duration of treatment sessions considered as an independent variable: two, eight, and 16 sessions. An overarching aim of these studies was to increase the level of precision of outcome-trials methodology as one possible resolution to the equivalence paradox.

The first Sheffield Psychotherapy Project was directly informed by Shapiro's meta-analytic work by comparing prescriptive (CB) therapy with exploratory (PI) therapy within the same experiment and by using a crossover design to control for patient, therapist, and common factors and giving each treatment an equal chance to demonstrate efficacy. In addition, it sought to address issues of treatment sequence effects within eclectic therapy by discovering whether the order of delivering the two different kinds of psychotherapy made a difference to outcome. The results favored prescriptive therapy, although this difference was moderate, and confirmed Shapiro's view that findings of equivalent outcomes may be due to poor control over extraneous therapist, technique, and patient variables that were well controlled in this study. The outcome was largely unaffected by the order in which the two methods were offered. However, further analysis showed that the differential effectiveness of the two treatments was confined to one of the two main therapists—a clear marker for current interest in therapist effects.

The design of the Second Sheffield Psychotherapy Project employed Shapiro and his team of clinician–researchers—Michael Barkham, Gillian Hardy, Shirley Reynolds, and Mike Startup—as therapists, together with a dedicated interviewer/assessor, in a more sophisticated study testing the impact of treatment length and severity of depression with a sample of 117 clients (Shapiro et al., 1994).

More specifically, the 1994 study focused on questions of modality—Is CB more effective and rapid in its effects than PI when delivered by investigators having no prior allegiance to CB?—and questions of duration—Are 16 sessions more effective than eight sessions? Crucially, the effect of initial severity was considered. Overall, the study yielded slight but not robust advantages to CB therapy, with only the Beck Depression Inventory (BDI; Beck, Ward, Mendelson, Mock, & Erbaugh, 1961) yielding a medium-size treatment effect and no evidence that either modality delivered a difference in rate of change. There was some evidence that 16 sessions were more effective than eight sessions, but data also suggested that therapist–client dyads adjusted the pace of therapy according to the duration available. There was, however, a significant interaction between severity and duration, resulting in more severely depressed clients faring worse when receiving eight rather than 16 sessions. Important, this result held for both PI and CB treatments. At 1-year follow-up, the significant difference was between eight sessions of PI, which performed worse than eight sessions of CB, and 16 sessions of PI or CB. In terms of informing the dose-effect curve, aggregated results from delivery of two, eight, and 16 sessions suggested a greater degree of linearity than originally proposed by the work of Ken Howard and colleagues (for a summary, see Shapiro et al., 2003).

Process Studies

Underpinning the design of the Sheffield studies and their comparative design was a focus on the underlying mechanisms of change. This work was hugely influenced by Shapiro's finding a companionship of ideas and ideologies with colleagues in SPR, notably Marv Goldfried, Bill Stiles, and Robert Elliott, collaborations with whom were sparked by Shapiro's attending the 1979 international meeting of SPR, held that year at St. Catherine's College in Oxford, England. All three brought differing theoretical and practice perspectives— behavioral/eclectic (Goldfried), person-centered (Stiles), and experiential (Elliott)—but were similarly committed to studying psychological processes within therapy and open-minded about the commonalities between, as well as distinctiveness of, differing therapy modalities.

Intensive process work on the first Sheffield Psychotherapy Project in collaboration with colleagues showed the immediate impacts of the two treatments to be consistent with their theoretical expectations, with exploratory sessions rated as deeper and more powerful, whereas prescriptive sessions were rated as smoother and easier. Differential impacts also appeared, whereby significant therapy events in prescriptive sessions were more likely to lead to problem solution and reassuranceand, in exploratory therapy, to awareness and a sense of personal contact with the therapist. Analyses led by Robert Elliott using comprehensive process analysis on selected insight events in exploratory and prescriptive sessions directly informed the development of the assimilation model by Bill Stiles and colleagues (1990).

Work arising from the Second Sheffield Psychotherapy Project focused on investigations of common factors as a means of explaining the equivalence paradox and of developing innovative research methods to study "encompassing" frameworks. For example, an experimentally rigorous but clinically sensitive method was devised for testing the assimilation model and showing how a problematic experience in PI therapy was successfully incorporated into a schema (see Shapiro, 1995). Much of the change occurred within a single session, a finding that anticipated subsequent work on "sudden gains." A further example of encompassing frameworks was the exploration, with Bill Stiles, of the concept of appropriate responsiveness as an explanation for the limitations of process–outcome "dose–effect" relationships. In addition to theoretical debate, evidence for such an explanation was obtained in observations of therapist behavior in the two contrasting therapies of the Second Sheffield Psychotherapy Project.

Shapiro's early interest in empathy and relationship factors as facilitators of change was further developed by doctoral students in Sheffield and Leeds through work on the therapeutic alliance. Innovative qualitative methods were used to develop alliance rupture markers and the cultural determinants of the relationship development. Work from the Leeds clinic showed that both the alliance and therapist competence independently predicted outcome, with client interpersonal style influencing therapy processes—evidence for the importance of common mechanisms in psychotherapy change processes.

However, although Shapiro's research was lauded in many circles, it was treated with some suspicion in others. This arose, in part, because Shapiro's conceptualization of CB therapy was not deemed sufficiently purist, even though his work on adherence within the studies was as thorough as in any psychotherapy study. Although Shapiro had a sharpness of mind in relation to the specifics of research design, implementation, and analysis, he would later acknowledge that he did not take realistic account of the prevailing academic context and climate (e.g., the rise of Beckian cognitive therapy in the early 1980s and its effect of marginalizing therapeutic approaches in which behavioral change and skill acquisition were the primary drivers).

Clinical and Service Delivery Research

Over 1992 and 1993, a review by the MRC determined that the Social and Applied Psychology Unit would be closed, and Shapiro was appointed professor of clinical psychology at the University of Leeds. In partnership with the local mental health services, the University of Leeds established a new research center—the Psychological Therapies Research Centre (PTRC)—of which he was director. This new partnership between the University of Leeds (scientific) and the NHS Mental Health Trust (practice) aimed to improve the quality of services to people needing psychological therapies by carrying out high-quality research. A research clinic was established, modeled on the research clinic in Sheffield but staffed by NHS clinical psychologists working one day per week at PTRC, and a protocol-based trial developed—the Leeds Depression Project. PTRC established a CBT clinic for depression that yielded significant work for the research group on phenomena such as sudden gains and the further development of the responsiveness inquiry.

Although the vision of PTRC signaled a bold and courageous venture, the changing climate led Shapiro to leave the University of Leeds in 1999 but retain the title of research professor of clinical psychology to 2001 and subsequently honorary professor at the Universities of Leeds and Sheffield from 2001 to 2007. During this time, he established an independent consultancy in research and training, with projects that included supporting the development and trialing of a computerized CBT self-help package called *Beating the Blues*—subsequently endorsed by the UK's Department of Health—and training and supporting a small group of NHS workers (not clinical psychologists) in delivering PI therapy.

David Shapiro formally retired in April 2007 to pursue what had been a developing passion for some years, photography, especially of musicians and artists more generally—exchanging, perhaps, the twin role of scientist–practitioner for that of technician and artist. The activity provides a rich environment for David's abundant skills, ranging from his obsession with fine detail to his ability to stand back and see the whole picture.

OTHER CONTRIBUTIONS

In the 1970s in the UK, the only journal focusing on clinical psychology was the *British Journal of Social and Clinical Psychology*, published by the British Psychological Society. In 1981, the journal was split into separate journals, and Shapiro was appointed the first editor of the *British Journal of Clinical Psychology*, a position he held for 6 years.

Shapiro's discovery in 1979 of the SPR meeting at St. Catherine's College, Oxford, made him a devoted conference attendee. He was also an astute organizer and was responsible for bringing the 1983 international meeting to Sheffield at very short notice. From this experience Shapiro saw the need and potential for establishing a UK chapter, and the decision was taken to establish a UK chapter of SPR and to hold a UK meeting in the following year. The selected venue, on the North Yorkshire coast, was one drawn from Diana Shapiro's childhood and infused the meeting with personal meaning for both Shapiros. David Shapiro was the first vice president of the UK chapter of SPR.

A further sphere of influence came with Shapiro's central involvement with the Mental Health Foundation Psychotherapy Initiative. Following a 2-day conference in 1993 at Balliol College in Oxford at which key speakers provided summaries of state-of-the-art issues, Shapiro and Mark Aveline coedited the book *Research Foundations for Psychotherapy Practice* (1995). His involvement in the MHF initiative led him to support subsequent research programs relating to the development of a core outcome battery, therapist competence, and adherence rating scales for CBT.

A key contribution made by Shapiro was to the establishment of the doctoral training program in clinical psychology at the University of Sheffield that started in 1991. Shapiro worked tirelessly behind the scenes to provide the argument for the course and its successful establishment. Its existence is a tribute to his selfless endeavours.

INFLUENCES

Many of the themes in Shapiro's work have been influenced by his parents, Monte and Jean Shapiro, both of whom were highly committed people with powerfully independent minds. Monte Shapiro (M. B. Shapiro) came to the UK from South Africa and became one of a powerful group of clinical psychologists (including Gwynne Jones, Victor Meyer, Jack Rachman, and James Inglis) in Hans Eysenck's department at the Maudsley Hospital in London in the late 1950s. Monte Shapiro's central axiom was his espousal of a stringent methodological approach to building a scientific basis for the assessment and treatment of psychological problems. The whole research culture intrinsic to the Maudsley and Institute of Psychiatry had a pervasive influence on David Shapiro's approach, informing but also showing the potential limitations of single approaches to practice and research. Beyond M. B. Shapiro, the influence of Bob Hobson is foremost as a researcher and practitioner, with his commitment to the supervision process and his encouragement to junior staff pervading Shapiro's own practice.

Shapiro developed lasting collaborations with Robert Elliott, William B. Stiles, and Marv Goldfried, and each had a considerable influence on Shapiro's work. Their differing theoretical orientations but common interest in researching client change yielded a highly productive program of

American Psychological Association publications using data from the Second Sheffield Psychotherapy Project.

David Shapiro was very generous in supporting postgraduate students and junior staff in developing their own interests and careers; all seven research clinical psychologists who worked in his team at the Social and Applied Psychology Unit subsequently becoming professors of clinical psychology. David and Diana also developed lifelong friendships with many UK clinical psychologists, especially those involved in training, including Chris Barker and Nancy Pistrang, John and Marcia Davis, Chris Leach, and David Kennard.

CONCLUSION

Through his investment in researching the process of outcomes and his commitment to methodological rigor, Shapiro has made a substantial contribution to psychological therapies research. Perhaps more than any specific research finding per se, the hallmarks of his work have been the combination of his philosophical approach and evenhandedness; the former based on his belief that insights are derived from examining the inextricable links between methods and findings, and the latter based on a social and scientific principle of providing a level playing field as the only basis for carrying out psychotherapeutic investigations.

REFERENCES

Aveline, M., and Shapiro, D. A. (1995). *Research foundations for psychotherapy practice*. Chichester, England: Wiley in associations with the Mental Health Foundation.

Beck, A. T., Ward, C. H., Mendelson, M., Mock, J., & Erbaugh, J. (1961). An inventory for measuring depression. *Archives of General Psychiatry, 4*, 561–571.

Shapiro, D. A. (1973). Naïve British judgements of therapeutic conditions. *British Journal of Social and Clinical Psychology, 12*, 289–294.

Shapiro, D. A. (1976). Conversational structure and accurate empathy: An exploratory study. *British Journal of Social and Clinical Psychology, 15*, 213–215.

Shapiro, D. A. (1985). Recent applications of meta-analysis in clinical research. *Clinical Psychology Review, 5*, 13–34. doi:10.1016/0272-7358(85)90027-3

Shapiro, D. A. (1995). Finding out how psychotherapies help people change. *Psychotherapy Research, 5*, 1–21.

Shapiro, D. A., & Firth, J. (1987). Prescriptive vs. exploratory psychotherapy: Outcomes of the Sheffield Psychotherapy Project. *British Journal of Psychiatry, 151*, 790–799. doi:10.1192/bjp.151.6.790

Shapiro, D. A., & Hobson, R. F. (1972). Change in psychotherapy: A single case study. *Psychological Medicine, 2,* 312–317. doi:10.1017/S0033291700042628

Shapiro, D. A., & Shapiro, D. (1982). Meta-analysis of comparative therapy outcome studies: A replication and refinement. *Psychological Bulletin, 92,* 581–604. doi:10.1037/0033-2909.92.3.581

Shapiro, D. A., Barkham, M., Rees, A., Hardy, G. E., Reynolds, S., & Startup, M. (1994). Effects of treatment duration and severity of depression on the effectiveness of cognitive-behavioral and psychodynamic-interpersonal psychotherapy. *Journal of Consulting and Clinical Psychology, 62,* 522–534. doi:10.1037/0022-006X.62.3.522

Shapiro, D. A., Barkham, M., Stiles, W. B., Hardy, G. E., Rees, A., Reynolds, S., & Startup, M. (2003). Time is of the essence: A selective review of the fall and rise of brief therapy research. *Psychology and Psychotherapy: Theory, Research and Practice, 76,* 211–235.

Smith, M. L., & Glass, G. V. (1977). Meta-analysis of psychotherapy outcome studies. *American Psychologist, 32,* 752–780.

Stiles, W. B., Elliott, R., Llewelyn, S. P., Firth-Cozens, J. A., Margison, F. R., Shapiro, D. A., & Hardy, G. (1990). Assimilation of problematic experiences by clients in psychotherapy. *Psychotherapy, 27,* 411–420.

Stiles, W. B., Shapiro, D. A., & Elliott, R. (1986). Are all psychotherapies equivalent? *American Psychologist, 41,* 165–180.

24

ROBERT ELLIOTT: COMMITMENT TO EXPERIENCE

RHEA PARTYKA

One of Robert Elliott's most influential contributions to the field of psychotherapy research has been his development of highly innovative and rigorous quantitative and qualitative research methods for the empirical evaluation of clients' accounts of change in psychotherapy. Early in his career he began to systematically explore clients' experiences of significant events in therapy. This research initiative paved the way for his further studies on the perceived helpfulness of therapist response modes and eventually led to the development of a taxonomy of helpful and hindering therapy events. To undertake a more thorough investigation of these events, he developed the comprehensive process analysis (CPA) method to more fully address the context in which significant events occur in psychotherapy sessions. This method was later applied in examining insight events in both psychodynamic and cognitive–behavioral therapy modalities. Brief structured recall (BSR) was then developed as a more focused method for measuring and collecting information on significant therapy events. In an effort to more fully understand causality in the change process, Elliott developed the hermeneutic single case efficacy design (HSCED). An adjudicational model of this method was later used for assessing psychotherapy outcome. Most recently, Elliott and colleagues introduced a new psychometric method—Rasch analysis—for the analysis of common therapy outcome measures.

In addition to his contributions in research methods, Elliott has also played a vital role in the development of process–experiential (PE) therapy (also known as emotion-focused therapy, or EFT) and its application to various types of clients and presenting issues. He has worked with colleagues to develop a model of how clients progress through experiential tasks, which has led to the publication of influential PE treatment and training manuals. In fact, he has become an internationally recognized expert in PE training and supervision. Furthermore, Elliott's research on PE therapy and depression has made a significant contribution to the recent recognition of PE therapy (EFT) as an empirically supported treatment of depression by APA Division 12 (Society of Clinical Psychology).

EARLY BEGINNINGS

The oldest of six children, Elliott was raised in California and describes his parents as intellectuals. Strongly influenced by his father, he attributes the use of humor in his work, as well as his desire to understand and help others, to experiences with his dad. Moreover, Elliott also shared a passionate interest in science fiction with his father and, as a young man, thought he would become a science fiction writer when he grew up. A turning point in his career aspirations occurred after he read Karen Horney's *Our Inner Conflicts* (1945) as part of a high school creative writing course. His mother and grandmother shared an interest in Jungian psychology, and his grandmother, a writer, was also quite interested in the field of parapsychology, hoping one day her grandson would become a parapsychologist. Although parapsychological concepts seemed too ephemeral and abstract to Elliott, he realized observable psychological processes, such as empathy and the therapeutic interaction, discovered in Horney's writing, could be equally powerful and intellectually challenging. He came to view empathy and therapy as "magical" in their power to transform human experiences, about the time he realized that he wanted to become a therapist—which he naively imagined as a kind of magician/healer—an insight he described as similar to a religious conversion.

Elliott's undergraduate training at the University of California–Santa Cruz (UCSC) was primarily humanistic in nature, especially as UCSC was home to several influential humanistic psychologists, including Ted Sarbin, Brewster Smith, Frank Barron, and Bert Kaplan. During college and graduate school, Elliott's goal was to become a therapist; however, his professors recognized his talent as a "natural academic" and suggested that he also pursue research. He began his clinical training in graduate school at the University of

California–Los Angeles (UCLA), however, with a perspective more consistent with that of a social behaviorist. At this time, he was also influenced by his advisor, Jerry Goodman, who provided Elliott with foundational training in client-centered therapy. Elliott's clinical externships included Veterans Administration hospitals, where he worked with acutely psychotic patients and a child and family guidance clinic. He completed his internship at UCLA's student mental health clinic. While attending his first conference for the Society for Psychotherapy Research (SPR) in 1976, Elliott met Leslie Greenberg and Laura Rice, and the following year he heard them present research findings on gestalt two-chair work for conflict splits and systematic unfolding for problematic reactions that inspired him to incorporate those methods into his practice. He acknowledges Rice and Greenberg's research as the strongest influence on his practice as a therapist. At the same time, he has consistently seen SPR as his key scientific organization and reference group; he has not missed an international SPR conference since his first in 1976!

By the time he completed his PhD and accepted an academic clinical faculty position at the University of Toledo, he identified himself as an eclectic–integrative therapist, utilizing a wide variety of therapy techniques conceptualized within a broadly psychodynamic framework. During that time, Elliott took pride in his ability to make sense out of complex phenomena, and he found enjoyment in developing and offering interpretations to clients; however, over time he became increasingly aware of his uncertainty regarding whether his interpretations actually helped his clients. He initiated the psychotherapy research program at the University of Toledo in 1978 and subsequently immersed himself in the study of client in-therapy experiences, close analysis of therapy process, effective ingredients in therapy, results of relevance to clinical practice and training, and development and testing of new measures and research approaches for capturing psychotherapeutic change processes.

ACCOMPLISHMENTS

Innovative Research Methodologies

While in graduate school at UCLA, Elliott and fellow students Chris Barker and Nancy Pistrang developed an application of Kagan's interpersonal process recall procedure for the systematic investigation of client experiences of particular moments in therapy (Elliott, 1986). During the course of this research, Elliott came to the dual realization that while therapists are often unaware of how their clients perceive the therapy process, clients are active, aware processors of their therapy experiences. This insight resulted in Elliott's becoming a more cautious, inquiring therapist. In addition, these data led him to develop an interest in significant change events in therapy. His early studies at the University of Toledo (Elliott, Barker, Caskey, & Pistrang, 1982) focused on the perceived helpfulness of therapist response modes. Through these studies, the existence of very helpful or "significant" therapist interventions was discovered. A subsequent study involved volunteer clients who were asked to identify and describe the impact of the most and least helpful therapist responses in brief counseling sessions. A cluster analysis of these client descriptions resulted in his highly influential taxonomy of helpful and hindering therapy events (Elliott, 1985).

Through the process of analyzing helpful and hindering therapy events, Elliott became increasingly aware of a need for developing qualitative procedures to more fully capture the nature of these events. Furthermore, he recognized a need to consider not only the events themselves but also the full context in which these events occurred. Accordingly, he developed CPA (Elliott, 1984), an interpretive, inductive qualitative research method that is based on the assumption that identifying and analyzing particular instances of a phenomenon is necessary in order to understand that phenomenon more generally. CPA involves the examination of three domains: context, key responses, and effects. *Context* refers to the factors and events that lead up to or are exemplified by the event, such as background, presession context, session context, and episode context. *Key responses* consist of four aspects of the most helpful therapist or client responses: action, content, style, and quality or skilfulness. *Effects* involve the sequentially unfolding consequences of an event, including its immediate effects within the episode, its delayed effects within the same or later sessions, and the clinical significance of the event.

For example, Elliott and colleagues' CPA of insight events in cognitive behavioral (CB) and psychodynamic interpersonal (PI) psychotherapies (Elliott et al., 1994) first entailed each analyst's independently explicating the implicit meanings in key therapist speaking turns and the client's postsession description of the event. Next, the analysts met to develop a consensus explication of these meanings. Third, each analyst independently used the CPA framework to analyze the individual events, and then the entire team of judges carried out a cross-analysis of six events with a goal of identifying common and discriminating factors. Common factors included the presence of what Rice and Sapiera (1984) called a *problematic reaction point* and a *meaning bridge*. Elliott and colleagues' analyses led to the development of a sequential model of insight reflecting the progression through *contextual priming, presentation of novel information, initial distantiated processing, insight,* and *elaboration.* The CPA analyses also established that a client's experience of insight may vary in different therapeutic modalities. Specifically, CB insight events were found to be primarily reattributional in nature, whereas PI insight events involved connection to a conflict theme and the expression of painful affect. These research findings have important implications for psychotherapy researchers interested in identifying core principles of change in psychotherapy.

Elliott and his colleagues eventually came to view the data they had been using to conduct CPA—therapy transcripts and postsession descriptions—as not detailed enough to support the method. This led to the development of BSR (Elliott, 1993; Elliott & Shapiro 1988), a form of tape-assisted recall used for the identification and description of significant client events in psychotherapy, utilizing both qualitative and quantitative collection procedures. The most basic BSR format entails the completion of a semistructured interview schedule that addresses the three major domains of CPA (context of event, major process involved, and effect of the event on the client). A more detailed format (Brief Structured Recall Version 3.5) utilizes rating scales to obtain numerical data on psychometrically evaluated measures of event helpfulness, therapist and client intentions, client feelings, and client reactions in addition to allowing for open-ended descriptions of experiences (Elliott, 1989).

Elliott's early CPA studies were based on several assumptions: Open-ended questions are largely used to gather descriptive data, words (as opposed to numbers) are used to describe phenomena, a small number of cases are intensively studied, and context is necessary to understand the experience. The CPA method formed the basis for a research method that later became known as consensual qualitative research (CQR), which also uses consensus and auditing procedures to reduce various forms of researcher error and narrowness. The full CQR method was initially applied in McGlenn's (1990) dissertation on clients' experiences of important weeping moments. Elliott passed this approach on to Clara Hill, who developed CQR further and applied it in numerous studies on a range of aspects of counseling (see Chapter 13, this volume).

Elliott also developed a greater interest in understanding the change process, and he was motivated to develop a method driven largely by data. The HSCED (Elliott, 2002) is an interpretive approach to evaluating treatment causality in single therapy cases. This particular approach uses a blend of quantitative and qualitative methods to create a network of evidence that identifies direct examples of causal links between therapy process and outcome and then evaluates plausible nontherapy explanations for apparent client change. The HSCED seeks to answer three questions: (a) Has the client actually changed? (b) Is psychotherapy generally responsible for the change? and (c) What specific factors (both within therapy and outside of therapy) are responsible for the change? The first prerequisite for the HSCED is a rich case record detailing aspects of the client's therapy. Several sources of data are typically used. First, *quantitative outcome measures* are utilized to determine the extent to which the client changed. Second, a *weekly outcome measure* is used to identify the client's main therapy-related problems or goals and to measure their weekly level of distress related to these specific issues. Third, a *qualitative outcome assessment* is conducted, during which clients are asked to provide descriptions of any changes experienced over the course of therapy as well as their attributions for these changes. Fourth, *qualitative information about significant events* is collected. Lastly, *therapist accounts of the therapy process* are gathered.

Influenced by Bohart's (2000) adjudicational model for assessing psychotherapy outcome, Elliott and his team then developed an adjudication model for the HSCED and applied it in a case study involving a male client with panic disorder (Elliott, Partyka, Wagner, Alperin, & Dobrenski, 2003). The first stage of this model entails the critical review of evidence that supports the conclusion that psychotherapy was a major causative source of assessed client change. Examples of direct evidence include restrospective attribution, outcome-to-process mapping, event-shift sequences, and change in stable problems. A valid evaluation of potential client change must also include a good-faith effort to identify evidence that refutes the causal role of therapy. Examples of such negative evidence include trivial or negative change, statistical artifacts, relational artifacts, expectancy artifacts, self-help or other self-correction processes, extratherapy life events, psychobiological processes, and the reactive effects of taking part in research.

As a final example of his scientific creativity and commitment to both qualitative and quantitative methods, Elliott and colleagues from the University of Toledo (Elliott, Fox, Beltyukova, Stone, Gunderson & Zhang, 2006) recently published an article illustrating the use of a powerful new psychometric research tool, Rasch analysis. The Rasch model is a type of item response model specifying that useful measurement consists of a single-dimensional concept arranged in a consistent pattern along an equal-interval continuum. Instruments calibrated using Rasch modeling enable one to determine the extent to which items have consistently measured a single variable. Further, Rasch statistics assist in the evaluation of the constructed metric. For instance, Rasch analysis can identify gaps in the construct continuum by identifying items and persons that are not well targeted. In Elliott and colleagues' (2006) study, several forms of Rasch analysis were applied to the Symptom Checklist-90-R (Derogatis, 1983) to obtain a greater understanding of the strengths and limitations of this common therapy outcome measure and to illustrate the utility of Rasch analysis for psychotherapy outcome measurement. In fact, Elliott has described Rasch analysis as "the next wave of psychometric research."

Development of Process–Experiential Therapy

On sabbatical in England in 1985, Elliott was influenced by the work of David Shapiro and the first Sheffield Psychotherapy Project, a complex process–outcome study comparing CB and interpersonal dynamic treatments of depression (Shapiro & Firth, 1987). While presenting at a conference in England, Elliott was confronted by a member of the audience, a psychoanalyst, who drew attention to the inconsistency between his willingness to offer an interpretation of his client's dreams and his unwillingness to make such high-level inferences regarding clients in his own research. This insight served as a key turning point in Elliott's development as a psychotherapist and reinforced his commitment to the value of understanding his clients' internal experiences. It was in light of this experience that Elliott also decided to focus his work as a therapist and researcher within a particular therapeutic approach, client-centered/experiential psychotherapy.

Upon his return to the United States, Elliott and his students decided to initiate a study parallel with the Sheffield project. Motivated by a need to broaden the range of treatments available for working with depression and recognizing the relative scarcity of recent work on humanistic or experiential therapies, they chose to use an integrative experiential therapy based on a task analytic approach (Rice & Greenberg, 1984). At that time, the task interventions did not yet amount to an internally coherent treatment, and a comprehensive theory of treatment and the change process had yet to be fully developed. Greenberg and Rice invited Elliott to collaborate on the further articulation of the therapeutic model, and together with Clark they drafted a treatment manual for depression (Elliott, Greenberg, Rice, & Clark, 1987). The primary research questions focused on change processes, particularly the identification of types of significant events and the factors that contribute to them, as well as assessment of the outcome and change processes in the treatment.

The emerging approach was called *process–experiential therapy* to distinguish it from other experiential treatments. This form of therapy set out to integrate key elements of client-centered and gestalt therapies. Elliott utilized his background of previous research on therapist response modes (Elliott, 1979, 1985; Elliott et al., 1987) to develop a description of the therapist's experiential response modes used in PE therapy. Elliott and his students conducted a process–outcome study of PE therapy with major depressive disorder. Through their work as therapists in the study, they were able to work toward the development of a general treatment model as well as its specific application to depression (Elliott et al., 1990; Greenberg, Elliott, & Foerster, 1990). This research served as a foundation for Elliott to collaborate with Les Greenberg to develop a description of practical treatment issues and propose a general model of how clients progress through the different experiential tasks. This work resulted in an extensive treatment manual (Greenberg, Rice, & Elliott, 1993), largely informed by research.

In 1992, Elliott undertook a sabbatical in Toronto and began work on a major review chapter addressing the efficacy of experiential humanistic psychotherapies (Greenberg, Elliott, & Lietaer, 1994). His decision to undertake a meta-analysis of all available outcome research pertaining to experiential–humanistic therapies resulted in the following conclusions: Clients who participate in experiential therapies show, on average, large amounts of change over time; posttherapy gains in experiential therapies are stable through both early and late follow-ups; clients in experiential therapies show substantially more change than comparable untreated clients in randomized clinical trials; and clients in experiential therapies show gains that are comparable to those in clients seen in nonexperiential therapies, including cognitive behavioral treatments. Based on these results, later updated and strengthened, Elliott et al. (2003) asserted that "the evidence is now strong enough for us to recommend that experiential-humanistic therapies should be considered empirically supported treatments. In fact, students' education as psychologists is incomplete without a greater emphasis on such training." It should be noted that, at the time of this writing, the process–experiential approach, now also known as emotion-focused therapy (EFT), will be recognized as an empirically supported treatment of depression by APA Division 12.

From 1993 to 2005, Elliott continued to develop and expand PE therapy. He also focused much of his attention on training students and wrote or collaborated on several books, including *Learning Emotion-Focused Therapy* (Elliott, Watson, Goldman, & Greenberg, 2004). After retiring from the University of Toledo in July 2006, he moved to Glasgow, Scotland, to become professor of counseling in the Counseling Unit at the University of Strathclyde, one of the largest person-centered therapy training centers in Europe. He describes his current interests as a culmination of his earlier research. In addition to conducting practice-based and interpretive case study research, he is also developing an emotion-focused therapy approach for individuals with social anxiety. In addition, he has also started on students' outcomes and change processes in therapy training. He is currently involved in encouraging similar efforts in Europe and North America.

PROFESSIONAL CONTRIBUTIONS AND CONCLUSION

Robert Elliott has held many leadership positions within the field of psychotherapy research. He served as president of the North American Chapter of the Society for Psychotherapy Research (SPR) in 1991, and he served as president of the international SPR in 2000–2001. He has served as North American editor of *Psychotherapy Research* (1994–1998) and as coeditor of *Person-Centered and Experiential Psychotherapies* (2002–2007). When describing his leadership positions and his role as a journal editor, Elliott stated, "It's a way for me to give back what has been given to me." Most recently, Elliott was named the recipient of the 2008 Carl Rogers Award of APA's Division of Humanistic Psychology.

Finally, it is important to note that Robert Elliott has significantly influenced the clinical development of numerous students and is an inspiring and trusted colleague to many seasoned researchers and clinicians. Simply stated, he is a person who cares deeply about his students and colleagues and embodies the values of genuineness, authenticity, and warmth that define the practice of person-centered and experiential therapies.

REFERENCES

Bohart, A. C. (2000, June). *A qualitative "adjudicational" model for assessing psychotherapy outcome*. Paper presented at meeting of Society for Psychotherapy Research, Chicago, IL.

Derogatis, L. R. (1983). *SCL-90-R administration, scoring and procedures manual-II*. Towson, MD: Clinical Psychometric Research.

Elliott, R. (1979). How clients perceive helper behaviors. *Journal of Counseling Psychology, 26*, 285–294. doi:10.1037/0022-0167.26.4.285

Elliott, R. (1984). A discovery-oriented approach to significant events in psychotherapy: Interpersonal process recall and comprehensive process analysis. In L. N. Rice & L. S. Greenberg (Eds.), *Patterns of change* (pp. 249–286). New York, NY: Guilford Press.

Elliott, R. (1985). Helpful and nonhelpful events in brief counseling interviews: An empirical taxonomy. *Journal of Counseling Psychology, 32*, 307–322. doi:10.1037/0022-0167.32.3.307

Elliott, R. (1986). Interpersonal Process Recall (IPR) as a psychotherapy process research method. In L. Greenberg & W. Pinsof (Eds.), *The psychotherapeutic process* (pp. 503–527). New York, NY: Guilford Press.

Elliott, R. (1989). Comprehensive process analysis: Understanding the change process in significant therapy events. In M. Packer & R. B. Addison (Eds.), *Entering the circle: Hermeneutic investigation in psychology* (pp. 165–184). Albany, NY: State University of New York Press.

Elliott, R. (1993). *Comprehensive process analysis: Mapping the change process in psychotherapy*. Unpublished research manual, University of Strathclyde, Glasgow, Scotland.

Elliott, R. (2002). Hermeneutic single case efficacy design. *Psychotherapy Research, 12*, 1–21. doi:10.1080/713869614 http://pe-eft.blogspot.com/2007/02/my-journey-as-therapist-as-symphony-in.html

Elliott, R., Barker, C.B., Caskey, N., & Pistrang, N. (1982). Differential helpfulness of counsel or verbal response modes. *Journal of Counseling Psychology, 29*, 379–387.

Elliott, R., Clark, C., Wexler, M., Kemeny, V., Brinkerhoff, J., & Mack, C. (1990). The impact of experiential therapy of depression: Initial results. In G. Lietaer, J. Rombauts, & R. Van Balen (Eds.), *Client-centered and experiential psychotherapy towards the nineties* (pp. 549–577). Leuven, Belgium: Leuven University Press.

Elliott, R., Fox, C., Beltyukova, S., Stone, G., Gunderson, J., & Zhang, X. (2006). Deconstructing therapy outcome measurement with Rasch analysis of a measure of general clinical distress: The Symptom Checklist-90-Revised. *Psychological Assessment, 18,* 359–372.

Elliott, R., Greenberg, L. S., Rice, L.N., & Clark, C. (1987). *Draft manual for experiential therapy of depression.* Unpublished manuscript, Department of Psychology, University of Toledo, Toledo, OH.

Elliott, R., Hill, C. E., Stiles, W. B., Friedlander, M. L., Mahrer, A., & Margison, F. (1987). Primary therapist response modes: A comparison of six rating systems. *Journal of Consulting and Clinical Psychology, 55,* 218–223.

Elliott, R., Partyka, R., Wagner, J., Alperin, R., & Dobrenski, R. (2003). *An adjudicated hermeneutic single case efficacy design study of experiential therapy for panic disorder: Case record and arguments.* Unpublished paper, University of Toledo, Toledo, OH.

Elliott, R., & Shapiro, D.A. (1988). Brief structured recall: A more efficient method for identifying and describing significant therapy events. *British Journal of Medical Psychology, 61,* 141–153.

Elliott, R. Shapiro, D. A., Firth-Cozens, J., Stiles, W. B., Hardy, G., Llewelyn, S. P., & Margison, F. (1994). Comprehensive process analysis of insight events in cognitive-behavioral and psychodynamic-interpersonal therapies. *Journal of Counseling Psychology, 41,* 449–463.

Elliott, R., Watson, J., Goldman, R., & Greenberg, L. S. (2004). *Learning emotion-focused therapy: The process experiential approach to change.* Washington, DC: American Psychological Association.

Greenberg, L. S., Elliott, R., & Foerster, F. (1990). Experiential processes in the psychotherapeutic treatment of depression. In N. Endler & D.C. McCann (Eds.), *Contemporary perspectives on emotion* (pp. 157–185). Toronto, Canada: Wall & Emerson.

Greenberg, L. S., Elliott, R., & Lietaer, G. (1994). Research on humanistic and experiential psychotherapies. In A. E. Bergin and S. L. Garfield (Eds). *Handbook of psychotherapy and behavior change,* 4th ed. (pp. 509–539). New York, NY: Wiley.

Greenberg, L. S., Rice, L. N. & Elliott, R. (1993). *Facilitating emotional change.* New York, NY: Guilford Press.

Horney, K. (1945). *Our inner conflicts: A constructive theory of neurosis.* New York, NY: Norton.

McGlenn, M. L. (1990). *A qualitative study of significant weeping events.* PhD dissertation, Department of Psychology, University of Toledo, Toledo, OH. . (Available from ProQuest, publication number AAT 9104085, Document ID 744819641.)

Rice, L. N., & Greenberg, L. S. (Eds.) (1984). *Patterns of change*. New York, NY: Guilford Press.

Rice, L. N., & Sapiera, E. P. (1984). Task analysis and the resolution of problematic reactions. In L. N. Rice & L. S. Greenberg (Eds.), *Patterns of change* (pp. 29–66). New York, NY: Guilford Press.

Shapiro, D. A., & Firth, J. (1987). Prescriptive vs. exploratory psychotherapy: Outcomes of the Sheffield psychotherapy project. *British Journal of Psychiatry, 151*, 790–799.

25

WILLIAM B. STILES: EMPATHIC REFLECTIONS, VOICES, AND THEORY BUILDING

MEREDITH GLICK BRINEGAR AND KATERINE OSATUKE

William B. Stiles has touched the field of psychotherapy through his research, teaching, and mentoring. Bill, as most people know him, has a quiet, unassuming presence that belies the impact his work has had on understanding therapy process, outcome, and related theoretical issues. This chapter summarizes his contributions, highlighting several major pieces: his work on verbal response modes, the assimilation model, process–outcome research, and the use of qualitative methods. A uniting element of his work has been generating theoretical explanations for existing psychotherapy findings, or what Bill calls *theory building*.

BEGINNINGS

William B. Stiles was born in Seattle, the first of four children, and grew up in the Washington, DC, area. He did his undergraduate studies at Oberlin, the historically liberal college in Ohio that his wife, parents, siblings, and many other relatives have attended. He had planned on majoring in economics but decided to pursue psychology because, he admits, his grades were good in that field and mediocre in everything else. In hindsight, Stiles speculated that his higher grades reflected interest in the subject, but at the time he interpreted it as differential aptitude. Stiles first became aware of his interest in psychology and personality when discussing his student paper on psychopaths with his clinical psychology instructor, John Thompson. A decision to pursue graduate studies seemed like a natural fit for him; he came from an academically minded family. His father was a specialized librarian, his mother a primary school teacher, his brother a biology professor, and his maternal grandfather (a junior high school principal) had always wanted to be a professor.

Stiles was accepted into the clinical psychology doctoral program at the University of California–Los Angeles (UCLA), where his interest in theory building gradually came to focus on psychotherapy research. He saw psychology as a science "not all thought through." It offered the challenge of explaining complex phenomena in a rich way, without oversimplifying and without losing methodological rigor. Stiles's UCLA training was half clinical and half neuroscience. His dissertation focused on a theory of human experience (e.g., grief, anger, sexual excitement) and was neurologically based. This early study foreshadowed his approach to explaining something as broad as human experience, by articulating theoretical concepts and grounding them in observations. Stiles's specific interest in psychotherapy research emerged out of doing, supervising, and teaching therapy. It reflected his attempt to understand more thoroughly what happens in therapy. He was strongly influenced by a clinical supervisor at UCLA, Jerry Goodman, who studied response modes: a classification of possible responses in an interview setting. Studying therapy offered Stiles a chance to explain real-world psychological processes, with both realism and precision.

By the time of his graduation, Bill Stiles had decided to look for an academic position in clinical psychology, finding the openness of the field appealing. After completing his internship at the Neuropsychiatric Institute at UCLA Center for Health Sciences, he became an instructor and then an assistant professor at the University of North Carolina, Chapel Hill. After reading Carl Rogers's work, he adopted a student-centered, nondirective form of teaching. He developed a career-long reputation for teaching classes in a radically nondirective way. His students had a hand in developing the syllabus, choosing their own readings, structuring group discussions, and evaluating themselves. Although this nontraditional classroom environment often elicited strong reactions (both positive and negative), Stiles's students had opportunities to learn and grow in ways previously unimagined. Stiles is well known for his use of empathic reflections: Usually accurate, they can be both irritating and therapeutic. A typical sequence reported by students who have been exposed to his manner of teaching is, first, feeling left to their own devices, then resenting it, deciding to fend for themselves, and then eventually discovering a new level of professional independence or developing a new level of skill. When Stiles's students—graduate or undergraduate—reflect on their experiences with him, they often observe striking similarities. Some express self-directed humor or new awareness into how this seems to have worked, others note some remaining guilt over their initial resentment, but almost all report gratitude for having been helped to discover a new level of professional autonomy they had not conceived of before.

Stiles's relatively pure Rogerian approach (an interest in the other person's experience and how it evolves, rather than in techniques to make people think or act in certain desirable ways) is present in all of his professional roles. For example, whether he is a teacher, mentor, supervisor, coinvestigator, or senior colleague, he offers an attentive and respectful way of listening, openness to different perspectives, and willingness to clarify those parts that seem hard to understand or explain. His consistency in interacting in this nondirective way, across domains, illustrates how well he has integrated this theory into his way of being.

Stiles returned to Ohio in 1979 to assume the position of associate professor at Miami University. While there, he served for a period as director of the departmental training clinic, overseeing clinically relevant research conducted by trainees. He also developed a practice of writing in the morning at home and then walking to the psychology department each afternoon to teach and meet with students. Although some days are more productive than others, Stiles has commented that this practice has had an enormous impact on advancing his thinking and productivity. Stiles's disciplined approach to writing seems to have paid off; he is the author of countless journal articles, book chapters, and conference presentations.

Stiles often organizes weekly research team meetings, currently known as the Assimilation Research Group (ARG). True to his client-centered roots, he allows the team to set the agenda, whereby, typically, Stiles and his graduate students take turns presenting research ideas, study results, or paper drafts for group feedback. He models how to be open to criticism and always honors student input on his own work, despite differences in experience level. For example, if a student felt confused by a certain idea or sentence he had written, he would note that this reaction likely represented a portion of how reviewers or other readers would respond, and he then would make changes accordingly. Stiles has a quiet, steady, and thoughtful presence. He responds to e-mail messages almost instantly—even from exotic locations—providing dependable communication to students and colleagues alike. He is also fairly unassuming—from his casual dress and sandwiches made on homemade bread, to his quiet manner of speaking and way of putting complex ideas in simple, jargon-free language. Interacting with him invites others to drop pretenses, making it easier to clarify and focus on what really matters to them.

When mentoring individual projects, Stiles has long remained committed to supporting students' own interests. Just like students in classes he teaches, his advisees often experience frustration with his lack of directiveness and tendency toward (usually accurate) empathic reflections. Over time, they typically appreciate the chance to find a project and style of working that truly fits them. Stiles's students often take longer finding their way but are rewarded with an increase in self-trust, autonomy, and an authentic research project that they truly own. To be sure, Stiles is not entirely nondirective in his mentoring. Any of his students who have received his feedback on writing will confirm that his edits, although usually helpful and respectful, are profuse, direct, and in color (these days, Bill uses the Track Changes feature in Microsoft Word: additions/comments in blue, deletions in red). Always respectful of the other person's experience, Stiles typically qualifies his numerous edits with "Use as you see fit."

A summary of Stiles's biographical details would not be complete without mention of his wife, Sue. They were married December 30, 1967, in New York City. Stiles recalls that afterward they took a train from Montreal to Vancouver and then drove down the coast to Los Angeles, where he was in graduate school. It seems appropriate that their married life started out with adventuresome travels, given that they have spent a good part of their lives since then in traveling the world together, for Stiles's research, for Sue's writing, and for pleasure. Following in the footsteps of her father and grandfather, Sue has training and experience as a journalist. Her focus has been on travel writing. Stiles describes her as his first and best editor and says that she taught him how to write clearly and succinctly. She has emphatically declared, however, that she is not a psychotherapy researcher. With Sue's talent for writing and her kind, unassuming presence, it is easy to see how they have developed a wonderful partnership.

ACCOMPLISHMENTS

Theory Building

Stiles's favorite aspect of studying psychotherapy involves formulating and honing a theory of human experience. In his view, scientific theories are built by gradually integrating various observations, not through a single act of discovering the whole truth. Knowledge is constructed on the basis of the assumption that the world is capable of being understood. The construction of truth is an iterative process; Stiles has explained that in his own theoretical pursuit, he had to repeatedly ask what was even meant by "truth" (Stiles, 1981, 2006). To this day, Stiles continues to refine his theories about psychotherapy and theories about theory.

One of Stiles's first theoretical forays was an article on the development of intense relationships.Humorously entitled "Psychotherapy Recapitulates Ontogeny: The Epigenesis of Intensive Interpersonal Relationships" (Stiles, 1979a), it drew a parallel between personal development in the relational context and biological growth, in which organisms repeat chronological stages of their species' evolution (i.e., ontogeny recapitulates phylogeny). On the basis of his experience facilitating nondirective process groups with undergraduates, Stiles proposed that intense interpersonal relationships contribute to personal growth by allowing people to recapitulate, and possibly heal, psychosocial conflicts in their prior development. To the extent that psychosocial development is similar across people (Erikson's "eight ages of man"), the evolution of a person's interpersonal stances, needs, and attitudes follows that same sequence in the context of relationships. Achievements at prior stages contain seeds of conflict at the subsequent stages. The model applies to therapy, teaching, business, friendships, and marriage. Typical of Stiles's work, this model has rich conceptual roots. It built upon prior Eriksonian thinking, broadening it to other psychological domains.

Verbal Response Modes

Much of Stiles's early work focused on verbal response modes (VRMs). The VRM system focuses on the microrelationships that people establish as they speak. It describes how speakers position themselves with respect to people or groups they address, whether they use their own frame of reference or others', and how they choose grammatical forms to heighten, soften, or enrich their intended messages. The main virtue of the VRM system may be that it allows interpersonal communication to be quantified and empirically studied. This has proved useful for studying verbal exchanges in therapy. For example, client and therapist speech could be placed into categories such as questions, advisements, and interpretations.

Stiles traced the idea of VRMs to a conceptual influence from Jerry Goodman, who introduced him to six different response modes intended to be helpful: questions, advisement, interpretation, reflection, disclosure, and silence. In his book, *Describing Talk: A Taxonomy of Verbal Response Modes*, Stiles (1992) recounted his initial attraction:

> I was attracted to the response modes at first by the therapeutic power of Reflections. I was fascinated by the process-facilitating effects of "simply" repeating a client's communication, in comparison to, say, the process-deflecting effects of Questions. Reflections were followed by deeper exploration; Questions were followed by a change in direction. In the tapes of therapy, in my work as a therapist, and in my own experience of being listened to, response modes seemed to make a dramatic difference. (p. 1)

Several years later, as an assistant professor, Stiles examined whether certain response modes were more therapeutic than others. Although he approached this question with an open mind as a researcher, he personally wondered whether responses in the client-centered tradition (e.g., empathic reflections) were especially useful. His research suggested that certain response modes were not inherently better than others (i.e., did not lead to better therapy outcomes), but it did lead to the classification of various kinds of therapist interventions.

VRM-based studies of psychotherapy showed that therapists of different orientations have dramatically different profiles of verbal interventions. That is, therapists predominantly rely on verbal response modes that are consistent with their theoretical orientations (Stiles, 1979b; Stiles, Shapiro, & Firth-Cozens, 1988). Each theory's therapeutic recommendations are consistent with and can be seen as prescribing and proscribing particular response modes. For example, the Rogerian approach, which focuses on the client's frame of reference, would rely on response modes such as Reflection and Acknowledgement rather than Advisement or Question. As it happens, clients use a similar profile of modes regardless of their therapist's orientation, with the most prominent client mode being Disclosure.

Equivalence Paradox and Responsiveness

The finding that VRMs did not directly predict outcome was consistent with the enigmatic yet common finding of null correlations between types of interventions and outcomes. These results influenced Stiles's thinking about one of the long-standing puzzles in psychotherapy research: the equivalence paradox. Also known as the Dodo verdict, it refers to the established finding of equivalent outcomes for therapies that use vastly different methods (Luborsky, Singer, & Luborsky, 1975; Stiles, Shapiro, & Elliott, 1986). To help understand this paradox, Stiles articulated the concept of *responsiveness* (Stiles, 1988; Stiles, Honos-Webb, & Surko, 1998). Responsiveness suggests that therapeutic interventions tend to be delivered to clients in ways that match their emerging needs on a moment-to-moment basis. That is, interventions are delivered responsively rather than rigidly as advised by therapy manuals. Stiles suggested that responsiveness to clients' needs rather than the amount of any type of intervention per se may be driving therapeutic success. For example, the fact that empathic reflection may generally be helpful does not always mean that more of it will yield a better outcome (the client may not need more). Explaining outcomes as driven by the nonlinear, complex patterns in which therapists responsively meet clients' emerging needs required qualitative approaches to capture interactions, timing, and context of interventions. This approach provided an alternative to the dose–response model, in which therapy is treated like a drug and analyzed to determine the optimal relationship between number of sessions and outcome.

Assimilation Model

Stiles's work with VRMs sensitized him to nuances of clients' verbal expression. This sensitivity, and an appreciation for the complex relationship between process and outcome variables, led him to explore common patterns of therapeutic change. His participation in an ongoing seminar with Robert Elliott and David Shapiro in Sheffield, England, in 1984–1985 furthered his thinking in this area and led to an early version of the assimilation model. The concept of assimilation can be explained in Piagetian terms: Experiences are assimilated into *schemas*—ways of thinking and acting that are developed or modified (accommodation) in order to assimilate the new experience (Stiles et al., 1990). Assimilation can also be described using the metaphor of *voice* (Honos-Webb & Stiles, 1998; Stiles, 1999) to emphasize that traces of past experiences are active within people. They seek to be expressed through actions, words, affective states, and so on. The previously assimilated, interlinked traces of experiences are considered as a community of voices within the person. Assimilated voices can be resources—available when needed—whereas unassimilated voices tend to be the unresolved problematic experiences that often bring people to therapy.

Difficult-to-assimilate experiences are referred to as *problematic voices*. The process of assimilating them into the community is described as building connections or *meaning bridges*. A meaning bridge is any sign (e.g., word, image, gesture) that means the same thing to both the problematic voice and the community. It is this process of building meaning bridges that allows clients to more fully experience and accept all parts of themselves and become less psychologically fragmented.

Eight developmental stages of assimilation have been outlined in the Assimilation of Problematic Experiences Sequence (APES; Stiles, 2002; Stiles & Angus, 2001; Stiles et al., 1991). The APES levels are (0) warded off/dissociated, (1) unwanted thoughts/active avoidance, (2) vague awareness/emergence, (3) problem statement/clarification, (4) understanding/insight, (5) application/working through, (6) resourcefulness/problem solution, and (7) integration/mastery. Both cognitive and affective features characterize each level. Levels represent anchor points along a continuum. Clients may enter treatment at any point, and any movement along the continuum is considered progress.

Stiles's interest in the assimilation of discrepant, traumatic, or unwanted parts of the self can be traced to his humanistic, client-centered foundation. Carl Rogers wrote a great deal about therapists valuing *all* aspects of clients, in turn allowing clients to do this for themselves.

> The therapist perceives the client's self as the client has known it, and accepts it; he perceives the contradictory aspects which have been denied to awareness and accepts those too as being a part of the client; and both of these acceptances have in them the same warmth and respect. (Rogers, 1951, p. 41)

Rogers noted that when individuals can come to "own" or "assimilate" experiences—without denying or distorting them—they feel more freedom and unity. And although Stiles would not suggest that client-centered therapy is the only successful way to assimilate problematic experiences (his research has shown that many therapies are useful in this way), it certainly helped provide a framework for understanding how change occurs.

Assimilation analyses have yielded a variety of examples of problematic experiences that were assimilated, to a greater or lesser degree, following the pattern described in the APES (for case examples, see Stiles & Angus, 2001). Each case was different and has confirmed, modified, and elaborated aspects of the model; their aggregate offers a substantial basis for confidence in the model.

Stiles has generously allowed and in fact encouraged his graduate students to conduct assimilation research in line with their own interests. He usually refers to the assimilation model as "our theory," not "my theory." His humility and openness have allowed the theory to be applied to fields outside of psychotherapy. For example, his theory has informed projects examining immigrants' adjustment, assimilation of sexual abuse, stages of rehabilitation of sex offenders, and consultative interventions in organization development.

Qualitative Research

Stiles and his research group have applied qualitative methods to studying therapy, particularly with the assimilation model. This work, along with Stiles's elaboration of the philosophy and rationale of qualitative approaches, helped establish qualitative inquiry as a scientific method in its own right rather than a lesser strategy used for lack of alternatives. Stiles addressed the issue of methodological rigor by articulating good practice standards (criteria of reliability and validity) in qualitative research (Stiles, 1993, 2003). Much of his recent thinking has centered on comparing and contrasting the epistemologies of qualitative versus quantitative approaches and promoting the use of case studies (Stiles, 2005, 2007).

Alliance and Session Evaluations

Stiles's Session Evaluation Questionnaire (SEQ), a brief, comprehensive questionnaire that can be completed by clients, therapists, and observers, is frequently used to measure session impact (Stiles, Gordon, & Lani, 2002). The SEQ measures session depth, smoothness, and postsession mood. Client–therapist agreement on SEQ ratings is generally weak, reminding us of the constructed nature of experience and the importance of checking in with clients about their evaluations.

Stiles has also contributed to the measurement of alliance, one of the strongest known predictors of therapy outcome. An example of this is his work on developing and testing the Agnew Relationship Measure (ARM; Agnew-Davies et al., 1998; Stiles et al., 2002), an alliance questionnaire similar to the Working Alliance Inventory (Horvath & Greeberg, 1986, 1989). Using the ARM, Stiles has articulated the relationship between patterns of alliance development and outcome (Stiles et al., 2004).

OTHER CONTRIBUTIONS

Stiles has been intimately connected with the Society for Psychotherapy Research (SPR) since attending his first conference in 1981 in Aspen, Colorado. In 1980, Al Mahrer invited him to participate in an APA symposium, "Psychotherapy Process Research: A Preview of the Next Decade." The other participants, Clara Hill and Robert Elliott, encouraged him to attend the next SPR conference. He has collaborated with numerous individuals from this organization, who have served as a valuable reference group. Stiles served as program chair for the 28th international annual meeting in 1997 in Geilo, Norway, and was president for the 1997–1998 year. In 2009, he received the prestigious Distinguished Research Career Award from SPR. Stiles helped establish a local area group, Ohio SPR, uniting three centers of psychotherapy research (Miami University, Ohio University, and University of Toledo) into a consortium. This small, intimate conference—geared toward grad students—met annually between 2001 and 2007.

Stiles's affiliation with SPR led to his service as associate editor and then editor for the organization's journal, *Psychotherapy Research*. He has engaged in editorial duties with his usual sense of quiet commitment and conscientiousness, hoping to ensure the integrity of the peer review process he has long valued. At this writing, Stiles is the coeditor of *Person-Centered and Experiential Psychotherapies* and associate editor of the *British Journal of Clinical Psychology*.

STILES'S LEGACY

Stiles's program of psychotherapy research has centered on several areas: VRMs, the assimilation model, process–outcome relationships, and qualitative methodology. Perhaps the broadest theme in all of his work is understanding human experience through evolving and ever-refining theoretical accounts. Stiles's deep and genuine interest in people (what they think, how they feel, where this comes from) is evident in everything he does: what he researches, how he supervises clinical trainees, how he mentors graduate students, and how he works with colleagues. He continues to challenge himself and others, asking difficult questions (What is truth? How will we recognize it? How does talking help?). His attempts to answer these questions have improved our understanding of whether and how psychotherapy helps and have inspired others to be just as curious.

REFERENCES

Agnew-Davies, R., Stiles, W. B., Hardy, G. E., Barkham, M., & Shapiro, D. A. (1998). Alliance structure assessed by the Agnew Relationship Measure (ARM). *British Journal of Clinical Psychology, 37,* 155–172.

Honos-Webb, L., & Stiles, W. B. (1998). Reformulation of assimilation analysis in terms of voices. *Psychotherapy, 35,* 23–33. doi:10.1037/h0087682

Horvath, A. O., & Greenberg, L. S. (1986). The development of the Working Alliance Inventory. In L. S. Greenberg & W. M. Pinsof (Eds.), *The psychotherapeutic process: A research handbook* (pp. 529–56). New York, NY: Guilford Press.

Horvath, A. O., & Greenberg, L. S. (1989). Development and validation of the Working Alliance Inventory. *Journal of Counseling Psychology, 36,* 223–233.

Luborsky, L., Singer, B., & Luborsky, L. (1975). Comparative studies of psychotherapies: Is it true that "Everyone has won and all must have prizes"? *Archives of General Psychiatry, 32,* 995–1008.

Rogers, C. R. (1951). *Client-centered therapy.* Boston, MA: Houghton Mifflin.

Stiles, W. B. (1979a). Psychotherapy recapitulates ontogeny: The epigenesis of intensive interpersonal relationships. *Psychotherapy: Theory, Research, and Practice, 16,* 391–404. doi:10.1037/h0088365

Stiles, W. B. (1979b). Verbal response modes and psychotherapeutic technique. *Psychiatry, 42,* 49–62.

Stiles, W. B. (1981). Science, experience, and truth: A conversation with myself. *Teaching of Psychology, 8,* 227–230. doi:10.1207/s15328023top0804_11

Stiles, W. B. (1988). Psychotherapy process-outcome correlations may be misleading. *Psychotherapy, 25,* 27–35. doi:10.1037/h0085320

Stiles, W. B. (1992). *Describing talk: A taxonomy of verbal response modes*. Newbury Park, CA: Sage.

Stiles, W. B. (1993). Quality control in qualitative research. *Clinical Psychology Review, 13*, 593–618. doi:10.1016/0272-7358(93)90048-Q

Stiles, W. B. (1999). Signs and voices in psychotherapy. *Psychotherapy Research, 9*, 1–21. doi:10.1093/ptr/9.1.1

Stiles, W. B. (2002). Assimilation of problematic experiences. In J. C. Norcross (Ed.), *Psychotherapy relationships that work: Therapist contributions and responsiveness to patients* (pp. 357–365). New York, NY: Oxford University Press.

Stiles, W. B. (2003). Qualitative research: Evaluating the process and the product. In S. P. Llewelyn & P. Kennedy (Eds.), *Handbook of clinical health psychology* (pp. 477–499). London, England: Wiley. doi:10.1002/0470013389.ch24

Stiles, W. B. (2005). Case studies. In J. C. Norcross, L. E. Beutler, & R. F. Levant (Eds.), *Evidence-based practices in mental health: Debate and dialogue on the fundamental questions* (pp. 57–64). Washington, DC: American Psychological Association.

Stiles, W. B. (2006). Numbers can be enriching. *New Ideas in Psychology, 24*, 252–262. doi:10.1016/j.newideapsych.2006.10.003

Stiles, W. B. (2007). Theory-building case studies of counselling and psychotherapy. *Counselling & Psychotherapy Research, 7*, 122–127. doi:10.1080/14733140701356742

Stiles, W. B., Agnew-Davies, R., Barkham, M., Culverwell, A., Goldfried, M. R., Halstead, J., . . . Shapiro, D. A. (2002). Convergent validity of the Agnew Relationship Measure and the Working Alliance Inventory. *Psychological Assessment, 14*, 209–220. doi:10.1037/1040-3590.14.2.209

Stiles, W. B., & Angus, L. (2001). Qualitative research on clients' assimilation of problematic experiences in psychotherapy. In J. Frommer & D. L. Rennie (Eds), *Qualitative psychotherapy research: Methods and methodology* (pp. 112–127). Lengerich, Germany: Pabst Science Publishers.

Stiles, W. B., Elliott, R., Llewelyn, S. P., Firth-Cozens, J. A., Margison, F. R., Shapiro, D. A., & Hardy, G. (1990). Assimilation of problematic experiences by clients in psychotherapy. *Psychotherapy, 27*, 411–420. doi:10.1037/0033-3204.27.3.411

Stiles, W. B., Glick, M. J., Osatuke, K., Hardy, G. E., Shapiro, D. A., Agnew-Davies, R., . . . Barkham, M. (2004). Patterns of alliance development and the rupture-repair hypothesis: Are productive relationships U-shaped or V-shaped? *Journal of Counseling Psychology, 51*, 81–92. doi:10.1037/0022-0167.51.1.81

Stiles, W. B., Gordon, L. E., & Lani, J. A. (2002). Session evaluation and the Session Evaluation Questionnaire. In G. S. Tryon (Ed.), *Counseling based on process research: Applying what we know* (pp. 325–343). Boston, MA: Allyn & Bacon.

Stiles, W. B., Honos-Webb, L., & Surko, M. (1998). Responsiveness in psychotherapy. *Clinical Psychology: Science and Practice, 5*, 439–458.

Stiles, W. B., Morrison, L. A., Haw, S. K., Harper, H., Shapiro, D. A., & Firth-Cozens, J. (1991). Longitudinal study of assimilation in exploratory psychotherapy. *Psychotherapy, 28*, 195–206. doi:10.1037/0033-3204.28.2.195

Stiles, W. B., Shapiro, D. A., & Elliott, R. (1986). Are all psychotherapies equivalent? *American Psychologist, 41*, 165–180. doi:10.1037/0003-066X.41.2.165

Stiles, W. B., Shapiro, D. A., & Firth-Cozens, J. A. (1988). Verbal response mode use in contrasting psychotherapies: A within-subjects comparison. *Journal of Consulting and Clinical Psychology, 56*, 727–733. doi:10.1037/0022-006X.56.5.727

IV

WHAT WORKS FOR WHOM?

26

SOL L. GARFIELD: A PIONEER IN BRINGING SCIENCE TO CLINICAL PSYCHOLOGY

LARRY E. BEUTLER AND ANNE D. SIMONS

The death of Sol Garfield in August of 2004 portended the end of an era in psychotherapy and clinical psychology. Sol Garfield was one of a handful of psychologists, largely educated in the years before and during World War II, who established clinical psychology as both a health profession and a science. With professional colleagues like Allen Bergin, Hans Strupp, Lester Luborsky, Kenneth I. Howard, Morris Parloff, and David Orlinsky, Sol worked to establish recognition for psychotherapy research as a legitimate scientific discipline and thereby firmly established the scientist–professional model of training and practice as an ideal for clinical psychology.

Facing the daunting task of challenging the giants of psychodynamic theories in the middle and late 20th century, Sol Garfield became a controversial man. Although often seen as a "kindly curmudgeon" (Beutler, 1998), he was vocally and notably in disagreement with many of the developments in clinical psychology and psychotherapy research that dominated the discipline in the 20th and early 21st centuries. He was a vocal critic of randomized clinical trials as the gold standard for determining psychotherapy's effects, of process research without first obtaining strong evidence of beneficial outcome, of the PsyD degree and the accompanying professionalization of psychology, of prescriptive authority for psychologists, and of the empirically unsupported practice of psychoanalysis. These issues troubled Garfield immensely, and he used the spoken and written word to try to hold clinical psychology on a course that would be true to its scientific foundations, as well as to keep the Society for Psychotherapy Research (SPR), a group that he cofounded, to its commitment to students and scholarship. Garfield viewed clinical psychology as "scientifically oriented" with a mission for "providing services to all segments of the public without a dominant interest in our own economic aggrandizement" (Garfield, 1991a; p. 119). His career was devoted to establishing this ideal, and it served as a model, for those of us who followed, of what we might become if we adopted his view of a worthy and accountable clinical psychology.

MAJOR CONTRIBUTIONS

During his career, which spanned more than 60 years, Sol Garfield published nearly 200 articles, chapters, and books. These contributions had an immense impact on the field, as noted by the extensive list of honors and awards that Garfield received during this time. However, none of his contributions match or exceed that of editing and publishing four volumes of *The Handbook of Psychotherapy and Behavior Change*, with his good friend and colleague Allen Bergin. The first of these volumes appeared in 1971 (Bergin & Garfield, 1971) and rapidly became the psychotherapy researcher's and clinical psychologist's bible. Among the most widely cited books in American psychology, the *Handbook* set the bar of evidence for effective practice. It left an indelible mark on two generations of clinical psychologists and researchers; and it became the definitive reference for the information and relationships "factually embedded" in scientific methods. Indeed, the *Handbook* ushered in the age of accountability in clinical psychology, expressed best by Garfield's (1994) words: "Let scientific evaluation make determinations about what treatments, provided by whom, are best applied to what types of client problems."

Sol Garfield provided some of the earliest work on the types and numbers of psychotherapies being practiced. The context for this work was the very rapid surge in different variants of psychotherapy dating from the 1960s. Surveying so many different therapies, Garfield and his longtime colleague at Washington University, Richard Kurtz, reported very interesting data on how therapists described their work, finding a large number who espoused eclecticism, rejecting any one particular theoretical orientation in favor of picking and choosing from a number of models (Garfield & Kurtz, 1977). Garfield's *Psychotherapy: An Eclectic Approach* (1980/1995) provided a way forward, advocating a form of eclectic treatment built on optimizing the common client, therapist, and intervention characteristics of all effective treatments (Garfield, 1987, 2000).

Through his work, Garfield established his reputation as a leading common factors theorist, arguing that these factors, however defined and operationalized, were more responsible for good outcomes in psychotherapy than any of the specific factors unique to a given model of psychotherapy. This position continues to generate considerable attention and research activity (Wampold, 2001) and a debate that one can only speculate that Garfield would welcome. Garfield was also a strong contributor to the lively debate on the merits of treatment manuals and the trend toward the identification of empirically supported treatments for different disorders (Garfield, 1996, 1998).

Garfield was very interested in client variables in psychotherapy and literally wrote the book on this area of research in his chapters for the different editions of the *Handbook of Psychotherapy and Behavior Change* (Bergin & Garfield, 1971, 1978, 1994; Garfield & Bergin, 1986). While he acknowledged that predictions regarding continuation and outcome based solely on client variables are unlikely to be successful, he identified some early predictors of continuation and benefit such as expectations, a client variable that continues to be the focus of contemporary psychotherapy research as they related to different aspects of therapy, particularly premature termination (Greenberg, Constantino, & Bruce, 2006).

Garfield's other research cut across a large number of topics, including the use of the Rorschach and the Thematic Apperception Test, measurement of performance among minority adolescents, intellectual measurement, clinical training, usefulness of psychological reports, classification and identification of those with mental retardation, drug effects on performance of patients with serious mental illness, and selection and training of aircraft pilots.

These were his numerous and extensive formal contributions, but his informal ones—the mentoring that he did for his students and colleagues—surely surpassed these sterile (by comparison) expressions of facts.

EARLY BEGINNINGS

Sol Garfield's acceptance of the mantles conferred with the various roles that became clinical psychology came in stages, and not always by his election and choice. He was virtually driven into psychology by the anti-Semitic attitudes of the time. However, Garfield developed his concern for people long before he obtained his formal education. While still in high school and college, he learned by experiencing the trials of helping to support his family—his parents and a younger sister—during the Great Depression. He gained an appreciation for struggle and pain by observing his father's efforts to overcome the financial failure of his grocery business and rise above it; he learned patience and empathy as one of few non-Black residents in his Chicago neighborhood;

and he learned the pain of rejection and the frustration of discrimination by experiencing the anti-Semitism of pre–World War II Chicago.

Born in 1918, growing up during the Great Depression, and educated during the war years, Sol struggled to help his family survive. When the failing economy of the early 1930s forced his father to give up his grocery store just as Sol was entering his freshman year at the University of Wisconsin, Sol came home to help his family. While he attended the Central YMCA College in downtown Chicago, this interest in psychology was piqued by the results of the Strong Vocational Interest Inventory. Taking this test helped move him to change career directions from prelaw to education. He wanted to be a secondary school teacher, but he would find that this role would elude him.

In a real way, Garfield's career in psychology was necessitated by his inability, as a young Jewish man, to obtain work in the teaching profession. When he failed to find a job after obtaining his baccalaureate degree from Northwestern University in 1938, he enrolled in graduate school to better prepare himself and improve his chances. But he subsequently found that an MA in education was no help, either—his ethnicity again precluded his being able to find work as a teacher or guidance counselor. Although he was discouraged by some of his faculty from entering the PhD program, circumstances and the persuasion of Paul Witty, a distinguished faculty member in the Department of Education and Guidance, contrived to help him earn the PhD. Although his PhD degree was in education and guidance, over half of the courses he took were in the Department of Psychology, and his graduate committee consisted of more psychologists than of education faculty. He was drawn to psychology, but it still took the intervention of chance and outside forces finally to settle his career choice. Indeed, it was the U.S. military that made him an official psychologist.

Garfield was inducted into the U.S. Army in December of 1942, where he was assigned to an infantry division. Enter again the constraint of anti-Semitism—he was denied entry to officer candidate school and assigned to the adjutant general's personnel consultant assistant school. His appeal to be reassigned was denied. He was trained and assigned to the psychology section. For the remainder of his service career and for the rest of his life, he was officially a psychologist.

Garfield served in a variety of locations while in the service. His first experiences as a clinical psychologist were at the Third Service Command in Baltimore, where he served on the neuropsychiatry unit, under the direction of the chief of service, Dr. Henry Brosin, a psychoanalyst and psychiatrist. With the encouragement of Brosin and several other psychiatric colleagues, Garfield learned about psychopathology, did many intake evaluations, and began conducting psychotherapy.

The war ended in 1945, and at the end of that year, Garfield married Amy Nussbaum, whom he described, with his inimitable sense of humor, as being "properly appreciative of my talents" (Garfield, 1991a; p. 104). He was discharged in 1946 and began work at the Mendota, Wisconsin, Veterans Hospital. It was there that Garfield's interest in teaching and training developed. He initiated both practicum and internship programs while in the Mendota VA and fostered the role of psychologists as psychotherapists.

Garfield left the Mendota VA after 14 months and entered academia as an assistant professor of psychology at the University of Connecticut, where he established a PhD program in clinical psychology. He left after less than 2 years to return to the VA, this time in Milwaukee, Wisconsin. Garfield's career in the following years moved back and forth between VA programs and academia as his interests in research were reawakened. Throughout, the red thread that defined his career never unravelled—the integration of research, education, and practice.

Three positions accounted for 28 years of Garfield's career, the longest lasting being his tenure at Washington University in St. Louis, where he ultimately retired as professor emeritus. His years (1957–1963) at the University of Nebraska College of Medicine cemented his commitment to the role of research in practice and furthered his commitment to a psychology that was distinguished from psychiatry. His years at Columbia University Teachers College (1964–1970) saw his career flourish as he achieved wide recognition for his research and scholarly writing on psychotherapy. His time at Washington University was a time of consolidation during which he finalized his stance as an eclectic psychotherapist and came to enjoy the fruits of his efforts. Here, Garfield's wisdom was recognized in the scholarly and wise contributions for which he ultimately was best known—the several editions of *The Handbook of Psychotherapy and Behavior Change*.

ACCOMPLISHMENTS

Sol Garfield's life reflects much of the American dream in the postwar years. He came from humble beginnings, as the child of immigrant Polish Jews who sought in America an opportunity for freedom from oppression and bigotry. The fact that this dream was not realized, given that Garfield experienced some of the anti-Semitism in Middle America that his parents had sought to escape in Poland, makes his achievements all the more impressive.

In Sol's self-reflections, he noted progressive dissatisfaction with his colleagues' psychoanalytic traditions and their authoritative, but meaningless, formulations of patients' problems. He also reported some satisfaction with the power of his own experience as an emerging psychotherapist who tried new things and with the evolution of his identity as an eclectic psychotherapist. At the Milwaukee Veterans Hospital, Garfield began to notice that different patients responded to different styles of intervention. In Milwaukee and after, he began to identify himself more and more as a psychotherapist and at the same time became more and more convinced that research was the answer to the question of "what worked." Indeed, it was his shift in research away from assessment and prediction of human performance and toward factors that predicted dropout that confirmed his reputation as one of the leading proponents of common factors approaches to psychotherapy integration (Garfield, 1991b; 1997). However, it was only a gradual development of interest and observation that led Garfield to become firmly and finally convinced that the many practices then in vogue could not be supported by research and to develop the conviction that empirical evidence should be the basis for practice. He wryly observed that few psychotherapists ever questioned the efficacy of their own psychotherapy practices, although they had doubts about the therapy of others (Garfield, 1994).

In 1952, when he was in charge of the training unit in the Downey, Illinois, VA, Garfield and a colleague conducted a study on outcomes of 1,216 patients who had been treated in an outpatient mental hygiene clinic (Garfield & Kurz, 1952). The results demonstrated a remarkable disparity between the perception of therapists who reported conducting "long-term psychotherapy" on their patients and the remarkably brief therapy that patients were actually receiving. Most patients received no more than 10 sessions of treatment, and fewer than 10% received 25 or more sessions. Early terminations were ignored, forgotten, overlooked, or denied by therapists.

The results of this study caught Garfield's imagination. While he continued his research on measurement and diagnosis, he was increasingly interested in how psychotherapy worked and failed to work. He published two studies on premature dropout (Garfield & Affleck, 1959, 1961) and then began to refine his focus on patient expectations in following years (Garfield, 1963; Garfield, Affleck, & Muffly, 1963; Garfield & Wolpin, 1963).

OTHER CONTRIBUTIONS

From 1963 to 1965, Garfield served on the advisory committee for a conference on the professional preparation of clinical psychologists for the American Psychological Association (APA), publishing his first article on training and psychology's search for identity (Garfield, 1966). A year later, he and colleagues (Garfield, Bergin, & Thompson, 1967) published the results of the Chicago Conference on Training in Clinical Psychology.

Garfield's contributions were not restricted to publications and research. He reported with some pride, his selection in 1959 to be the secretary–treasurer of APA's Division of Clinical Psychology (1960–1963; Garfield, 1991a). He later rose to serve as president of that organization (1965) and received this division's Distinguished Contributions Award. Among his many leadership roles, he also served as president of the Illinois Psychological Association in 1958; president of SPR in 1976–1977; and president of the Division of Clinical Psychology of the American Psychological Association (APA) in 1965. He served at least three terms as a member of the Council of Representatives of APA.

Among his many accolades, he was a recipient of the Distinguished Contributions to Knowledge Award from APA; the Distinguished Scientist Award from the Section on Clinical Psychology as an Experimental–Behavioral Science (Division of Clinical Psychology, APA); the Distinguished Research Career Award from SPR; and the Award for Outstanding Contributions to Clinical Training from the Council of University Directors of Clinical Psychology. However, of all his professional contributions, Garfield expressed special pleasure (Garfield, 1991a) at being asked by APA to serve on the advisory committee for a conference on professional preparation of clinical psychologists, which was focused on the development of practicum and internship experiences. This position ranked along with the awards and recognition that he received from the membership of SPR, which he had cofounded in 1962, for his work on the *Handbook* with his friend Allen Bergin, and for his work as editor of the *Journal of Consulting and Clinical Psychology* (1979–1984).

INFLUENCES

There were many who influenced Garfield throughout the years. Certainly, he was close to his parents, and after his marriage sought wisdom and support from his wife, Amy. His early mentor, Paul Witty, helped set him in a direction of research interest and education, a direction further encouraged by Professor A. R. Gilliland, who was then chair of the Department of Psychology at Northwestern University. In his postgraduate years, others came to influence him strongly. The list is endless, but certainly Ralph Heine, Craig Affleck, Allen Bergin, Jerome Frank, Leonard Eron, and his senior colleagues and coorganizers of SPR were among them. He spoke of these people often, both in his personal communications with colleagues (present authors among them) and in his personal reflective writings (Garfield, 1991a; 2000).

Sol Garfield was a mentor to many. He published with a large cadre of students, the last of whom is a coauthor of this chapter (Simons). Many of his previous students are now involved in clinical psychology training in various settings; all remember his insistence on empirical support for clinical work and have commented on how this insistence could be viewed as the precursor to the current zeitgeist of empirically supported treatments and evidence-based practice. His strength as a mentor also extended generously to junior colleagues, whom he encouraged, for whom he served as a model, and to whom he constantly gave of his wit and wisdom while opening doors and providing advice.

CONCLUSION

Sol Garfield is described in the subtitle of this chapter as "a pioneer in bringing science to clinical psychology." There can be no doubt that he blazed this trail at a time when it was difficult and unpopular to do so. Indeed, the zeitgeist of the time held that the mysteries of psychotherapy would not yield to the scientific method. Only a man of Sol's intelligence, courage, and conviction could succeed in truly changing the course and face of clinical psychology. The issues with which he grappled—What are the mechanisms of change in psychotherapy? How can we assess outcomes in psychotherapy? What are the client variables that influence clients to enter, continue in, and benefit from psychotherapy?—remain current today.

REFERENCES

Bergin, A., Garfield, S., & Thompson, A. (1967). The Chicago Conference on Clinical Training and Clinical Psychology at Teachers College. *American Psychologist, 22,* 307–316.

Beutler, L. E. (May, 1998). *A tribute to Sol Garfield.* Unpublished paper presented to the faculty and students at Washington University, St. Louis, MO.

Garfield, S. L. (1963). A note on patients' reasons for terminating therapy. *Psychological Reports, 13*(1), 38–42.

Garfield, S. L. (1966). Clinical psychology and the search for identity. *American Psychologist, 21,* 353–362. doi:10.1037/h0023529

Garfield, S. L. (1971). Research on client variables in psychotherapy. In A.E. Bergin & S.L. Garfield (Eds.), *Handbook of psychotherapy and behavior change: An empirical analysis* (1st ed., pp. 271–298). New York, NY: Wiley.

Garfield, S. L. (1978). Research on client variables in psychotherapy. In A. E. Bergin & S. L. Garfield (Eds.), *Handbook of psychotherapy and behavior change* (2nd ed., pp. 191–232). New York, NY: Wiley.

Garfield, S. L. (1986). Research on client variables in psychotherapy. In S. L. Garfield & A. E. Bergin (Eds.) *Handbook of psychotherapy and behavior change* (3rd ed., pp. 213–256). New York, NY: Wiley.

Garfield, S. L. (1987). Towards a scientifically oriented eclecticism. *Scandinavian Journal of Behavior Therapy, 16*(3), 95–109.

Garfield, S. L. (1991a). A career in clinical psychology. In C. E. Walker (Ed.), *A history of clinical psychology in autobiography* (pp. 87–123). Pacific Grove, CA: Brooks/Cole.

Garfield, S. L. (1991b). Psychotherapy models and outcome research. *American Psychologist, 46,* 1350–1351. doi:10.1037/0003-066X.46.12.1350

Garfield, S. L. (1994). Research on client variables in psychotherapy. In A. E. Bergin & S. L. Garfield (Eds.), *Handbook of psychotherapy and behavior change* (4th ed., pp. 190–228). New York, NY: Wiley.

Garfield, S. L. (1995). *Psychotherapy: An eclectic-integrative approach* (2nd ed.). New York, NY: Wiley. Originally published in 1980.

Garfield, S. L. (1996). Some problems associated with "validated" forms of psychotherapy. *Clinical Psychology: Science and Practice, 3,* 218–229.

Garfield, S. L. (1997). Brief psychotherapy: The role of common and specific factors. *Clinical Psychology & Psychotherapy, 4,* 217–225. doi:10.1002/(SICI)1099-0879(199712)4:4<217::AID-CPP134>3.0.CO;2-Y

Garfield, S. L. (1998). Some comments on empirically supported psychological treatments. *Journal of Consulting and Clinical Psychology, 66,* 121–125. doi:10.1037/0022-006X.66.1.121

Garfield, S. L. (2000). Eclecticism and integration: A personal retrospective view. *Journal of Psychotherapy Integration, 10,* 341–355.

Garfield, S. L., & Affleck, D. C. (1959). An appraisal of duration of stay in outpatient psychotherapy. *Journal of Nervous and Mental Disease, 129,* 492–498. doi:10.1097/00005053-195911000-00010

Garfield, S. L., & Affleck, D. C. (1961). Therapists' judgments concerning patients considered for psychotherapy. *Journal of Consulting Psychology, 25,* 505–509. doi:10.1037/h0046098

Garfield, S. L., Affleck, D. D., & Muffly, R. (1963). A study of psychotherapy interaction and continuation in psychotherapy. *Journal of Clinical Psychology, 19,* 473–478. doi:10.1002/1097-4679(196310)19:4<473::AID-JCLP2270190428>3.0.CO;2-3

Garfield, S. L., & Kurz, M. (1952). Evaluation of treatment and related procedures in 1,216 cases referred to a mental hygiene clinic. *Psychiatric Quarterly, 26*(1), 414–424. doi:10.1007/BF01568477

Garfield, S. L., & Kurtz, R. (1977). A study of eclectic views. *Journal of Consulting and Clinical Psychology, 45,* 78–83. doi:10.1037/0022-006X.45.1.78

Garfield, S. L., & Wolpin, M. (1963). Expectations regarding psychotherapy. *Journal of Nervous and Mental Disease, 137,* 353–362. doi:10.1097/00005053-196310000-00007

Greenberg, R. P., Constantino, M. J., & Bruce, N. (2006). Are expectations still relevant for psychotherapy process and outcome? *Clinical Psychology Review, 26,* 657–678. doi:10.1016/j.cpr.2005.03.002

Wampold, B. E. (2001). *The great psychotherapy debate*. Mahwah, NJ: Erlbaum.

27

LARRY E. BEUTLER: A MATTER OF PRINCIPLES

PAULO P. P. MACHADO, HÉCTOR FERNÁNDEZ-ÁLVAREZ,
AND JOHN F. CLARKIN

Larry E. Beutler has devoted his entire academic career to investigating and unraveling the complexity of change in psychotherapy. By doing so, he has systematically and strategically challenged the field of psychotherapeutic research to abandon the theoretical trenches and openly embark on a quest for the principles underlying the therapeutic endeavor. As a result, he has made significant contributions to our understanding of which treatment works for which individual and how therapists should select their goals and therapeutic strategies on the basis of patient characteristics rather than theoretical orientation or traditional diagnostic categories.

MAJOR CONTRIBUTIONS

It is difficult to assess the impact of Larry Beutler's countless contributions to the field of psychotherapy research. Those who have been lucky enough to have worked, collaborate with, or even chat with him are most probably impressed with his strong motivation for scientific discovery, as well his quest for how to best serve those in need of psychological services. Several areas of extensive and intense focus and concentration stand out, nonetheless, and these include psychotherapy research and systematic treatment selection. These two areas of concentration reflect his early career focus on both the art of helping others and a scientific approach to that endeavor.

The search for specific factors that would maximize treatment matching to a patient's individual characteristics was present in most of his scientific production and research projects, and it will probably become his most significant contribution to the field of psychotherapy research. Illustrative examples of this long-term commitment are the seminal book published with John Clarkin (Beutler & Clarkin, 1990) and later with John Clarkin and Bruce Bongar (Beutler, Clarkin, & Bongar, 2000) on systematic treatment selection and his research projects on the treatment of depression (Beutler et al., 1991), alcoholism (Beutler et al., 1993), and treatment matching (Beutler, Moleiro, & Talebi, 2002), and several papers in which he challenged the field to find and test principles that cut across theoretical orientation and perspectives and helped develop optimal interventions adapted to the individual characteristics of each patient.

EARLY BEGINNINGS

Larry E. Beutler was born on February 14, 1941, in a small private clinic in Logan, Utah. He was the younger of two children. After the bombing of Pearl Harbor, the family moved to San Francisco, where his father briefly worked in the shipyards. From there, they moved to Arizona and then back to Logan. His father continued to work in construction, taking the jobs he could find and farming with his brothers, as well. The period 1943–1944, as the war continued, was particularly hard for the family, with several severe losses over those 12 months. His step-grandmother died, his uncle was killed in the Battle of Okinawa, and then finally came the death of Beutler's mother from rheumatic heart disease. After that last loss, Larry and his sister were shuffled among various relatives, coming to rest with his aunt. They stayed with her for about a year, until his father remarried. The new family then moved back into one of the family dwellings, a basement house, a type of dwelling common at the time. They then moved to Ucon, Idaho, about 150 miles away, and lived in a one-room cabin while his father built a house for them. By then Larry was 5 years old, and his career as a cowboy was well developed in his head. All told, during the first 6 years of his life, he lived in eight different houses, four different states, and with four different families. Remembering this, Beutler commented, "No wonder I could never stand being in one place for a prolonged period of time."

During his early teenage years, which were marked by more family moves, illness, and separation, Beutler pursued his interests as a cowboy and horse trainer, taking summer jobs in Canada and Utah. After high school, where he graduated without distinction, he attended Ricks College, in Rexburg, Idaho (about 30 miles away), for 1 year before accepting an appointment as a Mormon missionary in North Carolina and Virginia in 1961.

Upon his return from North Carolina in September of 1963, Beutler discovered that his father had arranged for his marriage with a young woman. They married 4 months later, and he went back to school at Ricks College while working nights to support his new family. He graduated in sociology in 1963 and transferred to Utah State University. By that point Larry Beutler had had four different majors, but his interest had been piqued in psychology, and he was accepted into the BS program in psychology at Utah State.

At the beginning of his academic career, Beutler was drawn to a combination of social studies and more hard-core scientific studies such as mathematics and chemistry. His eclectic interests had led to a major in psychology and minors in sociology and business by by the time he graduated from Utah State University in 1965. He entered a master's program at Utah State while he applied to doctoral programs, having decided firmly by then that he wanted to get a PhD in clinical psychology and go into private practice. He earned a research fellowship from the university and was surprised by the end of the year that he was accepted into several graduate schools.

He chose the University of Nebraska, and he and his wife embarked on an adventure away from family and church. He entered the University of Nebraska–Lincoln PhD program in the fall of 1966 and completed it in three and a half years, including a one-year internship at Norfolk State Hospital and Regional Center. The experiences with his dissertation at the University of Nebraska influenced him to become a scientist–practitioner, and his career has been shaped around that model. His advisor, Dr. James K. Cole, who had been a student of Carl Rogers, influenced him in pursuing an academic career.

After completing his degree, Beutler moved to North Carolina, where he accepted a job at Highland Hospital, which was then a Division of Duke University Medical Center. Here his career began taking off under the tutelage of Dr. Dale T. Johnson, and within a year he was offered the job of director of research. He found that he was quite good at getting things published. His success got him introduced to Sol Garfield, who was then the editor of the *Journal of Consulting Psychology* (now the *Journal of Consulting and Clinical Psychology*). Garfield introduced Beutler to the Society for Psychotherapy Research (SPR) and later invited him to be on the review board of that journal. Garfield assumed and retained the role of Larry's mentor during the next several years and stimulated his career in psychotherapy research. His dissertation, a predictor of a career-long focus, had been on psychotherapist–patient matching.

These early academic areas of concentration suggest a combination of scientific and mathematical skills combined with a keen interest in helping others through counseling and psychotherapy. This dual focus on the art of psychotherapy and the awareness of and application of scientific methods would characterize his pursuits for many years to come.

ACCOMPLISHMENTS

Larry Beutler's main research always orbited around the development and testing of decisional models for matching specific psychotherapy procedures and formats with patient characteristics. His work focused on defining empirically based and cross-theoretical guidelines for treatment, matching interventions to various extradiagnostic patient qualities.

The energy and zeal that Beutler has brought to his research in psychology, like the breadth and productivity of that research, are extraordinary. He is the author of about 400 scientific papers and chapters and is the author, editor, or coauthor of more than 20 books on psychotherapy, assessment, and psychopathology. These works have explored multiple disciplines, including social psychology, the psychology of religion, chemical abuse, forensic assessment, childhood sexual abuse, sleep, depression, sexual disorders, rape, victimization of women, and various aspects of psychotherapy. His voracious appetite for knowledge about the human condition and its sufferings and possible ameliorations seems unlimited. Beutler has tended always to trust more in data than in theoretical arguments, and early in his academic career he was drawn to the exploration of the specific ingredients, or techniques, that were responsible for client change in psychotherapy.

Curiously, it was Sol Garfield's rejection of one of his articles, in the late 1970s, that made Beutler rethink what he was doing and turn his attention to the relationship between process and outcome in psychotherapy, as a function of the actions of the therapist. Years later, his attention returned to the issue of matching, now captured within the broader domain of integrating interventions, relationship factors, participant factors, and context. However, that rejected article, eventually published in 1979, was where this interest in integration began.

In this early article, titled "Toward Specific Psychological Therapies for Specific Conditions" (1979), Beutler laid the foundation for his career-long quest. Starting with the observation that psychotherapy research had been unable to clarify the idea that specific therapies would be most efficacious with specific disorders, Beutler took the position that traditional studies had always looked at main effects, ignoring potential interactions between patient characteristics and treatment. He offered a "speculative model for predicting deferential rates of therapeutic change" (p. 882). This model was based not solely on theoretical grounds but also on a careful review of the empirical literature available at the time. Starting with potential patient and symptom dimensions, specifically, symptom complexity, patient's defensive style and reactance, Beutler analyzed 52 comparative psychotherapy studies, looking for evidence of relationship between these dimensions and treatment outcome.

Revisiting these concerns, Beutler, now editor of the journal that had initially rejected his article, published another one, ironically titled "Have All Won and Must All Have Prizes? Revisiting Luborsky et al.'s Verdict" (Beutler, 1991). In this article, he again claimed that although psychotherapy research failed to find significant differences between treatment approaches, it would be premature to stop searching for differential effects. More than 10 years later, the number of available treatment brands had risen from close to 130 to more than 300, and researchers as well as clinicians struggled to find sound clinical decision procedures. Again Beutler's challenge to the field was to abandon theoretical labels and look for specific ingredients in treatments that could account for change and, most important, would interact with specific patient personal characteristics to explain differential effects that were lost when attention and resources were channeled to look for main effects of treatment. Given the herculean task of exploring all possible interactions between patient, therapist, and treatment variables, Beutler suggested the need for consensual models to guide the search for variables that would mediate treatment effect on outcome, making a strong argument for the development of "systematic eclectic models of treatment application" (Beutler, 1991, p. 231).

In his professional work, Beutler was also convinced that the work of the clinical psychologist (in the assessment and treatment of patients) should be guided by the application of research results in a systematic way. His book *Eclectic Psychotherapy: A Systematic Approach* (1983) was a manifestation of this effort. At about this same time, a similar book on an organized approach to the selection of the most optimal psychotherapy for the individual patient emerged from a medical and psychiatric setting. This book was *Differential Therapeutics in Psychiatry* (1984) by Alan Frances, John Clarkin, and Samuel Perry. Through contacts at SPR and other professional forums, Beutler and Clarkin combined to further explore the application of research results to principles and guidelines for the selection of treatment in clinical settings. This collaboration eventually led to the publication of another important book, *Systematic Treatment Selection: Toward Targeted Therapeutic Interventions* (Beutler & Clarkin, 1990). Later, joined by Bruce Bongar, they decided to focus the concepts of systematic treatment selection on the treatment of the depressed patient. In *Guidelines for the Systematic Treatment of the Depressed Patient* (Beutler, Clarkin, & Bongar, 2000) they presented guidelines in the form of hypotheses about the treatment of depressed individuals that they explored with the existing empirical information. The resulting guidelines were not limited to any one theory of the psychopathology of depression or any one school of psychotherapy but, rather, attempted to incorporate existing data. With an exhaustive review of the empirical literature, two levels of guidelines were generated. The basic guidelines could be applied independently of the therapist and used routinely by health care managers. In contrast, the optimal guidelines were more detailed and involved training and monitoring of the practicing clinician. The resulting guidelines incorporated both significant patient characteristics and corresponding aspects of treatment that had been investigated empirically. Thus, an exhaustive review of the literature on the depressed patient yielded six patient variables: functional impairment, subjective distress, social support, problem complexity and chronicity, reactance/resistance, and major coping styles. These patient relevant variables, assessed with the appropriate interview and instrumental assessment, were then matched to treatment variables to generate the basic and optimal treatment guidelines.

The resulting guidelines were nuanced and tailored to the individual patient, on the basis not only of the diagnosis of depression but also of the six patient variables emerging from the data. In addition, the guidelines went beyond treatment school labels to research-generated aspects of treatment delivery that are relevant across schools of information. These guidelines differed from those generated by official organizations, like the American Psychological Association (APA) and the American Psychiatric Association, in their thorough empirical basis and matching of multiple patient and treatment characteristics.

Beutler expressed his concerns with translating research findings to clinical practice in a talk titled "David and Goliath: When Psychotherapy Research Meets Health-Care Delivery Systems," the Rosalee G. Weiss lecture at the 1999 APA convention in Boston, and later in print in *American Psychologist* (2000). In this article, Beutler again addressed the question of translating scientific evidence to clinical practice and did that in a way that could be translated and applied to everyday decision making in selecting the best treatment option. The article finishes with a set of empirically derived basic guidelines that reflect the decisions resulting on patient prognosis, level of risk, and recommendations for use of various modalities and formats of treatment, as well as guidelines for treatment enhancement and optimization.

Larry's quest for scientific discovery is so ingrained in him that you can find him on both sides of some of the most recent discussions in our field. He was a member of the APA Division 12 (Society of Clinical Psychology) task force for empirically supported treatments and also a member of the Division 29 (Psychotherapy) task force on relationship ingredients. This means that he was a prominent figure in the empirically supported treatment movement that was initiated by the Society for Clinical Psychology within Division 12 of APA, but later also prominent in the empirically supported relationships movement with APA's Division 29.

However, not entirely satisfied with the outcome, he promoted a new movement for empirically based principles, trying to extract from research studies principles of change that could guide clinicians in their daily work with patients. This entailed a proposal to shift from focusing on manual-defined treatments to identifying empirically established principles to guide treatment. The structure and process of the movement's task force are presented in a coauthored article (Castonguay & Beutler, 2006a) and a coedited book (Castonguay & Beutler, 2006b).

It is fair to say that Larry's views have always been informed by scientific data and also infused with a sense of what others may be experiencing clinically. This preoccupation is clear when, in his numerous works, he states that the therapist should struggle to match the individual patient with the most optimal treatment. But what about the patient who feels that the treatment is not optimal and not producing results? That empathic perception led Beutler to write a helpful book (Beutler, Bongar, & Shurkin, 2000), originally titled *Am I Crazy or Is It My Shrink?* (reprinted as *A Consumer's Guide to Psychotherapy: A Complete Guide to Choosing the Therapist and Treatment That's Right For You*).

OTHER CONTRIBUTIONS

Larry Beutler can claim an impressive collection of acknowledgments of his scientific achievements. For example, he served as president of APA Division 29 and APA Division 12 (Clinical) and as president of the Society for Psychotherapy Research (SPR). Among his citations and achievements he can count the Distinguished Career Award from SPR, the Gold Medal Award from the American Psychological Foundation, and a presidential citation for achievement from APA. He has also been honored for his contributions by the states of Arizona and California. As noted, the scholarly publications that he has written or to which he has contributed number in the hundreds.

Larry Beutler has made continuous and major contributions to the renowned *Journal of Consulting and Clinical Psychology*. After serving on the editorial board from 1975 to 1983, he was associate editor from 1984 to 1989 and editor from 1990 to 1995. As editor, he not only published scientifically excellent research reports but also organized a number of special sections that brought together the best thinking in the field at the time on such topics as theoretical developments in the cognitive psychotherapies, single-case research in psychotherapy, curative factors in dynamic psychotherapy, smoking cessation, and the analysis of the process of change. Under his editorship, JCCP reprinted historic papers by Cattell, Eysenk, Super, and Rogers.

One of us (Clarkin) was fortunate enough to work for the editorial group under Beutler during the latter's involvement with the journal and observed his way of managing the difficult and often thankless task of editorship. The acceptance of outstanding articles for publication takes judgment and leads to joy and gratitude on the part of the authors. The rejection of articles can tear at the fragile sense of competence and self-esteem in young researchers. As editor, Beutler had to summarize the criticisms of the reviewers and deliver the bad news to those who were to receive rejection letters. His rejection letters were a beauty to behold. Like a good parent, effective mentor (caring horse trainer?), Beutler had a way of praising the author for the merits of the investigation and delivering the bad news with a strong ray of hope for future efforts.

His editorial contributions were not limited to JCCP, however. He served as editor, with Ken Howard, a longtime and dear friend deeply missed, of the *Journal of Clinical Psychology* and again promoted numerous special sections that became references in the field of psychotherapy research.

Larry Beutler is a powerful and influential force in psychology in the United States, but his influence is not contained by U.S. boundaries. He has traveled frequently and has developed long-term collaborations with groups in several countries and regions around the world. One of us (Fernández-Álvarez) witnessed the impact of these collaborations in the development of psychotherapy research in South America. Since his first trip to South America in 1992 to attend an international meeting organized by the Aiglé Foundation in Buenos Aires, Beutler has visited frequently, giving seminars that helped the development of the field in South America. Another of us (Machado) witnessed a similar process in Europe, namely, in Portugal and Spain, countries that Larry has visited over the years, having established close ties with the University of Minho in Portugal and the University of Granada in Spain.

In addition to these accomplishments, Beutler has always had an interest in the training of psychotherapists and psychotherapy researchers. Needless to say, he has written several publications on this topic, but mostly he has influenced several generations of students. As a mentor, he has always had a strong commitment to helping every student's personal and professional development. He has a long list of students not only in the United States but around the world, several committed to academic careers and the field of psychotherapy research.

CONCLUSION

The measure of an individual's contribution to a field of study is multi-faceted. If one judges the contribution from the number and extent of impactful research contributions to the field, Larry Beutler can be viewed as a giant in psychotherapy research. If the measure of contribution is the individual's role in the organizational and scholarly advance of the field of study, Larry is a provocateur by virtue of the challenges he presented to the field, but he is also a leader and a great team player. Finally, and most important, if the measure of contribution is the modeling effect of the individual on the next generation of researchers and practitioners in the field, Larry Beutler is a folk hero.

Currently, he is most likely to be found either in one of the academic campuses of Stanford or on his ranch in Northern California, where he lives with his wife, Jamie Blitzer (whom he married in 2004). In Northern California he seems to have the best of all worlds, given his academically stimulating environment in psychology and the opportunity to return to his childhood love of animals, working with horses and finding a sense of peace. When asked for some words of wisdom, he quoted one of the principles of working with horses, and he sees no reason not to use it as a metaphor for the delicate balance between the many facets of psychotherapy that occupied his long and fruitful academic career: "A horse doesn't care about how much you know, until he knows how much you care."

REFERENCES

Beutler, L.E. (1979). Toward specific psychological therapies for specific conditions. *Journal of Consulting and Clinical Psychology, 47*, 882–897.

Beutler, L. E. (1983). *Eclectic psychotherapy: A systematic approach.* New York, NY: Pergamon.

Beutler, L. E. (1991). Have all won and must all have prizes? Revisiting Luborsky et al.'s verdict. *Journal of Consulting and Clinical Psychology, 59*, 226–232. doi:10.1037/0022-006X.59.2.226

Beutler, L. E. (2000). David and Goliath: When psychotherapy research meets health care delivery systems. *American Psychologist, 55*, 997–1007. doi:10.1037/0003-066X.55.9.997

Beutler, L. E., Bongar, B., & Shurkin, J. L. (2000). *A consumer's guide to psychotherapy: A complete guide to choosing the therapist and treatment that's right for you.* New York, NY: Oxford University Press. (Originally published in 1998 as *Am I crazy or is it my shrink?*)

Beutler, L. E., & Clarkin, J. F. (1990). *Systematic treatment selection: Toward targeted therapeutic interventions*. New York, NY: Brunner/Mazel.

Beutler, L. E., Clarkin, J. F., & Bongar, B. (2000). *Guidelines for the systematic treatment of the depressed patient*. New York, NY: Oxford University Press.

Beutler, L. E., Engle, D., Mohr, D., Daldrup, R. J., Bergan, J., Meredith, K., & Merry, W. (1991). Predictors of differential response to cognitive, experiential, and self-directed psychotherapeutic procedures. *Journal of Consulting and Clinical Psychology, 59*, 333–340. doi:10.1037/0022-006X.59.2.333

Beutler, L. E., Moleiro, C., & Talebi, H. (2002). How practitioners can systematically use empirical evidence in treatment selection. *Journal of Clinical Psychology, 58*, 1199–1212. doi:10.1002/jclp.10106

Beutler, L. E., Patterson, K. M., Jacob, T., Shoham, V., Yost, E., & Rohrbaugh, M. (1993). Matching treatment to alcoholism subtypes. *Psychotherapy, 30*, 463–472. doi:10.1037/0033-3204.30.3.463

Castonguay, L. G., & Beutler, L. E. (2006a). Principles of therapeutic change: A task force on participants, relationship, and techniques factors. *Journal of Clinical Psychology, 62*, 631–638. doi:10.1002/jclp.20256

Castonguay, L. G., & Beutler, L. E. (Eds.). (2006b). *Principles of therapeutic change that work: Integrating relationship, treatment, client, and therapist factors*. New York, NY: Oxford University Press.

Frances, A., Clarkin, J. F., & Perry, S. (1984). *Differential therapeutics in psychiatry: The art and science of treatment selection*. New York, NY: Brunner/Mazel.

28

SIDNEY J. BLATT: RELATEDNESS, SELF-DEFINITION, AND MENTAL REPRESENTATION

JOHN S. AUERBACH, KENNETH N. LEVY, AND CARRIE E. SCHAFFER

Within the field of clinical psychology, contributors who are both psychoanalysts and leading empirical researchers are increasingly rare. Yet one figure who has made extensive contributions as an analytic clinician, as a researcher, and as a theoretician is Sidney J. Blatt. In addition to being trained as a psychoanalyst, he has conducted extensive research on personality development, psychological assessment, psychopathology, and psychotherapeutic outcomes. Along with his many students and colleagues, he has developed several widely used measures, both self-report and projective, for assessing depressive style, self- and object representations, and boundary disturbances in thought disorder. In short, Sid has been a wide-ranging and productive scholar in a career of more than 40 years' duration, and throughout this career he has been committed to the proposition that it is not only possible but also essential to investigate psychoanalytically derived hypotheses through rigorous empirical science.

SUMMARY OF MAJOR CONTRIBUTIONS

Sidney Blatt is known for two fundamental ideas: his two-configurations model, which delineates between anaclitic (or relational) and introjective (or self-definitional) forms of depression (e.g., Blatt, 1974; Blatt & Shichman, 1983) and his cognitive morphology of personality development and psychopathology (e.g., Blatt, 1991, 1995b). Regarding the two-configurations model, Blatt early in his career began to differentiate between relational forms of depression, which derive from interpersonal dependence and experiences of loneliness and loss, and self-definitional forms, which involve experiences of guilt, self-criticism, and failure. He has applied this distinction to psychopathology in general, personality development, and psychotherapy research. Regarding his cognitive morphology, Blatt proposed a psychoanalytically informed cognitive developmental model of personality, according to which psychological growth involves the maturation of underlying representational structures of interpersonal or object relations. Initially, these representational structures focus primarily on need gratification, and they progress toward representations that integrate this early focus on needs with abstract conceptual properties involving complex psychological states and intersubjectivity (e.g., Blatt, Auerbach, & Levy, 1997; Diamond, Kaslow, Coonerty, & Blatt, 1990). Blatt's broad theoretical ideas serve as the foundation for his psychotherapy research, with its focus on how personality style and level of development influence clinical outcome. In those studies, Blatt and his collaborators demonstrated how anaclitic and introjective patients have very different responses to psychotherapy, whether short-term or long-term, whether behavioral or psychoanalytic, and how the personality of the patient may indeed matter as much as or more than the type of the psychotherapy he or she receives.

EARLY BEGINNINGS

The oldest of three children, Sidney Blatt was born on October 15, 1928, to Harry and Fannie Blatt. Raised in modest circumstances, he grew up in a Jewish family in South Philadelphia, where his father owned a sweets shop; his family lived in the apartment upstairs. Sid recalls that every year he would accompany his father to the cemetery where his grandmother was buried, and there Sid would hold his father's hand and attempt to console him as his father wept over the grave. Sid also recalls that, at age 13, he accompanied his mother on a painful 2-hour bus trip to New Jersey as she responded to an urgent phone call informing her that her father had just suffered a heart attack. He tried to comfort his mother during the trip while she, correctly anticipating her father's death, grieved his loss. Regarding these childhood memories, Sid says that it is no surprise that he eventually was to become interested in studying depressive experiences that focus on separation and loss. He further recalls that, at age 9, he became disillusioned with his father for failing to support him in what he describes as some minor but symbolically important matter. Sid decided to run away from home. He defiantly packed his bags and left the house, but within a few blocks he became aware that he could not remember what his mother looked like; he ran home in a panic. Sid says that this terrifying memory may be one of the roots of his lifelong interest in the mental representation of the important people in one's life.

Sid's interest in psychoanalysis began in high school with his reading of Freud's "Introductory Lectures on Psycho-Analysis" (see Strachey, 1963). He was fascinated by Freud's descriptions of unconscious processes. Then, as a psychology major at Penn State, Sid extended his earlier interest in psycho-analysis to an emerging interest in projective testing. When taking a group Rorschach in one of his classes, Sid was intrigued by how much his responses revealed about himself.

Between his sophomore and junior years at Penn State he was introduced, by one of his fraternity brothers, to Ethel Shames. He and Ethel married on February 1, 1951, and were eventually to have three children, Susan, Judy, and David. Sid says that without Ethel by his side, his professional accomplishments would have been impossible.

In 1950, Sid entered the graduate program in psychology at Penn State and worked under William Snyder, a student of Carl Rogers. In 1952, he completed his master's degree and received honors for his thesis, later published in *Archives of General Psychiatry* (Blatt, 1959). In 1954, Sid entered the PhD program in psychology at the University of Chicago and found the "U of C an intellectual paradise," where he maintained an ever-increasing list of "must-read books and articles" (Auerbach, Levy, & Schaffer, 2005, p. 5). He did his predoctoral internship in 1955 and 1956, under the supervision of Carl Rogers, whom he still describes 40 years later, even after his analytic training, as a profound influence on his psychotherapeutic approach. From Rogers, he learned the crucial importance of empathy—of understanding how his patients experienced the world and of framing his therapeutic interventions from the patient's standpoint. He also worked as a research assistant for Morris I. Stein, who had been a student of Henry Murray's at Harvard and who served as the chair for Blatt's dissertation ("An Experimental Study of the Problem Solving Process"), completed in 1957 and retitled and published shortly thereafter (Blatt & Stein, 1959). The other major influence on Blatt's thought, however, was not one of his teachers but David Rapaport (1951), whose ideas gave Blatt a deeper theoretical understanding of the workings of the mind, a way of linking motivation and cognition.

After a postdoctoral fellowship at the University of Illinois Medical School and at Michael Reese Hospital's Psychiatric and Psychosomatic Institute, then headed by Roy Grinker Sr., Sid joined the Department of Psychology at Yale University as an assistant professor in 1960. He was also accepted for analytic training at the Western New England Institute for Psychoanalysis (WNEIP). At the WNEIP, Sid hoped to have a chance to work directly with Rapaport, whose intellectual contributions Sid had come to admire enormously. Rapaport died suddenly on December 14, 1960. Although crestfallen about losing the opportunity to work with Rapaport, Blatt had already established a relationship with Roy Schafer, his Yale faculty colleague. From Schafer, who had worked extensively with Rapaport (see Rapaport, Gill, & Schafer, 1945–1946), Blatt learned in greater depth the subtleties of Rapaport's thinking. In July 1963, he became chief of the Yale psychiatry department's Psychology Section, the position he holds to this day.

ACCOMPLISHMENTS

Two-Configurations Model

Although Sidney Blatt's earliest interests were in psychological testing and mental representation (e.g., Allison, Blatt, & Zimet, 1968), it was with his two-configurations approach to psychopathology, depression in particular, that he came into his intellectual own. In 1972, Blatt completed his psychoanalytic training, and his experiences with his two training cases led him to formulate the anaclitic–introjective distinction (Blatt, 1974). Although each of these patients suffered from depression, one proved to be highly self-critical and guilt-ridden, with much suicidal ideation, and the other was highly dependent, wanting nurturance and desperately seeking emotional contact. From these experiences, Blatt proposed that some depressed patients, whom he termed *introjective* because of their excessively harsh introjects, are focused mainly on self-criticism, guilt, failure, and a need for achievement and that others, whom he termed *anaclitic* because of their need to lean on others for emotional support, are concerned mainly with loss, separation, abandonment, and a need for emotional contact. Later, Blatt expanded this classification to apply to other forms of psychopathology (Blatt & Shichman, 1983), as well as to personality development (Blatt & Blass, 1990). As he expanded the scope of this model, he also became interested in attachment theory and intersubjectivity theory, primarily as a result of the influence of younger colleagues (see, e.g., Auerbach & Blatt, 2001; Diamond & Blatt, 1994; Levy, Blatt, & Shaver, 1998; Schaffer, 1993), and his terminology shifted from anaclitic and introjective to the more inclusive distinction between *attachment* or *relatedness* on the one hand and *separateness* or *self-definition* on the other (e.g., Blatt & Blass 1990). Thus, this tension between relatedness and self-definition has been central to Blatt's understanding of human life.

Blatt recognized that his theories needed grounding in empirical evidence. He and his colleagues therefore developed the Depressive Experiences Questionnaire (DEQ; Blatt, D'Afflitti, & Quinlan, 1976), a self-report scale that assesses the two types of depression, anaclitic (or dependent) and introjective (or self-critical). The measure has now been validated in numerous studies (see Blatt, 2004), and an adolescent version of the measure has also been constructed (Blatt, Schaffer, Bers, & Quinlan, 1992).

Representational Theory and the Cognitive Morphology

Although Blatt is perhaps best known for his work on the two-configurations model, he has always developed his cognitive representational understanding of personality and psychopathology in conjunction with his understanding of relatedness and self-definition. In 1974, he delineated a Piaget-influenced cognitive affective model of personality development. He proposed (e.g., Blatt, Chevron, Quinlan, Schaffer, & Wein, 1988; Blatt, Wein, Chevron, & Quinlan, 1979) that personality development proceeds from a sensorimotor-enactive stage, in which a person's object relations are dominated by concerns with gratification and frustration, through a concrete perceptual stage, in which object relations are based on what the other looks like, an external iconic phase, in which object relations involve mainly what others do, an internal iconic phase, in which object relations involve mainly what others think and feel, and finally, a conceptual stage, in which all previous levels are integrated into a complex, coherent understanding of significant others. Blatt used this model in developing the Conceptual Level Scale for rating open-ended descriptions of parents and other significant figures. Later, he integrated ideas from the two-configurations model with concepts from his representational model of cognitive development and from intersubjectivity theory in constructing the Differentiation–Relatedness Scale (Diamond et al., 1990; Diamond, Blatt, Stayner, & Kaslow, 1991), a measure that rates significant-figure descriptions from a more relational perspective. The theoretical assumptions underlying these scales are that cognitive development and the development of object relations occur in parallel and that the emergence of psychopathology is closely linked to disturbances in the development of object relations and cognitive organization (Behrends & Blatt, 1985). For example, low levels of differentiation–relatedness are usually found in psychosis, intermediate levels in borderline states, and higher levels in neurotic conditions and normality. Gradually, therefore, Blatt articulated his *cognitive morphology*, a comprehensive, integrated model of personality development, psychopathology, and therapeutic change that connects psychological maturation to the level of an individual's representation of significant interpersonal relationships (Blatt, 1991, 1995b; Blatt & Blass, 1990; Blatt & Shichman, 1983).

Psychotherapy Research

In recent years, Blatt has applied these theoretical ideas to concrete questions like what changes in treatment and how. Regarding his representational theories, Blatt and his colleagues found, in a sample of severely disturbed adolescents and young adults in long-term psychoanalytically oriented inpatient treatment, that changes in the structure and content of representations of self and significant others, in variables like conceptual level, differentiation–relatedness, and thematic content, were related to independent assessments of clinical improvement (Blatt, Auerbach, & Aryan, 1998; Blatt, Stayner, Auerbach, & Behrends, 1996). Specifically, they found that more positive and better articulated representations of mother and therapist, along with the expression of negative feelings about father, paralleled improvements in global functioning. They also found that more differentiated representations of the therapist are crucial for allowing patients to find and describe in others their own positive qualities and then to reappropriate these psychological strengths in a more integrated manner.

Blatt has also shown that relationally oriented and self-definitionally oriented persons have differential responses to psychotherapy. In his reanalysis of Wallerstein's (1986) Menninger Psychotherapy Research Project (Blatt, 1992), Blatt found that self-critical patients responded better to psychoanalysis and that dependent patients responded better to psychotherapy, with the increased support provided by face-to-face interaction. Meanwhile, his study (Blatt & Ford, 1994) of therapeutic change in long-term inpatient treatment at the Austen Riggs Center in Stockbridge, Massachusetts, found that dependent patients changed most with regard to interpersonal functioning, whereas self-critical patients, who tend to be ideational, rather than affective, in their orientation to the world, showed change primarily through improved cognitive functioning and decreased thought disorder. These studies showed that personality characteristics can crucially determine what kinds of therapeutic interventions prove to be effective.

Stronger support for his model, however, has been a series of reanalyses by Blatt and his colleagues (e.g., Blatt, Quinlan, Pilkonis, & Shea, 1995; Shahar, Blatt, Zuroff, & Pilkonis, 2003; Zuroff & Blatt, 2006; Zuroff, Blatt, Krupnick, & Sotsky, 2003) of the National Institute of Mental Health Treatment of Depression Collaborative Research Program (TDCRP). Blatt and his colleagues identified two factors in psychological functioning in the sample: perfectionism (a proxy for self-criticism) and need for approval (a proxy for dependence). They found that, regardless of the form of psychotherapy used (i.e., cognitivebehavioral, interpersonal, medication, and placebo), perfectionism had a negative effect on outcome in short-term treatment of depression, presumably because patients with high standards were unlikely to resolve their problems in just 15 or 20 sessions. These findings prompted Blatt (1995a) to argue that introjective or self-critical patients need long-term treatment to effect change. Thus, these research findings suggested not only that personality differences are important in response to psychotherapy but also that the short-term treatments that may be imposed on psychotherapy patients by managed care might have significant countertherapeutic effects on perfectionistic patients. In his reanalyses of the TDCRP, Blatt and colleagues also found, as have many psychotherapy researchers before him, that a positive therapeutic relationship, early in short-term treatment, predicted both symptom reduction and enhanced adaptive capacity, above and beyond patient characteristics and type of therapy. Thus, Blatt's reanalyses of archival data produced evidence that confirmed his psychoanalytically informed predictions that therapeutic alliance and underlying personality dimensions, not manualized treatments, are the chief determinants of therapeutic outcome (Blatt & Zuroff, 2005), and this is one of his most important contributions.

INFLUENCES AND INFLUENCE

Blatt's long-term colleagues, many of whom were students of David Rapaport and therefore as much influences on Sid as influenced by him, have included the members of the Rapaport–Klein Study Group, a small group that has met annually at Austen Riggs since 1963 to pursue Rapaport's and George Klein's efforts to extend psychoanalytic theory by putting it to empirical test. In addition, Blatt's approach to psychoanalysis was deeply influenced by Hans Loewald, for many years the preeminent analytic theorist in New Haven, and other important colleagues in New Haven have included Stephen Fleck, Jesse Geller, Theodore Lidz, and Jerome Singer.

Sid Blatt has influenced the field of psychotherapy not only through his ideas and his research but also through his relationships with 5 decades of colleagues, both those who came before him, many of whom we have already mentioned, and those who were his peers, undergraduates, graduate students, psychiatry residents, psychology interns, and postdoctoral fellows. To trace lines of influence from Blatt, perhaps the best known of his dissertation students is Paul Wachtel, who has himself become a leading contributor to the psychotherapy field. Other examples of Blatt's influence on colleagues can be found in a Festschrift (Auerbach et al., 2005) that summarizes the fruits of his many collaborations over the years. Particularly revealing of Blatt's influence is that more than 300 dissertations in the past 25 years have used measures that he and his colleagues developed. However, his most generative contributions, in our view, are two basic ideas: the two-configurations model and the cognitive morphology. These two concepts have influenced not only his many academic collaborators but unnamed practicing clinicians who think differently about psychotherapy and psychopathology because of them.

CONCLUSION

Sidney Blatt has integrated two main ideas into psychotherapy research: (a) the role of differences in patient personality characteristics and (b) the importance of changes in cognitive representational aspects of personality. Perhaps his most important contribution to psychotherapy is to have shown that anaclitic and introjective patients have differential responses to treatment that may have more influence on therapeutic outcome than the specific therapy or therapies to which they are assigned. Thus, the distinction between relatedness and self-definition that Sid Blatt, inspired by psychoanalytic theory, began exploring some 35 years ago has had relevance not only for psychopathology, personality theory, and psychoanalysis, as Sid originally theorized, but for short-term, nonpsychoanalytic approaches to therapy as well. In a field that remains divided by theoretical approach and that lacks the unified body of knowledge that characterizes physical sciences, it is no small accomplishment to have ideas that are relevant across theoretical boundaries. But this broad relevance is precisely the case in Sidney Blatt's work, perhaps because he has always worked to translate complex psychoanalytic ideas into concepts useful to clinicians and researchers of all theoretical persuasions—in essence, because he has lived with the tension of simultaneously asking deep questions about what it means to be human and submitting his ideas to empirical test.

REFERENCES

Allison, J., Blatt, S. J., & Zimet, C. N. (1968). *The interpretation of psychological tests*. New York, NY: Harper & Row.

Auerbach, J. S., & Blatt, S. J. (2001). Self-reflexivity, intersubjectivity, and therapeutic change. *Psychoanalytic Psychology, 18*, 427–450. doi:10.1037/0736-9735.18.3.427

Auerbach, J. S., Levy, K. N., & Schaffer, C. E. (2005). *Relatedness, self-definition, and mental representation: Essays in honor of Sidney J. Blatt*. London, England: Routledge.

Behrends, R. S., & Blatt, S. J. (1985). Internalization and psychological development throughout the life cycle. *Psychoanalytic Study of the Child, 40*, 11–39.

Blatt, S. J. (1959). Recall and recognition vocabulary: Implications for intellectual deterioration. *Archives of General Psychiatry, 1*, 473–476.

Blatt, S. J. (1974). Levels of object representation in anaclitic and introjective depression. *Psychoanalytic Study of the Child, 29*, 107–157.

Blatt, S. J. (1991). A cognitive morphology of psychopathology. *Journal of Nervous and Mental Disease, 179*, 449–458. doi:10.1097/00005053-199108000-00001

Blatt, S. J. (1992). The differential effect of psychotherapy and psychoanalysis on anaclitic and introjective patients: The Menninger Psychotherapy Research Project revisited. *Journal of the American Psychoanalytic Association, 40*, 691–724.

Blatt, S. J. (1995a). The destructiveness of perfectionism: Implications for the treatment of depression. *American Psychologist, 50*, 1003–1020. doi:10.1037/0003-066X.50.12.1003

Blatt, S. J. (1995b). Representational structures in psychopathology. In D. Cicchetti & S. Toth (Eds.), *Rochester symposium on developmental sychopathology: Vol. 6. Emotion, cognition, and representation* (pp. 1–33). Rochester, NY: University of Rochester Press.

Blatt, S. J. (2004). *Experiences of depression.* Washington, DC: American Psychological Association. doi:10.1037/10749-000

Blatt, S. J., Auerbach, J. S., & Levy, K. N. (1997). Mental representations in personality development, psychopathology, and the therapeutic process. *Review of General Psychology, 1*, 351–374. doi:10.1037/1089-2680.1.4.351

Blatt, S. J., Auerbach, J. S., & Aryan, M. (1998). Internalization, separation-individuation, and the therapeutic process. In R. F. Bornstein & J. M. Masling (Eds.), *Empirical studies of psychoanalytic theories: Vol. 8. Empirical studies of the therapeutic hour* (pp. 63–107). Washington, DC: American Psychological Association.

Blatt, S. J., & Blass, R. B. (1990). Attachment and separateness: A dialectic model of the products and processes of psychological development. *Psychoanalytic Study of the Child, 45*, 107–127.

Blatt, S. J., Chevron, E. S., Quinlan, D. M., Schaffer, C. E., & Wein, S. J. (1988). *The assessment of qualitative and structural dimensions of object representations* (rev. ed.). Unpublished research manual, Yale University, New Haven, CT.

Blatt, S. J., D'Afflitti, J. P., & Quinlan, D. M. (1976). Experiences of depression in normal young adults. *Journal of Abnormal Psychology, 85*, 383–389. doi:10.1037/0021-843X.85.4.383

Blatt, S. J., & Ford, R. (1994). *Therapeutic change: An object relations perspective.* New York, NY: Plenum.

Blatt, S. J., Quinlan, D. M., Pilkonis, P. A., & Shea, T. (1995). Impact of perfectionism and need for approval on the brief treatment of depression: The National Institute of Mental Health Treatment of Depression Collaborative Research Program revisited. *Journal of Consulting and Clinical Psychology, 63*, 125–132. doi:10.1037/0022-006X.63.1.125

Blatt, S. J., Schaffer, C. E., Bers, S. A., & Quinlan, D. M. (1992). Psychometric properties of the Adolescent Depressive Experiences Questionnaire. *Journal of Personality Assessment, 59*, 82–98. doi:10.1207/s15327752jpa5901_8

Blatt, S. J., & Shichman, S. (1983). Two primary configurations of psychopathology. *Psychoanalysis and Contemporary Thought, 6*, 187–254.

Blatt, S. J., Stayner, D., Auerbach, J. S., & Behrends, R. S. (1996). Change in object and self representations in long-term, intensive, inpatient treatment of seriously disturbed adolescents and young adults. *Psychiatry, 59*, 82–107.

Blatt, S. J., & Stein, M. I. (1959). Efficiency in problem solving. *Journal of Psychology, 48*, 193–213.

Blatt, S. J., Wein, S. J., Chevron, E. S., & Quinlan, D. M. (1979). Parental representations and depression in normal young adults. *Journal of Abnormal Psychology, 88*, 388–397. doi:10.1037/0021-843X.88.4.388

Blatt, S. J., & Zuroff, D. C. (2005). Empirical evaluation of the assumptions in identifying evidence based treatments in mental health. *Clinical Psychology Review, 25*, 459–486. doi:10.1016/j.cpr.2005.03.001

Diamond, D., & Blatt, S. J. (1994). Internal working models and the representational world in attachment and psychoanalytic theories. In M. B. Sperling & W. H. Berman (Eds.), *Attachment in adults: Clinical and developmental perspectives* (pp. 72–97). New York, NY: Guilford Press.

Diamond, D., Blatt, S. J., Stayner, D., & Kaslow, N. (1991). *Self-other differentiation of object representations.* Unpublished research manual, Yale University, New Haven, CT.

Diamond, D., Kaslow, N., Coonerty, S., & Blatt, S. J. (1990). Change in separation-individuation and intersubjectivity in long-term treatment. *Psychoanalytic Psychology, 7*, 363–397.

Levy, K. N., Blatt, S. J., & Shaver, P. (1998). Attachment styles and parental representations. *Journal of Personality and Social Psychology, 74*, 407–419. doi:10.1037/0022-3514.74.2.407

Rapaport, D. (Trans. Ed.). (1951). *Organization and pathology of thought.* New York, NY: Columbia University Press. doi:10.1037/10584-000

Rapaport, D., Gill, M. M., & Schafer, R. (1945–1946). *Diagnostic psychological testing* (Vols. I and II), Chicago, IL: Year Book Publishers.

Schaffer, C. E. (1993). *The role of attachment in the experience and regulation of affect.* Unpublished doctoral dissertation, Yale University, New Haven, CT.

Shahar, G., Blatt, S. J., Zuroff, D. C., & Pilkonis, P. A. (2003). Role of perfectionism and personality disorder features in response to brief treatment for depression. *Journal of Consulting and Clinical Psychology, 71*, 629–633. doi:10.1037/0022-006X.71.3.629

Strachey, J. (Ed.). (1963). *The standard edition of the complete psychological works of Sigmund Freud: Vols. 15 & 16. Introductory lectures on psycho-analysis.* London, England: Hogarth Press. (Original work published 1916–1917.)

Wallerstein, R. S. (1986). *Forty-two lives in treatment: A study of psychoanalysis and psychotherapy.* New York, NY: Guilford Press.

Zuroff, D. C., & Blatt, S. J. (2006). The therapeutic relationship in the brief treatment of depression: Contributions to clinical improvement and enhanced adaptive capacities. *Journal of Consulting and Clinical Psychology, 74*, 130–140. doi:10.1037/0022-006X.74.1.130

Zuroff, D. C., Blatt, S. J., Krupnick, J. L., & Sotsky, S. M. (2003). Enhanced adaptive capacities after brief treatment for depression. *Psychotherapy Research, 13*, 99–115. doi:10.1093/ptr/kpg012

29

WILLIAM E. PIPER: NEGOTIATING THE COMPLEXITIES OF PSYCHOTHERAPY

JOHN S. OGRODNICZUK

Successfully negotiating the complexities of the psychotherapeutic process requires a lifetime of unwavering commitment, ingenuity, skill, and leadership, which only a select few have demonstrated. One such researcher who exemplifies the commitment that is necessary to succeed in this area of research is Dr. William (Bill) Piper. With persistent dedication and a tenacious work ethic, Bill Piper has built a career out of answering complicated clinical questions about what works for whom, and why. This chapter briefly describes Bill's personal and professional journey to becoming a distinguished psychotherapy researcher.

MAJOR CONTRIBUTIONS

Much of Bill Piper's work has been progressive in nature, involving serial investigations that built upon each other in a systematic way. Thus, it is difficult and inappropriate to isolate particular studies as Piper's major contributions. Instead, it is more apt to highlight the major themes of Piper's research. Certainly, the most prominent theme of Piper's research program concerns his focus on psychodynamically oriented psychotherapies. Piper found the complexity of psychodynamic theories of normal and abnormal behavior to be attractive. Their emphasis on unconscious processes was intriguing and fit with his personal experiences and proclivity to think about underlying reasons for these experiences. Although Piper was not among the first to study psychodynamic psychotherapy, he was one of the early figures who consistently applied rigorous methodological practices to the scientific study of psychodynamic therapy.

William Piper's career began at a time when a shift was occurring in the field—a shift away from psychoanalytically based, long-term therapies to more structured and short-term therapies. Although it would have been logical for Piper to adjust his research program to this shift to survive as an academic, he did not relent (commitment is, indeed, one of Bill's endearing traits). His personal conviction that psychodynamic theory and therapy were appropriate and necessary for understanding and working with the richness and complexities of human mental development and psychopathology allowed him to stay the course he had set for his research. Furthermore, Piper saw opportunity. With the increasing emphasis on short-term and time-limited forms of therapy, Piper was intrigued by the opportunity to study psychodynamic forms of therapy that attempted to adopt such parameters. He went on to develop one of the most comprehensive research programs on short-term, time-limited dynamic psychotherapy in the field. Now, with the pendulum swinging back to the middle, there is an increasing appreciation and renewed interest in psychodynamic psychotherapy (Gabbard, Gunderson, & Fonagy, 2002). Piper's work in this area stands out as exemplary and is often referred to as a source for empirical support of psychodynamic therapy.

Another theme that runs through much of Piper's research, which has had a significant impact on the field, concerns his focus on group psychotherapy. The complexity of group dynamics and phenomena was intriguing and represented a challenge for Piper in terms of understanding how social processes can contribute to both the development and amelioration of mental illness. Group therapy research is also complex and not easy to conduct. Few have attempted it in a consistent fashion. From his early days as a graduate student, Piper has had an interest in groups. He was intrigued by the potentially powerful and unique change agents in groups. His work has examined sensitivity training groups for hospital corpsmen (Piper, 1972), long-term groups with mixed patient samples (Piper, Debbane, & Garant, 1977), comprehensive group-oriented partial hospitalization for patients with comorbid mood and personality disorders (Piper, Rosie, Azim, & Joyce, 1993), and short-term groups for people who have not adapted well to death losses (Piper, McCallum, Joyce, Rosie, & Ogrodniczuk, 2001), the latter of which is most dear to Piper's heart.

Piper's commitment to group therapy research has been praised as an example of how to approach work in this area. For example, Burlingame,

Fuhriman, and Johnson (2004) commented that "Piper and his colleagues on the Vancouver/Edmonton team have pursued one of the most progressive and comprehensive programs of group research" (p. 654). Given the continued growth of group therapy as a major treatment modality for people with psychiatric (e.g., major depression) and nonpsychiatric (e.g., breast cancer) difficulties, and the increased use of time-limited group treatments by behavioral health maintenance organizations (Taylor et al., 2001), Piper's work is sure to have a lasting impact on the field.

A third theme that runs through Piper's research is the concept of matching patients and treatments. To provide optimal treatment and maximize use of health care resources, therapists have argued for a more sensitive and clinically driven approach that matches patients to levels of care and treatment modalities, thus providing a range of options tailored to the qualities of individual patients. The patient–treatment matching paradigm has considerable potential for creating productive dialectic between theory, practice, and research, and it should ultimately result in enhanced and efficient care. Yet, despite its potential, research on patient–treatment matching in psychotherapy is still in its infancy, and its full promise has not been realized. Few researchers have attempted to systematically engage in this area of research, likely because of the significant investment of resources and time that it requires. Piper is among those who recognized the potential of patient–treatment matching and dedicated much of his career to using this paradigm in his research. His research in this area was an evolution. He started by attempting to identify important patient characteristics that influenced whether patients remained, worked, and benefited in psychotherapy. From there, he began to explore whether these different patient characteristics had differential impacts depending on the type of therapy that is provided. His patient–treatment matching studies involving individual and group forms of psychodynamic psychotherapy stand as some of the better examples of this type of research to date.

A recurring theme in Bill Piper's research is his attention to issues of therapy process. Piper continually challenged himself to go beyond the basic issue of whether a treatment worked and tackle the more complicated issue of how a treatment worked. Although knowing which treatments are effective is clearly important, Piper believed that clinicians would not be satisfied with this information only. Instead, they wanted and needed to know more about what to do during therapy in order to provide the best possible treatment to their patients. Thus, process analysis became an integral part of all of Piper's studies. Rather than looking at certain variables in isolation, Piper's research often integrated treatment variables, process variables, and patient variables in the same studies in order to examine more complex hypotheses about the mechanisms of action that contribute to benefit in psychotherapy. Change processes associated with psychodynamic theory and group therapy are particularly complex.

Piper was stimulated by the challenge of trying to elucidate these processes. The field is developing a greater appreciation of the importance of understanding psychotherapy change mechanisms (an example is the focus on "empirically supported relationships"). Thus, Piper's work in this area has served as a useful example of how to tackle such issues.

The final theme that characterizes Piper's work concerns the definition and measurement of important clinical constructs. Psychotherapy chiefly involves changing internal processes so that a patient can function more adaptively. These internal processes are not directly observable and are often described in complex, clinical terms. This makes psychotherapy research difficult. Clear operational definitions and reliable methods to assess constructs are required. Piper's efforts to define, observe, and measure various clinical constructs related to patient personality (e.g., quality of object relations), therapist technique (e.g., transference interpretations), and group processes (e.g., group cohesion) have helped to open doors for other researchers to study complex clinical phenomena.

EARLY BEGINNINGS

Bill Piper is the oldest of three boys from a middle-class family from Ohio. His father was a city fireman with a 10th-grade education who did not attribute much value to academics. His mother was a housewife until his parents divorced when he was 14 years old. She then went to work as a grocery store clerk in order to support the family. Bill did well academically and was also active in a number of sports, his favorites being basketball, tennis, and track. He was also active in church, where he met his future wife, Martha. After graduating from high school, Bill won a scholarship to attend a small liberal arts college in Wooster, Ohio. He initially chose to major in chemistry, at which he excelled. However, after having taken an introductory psychology course in the second semester of his 1st year, he decided that he found people more interesting than molecules and declared psychology as his major. During his undergraduate work, Bill completed an honors thesis that included a study of feedback mechanisms in small groups. Bill contends that he became curious about groups because he was shy. He recognized that he found group situations to be intimidating, and he challenged himself to master and overcome his fears by understanding group phenomena. After completing his undergraduate degree, Bill applied to graduate school in clinical psychology and was accepted at the University of Connecticut with a U.S. Public Health scholarship.

He was a graduate student in clinical psychology in the late 1960s, a time when sensitivity training was very popular. Sensitivity training groups (or T-groups, as they were called) were regarded as a relatively easy way to learn about interpersonal relations and processes in general and to gain insight about oneself in social situations in particular. Piper was keenly interested in having a T-group experience and did so. However, his interest in what he could learn about himself in T-groups was matched by a sense of danger. His graduate program was part of the more conservative East Coast culture of the United States, but he and his fellow students had heard about the uninhibited and unpredictable groups of the West Coast. Rather than discourage them, however, it all seemed to increase their curiosity about the varied effects of T-groups and the apparent double-edged sword of psychotherapy.

Training in group therapy was not a strong part of his graduate program's curriculum. Yet, there were plenty of groups and opportunities to join these different groups in the mental health system associated with his university. Among the opportunities that Piper took was an elective course on group therapy. Standing behind a one-way mirror with a small group of other graduate students, he first witnessed a therapy group in action. It was enough to capture his interest. He was struck by the potential of powerful and unique change agents in groups. Then he was called on to join a larger group.

In February 1968, he received his draft notice from the U.S. Army. He was able to negotiate an 11-month delay to finish his coursework and exams in Connecticut in exchange for serving for 3 years as a navy psychologist. In January 1969, he began the first of his 3 years in the U.S. Navy as a psychology intern at Bethesda Naval Hospital in Maryland. There he found plenty of groups: T-groups for the interns, therapy groups on the inpatient wards, and therapy groups in the outpatient services. Over the course of the year, Piper participated in a sensitivity group and was able to serve as a beginner cotherapist for two therapy groups. At the same time, he was in need of a dissertation topic and project. Following the dictum that "necessity is the mother of invention," he chose to seize an opportunity at the Naval Hospital, which was also a training center for a number of health service specialists. For his project, he studied the effects of sensitivity training groups on hospital corpsmen. Although the findings of his study did not provide much evidence for the effectiveness of sensitivity training groups in increasing interpersonal skills, the project proceeded smoothly and convinced him that randomized controlled trials involving groups could actually be conducted. Little did he know that such trials would eventually become a central component of his research activities. After Bethesda, he worked for the next 2 years in a psychiatric outpatient clinic at Marine Corps Base Quantico, Virginia, and there his involvement in group therapy lay somewhat dormant. In 1973, he left the Navy and joined the Department of Psychology at McGill University, where his involvement in group therapy was soon to revive.

Piper left the United States for Canada because there was an opening in the middle of the academic year (January 1973) that coincided with his departure from the U.S. Navy. He also knew that McGill had an excellent academic reputation and that Montreal was an attractive city with a unique European–North American culture. A few months after arriving in Montreal, he learned that a psychiatrist, Elie Debbane, at the Allan Memorial Institute was interested in creating a group psychotherapy unit that would promote training, research, and practice. Along with another psychiatrist, Jacques Garant, they forged a union that developed into a productive work group and set of friendships. Piper's early career was launched and continued with a remarkable trajectory.

ACCOMPLISHMENTS

Between 1977 and 2008, Bill Piper completed a series of eight large-scale, randomized clinical trials of psychotherapy. The studies' objectives, design, and methodology shared a number of common features. For example, each investigated the efficacy of one or more forms of dynamically oriented psychotherapy, most of which were short-term treatments. Also, in addition to including a large battery of outcome assessments, his studies always monitored one or more process variables during therapy, for example, therapeutic alliance and therapist technique. Finally, all involved the assessment of patient characteristics to help determine appropriate patient–treatment matches.

Each of these trials was significant in its own right, but a few stand out as particularly meaningful to Piper and, likely, the field in general. The first of these was conducted when Piper was at McGill in Montreal (Piper, Debbane, Bienvenu, & Garant, 1984). The trial compared four forms of psychoanalytically oriented psychotherapy: individual or group therapy that lasted either 6 or 24 months. What emerged as important from this trial was the particular form of therapy received, not the general type of therapy or the general duration of therapy. The results favored long-term group therapy and short-term individual therapy. This stands as a landmark study because it remains one of the few factorial designs in comparative therapy research.

A second significant trial occurred when Piper moved to the University of Alberta in Edmonton. This study compared two different forms of dynamically oriented, short-term individual therapy (Piper, Azim, McCallum, & Joyce, 1990). This was one of the first studies to use a patient–treatment matching paradigm. Specifically, the trial was designed to test the question of whether QOR (quality of object relations; see Azim, Piper, Segal, Nixon, & Duncan, 1991; Blatt, Wiseman, Prince-Gibson, & Gatt, 1991) had a differential effect on the outcome of two very different types of therapy. The hypothesis was that higher QOR patients were better suited for interpretive therapy and lower

QOR patients were better suited for supportive therapy. The findings supported this hypothesis. This study is among the better examples of this type of research to date.

Another significant trial that Piper conducted in Edmonton examined the efficacy of group-oriented partial hospitalization for patients with debilitating comorbid mood and personality disorders (Piper, Rosie, Azim, & Joyce, 1993). This type of intensive outpatient service held great promise. These patients typically failed in usual once-a-week outpatient therapy and often ended up in inpatient wards. Yet, inpatient treatment was not regarded as an appropriate level of care for such patients. A treatment that could provide an intermediate level of care was needed. The trial demonstrated that short-term, time-limited partial hospitalization had a powerful, lasting impact on patients, who improved on several aspects of functioning. This study remains one of the very few randomized trials of partial hospitalization.

Most recently, since his move to Vancouver and the University of British Columbia (UBC), Piper has led a large, multisite study. This trial was the latest in a series of studies that investigated different forms of group therapy for patients suffering from complicated grief and was designed to examine whether the composition of therapy groups had an effect on the outcome of treatment (Piper, Ogrodniczuk, Joyce, Weideman, & Rosie, 2007). The expectation was that patients who were in a group with similar others and provided a form of therapy that fit with their personality would do better than patients who were in a group with a mixed variety of patients, regardless of whether the form of therapy they were provided matched their personality. The findings, although not completely supportive of this hypothesis, did find that composition matters. In particular, the study found that the more high-QOR patients that are in a group, the better everyone in the group did, regardless of each individual member's level of QOR or the form of therapy provided. This study is important because it is one of the very few, if not only, clinical studies of composition effects in group therapy. Currently, Piper is engaged in a study that is attempting to identify variables that mediate the effect of group composition.

Finally, no description of Piper's accomplishments is complete without mention of his process work. A series of studies on the effect of transference interpretations best exemplifies Piper's efforts to understand how the processes of therapy impact patient outcomes (Ogrodniczuk & Piper, 2004). Transference interpretations are an important feature of psychodynamic psychotherapies. Despite their importance, the literature provides little guidance regarding the use of these powerful interventions in the treatment of different types of patients. Piper's research on the dosage and correctness of transference interpretations (and how these differ as a function of patient personality), however, has contributed to our knowledge of the appropriate use of transference interpretations. His findings argue for technical flexibility in the use of transference interpretations, with the particular needs of patients as the primary determinant.

Much of Piper's work can be found in several books that he has co-authored (e.g., Piper, Joyce, McCallum, Azim, & Ogrodniczuk, 2002), several of which in themselves represent significant contributions to the field. These publications offer a glimpse into the way Piper thought about the various issues at hand and his rationale for conducting his studies, how he designed his trials, the findings from the trials and their implication for practice and research, and clinical vignettes that give life to his work. Piper regards his books as a necessary final step that follows a series of trials—a mechanism that allows him to pull together his work in a way that appeals to both clinicians and researchers. In fact, he perceives this as his responsibility as a clinical scientist.

OTHER CONTRIBUTIONS

Bill Piper has been a strident advocate of psychotherapy research in his various administrative capacities. For example, as a member of the Randomized Controlled Trials Committee for the Canadian Institutes of Health Research, he helped bring greater awareness to the national health system of the value of clinical trials in psychotherapy. Similarly, as the president of the Canadian Group Psychotherapy Association, Piper was a strong voice for promoting research in venues that were traditionally resistant to research. Even locally, Piper has had a significant influence on the direction that mental health research should take and the role of psychotherapy research. His efforts helped in the creation of the UBC Institute of Mental Health Research, a $20 million endeavour (the largest of its kind in Canada), which has identified psychotherapy research as one its three pillars. Of course, as a past president of the Society for Psychotherapy Research, Piper was able to provide leadership and direction to a large, international coalition of psychotherapy researchers.

INFLUENCES

It is possible that all of William Piper's accomplishments in our field may not have happened, were it not for a few key people in Piper's early academic career. Piper attests that Mike Wogan was probably the most influential person with regard to steering him toward psychotherapy research. Mike was always receptive to Piper's ideas and conveyed excitement as Piper took on new challenges. Piper attributes his interest in groups to Herb Getter. Both Mike and Herb were advisors on Piper's master's thesis committee. Carl Wagner was also dear to Piper for being so helpful in facilitating his PhD work, which had to be completed early because of his military service commitments. Finally, Elie Debbane provided Piper with the support, encouragement, and camaraderie to launch his career as an independent academic at McGill.

Piper received caring and supportive mentorship during his academic training, which he, in turn, provided to his trainees. During his tenure at McGill University, Piper supervised a good number of clinical psychology graduates. Most of these graduates went on to become full-time clinicians. Mary McCallum, who went on to build a successful research career instead, stands out as an exception. Once Piper left McGill and went to the University of Alberta and then to UBC, his academic setting was in psychiatry, not psychology. He no longer had an opportunity to participate as a primary supervisor for trainees in the same way that had he enjoyed it at McGill. Nevertheless, while at the University of Alberta, Piper was able to take on two research trainees via a unique partnership between the Faculty of Medicine and Faculty of Graduate Studies. These trainees were Anthony Joyce and John Ogrodniczuk. To this day, he maintains a strong connection with them, and together they form a highly productive research team.

Throughout his career, Piper has enjoyed close, fruitful, and collaborative relationships with a number of clinicians, who were keen to contribute in whatever way they could. These people include Hassan Azim, Elie Debbane, John Rosie, John O'Kelly, and Rene Weideman. Piper has remarked on numerous occasions, "My accomplishments are theirs as well." He contends that these and other clinicians played crucial roles in the development of his research program because they were willing to evaluate the therapies that they practiced. They reinforced his interest in the psychodynamic orientation and introduced him to systems theory and to different ways to understand group phenomena. Piper's belief in the necessity of working with a team of people to accomplish important objectives in life is evident in the strong bonds had has developed and maintained with his colleagues over the years.

CONCLUSION

When one reads criticisms of the psychotherapy research literature, most often they focus on the failure to examine commonly used clinical treatment modalities, the failure to use experienced community-based clinicians, and the neglect of relationship and patient variables that influence the success of the therapeutic enterprise. Piper's research, however, has always addressed these issues and thereby has maximized the clinical relevance of his work. His clinical trials often focus on commonly used clinical treatments (e.g., individual and group therapy) and his process work has centered on clinical constructs widely viewed as central to dynamicallyoriented psychotherapy (e.g., transference interpretations), group therapy (e.g., cohesion), and all therapies (e.g., the alliance). In terms of important patient characteristics, Piper saw the importance of operationalizing the clinical notion of quality of object relations and has examined this variable in relation to both the process and outcome of psychotherapy. Many have recognized the value of and called for patient–treatment matching studies over the years, but Piper has been one of the few who have attempted such research. His work in this area has been second to none and stands as an example for others to follow.

The implications of Piper's work on the theory, practice, and research are plentiful. From a theoretical perspective, Piper's work compels us to think about how a person's internal representations of important people in his or her life and the wishes and emotions attached to these representations can be activated and modified within the context of a helping relationship to improve that person's life. With regard to practical implications, Piper's work demonstrates the importance of proper patient selection, matching patients and treatments, and monitoring one's technique during the course of treatment. Finally, from a research perspective, Piper's work shows us how we can move beyond the important but rather rudimentary issue of whether a treatment works, toward developing a better understanding of what kinds of treatment work with whom and how they work. Piper's theoretical innovation, dedication to helping others, and commitment to science are sure to stimulate and engage others to apply the highest degree of rigor for advancing the psychotherapy field.

REFERENCES

Azim, H. F. A., Piper, W. E., Segal, P. M., Nixon, G. W. H., & Duncan, S. (1991). The quality of object relations scale. *Bulletin of the Menninger Clinic, 55*, 323–343.

Blatt, S. J., Wiseman, H., Prince-Gibson, E., & Gatt, C. (1991). Object representations and change in clinical functioning. *Psychotherapy, 28*, 273–283.

Burlingame, G. M., Fuhriman, A. J., & Johnson, J. (2004). Process and outcome in group counseling and psychotherapy. In J. L. DeLucia-Waack, D. A. Gerrity, C. R. Kalodner, & M. T. Riva (Eds.), *Handbook of group counseling and psychotherapy* (pp. 49–61). Thousand Oaks, CA: Sage.

Gabbard, G. O., Gunderson, J. G., & Fonagy, P. (2002). The place of psychoanalytic treatments within psychiatry. *Archives of General Psychiatry, 59*, 505–510. doi:10.1001/archpsyc.59.6.505

Ogrodniczuk, J. S., & Piper, W. E. (2004). The evidence: Transference interpretations and patient outcomes. A comparison of "types" of patients. In D. Charman (Ed.), *Core processes in brief psychodynamic psychotherapy* (pp. 165–184). Mahwah, NJ: Erlbaum.

Piper, W. E. (1972). *Evaluation of the effects of sensitivity training and the effects of varying group composition according to interpersonal trust.* PhD dissertation, University of Connecticut.

Piper, W. E., Azim, H. F. A., McCallum, M., & Joyce, A. S. (1990). Patient suitability and outcome in short term individual psychotherapy. *Journal of Consulting and Clinical Psychology, 58,* 475–481. doi:10.1037/0022-006X.58.4.475

Piper, W. E., Debbane, E. G., Bienvenu, J. P., & Garant, J. (1984). A comparative study of four forms of psychotherapy. *Journal of Consulting and Clinical Psychology, 52,* 268–279. doi:10.1037/0022-006X.52.2.268

Piper, W. E., Debbane, E. G., & Garant, J. (1977). An outcome study of group therapy. *Archives of General Psychiatry, 34,* 1027–1032.

Piper, W. E., Joyce, A. S., McCallum, M., Azim, H. F., & Ogrodniczuk, J. S. (2002). *Interpretive and supportive psychotherapies: Matching therapy and patient personality.* Washington, DC: American Psychological Association. doi:10.1037/10445-000

Piper, W. E., McCallum, M., Joyce, A. S., Rosie, J. S., & Ogrodniczuk, J. S. (2001). Patient personality and time-limited group psychotherapy for complicated grief. International Journal of Group Psychotherapy, 51, 525–552.

Piper, W. E., Ogrodniczuk, J. S., Joyce, A. S., Weideman, R., & Rosie, J. S. (2007). Group composition and group therapy for complicated grief. *Journal of Consulting and Clinical Psychology, 75,* 116–125. doi:10.1037/0022-006X.75.1.116

Piper, W. E., Rosie, J. S., Azim, H. F. A., & Joyce, A. S. (1993). A randomized trial of psychiatric day treatment. *Hospital & Community Psychiatry, 44,* 757–763.

Piper, W. E., Rosie, J. S., Azim, H. F. A., & Joyce, A. S. (1993). A randomized trial of psychiatric day treatment. *Hospital and Community Psychiatry, 44,* 757–763.

Taylor, N. T., Burlingame, G. M., Fuhriman, A. J., Kristensen, K. B., Johansen, J., & Dahl, D. (2001). A survey of mental health care provider and managed care organization attitudes toward, familiarity with, and use of group interventions. *International Journal of Group Psychotherapy, 51,* 243–263. doi:10.1521/ijgp.51.2.243.49848

V

CONCLUSION

30

FUTURE DIRECTIONS: EMERGING OPPORTUNITIES AND CHALLENGES IN PSYCHOTHERAPY RESEARCH

LYNNE ANGUS, JEFFREY A. HAYES, TIMOTHY ANDERSON,
NICHOLAS LADANY, LOUIS G. CASTONGUAY,
AND J. CHRISTOPHER MURAN

With the publication of this volume, it is our hope that psychotherapy researchers and practitioners will not only enjoy the stories that enrich our shared past but will also have an opportunity to reflect on the emerging research and practice trends that are likely to shape the fields of clinical and counseling psychology, psychiatry, and social work in the years to come. Accordingly, in this final chapter we identify core research themes for the identification of key research issues that are likely to shape the future of psychotherapy research, training, and practice.

ASSESSING PSYCHOTHERAPY OUTCOMES— FROM RANDOMIZED CLINICAL TRIALS TO PRACTITIONER–RESEARCHER NETWORKS

No doubt influenced by Eysenck's (1952) challenging yet flawed review of psychotherapy effectiveness, a number of pioneers of the Society for Psychotherapy Research (SPR), such as Rogers, Luborsky, and Strupp, developed research programs aimed at measuring the outcome of insight-oriented treatments (the main target of Eysenck's review). Other researchers, such as Bergin,

Garfield, Howard, and Orlinsky, undertook the important task of collating, critically evaluating, and disseminating outcome research findings through the publication of landmark texts such as the *Handbook of Psychotherapy and Behavior Change* (Bergin & Garfield, 1978).

Irene Elkin's innovative effort to refine randomized controlled research designs for application in multisite collaboration psychotherapy research trials, the Treatment of Depression Collaborative Research Program, set the stage for the development of brief therapy approaches designed to address specific clinical disorders such as depression and anxiety. In addition to Elkin, numerous researchers featured in this book have conducted randomized clinical trial (RCT)-based therapy outcome studies that have contributed to the establishment of empirical support for psychodynamic (Blatt, Luborsky, Piper, Shapiro, Strupp), interpersonal (Strupp), client-centered/emotion-focused (Greenberg), gestalt/emotion-focused (Beutler), and cognitive behavioral (Beck, Beutler, Goldfried, Grawe, Shapiro) treatments for depression.

The number and variety of comparative treatment trials that have been completed over the past 30 years clearly attest to the impact that RCT designs and the evaluation of treatment outcomes have had on the field of psychotherapy research and practice as a whole. However, the equivalency of positive outcome findings achieved across different therapy approaches for the treatment of depression has led a number of researchers (Strupp, Goldfried, Elliott, Howard, Piper) to question whether future research efforts and funding should be focused on RCT designs that test differential treatment approaches for specific clinical disorders. Several researchers have encouraged the field to go one step beyond the question of whether one therapy is superior to another and have emphasized the importance of conducting studies to identify what forms of treatment might be more effective for particular types of clients or clinical problems (Beulter, Blatt, Grawe, Elkin, Jones, Kiesler, Piper, Stiles).

Influential contributors such as Frank, Bordin, Luborsky, Strupp, and Orlinsky have long advocated taking a new direction in psychotherapy research and funding that would entail the identification and empirical validation of key mechanisms of change—across therapy approaches—that are causally linked to efficacious treatment outcomes. Frank and Goldfried, along with Castonguay and Beutler (2006), have also suggested that if we are to understand how therapists can achieve more effective clinical outcomes with their patients, future research efforts should focus on the identification and empirical evaluation of a shared corpus of key principles of change that are evidenced in a diverse range of evidence-based practices. Understanding specifically how, when, and where key principles of change are most effectively used for productive treatment outcomes, across differing therapy approaches, will be an important future direction for this challenging research initiative.

Additionally, there is mounting criticism from key contributors to the psychotherapy research and practice field that the patient selection criteria used in RCTs is unduly restrictive and not representative of the complex symptom profiles that patients often present with in community-based settings. They also argue that the use of approach-specific therapist treatment manuals, mandatory for adherence ratings in RCTs, unduly limits the ability of therapists to responsively and flexibly meet the complex needs of patients who are often seen in community-based clinical practice. This is a particularly important issue for psychotherapy practitioners who may be required to use evidence-based therapy approaches with their patients. Taken together, critics have questioned the utility, generalizability, and validity of RCT-based research findings for clinicians who practice in real-world settings and have challenged major research funding agencies and clinical researchers to draw on sample practitioners engaged in community practices for future research trials. Indeed, a vitally important future research question remains to be answered in this regard: Can RCT experimental designs be adapted for implementation in community-based samples and still address key methodological issues such as random assignment to treatment, client diagnostic heterogeneity, and consistent adherence to specific treatment manuals? Alternatively, do psychotherapy researchers need to develop a new gold standard for the evaluation of effective clinical practices that not only accommodates but capitalizes on the heterogeneity of practice approaches and client diagnostic issues that abound in real-world clinical settings? Resolving these important key methodological and practice-based research issues will certainly shape the direction of psychotherapy research in the years to come.

In response to these criticisms and in light of influential contributions of Howard, Orlinsky, and Bergin, a new generation of psychotherapy researchers (e.g., Grawe, Lambert, Stiles, Elliott) have contributed to the development of session level patient outcome measures for application by practitioners in community-based settings (see Barkham et al., 2008). The collection of large samples and statistical advances in linear growth modeling has also allowed researchers to explore methods that can positively influence clinical decision making through feedback to therapists. For instance, Lambert and colleagues (2001) recently established that therapists in real-world practice settings and training centers are able to achieve more effective treatment outcomes when they are given post-session evaluations of their patient's symptom status and level of distress. The provision of patient feedback appears to significantly enhance treatment outcomes by reducing early dropout and allowing therapists to calibrate their treatment focus to better meet the needs of their patients. This important empirical finding should have a significant impact not only on current and future psychotherapy training programs—across treatment approaches—but also on real-world clinical practice wherein therapists are encouraged to draw on patients' postsession evaluations for more effective therapeutic outcomes.

As demonstrated by Lambert, the implementation of postsession evaluations in community-based settings also provides researchers with a golden example of how to develop broad-based practice-research networks for future research initiatives. In fact, several other practice-research networks are also proving the utility of large-scale collaborative efforts between therapists and researchers. For instance, the Pennsylvania Psychological Association's Practice Research Network (Borkovec et al., 2001) is a statewide effort to involve therapists in the process of clinically relevant research, from formulating questions to designing studies to collecting data. Furthermore, the Penn State's Center for the Study of Collegiate Mental Health (CSCMH, http://www.sa.psu.edu/caps/research_center.shtml) is a national collaboration in the United States among more than 125 university counseling centers to gather clinical data using a common set of instruments. The initial pilot study of the CSCMH, in which 66 counseling centers contributed one semester's worth of data, yielded a sample of more than 20,000 cases. Although projects of this magnitude require considerable time, coordination, and organization to even get off the ground, their potential benefits outweigh the efforts involved.

Additionally, representing a wide range of treatment approaches, Greenberg, Strupp, and Luborsky have cogently argued that traditional (i.e., comparative) treatment outcome studies have failed to provide definitive answers about the specific mechanisms of change that are causal to therapeutic outcomes. With the exception of dismantling, additive, or parametric designs, comparative treatment trials do not provide empirical validation of the treatment interventions so carefully spelled out in RCT treatment manuals (Borkovec & Castonguay, 1998). As a consequence, there has been an increasing call for the assessment of therapist and patient factors, within and across sessions, that may be able to provide at least approximate causal explanations for specific therapy outcomes (Kazdin, 2008). The immediate future seems to offer an opportunity for experiential/humanistic, integrative, interpersonal, psychodynamic, and CBT process researchers—many of whom have had a strong presence within SPR and have contributed to this book—to continue to focus their expertise on evidence-based treatments, for the identification and measurement of mechanisms of change operating in their respective therapy approaches.

FROM PROCESS TO PROCESS-OUTCOME STUDIES
AND THE IDENTIFICATION OF KEY MECHANISMS
OF CHANGE IN EVIDENCE-BASED THERAPY APPROACHES

Beginning with early investigations of generic change processes and relationship conditions (Rogers, Strupp, Orlinsky, Howard), many of the seminal researchers in this volume addressed specific measurement issues (Elkin, Kiesler, Elliott, Stiles), sometimes by utilizing observational tools that measure at a detailed level (Benjamin, Elliott, Jones) and at other times through qualitative research strategies that prize patients' first-person accounts of experiences of change (Hill, Elliott). It is clear that psychotherapy process research methodologies have significantly changed over time. In particular, there has been a gradual shift to more specification of individual change processes observed and assessed within and across therapy sessions and an increasing focus on tools that capture the patient's experience of therapy. For instance, Grawe used therapy spectrum analyses to formulate empirically validated heuristics that specified a mixture of resource- and problem-focused interventions suited to the different phases of therapy and guided the therapist's session-to-session decisions for the continual adaptation of treatment procedures. The Client Experiencing Scale (Gendlin), Rice's Client Vocal Quality Scale, Stiles's Verbal Response Modes, and Hill's efforts to measure therapist intentions and response modes, as well as patient reactions and behaviors, all share an appreciation of the multifaceted ways in which language can and does play a role in the change process.

Additionally, because most—if not all—of these measures emerged from the intensive, inductive analysis of actual therapy sessions, they have had considerable impact on clinical practice. For instance, Rice's systematic, intensive case analysis of specific client vocal markers (1967) ultimately contributed to the development of a new, process directive approach to conducting humanistic psychotherapy, emotion-focused psychotherapy. The intensive single-case analyses of actual therapy sessions—as demonstrated by Orlinsky, Rice, Rogers, Hill, Stiles, Elliott, and Kächele in their respective research programs—may in fact serve as an important first step and methodological bridge for future psychotherapy researchers who are interested in identifying evidence-based mechanisms of change. Specifically, the possibility of conducting multiple, intensive single-case analyses of dyads that have participated in RCTs opens the door to the identification (and with enough multiple cases, possibly verification) of key mechanisms and/or core principles of change for clients and therapists who have achieved clinically significant change at therapy termination. The intensive, contextual analysis of key change processes—interpersonal, patient, and therapist factors—within and across therapy sessions in turn provides researchers with an opportunity to develop a much more differentiated understanding of the complex factors that contribute to productive patient outcomes in the context of evidence-based therapy practices. Importantly, these findings may then inform the development of practice guidelines and training programs for the effective implementation of evidence-based approaches in community settings—an important and challenging future direction for psychotherapy research and practice.

Methodological flexibility that embraces a creative openness to unexpected findings is a recurring theme that seemed to define many of the process and outcome researchers included in this book. When one set of research tools proved inadequate to illuminate answers to research problems, they were flexible enough to consider alternative approaches. The problems that these researchers were studying were quite complex, and as complexity per se appeared to explain particular research findings, these researchers applied methods that were better suited for capturing this complexity.

For instance, Strupp began his career using analog procedures to make inferences about psychotherapy, then conducted carefully designed experiments using actual clients before turning to case study methodology to explore puzzling findings from Vanderbilt I. Findings from the intensive case analyses of actual therapy sessions in turn facilitated the development of hypotheses used for a new RCT about training. Kächele's intensive analysis of psychoanalytic therapy sessions also involved a hybrid approach that mixed various levels of observation, ranging from group-level measures to detailed and complicated analyses at the level of the individual word. Stiles turned to qualitative strategies in order to identify assimilative processes, whereas Hill adapted qualitative methods to understand more fully what clients experience during therapy sessions. Similarly, Greenberg turned to task analysis when he needed to identify specific change processes entailed in productive empty-chair and two-chair interventions. It is clear that the capacity to flexibly adapt standard research methodologies for the evaluation of emerging research questions has been key to the generation of new knowledge and effective intervention practices that have significantly affected the field as a whole.

It is also important to note that key research innovators such as Rogers, Luborsky, Goldfried, Strupp, Beck, and Greenberg have all practiced as psychotherapists throughout the course of their highly generative research careers. Understanding the essential contributions of therapy practice for the development of innovative, generative psychotherapy research programs must continue to inform how we educate and train future generations of psychotherapy researcher–practitioners.

While the first generation of outcome researchers saw little or no need to address within- and across-session change processes, it can also be said that process researchers (Kiesler, Rice, Gendlin, Rogers) were not initially interested in evaluating session or treatment outcomes when undertaking intensive process analyses of therapy sessions. The two worlds of psychotherapy research began to move closer together, however, when outcomes among different therapy approaches were found to be equivocal and could not be explained. Building on the integration of psychotherapy process and outcome research methodologies, researchers have become increasingly interested in understanding of the contributions of the therapeutic relationship to overall therapy outcomes at treatment termination and follow-up. Orlinsky and Howard's Therapist Session Report, Strupp's Vanderbilt Psychotherapy Process Scale, and Luborsky's Penn Helping Alliance Scales have set the stage for the development of the many alliance measures that have both sprouted and become deeply rooted throughout treatment research during the past generation.

In turn, the broad-based administration of reliable, pantheoretical self-report measures of the therapeutic alliance (Bordin, Luborsky), such as the Working Alliance Inventory (Horvath & Greenberg, 1989), has resulted in accumulating research evidence that patients' reports of a strong, collaborative alliance early in therapy are consistently correlated with overall positive therapeutic outcomes, across diagnostic subgroups (dysphoria, personality, anxiety, substance abuse) and therapy approaches (client-centered, psychodynamic, interpersonal, emotion-focused, CBT; Castonguay & Beutler, 2006). However, given the consistently modest effect sizes across diagnostic samples and therapy approaches, several researchers have cautioned that we still do not understand if a strong, early alliance is an essential "glue" of therapy that activates and helps to sustain other change processes or if it is the fundamental ingredient of therapeutic change itself (A. O. Horvath, personal communication, 2008). Investigating this research question and understanding how therapists help clients engage in the fundamental tasks of therapy will be an important focus of future process and outcome research that will likely influence psychotherapy training and clinical practice.

Recent developments in computerized DVD-based software systems that enable the simultaneous coding and analysis of relational processes occurring during therapy sessions may contribute to future research efforts addressing the contributions of client and therapist interpersonal processes for effective therapeutic outcomes. It is now possible for psychotherapy researchers to intensively investigate microlevel, interpersonal process patterns that are associated with positive, early alliance ratings, as well as therapeutic gains, using these observer-based coding systems. The development of new coding methodologies may in fact open the door to future innovative applications of standardized measures such as Benjamin's Structural Analysis of Social Behavior and the Client Experiencing Scale (Gendlin), as well as further refinement of concepts such as the therapeutic alliance. As demonstrated by Kächele's textual analysis of long-term psychodynamic therapy sessions, computer-assisted technology has already made a significant impact on psychotherapy process research, and advances in voice recognition and text conversion software may one day soon allow for live computer analysis of text and the potential for immediate feedback to therapists and trainees.

THERAPIST CONTRIBUTIONS, PSYCHOTHERAPY TRAINING, AND INTERNATIONAL RESEARCH NETWORKS

Interestingly, psychotherapy research has focused mainly on treatment methods and on clients' characteristics, in-session behaviors, and clinical outcome—while the person of the psychotherapist has remained largely unexplored. To address this gap in the research literature, Orlinsky and colleagues recently cofounded the SPR Collaborative Research Network (CRN) to conduct an international study of the development of psychotherapists. Meeting intensively before and after SPR conferences, a group of colleagues from different countries, professional backgrounds, and theoretical orientations worked together to construct the Development of Psychotherapists Common Core Questionnaire (DPCCQ). The DPCCQ has been translated into 20 languages to date and has been used in more than two dozen countries to collect reports about work experiences and professional development from nearly 9,000 psychotherapists. A theoretical integration of research findings resulted in a "cyclical-sequential model of psychotherapist development" that has resulted in empirically grounded recommendations for clinical training, supervision, and therapeutic practice. Orlinsky and his CRN colleagues are expanding data collection in previously unstudied Western and non-Western countries, examining the distinctive characteristics shared by therapists of specific orientations and exploring aspects of therapists' personal lives, such as the nature and impact of their religious background and experiences.

In addition, Bruce Wampold's (2001) work has exerted considerable influence on the field, emphasizing the importance of therapist, relational, and contextual factors in psychotherapy outcome and calling into question many of the assumptions of RCTs. Like Frank and Garfield before him, Wampold also questions the supposition that technical factors are largely responsible for change. As multilevel modeling and other similar statistical techniques become more widely accepted, understood, and utilized, researchers will be able to make continued advances in determining the relative contributions of these factors to treatment outcomes.

Taken as a whole, the CRN project presents the field of psychotherapy research with a highly innovative demonstration of the rich possibilities that may ensue when broad-based international research collaborations are created to address key research questions central to psychotherapy training and practice. We anticipate that SPR will continue to serve, as it has served in the past, as a key international forum for the creation of collaborative research networks that foster the development of innovative, rigorous research methods, measures, and research strategies that result in more effective training and delivery of evidence-based clinical interventions in community-based settings.

The CRN initiative dovetails with a growing interest in the psychotherapy research field at large regarding the contributions of psychotherapy supervision and training for effective therapeutic outcomes. Developing methods to systematically measure core competencies and productive training outcomes will be critical for this future research initiative. Additionally, Goldfried has also highlighted the critical importance of more fully addressing sexual orientation issues when educating psychotherapy researchers and practitioners, and he has organized a curriculum review initiative to achieve this outcome. In so doing, he has set the stage for future psychotherapy researchers to continue to attend to key multicultural issues such as race, gender, and nationality when conducting psychotherapy research investigations.

CONCLUSION

The field of psychotherapy research has been generative—and regenerative—in an almost benevolent way. The extraordinary scholars featured in this book are more than researchers and/or practitioners—they are also committed mentors, giving of themselves and their accumulated wisdom for the benefit of the profession and, more immediately, for those who are fortunate enough to study and work directly with them. Many of the chapter authors, and indeed the editors of this volume, can trace their own lineage to contributors featured in this book who were instrumental in introducing them to SPR at early points in their professional careers. The origination of our own collaborative research programs can be directly traced back to early engagement in SPR meetings and the respect for diversity, intellectual curiosity, and methodological rigor that permeates the society as a whole. And in this regard, it seems to us that SPR is unique in its explicit nurturing and valuing of collaborative research initiatives and its support for students and young scholars. We are truly indebted to those who have come before us, especially SPR cofounders David Orlinsky and Ken Howard, and this debt of gratitude is willingly paid in the form of a commitment to mentoring the next generation of psychotherapy researchers and ensuring the vitality and generativity of SPR for generations to come.

REFERENCES

Barkham, M., Stiles, W., Connell, J., Twigg, E., Leach, C., Lucock, M., . . . Angus, L. (2008). Effects of psychological therapies in randomised trials and practice-based studies. *British Journal of Clinical Psychology, 47*, 397–415. doi:10.1348/014466508X311713

Bergin, A. E., & Garfield, S. L. (Eds.). (1978.) *Handbook of psychotherapy and behavior change: An empirical* (2nd ed.). New York, NY: Wiley.

Borkovec, T. D., & Castonguay, L. G. (1998). What is the scientific meaning of "Empirically Supported Therapy"? *Journal of Consulting and Clinical Psychology, 66*, 136–142. doi:10.1037/0022-006X.66.1.136

Borkovec, T., Echemendia, R. J., Ragusea, S. A., & Suiz, M. (2001). The Pennsylvania Practice Research Network and future possibilities for clinically meaningful and scientifically rigorous psychotherapy effectiveness research. *Clinical Psychology: Science and Practice, 8*, 155–167. doi:10.1093/clipsy/8.2.155

Castonguay, L. G., & Beutler, L. E. (Eds.). (2006). *Principles of therapeutic change that work*. New York, NY: Oxford University Press.

Eysenck, H. J. (1952). The effects of psychotherapy: An evaluation. *Journal of Consulting Psychology, 16*, 319–324. doi:10.1037/h0063633

Horvath, A. O., & Greenberg, L. S. (1989). Development and validation of the Working Alliance Inventory. *Journal of Counseling Psychology, 36*, 223–233. doi:10.1037/0022-0167.36.2.223

Kazdin, A. E. (2008). Evidence-based treatment and practice: New opportunities to bridge clinical research and practice, enhance the knowledge base, and improve patient care. *American Psychologist, 63*, 146–159. doi:10.1037/0003-066X.63.3.146

Lambert, M .J., Hansen, N. B., & Finch, A. E. (2001). Patient-focused research: Using patient outcome to enhance treatment effects. *Journal of Consulting and Clinical Psychology, 9*, 159–172.

Rice, L., & Wagstaff, A. K. (1967). Client vocal quality and expressive styles as indexes of productive psychotherapy. *Journal of Consulting Psychology, 31*, 557–563.

Wampold, B. E. (2001). *The great psychotherapy debate: Models, methods and findings*. Mahwah, NJ: Erlbaum.

INDEX

Marvin R. Goldfried, 136
Clara Hill, 159
Enrico Jones, 267
Michael J. Lambert, 147
David A. Shapiro, 279–280
William B. Stiles, 303
Effectiveness research. *See also* Outcome
    research; Process–outcome
    research and studies
    patient-focused research vs., 95
    personality in, 334, 335
EFT. *See* Emotion-focused therapy
EFT-C (emotion-focused therapy for
    couples), 192–194
Elkin, Irene, 25, 77–86, 354
    accomplishments, 80–85
    and Edward S. Bordin, 199, 203
    early beginnings, 79–80
    legacy of, 85–86
    major contributions, 78
    and TDCRP, 8
Elliott, Robert, 175, 283–291, 303
    accomplishments, 285–290
    early beginnings, 284–285
    and Leslie Greenberg, 186, 191
    legacy of, 291
    professional accomplishments,
        290–291
    and David A. Shapiro, 275, 277, 280
    and William B. Stiles, 301
Ellis, Albert, 71, 108, 109
Emotional experiencing, 132–133
Emotional injuries, 192
Emotional processes, 186, 189–191
Emotional vocal quality, 179
Emotion-focused therapy (EFT), 186,
    189–194. *See also* Process–
    experiential psychotherapy
    (PE-EFT)
Emotion-focused therapy for couples
    (EFT-C), 192–194
Empathy, 9, 274, 278
Empirically-based research (empiricism)
    Aaron T. Beck, 65–66
    Larry E. Beutler, 325
    Irene Elkin, 79
    Kenneth I. Howard, 95–96
    in psychology, 3–4
Empirically-supported treatment (EST)
    movement, 8, 9
Encompassing frameworks, 278

Engagement, of clients, 179
Equivalence paradox, 300–301
Erikson, Eric, 42, 67
Errors, Type I, 97
EST (empirically-supported treatment)
    movement, 8, 9
Ethnic matching, of therapist and
    patient, 262–263
Events-based research paradigm, 186
Evidence-based therapy
    Allen E. Bergin, 107
    Kenneth I. Howard, 96
    mechanisms of change in, 357–360
Evocative unfolding technique, 180
Evoking messages, 215
Expected treatment response, 95
Experiences, of clients and therapists,
    90–91, 235–237
Experiencing
    Eugene Gendlin, 167–170
    Marvin R. Goldfried, 132–133
    Leslie Greenberg, 189
Experiencing Scale, 168–170
Experiential phenomenology theory,
    166–167
Experiential therapy, 22, 25, 26
Experimental case study approach, 106
Exploration stage (of helping skills
    model), 157
Expressive Stance Measure, 179
Externalizing vocal quality, 179
Eysenck, Hans
    on effectiveness of psychotherapy,
        104, 353
    in history of psychotherapy, 5–6
    and Donald Kiesler, 213
    and Lester Luborsky, 43

Families, working alliance in, 206
Feedback, 355–356
    Klaus Grawe, 119–120
    Michael J. Lambert, 146–147, 149
Fetzer Institute, 222
Figuration analysis, 119
Focused vocal quality, 179
Focusing Institutes, 166
Focusing-oriented psychotherapy, 170
Forgiveness, 186
Frank, Jerome D., 29–36, 354
    accomplishments, 30–36
    early beginnings, 29–30

Psychotherapy Session Project, 90–91, 235–237

QOR. *See* Quality of object relations
Qualitative research
Robert Elliot, 286–288
Clara E. Hill, 159, 358
Carl Rogers, 23–24
William B. Stiles, 302–303, 358
Quality of object relations (QOR), 344–345
Quantitative naturalistic research
Kenneth I. Howard, 96–98
Laura Rice, 178–179
Quantitative outcome measures (in HSCED), 287

Race, 260, 262–263
Randomized clinical trials, 22, 31
William E. Piper, 344–346
Irene Elkin, 354
Sol L. Garfield, 309
outcome studies based on, 354–355
Randomized Controlled Trials Committee for the Canadian Institutes of Health Research, 346
Rank, Otto, 20
Rapaport-Klein Study Group, 335
Rasch analysis, 284, 288
Rationale (in common factors model), 35
Rationalism, 4
Realism, 3–4
Realizations, therapeutic, 92
Recording, of psychotherapy sessions, 21, 272
Reductionism, 106
Regressive loyalty and Regressive Loyalists, 205, 228
Rehabilitation phase (of outcome phase model), 94
Relational disorders, 225
Relational form of depression, 329, 330, 332, 333
Relationship factors, 177
Relationship patterns, central, 40
Remediation phase (of outcome phase model), 94
Remission, spontaneous, 141, 142, 144, 145

Remoralization phase (of outcome phase model), 93–94
Repetitive interaction structures, 260
Representational theory of personality, 333, 334
Responsiveness, 300–301
Rhesus monkeys, 223
Rice, Laura, 9, 24, 175–181
accomplishments, 178–181
Client Vocal Quality Scale of, 357
early beginnings, 177–178
and Robert Elliot, 285, 286, 289
and Leslie Greenberg, 185–189, 191
legacy of, 181
major contributions, 176–177
Ritual (in common factors model), 35
Rogers, Carl, 17–26, 331
accomplishments, 20–22
and Lorna Smith Benjamin, 223
and Allen E. Bergin, 102, 109
and Edward S. Bordin, 200–202, 204
early beginnings, 19–20
and Irene Elkin, 80
and Eugene Gendlin, 165, 166, 168
and Leslie Greenberg, 188
in history of psychotherapy, 5
and Kenneth I. Howard, 90
and Donald Kiesler, 211–213
and Michael J. Lambert, 144, 148
legacy of, 24–26
major contributions, 18–19
process–outcome research, 23–24
and Laura Rice, 175, 176, 178
on valuing clients, 302
Rorschach test, 21, 179, 311
Rosenzweig, Saul, 45, 48

SANE (National Committee for a Sane Nuclear Policy), 30
SASB-based Intrex questionnaire, 225
SASB model. *See* Structural analysis of social behavior model
Scale for Suicide Ideation, 71
Schemas, 64–65, 301
Schema Theory, 117
Schizophrenia, 70, 80, 169. *See also* Wisconsin Schizophrenia Project
SCID-II (Structures Clinical Interview for *DSM–IV* Personality Disorders), 222

ABOUT THE EDITORS

Louis G. Castonguay, PhD, is a professor of psychology at Penn State University. His work focuses on the process, outcome, and training of psychotherapy, as well as on the development of practice–research networks. He has coedited three books: on psychotherapy integration (with Conrad Lecomte), on principles of therapeutic change (with Larry Beutler), and on insight in psychotherapy (with Clara Hill).

J. Christopher Muran, PhD, is associate dean and professor, Derner Institute, Adelphi University, and director, Brief Psychotherapy Research Program, Beth Israel Medical Center. His research has concentrated on alliance ruptures and resolution processes and has resulted in several book collaborations, including *Negotiating the Therapeutic Alliance*, *Self-Relations in the Psychotherapy Process*, *Dialogues on Difference*, and *Therapeutic Alliance*.

Lynne Angus, PhD, is a professor of psychology at York University in Toronto, Canada. She is the senior editor of the *Handbook of Narrative and Psychotherapy* (with John McLeod). Her research focuses on the investigation of narrative and emotion processes in psychotherapy, and she has developed the Narrative Processes Coding System (with Heidi Levitt and Karen Hardtke) for application in differing treatment approaches.

Jeffrey A. Hayes, PhD, is a professor of counseling psychology at Penn State University. His scholarship focuses on the psychotherapy relationship, with an emphasis on therapist factors and the integration of spirituality and psychology. He has coauthored two books with Charles Gelso, *The Psychotherapy Relationship* and *Countertransference and the Therapists' Inner Experience: Perils and Possibilities*.

Nicholas Ladany, PhD, is a professor of counseling psychology at Lehigh University in Bethlehem, Pennsylvania. He is the author of three books on supervision and training: *Critical Events in Psychotherapy Supervision: An Interpersonal Approach; Counselor Supervision: Principles, Process, and Practice;* and *Practicing Counseling and Psychotherapy: Insights from Trainees, Clients, and Supervisors*.

Timothy Anderson, PhD, is an associate professor of psychology at Ohio University in Athens. His current research is on the identification of common therapist factors that predict therapy processes and outcome. He is the recipient of the 2004 Distinguished Early Career Award from the International Society for Psychotherapy Research.